Praise for *Insight into a* [Bright Mind]

Nicole Tetreault has synthesized and translated [...] *the neuroscience field, beautifully illustrated through truthful personal stories, memoir, vulnerability, a good dose of humor, and heartfelt letters to the reader. This is an extraordinary creative book, perfectly suited for the gifted, talented, and twice-exceptional, as well as anyone who's curious how their unique brain works.*

—Scott Barry Kaufman, Ph.D.,
Humanistic Psychologist and author of *Transcend*

Nicole Teatreault's Insight Into a Bright Mind *is a true gift to the differently wired community! By blending neuroscience, evidence-based research, anecdotes about twice-exceptional children and adults, and lived experience in a warm, accessible way, Nicole offers an insightful companion for anyone interested in better understanding the complexities and strengths of neurodivergent humans.* Insight Into a Bright Mind *is a hopeful and practical must-read for any parent raising an exceptional child.*

—Debbie Reber, founder Tilt Parenting, author *Differently Wired*

Dr. Tetreault will capture the mind of readers. She writes knowingly about the brain, "a composite of emotions, words, stories, bodily sensations, our environment, experiences, and genetics, orchestrating the development of our authentic self." She also reveals her own self, complementing her extensive knowledge with personal revelations. These are riveting, memorable, and even poetic. Insight into a Bright Mind *is incredibly informative and beautifully written and, much like a "brain-print," it is totally unique.*

—Joanne Foster, Ed.D., author of *ABCs of Raising Smarter Kids, Not Now, Maybe Later, Bust Your Buts, Being Smart about Gifted Education,* and *Beyond Intelligence*

Nicole Tetreault's Insight into a Bright Mind *makes a wonderful contribution to our understanding of gifted and twice exceptional students. I found Tetreault's writing engaging. Her use of metaphors and personal stories make the content come alive as the reader is introduced to both the neuroscience of differently wired brains and the benefits of neurodiversity in how humans think. Peppered throughout with relevant research, quotes, and practical examples, this book will not disappoint. It promises to excite and enlighten all who choose to dive into this new territory.*

—Susan Baum Ph.D., Provost of Bridges Graduate School
and author of *To Be Gifted and Learning Disabled*

Insight into a Bright Mind *is a must read book for those who are, support, educate, or parent a gifted person. Dr. Nicole accomplishes the difficult by making the neuroscience of giftedness, personal, understandable, and functional. This book is a life changer.*

—Barry Gelston, M.Ed., GHF Board President

One of the most important components to raising/educating a neurodiverse child is to understand their atypical meta-physical development. This is the foundation upon which everything else is dependent. Dr. Nicole Tetreault has given us a comprehensive guide to understanding both our neurodiverse children (and perhaps even ourselves) in an accessible, yet intelligent manner with her thorough exploration of "Bright Minds". As a professional working with neurodiverse individuals, Dr. Tetreaullt is one of my "go to" sources for reliable information. Congratulations and kudos on an excellent book!

—Michael Postma, Ed. D., President & Owner,
Gifted & Thriving, LLC. & Programming Director

Dr. Tetreault takes us on a journey beginning with her childhood experience in noting that her own brain was different than her peers', or what others expected it to be. Teaching us that brains are as unique as fingerprints, Dr. Tetreault looks at the gifted experience, the unique "brain prints'" that may accompany it and shows us the connection between neurology, behavior and perspective. Dr. Tetreault's overall message of the age old adage—"Don't judge a book by its cover," allows us to discover that to be human is to be neurodivergent.

—Julie F. Skolnick, M.A., J.D.,
With Understanding Comes Calm, LLC

As the parent of three 2e kids I felt like this book was written for me. There is so much valuable and comprehensive information, and the book deals with the whole child. 2e kids are a mix of so many overlapping aspects and profiles. This book recognizes that and lays out so much useful information in such a kind and supportive way that it's easy and not intimidating for me, as a parent, to read.

The book is as educational and far-reaching in its complexity as our 2e kids are. It covers complicated subjects like anxiety and sensory issues at school which are often misunderstood, including the brain-gut relationship and all the neuroscience behind it all. With Dr. Tetreault's being 2e herself, with a 2e family, having the understanding of the neuroscience, and embracing with kindness individual's strengths and differences, this book is a must-have on every parent's, educator's, or professional's book shelf or iPad.

—Harri James O'Kelley, The O'Kelley Lab

Neuroscience about the high IQ brain is just exploding. Accessible, fresh, and richly textured, Dr. Tetreault expertly guides the reader through insight after insight, interwoven with examples of how they can manifest at home and in the classroom. An invaluable guide.

—Austina De Bonte, M.Eng., Consultant, Smart is not Easy, Past President, NW Gifted Child Association

I recommend this book to all professionals, teachers and parents who are longing to get a better understanding of the gifted brain. It is a valuable resource filled with insight and research, though also personal stories that make it applicable in daily practice. In that, it gives us hope for a happy and healthy future for gifted minds.

—Femke Hovinga-Tiller, Development Director SCALIQ, Executive Director Talentissimo 145+ IQ platform

Insight into a Bright Mind:

A Neuroscientist's Personal Stories of Unique Thinking

Nicole A. Tetreault, Ph.D.
Foreword by Susan Daniels, Ph.D.

Gifted
EDUCATION
A BRANCH OF GIFTED UNLIMITED

Edited by: Lesly Dahl
Interior design: The Printed Page
Cover design: Kelly Crimi

Published by
Gifted Unlimited, LLC
12340 U.S. Highway 42, No. 453
Goshen, KY 40026
www.giftedunlimitedllc.com

ISBN: 978-1-953360-03-8

For Billy and Spencer, thank you.

Contents

Foreword

Nicole Tetreault is a bright and complex woman. She has an amazing brain—as you yourself will soon discover while reading this amazing book. She is a neuroscientist, a teacher, an author, a mother, a valued colleague, and fabulous friend. She has written Insight into a Bright Mind from all of those perspectives—beautifully synthesized.

Insight into a Bright Mind is a smart and complex book—part research tome, part memoir, part poetry anthology, and part guidebook. Nicole makes tremendously complex material readable, accessible, and oh so interesting. Personal stories and insights, rich with details of living with a bright mind abound, and these are beautifully integrated with support and explanation from key studies conducted in the neurosciences.

Nicole shares her own experiences with neurodiversity along with her vast knowledge of neurodevelopment, and she does so in a friendly and approachable way. Vignettes of discovering her son Spencer's unique brain-based strengths and challenges help us make connections along a continuum from childhood through adult experiences of twice exceptionality (2e). Nicole writes honestly and from the heart about the joys and challenges of living with a range of personal strengths and challenges. Truly, this is quite a lot of rich material to integrate—quite an accomplishment and one that reflects who Nicole is as a person.

Nicole and I had the good fortune of meeting a few years ago at a conference and soon became colleagues and friends. We have presented workshops on creativity and neurodiversity together—at local and national conferences as well as online, and Nicole was my meditation teacher for quite some time—meeting virtually and meditating together each week. I always learn something from

Nicole—whether it be at a conference together, through meditation, or over a cup of coffee. It is with this knowledge of Nicole as a scientist, as an author, and as a bright and enlightened person that I am delighted to have been asked to write this foreword.

To elaborate just a bit more, there's one other impression I'd like to share. In addition to being a professor and author myself, I am a mixed media artist. In my art, I strive to integrate a variety of colors, materials, words and designs into a meaningful whole—to express big ideas and deep feelings. There are parallels and connections between my art processes and the artistry of this book. While writing clearly about big ideas and studies from the hard sciences, Nicole has also integrated her own poetry with stories and vivid descriptions from her own life. Her stories are rich, descriptive, and applicable. And so, I am entirely confident that her writing will draw you in.

With that in mind, I encourage you to get a warm cup of your favorite beverage and settle in for awhile. This is an uncommon book that you won't want to put down. Enjoy.

—Susan Daniels, Ph.D., Professor Emeritus
Cofounder of the Summit Center
Coauthor of *Living With Intensity and Raising Creative Kids*

Introduction

When my son, Spencer, was in third grade, I learned he read at college level, and that he was gifted. I wasn't surprised; he was a bright kid. But there was another story there. As a neuroscientist and his mother, I knew he saw the world differently. That same year, I'd learned he spent most of his recesses and lunch times in the library reading. My heart sank because I worried that he suffered from social isolation and exclusion. When I asked him about it, he said, "Mom, sometimes I need a break from the other kids. They're too much and too loud and the library is quiet." He also told me he didn't enjoy participating in team sports because he was afraid of running into other kids and injuring them. Again, this worried me. I thought he should be socializing with other kids that he should be an athlete like his father and me. I was filled with anxiety because I didn't understand. I feared he would always be alone and not connect with other kids. I had an expectation of what was normal. And I felt we were not that. Then, during a parent-teacher conference, I had a light bulb moment. His third-grade teacher insightfully said, "Spencer knows how to self-regulate, if he needs quiet at lunch time and the library relaxes him, let it be his way to recharge."

I was struck by how simple and true that was. He did not need to change or conform to what anyone else thought a third grader should be doing. He was perfectly right being exactly who he was, going to the library and reading during lunch time, and socializing with the librarian and teachers. Spencer had his own speed and his way of navigating the world was exactly right for *him*. I needed to listen to what he needed and follow his lead. I needed to step out of the way and watch him embody his essence. I needed to trust. I needed to wake up and see Spencer in all his complexity and individuality.

The most humbling part of being a parent is when your child challenges you to step out of your comfort zone and see them, accept them, and advocate for them to be who they are, exactly as they are. During that same conference, my husband and I learned that Spencer's reading goal for the year was to "read at appropriate times." His desk was stacked with eleven books and to this day he is happy reading for hours and playing Lego.

Spencer came into sports later. Beginning in 8th grade he played basketball and soccer on multiple teams and holds the school record for the fastest mile. Even so, he is still cautious on the field and court and opts out of scoring if it means possibly injuring another player. And I wouldn't have it any other way.

In high school, Spencer discovered his passion for cross country. He paces himself, runs with teammates that he now considers friends, and each time he runs a race he focuses on his personal record (PR) for his race time. He came into his own on his own terms, and his own time, and from him I learned how to understand and accept differences in the way he navigates in the world. Spencer continues to teach me to be better and to open my eyes to human diversity. This book was born to understand neurodiversity through the lens of science, to challenge our entrenched ideas of intelligence, and to challenge each of us to think outside the box. And to be better.

These are human and science stories centered on people who are thought to be outside that "box." What if the very box we are thinking of is not a box at all, but rather a series of never-ending circles evolving and expanding like a kaleidoscope? What if the mind's capacity is far greater than we can imagine?

Neuroscience studies are expanding our understanding daily, shaping our ideas as a society, and we are only scratching the surface. My hope is that you will be inspired to embrace your diversity, speak your voice, and embody being in your essence. Once we fully embrace our essence, we are open to the infinite and the collective as we live the life we imagine.

-Nicole A. Tetreault, Ph.D.

Dear Imagined,

You are perfect and imagined. Beautiful. You are full of light and dark. Both are your teachers; without light there is no darkness and without darkness, no light. There is a spectrum of light full of shades and shadows. You hide in the shadows. You fear.

Shed your fear. Holding on to your fear is a mind game. But you will find it is a mine field of material once you realize it is the exact direction you need to go headfirst into. Go into the darkness and illumination will appear. It may all be wrong. You learn from the good, the bad, the ugly, the brutality, neutrality, and equanimity. Find the compassion and wisdom in each lesson. That is progress.

You will fail time and time and time again to build <u>you</u> into who you are meant to be and what you are meant to do. When you are chosen, take that moment of grace and luck. All your dedication will come together. Continue to imagine with your head in the clouds, leaping into the unknown.

Life is entropy. There are few steady states—perhaps none. Ever changing, ever remaining the same.

You will experience pain. What you create from your pain is what matters. It is how you heal, how you provide healing for others. It is how you teach others to heal. It is how you create the universal from the individual. Share with everyone and they will, in time, heal.

Erase from your mind what you think you know about others. Instead, watch them closely. Listen to their speech. Watch their actions. Give them time, space, and silence to reveal themselves in their coming out. Let it be their rebirth. You their witness.

You are the deer and the lion. At times, you will need to be gentle with yourself and others; other times will call for the lion's roar. Trust you know when to be bold and gentle, where the circumstance and energy will guide you. You have to be both equally compassionate and fierce to protect all that you love. Love boundlessly like the vast ocean. Follow the waves and the current will lead you to your truth; ride the waves of self-doubt. Know it too will end as the wave carries you, the current settles. Love yourself boundlessly. We love you. You are glorious. You are imagined. You are hope.

Love Eternally,

Dreamer

CHAPTER 1:

A Lens into Neurodiversity

It is time for parents to teach young people early on that in diversity there is beauty and there is strength.
—Maya Angelou

In nature, we observe various divergent patterns, behaviors, and unique specializations. Biodiversity, the variety within an ecosystem, develops for symbiosis and the survival of the entire planet among plants, animals, and the natural landscape. Without variation, adaptation and evolution, we cease to exist. The origins of human cultural and biological diversity allow us to grow and expand as a society. Neuroindividuality is ingrained in our biology from conception. To our unique genetic profile, we add personal diversity through our memories, sensory processing, behaviors and actions, and our environmental influences. Together this creates a distinct brain, body, vision, nervous system, and one-of-a-kind individuality. No two humans are identical.

We each have diverse configurations, from the double helix of our DNA, to our one-of-a-kind fingerprints, to light activating photoreceptors in our retinas that ignite our senses and perceptions. Human diversity is beautiful; it builds the collective and is necessary for our expansion as a whole species. Judy Singer introduced the idea of neurodiversity in 1988, which advocates that brain differences are simply part of human variation that represent the spectrum of cognitive differences in social, emotional, attentional, learning, and other mental functions.[1] The term was popularized when Harvey Blume published a column in the *Atlantic* magazine about a parody website developed by individuals with autism called "The Institute for the Study of the Neurologically Typical." Blume said, "Neurodiversity may be every bit as crucial for the human race as biodiversity is for life in general. Who can say what form of wiring will prove best at any given moment? Cybernetics and computer culture, for example, may favor a somewhat autistic cast of mind."[2]

Neurodiversity guides us to accept and see one another for our cognitive variations. Each of us views the world through our very own exceptional lens. Possessing unique brain pathways and diverse abilities makes each of us no better or worse as people, but simply different, and these differences nurture our rich human tapestry. We need to embrace neurodiversity through a lens of equality and inclusion, where individuals are empowered to share their cognitive diversity and live a life free from stigma. We need to open our minds and hearts and revel in the magic of cognitive diversity.

Neuroindividuality is the New Normal

The "Goldilocks" setting for the brain, mind, and personality to fit into the range of normal is a part of our earliest teachings and comes from our family, school, community, and culture. Agreed upon socially accepted ideals form an expectation of what you should be, represent, and even become or not become.

At some time in most of our lives, we have felt the restraint of being expected to fit into a box. We feel we are suffocating in a coffin, hiding our true selves, hiding from the world where we only dare to emerge after dark to lurk in the shades of night. I am talking about camouflaging the true essence of who we are because others may see our behaviors as quirky, strange, and even flat-out wrong. We hide because we tell ourselves the fear story of not being accepted. But from a young age, we also learn a conflicting story: that each of us is unique and no one in the universe will ever be exactly like us. I believe that is absolutely true. However, we spend a good amount of time washing away our true selves to fit into the safe zone of homogeneity.

What if we were to reshape the discussion and tell children, adults, and all humans that we each exceed the confines of a box? Nature has many arrangements, like an artichoke displaying the number phenomena of the Fibonacci sequence and the various hexagonal columns of ice crystals forming distinct snowflakes. As biology naturally takes shape, we learn there is vast heterogeneity.

Through brain imaging, neuroscience studies are teaching us that no two brains are alike. Each brain has a distinctive signature, like a fingerprint. David Van Essen and Matthew Glasser reported from their group's findings that they had discovered and mapped 180 distinct brain areas in the human cortex. This is more than three times the number identified by Brodmann, the father of the human brain atlas.[3] Increasing the number of brain areas identified means greater precision and detail to identify the function of each specific brain area. In the study, they distinguished 97 new cortical regions, in addition to the 83 previously-known regions.[4] This new brain mapping software allows neuroscientists to identify with considerable accuracy the function and output of each brain area, shedding light on human brain individuality. The software creates an automated map of an individual brain, like a distinct fingerprint, and we know no two fingerprints are alike. Neither are brains. We each have our very own brain-print. This uniqueness arises from our genetics, experiences, and environment.

When this study came out, it rocked my world. I had studied individuals' brain tissue under the microscope and learned I could identify an individual subject based on the neuroanatomy I saw. I assumed my observation was because I had spent hours peering through the microscope and had memorized their brains. Each individual had their very own landscape of connections. Now, with the discovery of better parcellated brain regions and software, I know that every brain has an individual signature.

Another study, by Valizadeh and colleagues, found that they could identify the brain of an individual based on neuroanatomy from their brain scans.[5] They examined the brains of 191 elderly subjects by scanning their brains three times over a two-year period and assessing 450 neuroanatomical features, including total volume of the brain, thickness of the cortex, and volumes of grey and white matter. They found that a person was matched to their brain with greater than ninety percent accuracy by computer program. The study established that each human brain is absolutely unique. We know we are unique beings, and neuroscience is showing that we have distinctive brain signatures. Our experiences are myriad within our mind, a composite of emotions, words, stories, bodily sensations, our environment, experiences, and genetics, orchestrating the development of our authentic self. Human diversity encompasses neurodiversity, and science shows our diversity originates with our brains.

More than ever, we have scientific proof emphasizing our need to embrace human diversity, from gender to personality to ethnicity to creative genius to individuals who live with extraordinary challenges. There is great richness in human diversity and it is vitally important that we allow space for exceptional minds to open, to explore extraordinary ways of seeing, being, and navigating in the world. Our outside package is just a glimpse of what is going on in our mind and body. There is no box or geometric shape that can encompass the wide range of human experience. Rather, the human mind is a spectrum of light, each of us illuminating at our own wavelength, some of us in shadow, some of us in brightness, and some us even in ultraviolet light.

Neural Plasticity

Neural plasticity is the ability of the brain to change throughout an individual's life. We are taught the Hebbian notion that "neurons that fire together, wire together."[6] A common firing pattern creates a circuit and memory that shapes and develops the brain based on experience, environment, and memory. The brain is flexible, and we can guide children to reach their potential with the ability to learn at the level that suits them. The brain is a dynamic organ and has the ability to grow based on experience, environment, and genetics. The environment can support positive neural connections and strengthen development, or it can hinder development.

Neural plasticity is the process by which the brain can develop and organize networks in relation to use, function, training, and specialization. Think for a moment of a drummer's brain. The drummer will have brain expansions based on playing, listening, and practicing the drums. Specialized brain expansions will be in the auditory cortex (listening to music), motor (playing the drums), emotional (emotions when playing music), sensory (tactile for playing the drums), and cerebellum (timing and rhythm of creating the beat), each of which will expand and develop the more the drummer trains, practices playing the drums, listens to drums, and thinks about playing the drums.

Neural plasticity is the building block for developing neural circuits. We now know that the frontal cortex—the area of the brain essential for decision making, emotional processing, and executive functioning—continues developing throughout our thirties. More and more studies are showing the vast ability of neural plasticity, where the brain can change because of experience, neural patterning, behaviors, the environment, and openness to the mind's capacity.

There are several studies that show how through training the brain can develop networks that are expanded based on the specific training. The most famous of these findings involves London taxi drivers who memorize locations and names of over 25,000 streets, known as the "Knowledge." These drivers have an expanded brain area for spatial navigation and memory in their brains. This is the region of the hippocampus.[7] Eleanor Maguire and team found that the longer the driver was on the job, the greater the driver's grey matter growth in the area of the hippocampus involving spatial navigation and considerable knowledge. This is a powerful example of neural plasticity in the adult brain. In a follow-up, Eleanor Maguire and team conducted a longitudinal study over four years that measured the hippocampus prior to acquiring the Knowledge. Individuals who passed the exam and acquired the Knowledge compared to individuals who did not pass the exam showed greater hippocampus growth after the four years. Moreover, at the outset of the experiment the hippocampi were all the same volume, but the passing drivers' hippocampus expansion was specific to memory of spatial navigation. Additionally, the study found that the taxi drivers who passed did better on spatial memory tasks than the other participants, but they did not do better on all memory tasks—in other words, the brain expansion was particular to spatial navigation. The expansion of the hippocampus was particularly related to the activity involved and the specific knowledge absorbed by the drivers.

More recently, a study reported that brain expansions are based on spatial navigation for the task at hand and that the hippocampus is not expanded for all of memory. Rather, it is in relation to the specific activity.[8] The neural plasticity and growth are specific to the task at hand, so brain training only improves brain functioning for the practiced task.

Now, obtaining knowledge through training is of course multidimensional and multifaceted, which in turn will over time help with one's survival, but when it comes to neural plasticity, it is important to understand the process is highly individual, based on practice, cognition, intention, and the specific activity and brain process involved in acquiring new skills. Specifically, the London taxi drivers' brain expansions will differ from those of a classically trained musician because that activity, experience, and knowledge is particular to the skill and experience at hand. Neural networks reconfigure and expand based on training and neuronal activity by dedicating more neurons, glial cells, and dendritic processes for the practiced task. Within the fields of development and aging, these findings are promising potential ways to aid in brain growth and development of neural networks, and to repair the brain through specific activity. It is imperative that we understand that neuroplasticity is highly individual. To fully understand what is happening "under the hood" at the time of the brain expansions we must study these processes at the microscopic level where brain scans provide a wide-angle view of the macroscopic structure during neural plasticity. In the mind of brain expansions and neural plasticity there is more than meets the eye.

Wired for Plasticity*

You are capable of more than you know.
—Glinda the Good Witch[9]

Our mind is composed of knowledge (perceptions of the present moment made tangible through our five senses and our

---

* Previously published online by 2e News (at https://www.2enews.com) and in *Variations Magazine*

autobiographical memories) and energy flow (electrical pulses that fire across neural paths and transfer information). The way we perceive information is directly related to the attention and intention of how we choose to cultivate our neural pathways. Neural pathway development is similar to Dorothy's journey on the yellow brick road—unbound, uncharted territory, and full of possibility.

Life is not always rainbows, sunshine, and happy endings. But when we encounter unexpected showers we can gain wisdom from walking in the rain. We learn to avoid puddles (unless we are the few that leap frog puddle to puddle). Or we may choose a path lined with trees to deflect the rain drops. Building mental flexibility, neural strength, and connections allows for innovation and new patterns which in turn allow for greater adaptation. With enhanced mental flexibility, and gifted with a moment of insight, we can spontaneously discover a new highway leading to a shortcut home. Our growth is directly related to our openness which can amplify (or hinder) our neuroadaptation.

Neuroindividuality is at our forefront. Each of our brains has its own entire Land of Oz illuminating distinct yellow brick roads. The minds of our bright adults and children are just that, a place where pathways have unexpected detours, back country roads, and high-speed interchanges. The yin and yang of brain expansion is through time and space. Brain development is asynchronous—throughout our lives, our brains have the ability to change throughout our lives based on attention, intention, and experience.

Mental flexibility and neural plasticity go hand and hand and inform how we choose to nurture our mindset. Parents, educators, and community directly shape and build the roadways in our children's brains.

Positive neural plasticity is the process for building and strengthening neural patterns in the brain. A common firing pattern creates a circuit and memory that shapes and develops the brain. These pulses across the brain relay information of our perceived environment. The next step is our mindset—how we choose to pay attention to information, whether we are engaged in the present moment or not, can either encourage or inhibit the growth of a neural pathway.

Can we build neural connections for new skills from scratch? Yes, but it may take more time to develop a completely new neural pathway. A recent study in Richard Anderson's laboratory at Caltech showed that learning a new skill is easier for the brain if a common neural pattern has already developed. The lead authors, Sofia Sakellaridi and Vassilios Christopoulos, used a brain machine interface paradigm to track learning and individual neuron firing. They found that learning is restricted by pre-existing neural patterns. When the participant was acquiring a completely new skill, the neural framework was not in place and adaptation for neuronal firing in learning a new skill was being developed, as compared to skills that build upon or adapt skills already learned.[10] For example, a violinist can learn to play the bass guitar more easily than the drums, because the neural pattern involved with playing a string instrument has already developed. Having the pavement for the pathway helps when learning a new similar skill. However, when learning a new skill that does not have as well-paved a neural path, it takes time to build the road through repetition and practice of the skill, where attention and intention are paramount.

Often, bright children have a high level of disconnect when learning new skills. They may already have a roadway built for excellent spatial memory while their peers require months or perhaps even years to develop a similar ability. On the other hand, they may not have the brain infrastructure necessary to raise their hand, then wait to be called on. They cannot wait their turn and end up speaking out of turn. Behavior does not match the attention and intention of the child, and learning the appropriate behavior can be challenging and frustrating. In extreme cases, failing time and time again to learn a new skill can be demoralizing to a child, lowering self-image and esteem if the skill is not taught with compassion and patience.

This is where the connections with family, teachers, and community are key. Dr. Pamela Cantor and her colleagues found that emotional connection is the greatest factor helping children to learn.[11] Specifically, when a child is supported and has the emotional equanimity at home, in the classroom, and in the community, the child thrives and knowledge is easily acquired. Children need to feel engaged with material that is meaningful to them, and the bridge can be an emotional connection. When a child has an emotional connection and a sense that there is meaning in the material to learn, the child can easily absorb it.

By contrast, Cantor reports that negative reinforcement and trauma hinder learning. This makes sense. When our minds are stressed, we lack openness to obtain a new skill or information. Instead, our minds and bodies are absorbed in the fight, flight, or freeze responses associated with anxiety. Often this experience leads to a voice of negative self-talk. The mind is off-line, unable to connect with the present moment and material. As Dorothy says to the Scarecrow, "How can you talk if you haven't got a brain?"[12]

Importantly, the environment can support positive neural connections and strengthen development, or it can hinder development and determine whether the brain is primed and ready for learning. Positive neural circuits can reinforce further positive development. Positive reward for internal states that are related to meaning can allow for a change to positive neural circuits and positive behaviors.

In a striking example, Mariale Hardiman and her team have found that arts instruction enhanced learning and integration of science content and concepts.[13] Instructors in fifth grade classrooms in Baltimore, Maryland taught environmental science and astronomy along with singing and dancing. The arts-integrated students retained the scientific information ten weeks later with greater accuracy than students who had studied the same material without arts instruction. The students reported that the pop songs helped them learn the material for the long term. This demonstrates how learning works across three domains: first, learning novel information becomes meaningful and engaging when it is learned with music and dance by activating our senses; second, our brains are wired for retention when there is an emotional connection; and third, when we have an emotional connection to material we retain it better because it is integrated in our senses, emotions, and body. This is corporeal and neural learning. Learning that activates our mind, body, and true nature is everlasting.

Each of the characters in *The Wizard of Oz* searched for something outside of themselves, only to discover it had resided within them all along. We can build positive neural plasticity when our mind is open, awareness is present, and our intention is clear, and when we learn with emotional engagement of novel information. Trust your neurodiverse yellow brick roads. Take yourself on an adventure, get lost, have fun, and walk joyfully along the glistening path you are on. These golden bricks are the building blocks that enhance the neural plasticity of your mind.

As the Wizard of Oz explains to the Scarecrow: "Experience is the only thing that brings knowledge, and the longer you are on earth the more experience you are sure to get."[14]

Neuroscience 101

Before we examine these remarkable brains, I would like to provide a field guide to the brain and the study of neuroscience.

What is neuroscience? It is the most amazing scientific field to be studying in the twenty-first century—or ever.

Neuroscience is the study of the function of the brain and nervous system and encompasses a broad array of topics including neuroanatomy, neurochemistry, neurophysiology, neurobiology, neurogenetics, molecular biology, developmental biology, behavior, experimental psychology, and behavioral psychology. Neuroanatomy refers to the regional specification of a brain region related to function of a brain area. Neurobiology is the study of the central nervous system related to genetics, development, behavior, environment, and emotions. Neurogenetics is the study of the intersection of genetics and the development of the brain.

The main systems of focus in neuroscience are the central nervous system, which is composed of the human brain and the spinal cord, and the peripheral nervous system, which includes all the cranial nerves and ganglia in the body outside the spinal cord, from the nerves and ganglia in the face all the way to the tips of the toes. The nerve fibers are connected like tunnels for information to travel from one part of the nervous system to another. It is important here to imagine how the nervous system is integrated in all parts of the body, and that as a system, it is like a connected lattice where the emergence of the brain, body, and mind converge and meld information.

The study of neuroscience as a field is heavily influenced by the historical figure Phineas Gage. Phineas Gage was not a professor, nor a scholar. Mr. Gage was an unfortunate railroad construction worker who in 1848 was badly injured in an accident. A misplaced explosive blast caused an iron rod (a "tamping iron") to fly like a bullet, shoot through his left cheek, pierce his orbital bone, travel through the front part of his brain, and exit through the top of his skull.[15]

To the surprise of clinicians, Phineas Gage survived this horrific injury, stunned, but conscious. And forever changed. Doctors and family members retained detailed accounts of his extreme behavior changes. A kind, gentle, and joyous man before the accident, Phineas Gage lost his personality as others knew him. After the accident, he often lost his temper, was agitated, and lacked the ability to make sound decisions or see any actions completed. The reason for the dramatic change to his personality and cognition was that the metal rod that injured Phineas Gage created a lesion that was most likely specific to his frontal cortex, an area we now understand as crucial to higher level reasoning and function.

Much of our modern understanding of brain functioning is based on lesioning studies, where a portion of the brain is no longer functioning. It would have been a small consolation to Mr. Gage that his suffering and surviving of a serious brain injury made way for a new understanding of our brains, but we are nevertheless indebted to him.[16]

The human brain is composed of the cerebral cortex, cerebellum, the medulla, and the pons. The cerebral cortex is divided into hemispheres and has brain functions associated within the regions of the cerebral cortex.

The frontal lobe of the cerebral cortex, the frontmost part of the brain behind the forehead, has functions involved in reward attention, planning, short term memory tasks, and motivation. Historical neuroscience presumes that Phineas Gage may have suffered a substantial loss of the frontal lobe of his cerebral cortex.

The parietal lobe is located at the top of the head and integrates sensory information including spatial navigation and touch, mechanoreception (reception of touch from mechanical pressure on the body), and major sensory inputs for skin that include touch, tactile information, temperature, and pain receptors. This region of the brain is activated as we touch a warm cup of coffee, when a fly lands on our arm, when we get chills, or when we navigate down a hallway, and walk through a door. Lesion studies of the parietal lobe show that injury to this part of the brain causes an individual to have a deficit—on the opposite side of the body—in perception for spatial navigation, imagery, and ability to grasp visual objects.[17] Importantly, a lesion of the left hemisphere causes issues with mathematical problem solving, decoding symbols, and reading.[18] Lesions of the parietal lobe interfere with spiritual and transcendent experiences.[19]

The temporal lobe functions include retention of appropriate visual memories, language processing, and emotional connection. One of the most classic disorders of the temporal lobe is Pick's disease, which is the atrophy of the frontotemporal lobe. In Pick's disease, the person experiences mood changes, lack of emotional regulation, low attention span, expresses aggressive behavior toward themselves and others, loses language and speech, writing ability and motor deficits, all of which eventually lead to a loss of any ability to move.[20]

The occipital lobe is the first and main visual processing region for visual information. This is where the retinal ganglion cells share information about their visual field in the brain. Lesions of the occipital lobe may have impairment in visual information, sight, and the visual field.

The cerebellum is known as the hindbrain, the little brain, the structure behind the cerebral cortices which is involved in movement, coordination, timing, precision, and fine motor actions. Lesions of the cerebellum may produce mutism, altered coordination, equilibrium, fine movement, posture instability, and altered movement learning in humans.[21]

Atlas of the Brain

Neuroscience's great advancements in studying the human brain, behavior, and cognition is in part due to the vast studies using magnetic resonance imaging (MRI). This technology is used in modern medical science to view internal representations of the human body. In MRI studies, brain scans of an individual are acquired with millimeter accuracy of brain regions, structures, and functions. Often a group of individuals are accessed for MRI study. Functional MRI is the technique where individuals are scanned while undergoing behavioral, emotional, or cognitive tasks, which provides a visualization of activity by the blood oxygen level dependent ("BOLD") signal. MRIs provide insights of how the brain works as a whole during various behavioral and cognitive activities.

Brain maps facilitate visualizing the brain while measuring the relationship of the brain by cognitive tasks and performance. The structural images of the brain allow for regional representations of grey matter and white matter. Grey matter is composed of neurons and glial cells, which allows for information processing. Humans have approximately 100 billion neurons that construct complex networks for information processing, and that provide a broad range of individual variation for a human experience. Neurons release neurotransmitters for communication to other neurons via electrical signals. There are approximately one hundred known neurotransmitters that have the properties of excitation and inhibition. Importantly, the neurotransmitter receptor dictates the action of the neurotransmitter. Neurons provide a network for information convergence, manipulation, processing, and storage. Glial cells actively protect the brain by eliminating debris and aid with neuroinflammation and neurodevelopment. White matter measurement in the brain reflects axonal projections and thickness and is involved in information flow and efficiency. White matter tracts are the freeways of the brain where the white matter between two regions allows for the relay of information, and the brain regions are like different cities. The speed of the information varies on the white matter tracts themselves, such as the abundance, the distance and the strength of the connections across brain regions. Sensory systems include auditory (hearing), visual (sight), gustatory (taste), olfactory (smell), somatic sensation (touch), and vestibular (balance and movement) processing, which converge their sensory receptors and information on a single organ—the brain. The brain interprets sensory information in varying degrees that create the scaffolding of perception. Advancements in neuroscience have given us a great understanding of the human brain, its wiring, the remarkable uniqueness of each brain and the processing and the integration of unique individual experiences.

Degendered Brain

For years, the myth has persisted that there is a "typical male brain" that differs from the "typical female brain." Neuroscience is now debunking that notion. In fact, there is no such thing as a gendered brain. The brain is a dynamic mosaic. Its development and neural plasticity is tied to our genetics, upbringing, experience, environment, epigenetic factors, emotionality, bodily and sensory responsivity, and our autobiographical memories.

Unfortunately, myth of a gendered brain creates a false narrative flowing in our culture like a flooded pool spilling into everything and carrying an undercurrent of sexist stereotypes. The media and culture enjoy a catchy story that makes determinations about the sexes by exaggerating scientific findings to build a foundation of sex and gender differences. The problem is when a myth centers its foundation on soft science and is represented as fact, the mythology self-perpetuates into a cycle of anecdotal storytelling, building sexist ideas of a gendered brain and behaviors. In many cases, false narratives confine both genders to stereotypes within our culture limiting both boys and girls, dictating what they can or cannot do, how they should behave, who they should become, whom they may love, and how they see themselves in society.

When a people do not see a representation of themselves in the culture, it is as if they do not exist. It is particularly damaging to an individual's well-being and life trajectory. The false narrative of the gendered brain is a damaging kind of storytelling that must stop. It undermines the existence of diversity and detracts from seeing the gifts of an individual. I will say this: women can do math, science, and manual labor just as males can cook, crochet, and be the primary care-takers of children. Culture in the past has shaped the roles of gender division, but when it comes to our minds, there are no gender labels that predict that the female brain is better at something than the male brain, or vice versa. One's skill or ability to do any particular thing is highly individual and independent of one's gender, and we need to instill in people the truth that any person can be or do anything.

Our neuroanatomy reflects this truth. According to the latest large-scale studies reviewing both male and female brains, scientists are finding that there are no major anatomical distinctions between male and female brains. The research is deciphering the enigma of the brain. We are learning that the human range and potential are more wide open than previously imagined. Particularly, brain function and processing is centered on the principle of neuroindividuality—not using one's gender as the sole description of one's behavior and ability. Foundational principles of neuroscience are now being reevaluated, questioned, and rewritten right before our eyes with greater numbers of subjects participating in studies, more accurate MRI analyses, and advanced programing to explore the mysteries of the mind.

In a groundbreaking study involving an international collaboration, Professor Daphna Joel and team at University of Tel Aviv conducted extensive examinations of 2176 participants using three forms of analyses of brain scans. These revealed that female brains are almost as likely to be categorized as "normal male brains" as are male brains. The same was true for male brains: they were equally as likely to be identified as a female brain.[22] Only sex differences were found in some rare brain types on the extreme ends of the spectrum. Scientists found that sex categorization was not a major predictor of the variability of human brain structure, morphology, and neuroanatomy. This study highlights that gender is not a predictor for brain differences.

In another investigation to understand the human brain and gender, Joel and her team report in their article, "Sex beyond the genitalia: The human brain mosaic," where they reviewed 1,400 human male and female brain scans and revealed wide overlap for all brain connectivity, gray matter, and white matter in both male and female brains.[23] These findings are robust across groups, age, MRI technology, and analyses. Across the dataset, it is highly rare that a brain would show extreme femaleness or maleness. In fact, the human brain is comprised of a mosaic dependent on various factors like genetics, environment, experience, and epigenetic factors. Scientists stress that even though there are sex/gender variances in the brain, the human brain does not fit into a classification with one of the two groups, male or female. Instead, every brain belongs to a single class: human.

Looking into specifically the hippocampus, an area of the brain responsible for long term memory formation and consolidation, emotional and sensory processing, Dhruv Marwha and Meha Halari, scientists in Dr. Lise Elliot lab at Rosalind Franklin University, co-authored a meta-analysis study comprised of seventy-six academic papers encompassing analysis of the brains of over 6,000 male and female participants. They found that both male and female brains were of equal size in the hippocampus.[24] This study breaks the barriers of neurosexism—the idea of sex-brained behaviors based on a person's genitalia—and shows that sexist assumptions are factually untrue.

Previous studies reported that females' brains have larger hippocampi, espousing a false narrative to promote sex-based behavioral stereotypes, like the idea that females have greater verbal communication, enhanced emotionality and expression, and better interpersonal relations and the stereotype that males speak less, have less emotional expression, and have decreased ability for personal relations. These faulty assumptions are not scientific, and they undermine both females and males by prescribing that their gender provides for a set of fixed behaviors.

The truth is that, in our society, females and males can verbally communicate equally well, have an equal range of emotions and expression, and have the same abilities for interpersonal relations. Unfortunately, our society reinforces behavioral stereotypes with misinformation providing for behavioral conditioning and gender phenotyping. From birth on, males and females are programmed for sets of behaviors that define who they are in the world with such nonsense as *boys don't cry* and *be strong* and *good girls play nice* and *wait your turn to speak*, rather than telling every child, whether boy or girl, agender, bigender, or gender fluid, you can grow into who you are meant to be. This is a time in our culture when we can begin to reshape our ideas, stop minimizing and characterizing all genders, and erase these ideas of behavioral phenotyping based on sex.

Where did all this misinformation grow from and how? In the early 1990s and 2000s, when brain imaging had its birth, many of the first studies to understand the human brain opened the window to the impossible. But the foundations of these hypotheses were focused on group differences with a small number of participants and new technology. It seemed exciting to provide data and answers for male and female differences based on brain differences. And the media and culture loves a good story or a catchphrase like *Men are from Mars, Women are from Venus.* It became so tempting for the media to repeat the stereotypes that males are better problem solvers, think faster and thus they have more gray matter whereas women are more emotional, talk more, and can multitask because of their greater white matter and bigger corpus collosum for communication and relaying information across their hemispheres. All of these findings are incorrect, and have led to years of misinformation and brain sexist ideals. We know now that both male and female brains are much more alike than not. It is very important to understand that studying with small sample sizes gave results that were skewed and not representative of both populations. Now these gendered brain myths have been debunked, breaking the barriers of stereotypes surrounding the notion that there are female and male brains. That, my friend, is a myth with questionable evidence. New research studies are shattering what we once thought to be true of the human brain in relation to males and females; our understanding is now being reframed and redefined.

It is critical to make the distinction that although neuroanatomy appears as a mosaic of the human brain, sex hormones released by the sex organs of male and female gonads do have an impact on the brain, behavior, and even functioning. When it comes to neuroanatomy in large-scale studies, scientists are finding that there are no major distinctions between the male and female brain.

How hormones regulate functioning and behavior in males and females relates to the brain and behavior. That said, men's and women's sex organs (gonads) release hormones that influence behavior. But even that is highly individual. For example, hormonal secretion can regulate two people differently, even though both are female. Hormones are known to regulate behaviors, and there is a wide body of evidence for behavioral regulation focused on mating behaviors that can be manipulated in both the male and female brain with the presence of hormones and cause epigenetic events that account for behavioral differences.[25] It is essential to realize that behavior can show differential regulation based on hormonal release. But, more often than not, what we are looking at in our society is gender learned roles that divide both males and females for abilities, functioning, and life outcomes.

A more important point is that male and female brain and neuro-anatomy is similar and there are no brain differences that divide males or females into a specific brain type for a gender. Brain development is nuanced and neuroindividual. I believe it undermines both sexes to oversimplify by assuming that stereotypical behaviors are a function of neuroanatomy. Much of the so-called differences we see between males and females are driven by how culture feeds into stereotypes of males and females and by our socialization. I think we need to come away from this with greater awareness so that we don't jump to oversimplify complicated behaviors as female or male based on the brain's functioning and wiring and instead open our minds to individual differences that do not reduce males, females, agender, bigender, and gender fluid people to stereotypes.

Math Girls, Math Boys—Their Brains Look Identical when They're Doing Math

The challenges we face in our culture about gender and related abilities stem from ignoring facts and hard evidence and thereby allowing misinformation and opinions to feed into the language of stereotypes about girls and boys. But the truth is that girls' and boys' minds are equal when doing math from a young age. Our attitudes and speech remain among the key symbols of our solved and unsolved problems of gender gap. Our culture needs to become schooled in the latest neuroscience studies of math and the developing brain. Professor Jessica Cantlon of Carnegie Mellon University, lead author, Alyssa Kersey, and a team of neuroscientists conducted a study with 104 children, ages three to 10, to access the brain activity in boys and girls while they were engaged in math exercises. The team found that both girls' and boys' brains were equally stimulated and capable of solving math problems.[26] This was evidence that girls and boys possess equal capabilities for doing math at young ages, and that math abilities are not dominated by a single gender but rather equally across genders. Math abilities are ungendered in the brain. In an MRI scanner, children watched video clips of *Sesame Street* showing math concepts such as addition and subtraction. Both boys and girls had similar brain activity of the intraparietal sulcus, a region in the brain dedicated to math concepts such as number and object assignments, math predictions, word assignments of numbers, and the concept of adding and subtracting. This study challenges the kinds of stereotypes that so often discourage girls from going into the STEM fields, and that are perpetuated with nonsense such as Teen Talk Barbie dolls programmed to tell young girls, *"Math class is tough. Let's go shopping." "Okay, meet me at the mall!"*[27]

Alyssa Kersey, the lead author, highlights in their report: "Across all analyses girls and boys showed significant gender similarities in neural functioning, indicating that boys and girls engage the same neural system during mathematics development." In an earlier study, she, Jessica Cantlon, and team explored in a meta-analysis of five studies that included more than 500 children from ages six months to eight years, developmental mathematic abilities of the genders in three domains: perception of numbers, counting, and math concepts.[28] This elucidates that both boys and girls did not differ developmentally in math concepts and quantitative abilities. Further, this points out that boys *and* girls have the capacity to equally reason math cognition in childhood. Both studies reaffirm findings in earlier studies that showed equality. A massive wide-scale study that included over a million subjects and compiled data from 242 studies published from 1990 to 2007, established that males and females perform the same in math cognition.[29]

These findings are part of a wide body of evidence that females and males have equal math abilities. One of the most disheartening points is the gender stereotype-based language that surrounds abilities of males and females and limits individuals and, more important, discourages neuroindividuals from sharing their given gifts and talents with the world due to the self-limiting beliefs that arise as a result of the stories transmitted through our culture. The language of division, saying boys are better at XY and girls are better at XX, needs to change. We should listen to the voices of our children, hear their interests, and guide them on a path that will empower them to explore uncharted geographies, experience their unbound minds, enjoy their unlimited gifts, and set off into the sunset as trailblazers to discover the greater unknowns.

The Dark Art of Fitting Out

Sam Christensen, my mentor, once said to a class, "I know you all know Nicole is smart, but she is much smarter than she looks. Nicole, I hope you don't take that the wrong way, where that offends you. I say this because you are really smart, and they need to know."

Much of my life I have been out of sync with time, living through my own version of quantum entanglement. I was born the youngest of five children. My four siblings fit into their own tight pack, seven to 11 years older than me. Being highly verbal and articulate, I sought out conversations with adults. One of my favorite friends in elementary school was our neighbor, Mr. Sunday, a retired geology professor who showed me the world of natural and polished stones, rose quartz, turquoise, meteorites, and pieces of the earth's core. We had weekly chats in which he opened the world of minerals to me, and afterward we would visit with his wife in her hospital bed and I would hold her hand. Most children would not have had the patience for this, but I did.

As a child I often spent time alone in my room where I lived in my imagination and wrote stories, collected facts, and tried to understand how things worked. I drew months' worth of moon phases and cycles to understand patterns and rotations. When I took my moon phase journal into my 4th grade class and my teacher was unresponsive to my moon investigation and acted as though it were not amazing that we are continuously spinning on an axis. She missed my passion. That year, I decided I wanted to be an astronaut.

Even though my mother, father, and siblings encouraged my storytelling and talking, each of us knew that during dinner conversations, if we didn't capture everyone's attention, someone else would cut us off and take the spotlight. We learned to speak about things of value for us. We learned that our voices mattered. We learned that we all had something to share. We learned that at home we were safe. We learned that we could speak. At home I had unbound freedom to imagine, create, and speak. But at school, I did not feel free.

Quiet girls are good girls—something we are fed from our earliest days. If a voice if is not nurtured it will either burst into a wild forest fire or wilt away into ashes, scattered, diffuse, and immaterial. Girls are told to be quiet, to sit still, raise their hands, and wait their turn. If, time after time, they are not called on, they begin to choke and their voices—their thoughts, their ideas—get stuck at their collar bone for days, weeks, years, even decades.

The other thing I had to deal with was the cultural expectation that I'd be good-natured and nice because I was blonde and pretty with big green eyes. Too often, people focused on the way I looked and offered compliments on what a "pretty little girl" I was. Outside of my home, I rarely received the message that I was smart. In middle school, in all those times when quantum entanglement captures you with growing into adolescence and moving out of imaginary play into becoming a young woman, my 8th grade teacher Mrs. A had to highlight this.

In math class, I was at the chalkboard showing my proof of having solved the unsolvable problem. No surprise here, my father was an aerospace engineer and I loved math. As I smiled with excitement for having figured out the problem, Mrs. A called me over to her. Me, being a "good girl," obeyed. She turned me to face her and tucked my white uniform shirt into my green plaid skirt as everyone watched. We stood away from the board, away from my proof, my solved math problem, while the whole class stared at me and my body. When she was done tucking in my shirt and arranging my clothes, she remarked for all the class to hear about how my body looked nice and slim when my shirt was tucked in, rather than sloppy because my shirt was too baggy. I was horrified. I had started to develop and wore my shirt loose to mask my breasts. I'd already had a good amount of attention directed at me by the boys and my baggy shirt had solved that problem. Now the entire class was focused on how I looked—not on the fact that I'd gotten that problem right, the problem that no one, *not one person in my class*, had been able to solve.

That was not a story I told at the dinner table that night. I was too shattered and embarrassed. And a little broken. It was another message telling me that *good* girls are quiet, pretty girls. Mrs. A was caught up in her very own quantum entanglement and feeding into the stereotype that if you are girl and blonde, then math doesn't matter. But for me, a girl, *and* blonde, math had always been fun. For me, math was and still is a secret language on paper that has proof.

I am a rebel and follow my own timeline. At home, when I could explore my imagination, my Barbie had much more than kick-ass outfits, she had brains. In my Barbie's universe, she was the lead, the head honcho, the main character with limitless ability to innovate and succeed. My Barbie loved math. She had a career as a lawyer, a doctor, an explorer, an astronaut, a humanitarian; she solved problems and even through difficult times, she persisted. Barbie always persisted. And in some cases, she even had a shaved head.

Luckily for me, graduation approached and there was light at the end of that middle school tunnel. In high school I was selected for honors math and fast-tracked to reach college calculus in my senior year. In high school, I was filled with messages that girls could do anything. Time caught up with my mind, and even though I still often live out of sync, I have found my voice. I sometimes speak out of turn, sometimes say things that cause discomfort, but I always adhere to the truth that girls can do anything. Boys can do anything too. And agender, bigender, and gender fluid people can do anything. Bright children are often out of sync because they are years ahead with their cognition and abilities when quantum entanglement requires patience and practice learning some people will miss your full being because they are stuck in time.

> *"Life can only be understood backwards; but it must be lived forwards."*
>
> —Søren Kierkegaard

Neuroscience of Asynchronous Development in Bright Minds**

There is a great body of evidence in neuroscience indicating that our individuality originates within our unique brains. Recent studies

---

** Previously published online at 2e News (https://www.2enews.com) and in *Variations Magazine*

demonstrate that each of our brains is as distinctive as a fingerprint; we could even say a brain-print. With advances in brain mapping and imaging software, we know no two brains are identical—which makes sense. We each have our own genetic makeup, process information from our environment through our five senses, express unique ways of emotional processing, and are composed of our specific autobiographical memories. As a neuroscientist, I believe we are barely scratching the surface in our understanding of the human brain, both what we think we know and the vast world of the unknown. If you happen to be bright and have quirky behaviors, then your brain, body, and particular physiology may be at the core of how you navigate the world.

Early in 2006, a foundational study by Shaw and colleagues at UCLA Imaging Institute had followed more than 300 children for 12 years, mapping brain development and growth.[30] They created three-dimensional brain maps and calculated measurements of grey and white matter from brain scans from ages seven to 19. In the study, the children completed an IQ test and the participants were placed in three groups: average, high, and superior intelligence.

The researchers found that the children showed asynchronous brain development, meaning that regions of the brain grew at varying rates and various time points based on development. Brain growth was specific to the onset of puberty, when there is known to be vast brain expansions and major changes in the brain and body's hormonal systems. Children in the superior intelligence group had an even greater increase in brain growth—specifically in the frontal cortex—from age eight and a half through age 14.

The frontal cortex, which develops in humans all the way through the third decade of life, is the holy grail for executive functioning, intuitive problem-solving, communication, and emotional saliency. This is the mother lode for behavior and cognition, as well as planning, completing, and focusing on any sort of task. In bright children, a common challenge is remaining focused and being productive where there is a disconnect between their ability, functioning, and natural talents.

As we know, bright children often express extraordinary gifts but also have great challenges, which they either mask or are unaware of.

Standard measures of intelligence, such as IQ tests, pose issues for "twice-exceptional" (or "2e") students, who have both high intelligence and learning challenges, because their weaknesses can preclude them from demonstrating their strengths. For example, a child reading at college level who struggles with handwriting may not be able to show the depth and complexity of her textual understanding. Or, my son for example, who was known as the absent-minded professor in middle school because he did his work ahead of time but forgot to turn it in. Missing those assignments was not a true evaluation of his abilities or even a remote understanding of his brainpower and functioning.

Asynchronous brain development may be at the heart of what we are seeing in these bright children. There may be one or more greatly over-expanded and well-developed brain regions amid other regions that are developmentally behind, compromising cognitive processing and executive functioning skills. These are the emerging perspectives about neurodiversity. To take a look at this more closely, imagine a three-year-old child with a well-developed brain area for audition (sensory processing for sound). For him, sounds are heard louder, sooner, and in some cases the sounds can reach a threshold of pain for the child. Given the child's age, an underdeveloped frontal cortex could make it difficult to regulate this threshold, resulting in "bad behavior." A child could be tagged as a problem case rather than understood as having a specific disability that causes the child to suffer. This misidentification and misunderstanding could cause greater stress in the child and everyone around him because the actual issue is not addressed.

Understanding that the frontal cortex greatly expands in puberty could be key to understanding asynchronous behavior in gifted and 2e children. When we see these troubling behaviors, it is critical that we completely understand their causes.

Are we doomed if we have a bright child? No, we simply have to pay closer attention to their particular ways of navigating in the world. We need to pursue positive strategies and learning opportunities for the child. We know that learning requires an emotional connection to create positive associations and positive neural plasticity. The best ways to support a bright asynchronous learner are:

○ Have compassion for asynchrony

○ Provide safe spaces and communication

○ Listen to their needs

○ Identify their learning styles

○ Provide appropriate supports in and out of the classroom

○ Allow them to learn at their own pace

○ Nurture strengths and challenged areas equally

○ Provide more opportunities for success than failure

○ Encourage unique thinking

○ Help them identify their passions

○ Give them opportunity to engage in activities with like-minded peers

For my little absent-minded professor, a simple solution was creating a single homework folder that was turned in to his home-room teacher at the start of the day. This gave him a foundation and a simple repetitive task, which then translated into positive behavior and feelings of success. Ultimately, we changed the mind-body connection with a positive solution. Also, this coincided with his natural development, as his executive functioning skills caught up with his neurodiverse mind. Mary Oliver wrote, "In creative work—creative work of all kinds—those who are the world's working artists are not trying to help the world go around, but forward."

It is our job as a society to find creative solutions to help these children thrive and move forward into the space of imagining a future with all shapes and sizes of neurodiversity as a way of life. As guides, we need to allow space and time for the bright mind to break free from the ordinary, experience the extraordinary, and then awaken to life.

Spectrum of Light

There is a sweet spot in human sight for visualizing color in the range of 390 to 700 nanometers, but the spectrum of light is much greater, including unseen (to us) infrared and ultraviolet light. We know now that the spectrum of light goes far beyond our actual visual abilities. This limitation of our humanness became apparent to me when I began to label and study fluorescent neurons under the microscope.

For the process of fluorescent neuronal visualization, the entire microscope room must be dark. But before that step, staining the tissue is also done in darkness so there is no way to know whether an experiment has worked until it is seen under the microscope. The only illumination is from a fluorescent bulb emitting light onto treated tissue that is placed between two very thin pieces of glass. Under the microscope, neurons light up my visual field like a constellation of stars. Seeing light beyond the human range is achieved through science, modern technology, and creativity. The act of scientific discovery shapes our perception as we know it. This defies the limitations of the human visual range and allows for an entire landscape within an imagined range.

Underwater, our vision is blurred, out of focus, blunted, and we are creatures out of our element and ordinary experience. Underwater, light slows, blends, and changes color. Our visual system developed for us to see in air. To see underwater, we need to wear goggles with air in the space between our eyes and the water. Even then, colors underwater change, morph, and bend. Just under the surface, color is similar to that above water, but as we descend farther into the depths of the sea, colors escape our visual frequency.

When we are submerged in pure darkness, we first lose sight of red, then orange, yellow, green, and finally blue. To see in the deep of the ocean we need a flashlight to illuminate objects. We weave in and out of color fields and planes underwater, in space, and on land and at times we will need a flashlight to see what is there in the darkness to be revealed.

We also know that sight is a matter of perspective. No two people actually see the same flower the same way, or the same colors in the flower exactly the same way. At first glance, sight is a single modality. What we think we are seeing is our perception. The way our brain— the primary sensory organ in our skull—stores information is from our past, our emotions, our genetics, our experiences, and our sensory experiences all at the same time.

At birth, infants have limited vision. The visual pathway in humans develops after birth, and we know that, at birth, the visual cortex—the region of the brain for visual processing— has all cell layers and cytoarchitecture (the landscape of the cellular layers) fully developed. Even individuals who are blind at birth have fully developed and ordered cellular organization of the visual cortex.[31] It is through the use of the eyes, genetics, intricate developmental stages, neural processing, connectivity, and behavior that infants begin to see with greater clarity in their first six months. This period is known to be a critical time for brain development.

Once, while I was giving a lecture, a mother raised her hand and asked: "Can you go over in detail all the critical time periods for brain development?"

I told her, "All time is critical for development of the mind. In all the time in the universe you and I will never have this same discussion again. Each person's brain develops in its own way through genetics, environment, and training."

I was recalling what the Greek philosopher Heraclitus said: "No man ever steps in the same river twice, for it's not the same river and he's not the same man." No experience can ever be perceived exactly the same way twice. For example, the flow of the water in a river is amorphous and constantly changing. None of the molecules are ever the same. It is a new experience every moment. And no moment is ever fixed.

Heraclitus was expressing a truth that neuroscientists can now explain with precision: that a pattern of neuronal firing in the prefrontal cortex is unique to each experience. Each experience is truly "novel" in our brains. As I explained to the mother at my lecture, our conversation happened at a specific moment in time and was experienced uniquely in both our brains, never to be repeated. Experience is essential for adaptation, learning, and mental flexibility for new situations. This doesn't mean we don't have memory, but each experience must have its own unique pattern to adapt to different situations.

For example, a recent study conducted in mice recorded the electrical activity from 300 neurons in the frontal cortex. The investigators found that even though an identical activity was repeated by the mice, the brain perceived each experience as novel, each time, over many repetitions with distinct neuronal firing patterns.[32] Nothing is ever perceived twice. For that very reason, be here now, be present because every moment is unique. Pay attention to the actual moment you are in.

The rest of the answer to her question, the scientific truth, is that the human brain develops and changes continuously throughout our lives. We know there are times of rapid brain growth *in utero*, the first three years after birth known as critical period (blunt beginning and end) with sensitive period (gradual beginning and end) for brain development through age five. Thus, there is wide ability for neuronal development in the early years of life. For example, language acquisition has a sensitive period from three to seven years. Likewise, there are rapid brain expansions happening during puberty from hormonal changes that occur in the body, and in particular, the frontal cortex continues to develop through our mid-thirties. The brain has the ability for growth and expansion throughout life. As biologists, we have a road map of the brain, body, and mind expansions, but how each person develops is unique to their specific genetics, environment, and timing. We now know the brain and its processing is more malleable than we ever thought, and it can be developed through neural plasticity and training.

The brain is the control center of the nervous system. The mind is the intersection of the brain, where all our thoughts, experiences, emotions, bodily sensations, and perceptions converge with information from our present and future actions, our imagination, our conscious and subconscious states that guide mental and physical behaviors, the driving forces of our nature, the who, what, where, and why of our existence. Our individuality shapes our perception, our neural patterning, and our mind.

Like our minds, science is a matter of trial and error, of hypotheses testing. By the time you read a study published in a popular science magazine, a team of people has spent countless hours, days, years, even decades arriving at that single discovery. And the person, the first author, who took the study through the finish line, has the mental stamina and determination of an ultra-marathoner. What you read in popular science is not there by accident. It takes a great deal of creativity and faith to imagine a discovery after hundreds of failures.

Science is a highly creative process. A transformation of the unknown. Artistry is required to design an experiment, imagine possible outcomes, question methodology, retest parameters, relive failure, and rebirth new ideas. My favorite science studies and discoveries are those that leave open-ended questions for the next individual to test, the studies that find one small discovery that has us looking at things with a new slant, a discovery that opens years of questioning and provides insights on how to be better as a whole. But my favorite studies reveal what remains unseen.

Dear Big Think,

You are magic. Everything you imagine exists in you. There is nothing broken. Nothing to fix, change, improve, or erase about you. A flicker of light—your essence, your magic. Enveloping the chaos of the universe—you are complete and whole. You are everything of ordinary transcendence, a spark, an ignited flame of a match striking the side of a matchbox, a chemical reaction of red phosphorus to white. Pure light. Always remember you are magic.

Love forevermore,

Head Forest Fairy

CHAPTER 2:
You're Gifted, Now What?

Where we get it all wrong with gifted is the word "gifted" itself, the language or lack of language around giftedness, the disconnected dialogue, and the societal story of gifted. Inevitably, when I tell people I study giftedness, I hear their personal story of a child they once knew, perhaps a neighbor's child, classmate, a friend of a friend, or someone they grew up with who was a child piano prodigy. And yes, that is an accurate example of giftedness, but it is only one type of giftedness. People often think of giftedness as an extraordinary skill and achievement, one that can be seen by others and where there is a performance or other measure for the giftedness, specifically an external measure. Although that description is true in some cases, the "extraordinary achievement" model is far from the truth for all cases. As a society, we make observations and create identifications within groups—and sometimes we miss the entire spectrum. We are limited by viewing only a single wavelength.

As we discussed in chapter one, the concept of neuroindividuality centers on the fact that our uniqueness is ingrained in our biology. Our genetics, perceptions, experiences, emotions, and epigenetic events work together to make each of us unique individuals. Individuality is woven in our brain, body, mind, nervous system, and DNA. Often, we look at giftedness as a "group," but because there is vast individuality among those who are gifted, it is very challenging for us to identify a child who is gifted who does not fit the ideals we have societally defined as gifted. Additionally, asynchronous brain development creates a wide disconnect when we try to identify gifted children because what determines giftedness is continuously developing and, due to their asynchrony, their intelligence and gifts can be masked. Because of asynchrony of the brain and body development, the path for a bright child is an unchartered one and a struggling child may be how a gifted child presents in their giftedness. Every child develops in their own way and on their own timeline and there needs to be continuous adjustments by their parents and educators to ensure they are optimally engaged when exploring and learning. Identifying the origin and the underlying cause of challenging behavior is the turning point in identifying solutions to help the child thrive. Defining gifted is not one single thing, it is a range of light.

Gifted Talk

The word "gifted" is defined in Webster's dictionary as, "having great natural ability; revealing a special gift." When talking about intellectual, athletic, emotional, sensory, or any form of giftedness comes across as bragging, it is off-putting and taboo. The word gifted is loaded.

Because of this gifted disconnect, gifted persons are seen as awkward, misfit, weird, eccentric, and nerdy. Gifted people are highly misunderstood, misidentified, and misdiagnosed. There is a large confusion with elitism, success, and achievement that interferes with understanding giftedness. Because of the array of misunderstandings, gifted persons tend to experience social isolation and exclusion.

A person who is not understood and who lacks visibility because of exclusion can suffer devastating consequences to the brain, body, mind, and psyche. Specifically, social isolation activates the pain centers in the brain as physical pain has a signature in the brain, pain regardless of the source activates the same brain pathways. Simply put, pain is pain.[1] When individuals are suffering, they not only have challenges, they develop maladaptive behaviors and are seen as acting out.

It is essential that we reframe the gifted discussion to allow for openness and enough space to encompass neuroindividuality—to create a setting with the intention of understanding a large, diverse group of people, there needs to be space without boundaries. We need to open the discussion of giftedness, we need to share our voice, to talk and talk about giftedness.

New World Order Redefining Gifted

The gifted definition that will be the focus of this book mirrors the definition of the National Association for Gifted Children (NAGC), which describes gifted as:

> *"Gifted individuals are those who demonstrate outstanding levels of aptitude (defined as exceptional ability to reason and learn) or competence (documented performance or achievement in top 10% or rarer) in one or more domains."*

Based on this definition, approximately 10% of our population is identified as gifted, which is something we need to pay attention to for the future of the well-being of all people. In particular, this definition makes a critical distinction because an individual who has an enhanced specialization in a specific modality, like visual processing, distinctly interprets the world differently than do others.

Gifted diversity begins with the brain, body, and a different experiencing of the world. In particular, gifted individuals are "hardwired" differently. Their differences encompass brain anatomy, bodily perceiving, sensory processing, levels of intensity, increased sensitivities to bodily sensations, emotional intelligence, and elevated responses to the environment. Gifted individuals must understand their own being to live a healthy and fulfilled life. When the range of possibilities for gifted individuals to fit in is narrow, and their giftedness is limited to education, achievement, and success, they may not be able to cultivate true meaning and integrate all facets of their personality, and therefore not meet all their social, emotional, mental, intellectual, creative, physical, and sensory needs.

Here is my cocktail party version of the message: Gifted individuals see and experience the world uniquely. They have a unique biology, from their brain maps to their genetics to their sensory processing to their emotional processing to their biorhythms. Every individual navigates in his or her own way, and in the human population, there is a vast array of ways to do that.

As Catherine Pulsifer insightfully noted, "We are all different, which is great because we are all unique. Without diversity life would be very boring."

We are expanding, evolving beings, ever changing, ever growing. We can ignite our imagination to embark into the impossible and find space for a new gifted story. I invite you to open to a gifted pain, diversity, and beauty story, where the gifted voice is often lost, misunderstood, and marginalized. I am inviting you to open a dialogue with your family, friends, teachers, professionals, and with the entire world to give visibility to the gifted community and really see it for what it is—beauty. As a community, let's expand our awareness to respect one another in our differences, truly help one another, and compassionately engage in a dialogue that includes the latest scientific findings and gifted stories.

Our Deceiving Perceptions

I have been a cross country runner for much of my life. I was a good runner, usually placing in the top three in cross country meets. But I had a limit to my maximum speed: no matter how hard I trained, I had an innate threshold. I simply did not have the biology or gift to become a professional runner. My biological make-up is different than that of an elite Olympic marathoner. Olympian runners' prime unique physiology, which includes their physique, kinesthetic performance, and most important, a maximal oxygen uptake VO_2max (the quantification of an individual's maximum oxygen consumption during vigorous exercise) allows them to run a five minute mile.[2] I do not have, and will never attain, the ability to have a VO_2max of an elite runner like Jemima Jelagat Sumgong, from Kenya. Her genetics and environment, combined with her intensity and passion to train won her the gold medal at the 2016 Olympics in Rio.[3] Jemima Jelagat Sumgong has a remarkable gift.

A gifted athlete has a unique physiology. So does a gifted nine-year-old child who reads at college level. Specifically, the young child who reads at college level has an intensified intellectual ability that is specific to biology, originating from genetics and environment that develop expanded brain circuits and create an intensified intellectual ability. Brain research and imaging shows that high IQ individuals have expanded cortical brain volumes, regional expansions, and connections for intellectual processing—in other words, gifted individuals are "hard-wired" differently.

Gifted Expectations

Another area where we get it all wrong with giftedness is the hyperfocus on gifted academic success and achievement, as if we somehow get the academic achievement puzzle put together the gifted appetite will be satisfied. Gifted academics is one aspect of a gifted person. Academics and achievement measures cannot be the sole focus for a gifted person. An appropriate level of engagement and challenge is absolutely necessary for the purpose and satisfaction of life for a gifted person, but academic or professional achievement is only one area or domain. There are many other aspects that make up an individual.

We have an expectation that gifted children and adults should be able to obtain consistent success. As a result, in our minds we don't allow for failure or mistakes, and that mindset in turn doesn't allow much room for gifted people to grow. Often, when a child has an extraordinary gift, that child is praised for their gift and that kind of very specific praise leads to an overidentification with the actual gift. When gifted children learn something new, but are not extraordinarily adept at it, learning can be exceptionally challenging unless they have been appropriately trained in resilience and self-acceptance for a perceived failure.

This is where we are left with that double-edged sword of the label "gifted." Gifted children are packaged as though they should be meeting continued academic success without setbacks. This unreasonable expectation can be inherently stressful for the child and it is not practical. Gifted children who lack support for their failed efforts will ultimately flame out due to the stress of these great expectations and the paralysis of perfectionism.

The expectations of being gifted include a false idea that the gifted person is supposed to be good at everything and expected to be "better" compared to others. This false mindset causes deep misunderstanding within the gifted population. The gifted label creates expectations to perform and to always be successful. These expectations inherently create a false identity for the child and within society of what it means to be gifted. Gifted is no better, no worse, but actually neurodiverse. Gifted is a unique way of experiencing and absorbing the world.

Testing outside of the Box

Standard intelligence testing measures capture a good number of bright and gifted people, but the tests are imperfect. They do not capture *all* bright people. Standard intelligence tests can be a good starting point to identify gifted people, but by no means are these the only measure for giftedness. A test is simply what our society has constructed for order, classification, and quantification. While standard intelligence measures may be helpful or even necessary, the existing tests are far from a holy grail that can measure and predict a person's total ability and functioning for all the factors that contribute to a broad and inclusive definition of giftedness. Most important, testing is limited in its ability to identify a bright person with a learning difference ("twice-exceptional" or "2e" learners), and intelligence tests have been shown to be confounded by sexism, racism, and cultural and economic factors.

One of most commonly known "aptitude" tests, the SAT, is promoted by its publisher, the College Board, as predictive of the grades students will earn in their first year of college as well as their rate of retention in their second year of college.[4] This test is often an indicator for attrition in college. Students who score over 1150 have almost no attrition.

The inherent problem with the SAT is that it may not reflect aptitude at all but rather access to resources. Families who can afford to pay for test prep courses are promised a score increase of 200 points on average, while students with fewer economic resources have little to no access to these resources and may lack an environment that supports maximizing their test-scoring potential. Could the college attrition rate be similarly tied to access to resources? If so, what are some of the best practices to address this inequity?

A series of studies by Herman Aguinis and colleagues have challenged the validity of this assertion, demonstrating a statistical error rate between 16 and 19 percent, depending on the college.[5] Moreover, variation in SAT scores are highly correlated with wealth and race. Students who are poor, especially students of color, score significantly worse on the SAT than white, wealthy students with similar academic profiles[6]. In 2019, Robert Schaeffer, the Public Education Director of the non-profit FairTest, the National Center for Fair & Open Testing, summarized the demographic statistics: "Whether broken down by test-takers' race, parental education or household income, average SAT scores of students from historically disenfranchised groups fell further behind their classmates from more privileged families. The SAT remains a more accurate measure of a test-taker's family background than of an applicant's capacity to do college level work."[7]

In addition, affluent high school students benefit from expensive private tutoring and test preparation classes to prepare for these high-stakes tests, fueling a billion-dollar test preparation industry.[8] As a result of these issues with equity and access, a growing number of U.S. colleges and universities have made standardized tests optional for their admissions application. In June 2020, in part due to the coronavirus pandemic, Caltech announced that it would suspend standardized test requirements for two years, joining nearly half of U.S. colleges and universities that have made the test optional for fall 2021. Nevertheless, the SAT and similar standardized tests remain a qualifying gatekeeper for tuition-based "gifted" youth education and enrichment programs like the Center for Talented Youth at Johns Hopkins University.[9]

The differences in access to programs like CTY, limited by standardized tests and wealth differences further contribute to economic and racial inequality among the identified "gifted" population, limiting access and opportunity, and defining giftedness in terms of academic test-taking rather making room for a holistic and comprehensive view.

The gifted mind is incredibly challenging to understand. There can be different levels and forms of giftedness, and the uniqueness of our inherited gifts make the gifted spectrum all the more richly diverse.

Even more important, there can be a disconnect between raw talent and intellect and performance, achievement, ability, and functioning.

In scientific studies, intelligence is defined with reference to testing measures like Raven's Progressive Matrices test, WISC/WAIS, full-scale intelligence quotient FISQ and subsets of the WISC/WAIS. It is important to note, like the SAT, standardized IQ scores provide little more than an approximation of intellect and each test can only measure a specific type of aptitude, ability, or intellect. A gifted individual may be bright or even brilliant, but a standard intelligence test profile simply will not fit some unique thinkers. They may not perform in a testing environment, may be negatively impacted by testing bias, or simply fail to show their true level of functioning or even competency according to standard intelligence measures.

The dilemma in being gifted is nonstandard thinking, which makes identification challenging. Some gifted people may respond well to a test and yield remarkable scores across the board, so their identification is clear using standardized IQ tests. But often, gifted people present a myriad of gifts, performances, and sets of challenges, that can in some cases mask their true abilities and challenge the measures that could identify their giftedness.

Asynchronous Testing and Development, Look Beyond IQ Test

Gifted people often have asynchronous brain development, meaning that their brains do not develop uniformly at a single time and space, or at a consistent pace, but rather vary over time due to genetics, epigenetics, environmental interactions, learning, and nurturing. In particular, a great difficulty is presented by expanded brain development and functioning in gifted individuals that does not apply in all areas. For example, a child may have extraordinary gifts in the visual arts and have capabilities and talents far beyond their time. Additionally, that same child may have an underdeveloped brain processing for written material or have a delayed processing speed. This may be extremely frustrating for a gifted child who is a writer but who has dysgraphia and whose hand cannot keep up with their brain. When testing younger children, fine and gross motor skills could alter their scores due to the asynchrony of development. Often, because of asynchronous development, a child can be misidentified—or not identified at all.

If the child is tested by a tester not aware of the performance differences in gifted persons there may be serious consequences that could derail their life trajectory. A gifted child may test all over the map due to asynchrony of the mind, brain, and body development.

Test scores can be altered by a variety of factors unrelated to intelligence, such as:

- motor skills
- visual and auditory processing
- language skills
- imagination
- processing speed
- asynchronous processing
- attention
- learning, and
- memory.

Each of these areas can interfere with performance, functioning, and ability. Common behaviors may interfere and produce artificially low-test scores, such as increased testing of boundaries and limits, increased defiant behaviors, and greater emotional fluctuations. Additionally, a gifted child may show more demotivation, frustration, or defiant behavior because the kinds of test scores they receive do not reflect their own knowledge of their abilities. On the other hand, gifted people can sometimes easily score well.

This brings us to an important point: understanding the difference between performance, functioning, ability, and achievement. It is critical with any individual that they define their passion and the level at which they are comfortable pushing themselves. Often gifted children are misguided about where they may have raw talent, say in math, and are told they should become a doctor or engineer, even if those careers don't interest them.

IQ tests are one measure for intelligence, but gifted children, being outside of the box, do not always meet the standards for IQ tests. It is evident that IQ tests capture intelligence, but if the test is not administered by someone educated in giftedness and learning disabilities, a child can be mislabeled, misidentified, or completely missed as being gifted.

Our society fails our brightest and most innovative children when we are too focused on their ability, achievement, competency, performance, functioning, and capacity. Each of those external measures mute, rather than allow for, a commitment to creativity and divergent thinking. Gifted individuals need to find what they are passionate about so they can develop personal goals and engage in meaningful projects, either individually or within a group. We need to be able to really see the person and recognize their remarkable potential. We need to educate the whole person, not saddle them with a label that puts them in a category of inability or a disability, but rather look at the spectrum of what their potential can bring to society. Embracing creative and divergent thinking will allow for endless possibilities. You are more than your circumstances. Always remember that simple truth. As the magnificent Stephen Hawking said, "Although I cannot move and I have to speak through a computer, in my mind I am free."

Coming Out as Twice Exceptional

Twice-exceptional (2e)—sounds special, right? In some regards it is and in others it is incredibly taxing. 2e is defined where an individual is gifted and has a learning disability/difference. This can cause all sorts of confusion with ability and achievement measures. Here is how I came to understand my own 2e lens. From a young age, words have come to me like a flooding river, the kind that rages in a storm. I don't always know why the words, or lists of words, bounce around in my cerebral hemispheres for a few days, weeks, months, even years. Then, *BAM*, as I am writing, the words float into a sentence, like a network of stars filling a constellation. Words can churn in my brain like a song on auto play. As a child, I wrote poetry and stories as they came to me, and I was consumed with writing for hours at a time. I still prefer to be quiet in my imagination, making connections or disassembling networks of words. Writing stories was not really encouraged or even valued when I was in grade school, so I kept my journal and stories to myself. I never had exceptional grades in language or English classes and I was often bored. At home, I felt at peace when I was writing and imagining.

In high school, I woke up before the rest of the house as the sun rose over Angeles Crest and had the satisfaction of completing a four-page theorem in calculus—a universal language that made sense to me. There was a general sense of order within the proof on the pages, a safe space within the lines. I was highly driven, I enjoyed homework, studying, and engaging with intellectually challenging material. While caught up in intellectual flow, I bathed in the quiet chaos as math swirled in my mind. My grades improved in high school although I never achieved straight As. I was a good student and considered a bright kid but my grades did not reflect a fraction of my ability and intellect. There was always a mismatch.

At UC Davis, I had fantasies of designing novel medications for patients who lived with Parkinson's disease, the disease that plagued my mother. In my mind, I aspired to be an organic chemist. When I took my first organic chemistry test something terrible happened, I did not finish the test. I left a thirty-point stoichiometry problem blank. I got a sixty-three on the exam. The remainder of points lost were because of an error in copying a benzene ring reaction. I'd left off carbon chains and created a non-existent compound. My heart sank. I went to my professor after class, embarrassed, and showed him my grade. He smiled and said, "Pretty good. You passed since the class average was a fifty-eight." That was not the reaction I wanted. I knew something was deeply wrong. I called my parents sobbing and wanting to leave college. I wanted to drop out. I felt like such a failure. Even now as I write this, remembering this brings on strong feelings of sadness because I don't want what happened to me to happen to other kids unnecessarily. I was baffled, what happened on the test? Where did I go wrong? I was tutoring my study group before the exam, so how had this happened? I thought I'd mastered the material. Then my mom said, "I think you have a learning difference, you may have dyslexia. Go to the student center and get tested."

A week later, I was tested and learned that it took me twice as long to process visual material as it did my age-matched peers. A major deficit. I had a slow visual processing speed, and visual processing memory. I was, and am, identified as 2e. Having scored in the 99th percentile in other domains, my visual processing was miles away near the 49th percentile. That is what makes me 2e. Until that point in my life, I was totally unaware I was 2e, I had no idea that I'd been overcompensating, no idea that I literally saw and experienced the world differently. Now my eyes were wide open. Understanding that I was 2e allowed me to accept my neurodiverse way of processing the world. I opened up to greater self-compassion and acceptance of being 2e. I had a foundation for knowing my strengths and how to support myself in learning information that suited *my* brain and *my* particular processing.

Once I identified all the unnecessary energy and learning habits that interfered with my studying and working because of my divergent visual processing, I honed in how to study and work better with my specific learning style. I taught myself how to study more effectively and began to feel greater energy flow. Studying became an invigorating activity rather than a challenging and draining one. Discovering learning accommodations, tools, and tricks enhanced my process and increased my confidence. I was able to master material more quickly and effectively, and I was more engaged with greater enjoyment because I was no longer struggling. And, through trial and error, I was optimizing learning for my unique brain. I embraced and trusted my whole being, the polarities and spectrum of my neuroindividuality—the gifts, the strengths, weaknesses, challenges, and creativity—my whole being full of passion and compassion.

Seeing through 2e Lenses

In my experience, the path of a 2e person it is not the easiest road to travel. Even though I have experienced success, I have had equal experiences of failure, frustration, and pain. Being 2e, I was not aware of the underlying nervous system triggers that activate the low-level anxiety and stress responses I experienced daily because I saw the world differently. As I studied the nervous system, I learned how my visual processing repeatedly activated both visual and auditory shifts in focus and attention. I also learned that visual and auditory stimuli initiated stress triggers in both my mind and body, and on some occasions these sensory experiences reached the level of pain.

It is well documented that people with visual processing differences such as dyslexia have differential neuronal migration patterns during development, which cause atypical neural patterning and brain circuitry for sensory processing.[10] Specifically, during early brain development, when the brain has a high level of neural plasticity and growth, atypical neuronal migration patterns shape neurocircuitry and brain networks for sensory perception and processing for vison and hearing that differ in people with dyslexia. There are known genes involved in axon guidance and development of neuronal pathways. In particular, people with dyslexia have differential gene expression for axon guidance (specific groups of genes and proteins that allow for guiding neurons and pathways in the brain). Basically, genetics drives different neural development and pathways in the brains of people with dyslexia and other visual processing differences. The change in axon guidance cues causes the different neuronal migration patterns to differ and the brain develops alternate brain pathways. These reshaped neuronal networks create divergent series of pathways in the brain where these differences occur in experiencing sensory information. These changes in neural plasticity are not unique to the visual system, there are shifts in patterns of the auditory system as well. These changes in both visual and auditory pathways provide for experiencing and perceiving sensory inputs from the environment differently in individuals that have visual processing differences such as dyslexia. This translates to differential behaviors related to both vision and hearing. These sensory experiences can be perceived at an elevated level and heightened awareness, which can be observed as irritating, distracting, overstimulating, and painful. And, on the flipside, can be experienced as ecstasy, joy, rewarding, and highly stimulating. It is critical to identify the intensity level of experience for the sensory processing in an individual.

Much of the time, when children exhibit behaviors of ADD/ADHD they can be responding to a sensory input that is distracting and painful. Imagine a sound that gives you a headache, how do you respond? A person can respond by withdrawing from the sound and tuning it out (perceived as inattentive/withdrawn ADD or ADHD) or the person can respond by experiencing overstimulation to the sound (perceived as overactive ADHD). A child can be misidentified as having ADHD when in reality they are experiencing a stress response to an auditory stimulus. In this case, it is essential to determine source that is the reason for the behavior rather than jumping to a diagnosis that can affect the child's life trajectory when behaviors are misidentified.

For example, I was completely unaware of how particular wavelengths of light caused unintentional shifts in my focus and, because of my visual processing, were overstimulating. This overstimulation and attentional shift activated a low-level stress response throughout my mind and body. Over time, this overstimulation and stress produced anxiety symptoms, where sustained focus for reading and visual information became so taxing that the workload became increasingly overwhelming. My mind and body were shutting down due to stress signals, and studying in and out of the classroom caused exhaustion because my mind and body responded to what I perceived as harmful stimuli—different wavelengths of light that I experienced as stressors.

In particular, my visual system has developed and adapted for visual processing that centers on continuous quick scanning across a wide distant view such as a meadow, and not for close-up visual input of black and white print in unnatural light. Unknown to me, fluorescent lights sent me into a tizzy; I would get dizzy from the light. When I had prolonged exposure to unnatural light, I experienced visual migraines with an aura clouding my visual field and my surroundings faded into a white light. Patterns on clothing with black and white stripes or checkers make me dizzy and nauseated. I learned when I read, my eyes were out of sync and word images were incongruent. This signaled a single eye dominate, where the other eye periodically did not take in visual information and shut off. This made reading exhausting because a single eye hyper-focused to take in the information from my environment. Now I when I read, I wear special glasses with colored filters and prisms to better help my eyes both track and focus while scanning black and white print.

In addition, I experience unnatural sounds such as traffic or leaf blowers as painful and highly distracting. At times, even a clock ticking can be overstimulating to my nervous system. Now research describes that both axon guidance and development for visual and auditory processing differ in people who are dyslexic. This is due to the development of divergent sensory pathways for both vison and sound. This is particularly difficult within young children if they cannot express or have the language skills to describe what they are experiencing. What is necessary when we think about the bright mind is that it is a unique mind and way of thinking. These specialized divergent networks allow for truly different ways of thinking and patterning that are not common in our culture, our homes, and schools.

Unconventional networks and patterning are common across many 2e domains. For example, Temple Grandin, the leader of the neurodiversity movement, describes how she sees the world in pictures, not words, and her language is through pictures in her mind. Language through pictures is unconventional but it exists and is in the spectrum of our diversity.

Being 2e allows for having a high ability in a single or many domains while experiencing challenge in other areas. Specialization in the brain comes at a cost for remarkable network processing in a single domain, where another domain unconventional path is not as fluid and there is a lag in development. That is the definition of asynchronous brain and body experience, where the development is not uniform across all domains. These differences in specializations are critical because they allow for thinking outside the box, which is essential for our advancement. It is important to encourage young children to embrace their differences and find strength in their uniqueness, while helping them thrive in their own manner and identifying where they need support. Once a person is free, seeing through 2e lenses can spark unbound imagination and exploration.

Uncolored Phonics Book and the Art of Scribbling

It was first grade, Mrs. R's class, and it was the point in the semester when she corrected our phonics books. When she got to mine, I was in trouble. All the phonics exercises were complete, but the pictures on the pages were completely devoid of any color. Not just one, all of them—close to eighty pages in my phonics book were not colored.

First, in my defense, I was in first grade and had already mastered the skill of coloring inside the lines. Second, it seemed like a waste of time to color in my phonics book; the subject was phonics, not coloring. Third, who wants to color in the spring when you can be outside and ride your bike up and down the hills and imagine you are traveling to a faraway land? Also, who really wants to color when they have already mastered coloring inside the lines?

Unfortunately, Mrs. R did not see it that way, nor did she find any of my defenses valid. Instead she sent me to library to color during group reading time—an exercise, it turns out, I needed much more than coloring because I am dyslexic. Going to the library did not turn out to be that bad. The librarian took pity on me and let me read *The Giving Tree* and *Hansel and Gretel* and even check them out of the library before I was sent back to class. In total, I colored two and a half pages.

At the end of the school day, Mrs. R met my mother in the parking lot and informed her of my defiant and unmotivated actions in not coloring my phonics book. She also told my mother I needed to have all the coloring done by end of the week or I would get a lowered grade and might not even pass.

Yes, passing my language class was contingent on my coloring all the pages in my phonics book.

So, my mom took me to the Marie Callender's restaurant where we ate pie and colored my phonics book together. My mother, being a preschool teacher's aide, explained that in life there is something called "busy work" and that was what coloring a phonics book was. But, she stressed, in life busy work and following directions were things I would be challenged with, and I would have to do the busy work so that I could jump through the hoops that would take me to the other side where better things waited. She agreed that busy work was a bore but sometimes you still had to do it.

The other thing my mother taught me was that you can do busy work quickly, with minimal effort, and make it fun. She colored with me and we made up stories about the pictures. She showed me how to fill in the pictures by scribbling fast and pressing the crayon lightly, with minimal effort, while at the same time feeding herself bites of peach pie with her right hand. She was a lefty and ambidextrous. I remember as I ate pie and colored with her that I was *not* bored and my mind was engaged as we made up stories. And I also remember laughing and laughing and laughing.

This is a classic case of a bright kid who appeared to be unmotivated. But I was bored, not lazy. When I was bored, my mind was not engaged with the material. My brain wasn't able to do what it was meant to do: think, and think with engagement. This left me disengaged because I'd already mastered the art of coloring and because the material had no applicable meaning for me. I was not challenged and not learning something new. I was hungry for engaging and challenging information but not for rudimentary preschool coloring. I was in first grade, after all, far beyond that coloring stuff.

Studies show that once a person masters a skill, brain activity decreases and is dulled each time the mastered skill is repeated.[11] Conversely, when a person is learning a new skill the brain has greater activation and engagement. Activity of the brain is directly correlated with the level of novelty and the level of engagement with the material and task at hand. When a brain is engaged with meaningful material, motivation increases because the reward system is activated creating a surge of positive neurochemicals like dopamine and produces a cycle of reward and motivation. Dopamine is a happy chemical related to reward processing, motivation, and focus. When a person has rewarding and stimulating material, a positive loop drives motivation and behavior when this behavior matches what is happening in the brain. Basically, for the brain to be engaged, material needs to be at an appropriate level and novel enough for optimal brain activation, focus, and motivation. When the brain is engaged there is a release of positive neurochemicals, the circuitry for reward is engaged, and the individual is motivated. But when the child or adult is not appropriately challenged the brain is less engaged, learning is dulled, reward processing is decreased, and demotivation follows. It is important to think that with the brain, mind, and body engagement, energy goes where energy flows and when energy is blocked the mind-body is blocked. The brain's overall experience and performance is muted and motivation deceases because a repeated task that is already mastered reduces brain activity, which then causes a lack of positive neurochemicals to be released. The child/adult then has behaviors that parallel brain processing and the child is soon bored out of their mind and will search for other avenues that allow for the brain to be engaged. This response may translate into maladaptive and disruptive behaviors.

Was Mrs. R bad? No, she didn't know how to engage my brain, she didn't know I was suffering from boredom. And, she was teaching me something different than what I wanted to learn. She was teaching me that punctuality, task completion, and following directions were of the greatest importance in her classroom. Things that at the time I felt didn't matter. In my mind, completing the phonics was the important task. To Mrs. R, my behavior of not coloring the pictures in my phonics book indicated laziness and defiance and she wanted me to follow the rules of her class. But what she missed was that my lack of engagement was due to boredom and not intentional irreverence or disrespect. She misinterpreted my behavior. She needed to understand what motivated me instead of focusing on having me conform while I was demotivated. Better would have been if she had talked with me and tried to identify the reasons for my behavior.

This a call to action to encourage educators, parents, psychologists, and mental health professionals to define what is at the core of a child's apparent (or perceived) lack of motivation, defiance, laziness, rebelliousness, and failure to work at "their level." A potential origin for these behaviors is that they are bored and not engaged with the material offered, and they need to have material that matches their intellectual ability so that their brain will be entirely— or even remotely—engaged. That when information and experience is not at their level, they will act out to seek intellectual reward from other sources and their behaviors are an indication that they are suffering. An engaged brain produces a surge of positive rewarding neurochemicals that turns on the motivation circuitry and a positive loop of dopamine. Activated neural circuitry and enhancement of positive neural plasticity happens and stimulates their learning, keeping them motivated. In these circumstances, they can thrive and work on a rewarding intellectual, emotional, and social level.

Stanford Scientists Agree with Six Year Old Me, No More Homework

The truth about homework and learning is…drum roll please… too much homework has negative effects on learning and engagement. Counter to everything we've been taught, Stanford scholar Denise Pope and colleagues are now illuminating the truth that too much homework negatively impacts learning. Studies show that when students have a homework load that does not match their developmental and emotional level, the homework can cause significant stress and anxiety for children and their families. According to the National Education Association, homework should match maturity, with ten minutes per grade level so that first graders have ten minutes of homework and high school seniors can handle homework up to two hours a night. In a survey, parents report that their kindergarteners are coming home with homework that takes twenty-five to thirty minutes. In fact, kindergarteners should not have *any* homework. In many communities, parents are revolting against the homework and expectations that are placed on their children and refusing to have their children do homework. Where was this movement when I was in Mrs. R's class? I sure could have benefited from a no-homework movement and I bet the majority of my classmates would agree. Well, all but that one teacher's pet with perfect handwriting and every assignment completed on time. A rare exception, perhaps even a fiction or figment of imagination. Does a perfect student actually exist?

Look at this, I was right all along to trust my instinct and refuse to do busy work because it was boring, had no meaning or purpose except to accumulate pointless points and be a cushion to boost a grade—or in my case, drive my grade into a deep hole that I had to climb out of to see the light and meaning. I'm still digging. Why do I have to do this assignment? It is boring.

Education scholars and neuroscientists agree with six-year-old me that homework that is merely busy work actually discourages learning and ultimately leads to negative consequences for educational engagement. Educators, teachers, parents, can we please stop with the homework and let children do activities they love? Like play, socialize with other kids, enjoy being captured by their imagination? Can we free them from the homework and stressors related to late night busy work for brainless points? Allow children to live as anxiety free as possible, and let them be kids.

We all know the lyrics, "*We don't need no education,*" from Pink Floyd's song, "Another Brick in the Wall." Even Pink Floyd agreed with me! They channeled their free time into their music, and they became one of the greatest rock bands of all time. Denise Pope and colleagues discovered that when high school students were overloaded with too much homework, the students experienced decreased behavioral engagement and negative effects on their well-being. The survey was conducted in high school students from ten high-performing schools in California where they evaluated student's quality of life and behavioral engagement in relation to homework load. The group of 4,317 students collectively averaged 3.1 hours of homework in the evening. Particularly, the study found that that amount of homework interferes with learning and well-being. Often these children work into the late hours of the night in social isolation which restricts their time with family, friends, and their community, as well as their ability to engage in activities they would like to participate in and experience. Fifty-six percent of the students reported that homework was a primary stressor, while 43% said that taking tests was the number one stressor. Only 1% of students said homework was not a primary stressor.

In the free response portion of the survey, students stated they experienced sleep loss due to too much homework and had other health issues like headaches, stomachaches, and weight loss. Sadly, because homework takes so much of these students' time, they have less time for social interaction and connectedness. This leads to students suffering from greater social isolation and increased anxiety and depression. Too much homework interferes with quality of life. We need to teach our children to have greater enjoyment and engagement in the activities they find rewarding and motivating. Dr. Denise Pope urges against assigning pointless busy work just for points because it is not conducive to learning, rather it is discouraging and has negative mental, emotional, and behavioral consequences. Specifically, homework needs to be purposeful and centered on engagement and learning.

And what does all this mindless homework add up to? The test? State standards? A 2019 article in the *LA Times* by Sonali Kohli pointed out that less than half of California's public school students who had participated in the state's standardized test met grade level standards for language. And only 40% of students met the math standards for their grade level.[12] Where are we going wrong?

Unfortunately, this highlights additional problems we are facing in the education system. Dr. Susan Baum, Provost of Bridges Graduate School, revolutionary advocate for twice-exceptional education, points out that the state standards are exceedingly demanding each year and are overwhelming for children to learn. She notes that the standards are developmentally out of sync with children's learning abilities. This is happening across all schools where children are required to learn information above their level of development, leading them to miss much of what the lessons and information the standards are testing. She urges that we begin to test children and meet them where education and development are in sync.

Another issue is that a number of these students represent the growing population of our lower income communities where these students are at a vast disadvantage. For example, approximately 20% of children in California live in households that lack the resources to meet their basic needs, and nearly 80% of Californians experiencing poverty live in a household with at least one working adult.[13] These children growing up in financially impoverished homes are not just slipping through the cracks, they are in sinkholes with very few resources available to them, especially the most needed resources of time, attention, and guidance. These children are at considerable risk for improper identification and misdiagnoses because they have little access to educational interventions and resources. It is undeniable that stressors in a lower income community can interfere with a child's educational success, and their emotional, mental, physical and behavioral well-being. This is of special concern because it is estimated that 20% of our school-aged children are neurodiverse.[14] That is one out of five children in a classroom. The constraints placed on educators, who are managing thirty to forty students in a classroom, leaves little room for individualized education for gifted and 2e learners. These children are misidentified or missed all together. Limited resources and funding presents a major concern for the future of these children and for society as a whole.

There are no easy solutions to the financial constraints placed on academic institutions but we need to wake up because 40% of our children in California's public schools are not meeting grade level math standards. We need to make sure these children understand concepts such as compound interest and balancing a budget. These children are going to be part of our society and essential in our communities and they will be voting and implementing laws. They are becoming— and are—our future. Education, resources, and opportunity should not be a privilege; they are basic human rights. It is time for us to recognize this and help make changes for these students who are at the greatest risk of dropping out of school and even out of society all together. We need to give educational institutions and teachers the financial, emotional, and mental support they need to safely guide and nurture students in the classroom. We need to come together for positive solutions so that these students can flourish and thrive in school, and in all aspects of their lives.

Emotional Roller Coaster of 2e

As a child, I felt that entire shades of my core being were locked in a vault, invisible to the rest of the world. It was a combination of being in my own skin and the array of negative feedback I received about how I did not fit into normal, especially in the classroom.

When I went to elementary school, I was missed. There was a vast disconnect between the complexities of my mind and what appeared on paper, group work, and in my test performance. I admit, I was not a fan of group work. The negative message that I was considered "difficult" was evident to me. I would jump ahead in class, bored with the topic at hand, and forget the rules about raising my hand before running through my endless questions. How does this all work? How does this all relate? Why does this matter? Over time, I silenced that part of me because I was so often greeted with an eye roll or, worse, detention simply for asking too many questions. So, that voice in me began to quiet, I became disengaged and hid my gifts.

My work was disorganized, sloppy at times, sprinkled with misspelled words, unfinished assignments—the list goes on. I didn't fit into any sort of rectangular shape of a "good student." Because I wrote with an elevated vocabulary, spelling complicated words was challenging. And, my hand just couldn't keep up with my mind and its flood of words and sentences. This remains true to this day. I cannot write all that I think and sometimes feel as if my thoughts are wild horses that cannot be corralled onto the page. My motor output can't meet the speed of my galloping thoughts.

The underlying message I received time and time again was, "You are a pain in the ass," and "Can I get you to stop interrupting my classroom?" Basically, I was told I needed to sit still, be quiet, be a minion and get my work done, and repeat that cycle over and over and over to be successful—or at least in my case, not get into trouble. Over time, I began to believe I was not smart, my intellect was not valued, and asking questions was annoying, especially when I was questioning authority. Because of this negative cycle, I withdrew from standard grade school academics. I began to shut down and held back from ever voicing my curiosity in the classroom; I faded into chalkboard dust. Worse, I began to doubt my ability. Because my visual processing difference was not identified, I thought I was not smart and I began to suffer from shame, anxiety, and depression.

Doubt and Depression Not Knowing and Navigating with a Visual Difference

You place enormous of judgment on yourself when you do not perform to your true ability, and there is an uncoupling when you know that you do not externally measure up to your internal ability. I lived with a great deal of shame because I did not know I had a visual processing difference. I lived with a ton of negative feelings about myself and boatloads of self-doubt about whether I could live in the so-called normal range and within the status quo. I knew I was capable and often mastered material in my mind, but couldn't express my understanding of it, and I didn't understand why. This left me with a constant feeling of failure and frustration. Because I was overcompensating, and working in some cases double the amount, I could never really reconcile the ability I knew was inside me with my performance.

When I was identified as 2e, I developed a better understanding of myself and could reframe my thinking and self-perception. My visual processing differences allow for my alternate ways of spelling and writing and are centered around the biology of my particular brain wiring. Once I understood my learning differences were specific to my distinctive brain patterns and processing, I could hold space for the beauty in my difference. I was able to tame the voice of criticism and negative self-talk and reframe my thinking and self-perception, thus freeing myself from the stigma of being wired differently.

Spelling Bee Shame

I dreaded the yearly spelling bee. Often, I was already out in the early rounds and had to take the both welcome and dreaded seat of failure and public shame. In what other realm does public shaming occur while you remain seated in failure before an audience? For me, it was always the case that the children adjacent to me had been given words I could easily spell, but when it came to my word, I was stumped. I doubted every letter I wanted to attribute to the word and then just flat-out blanked. The letters jumbled in my head and I second-guessed myself, inevitably messing up the word. And simple as that, I was out. Seated in shame. Nothing was like the initial embarrassment of missing the word. A teacher once remarked that I'd had all the letters, just jumbled and out of order.

As more and more students took a seat and joined me on the other side of failure, I realized we made an army.

What we didn't know at the time is that we could have collectively revolted. We did not know we had the option of saying "I take a pass." Imagine if we'd all refused to spell and agreed instead to simply say the letter "A" for each word that came up. Eventually the teacher would get the message: we collectively did not like spelling bees.

Or instead, conduct the spelling bee only for those students who are excellent and thrive at it, who will practice and develop their skill to strengthen their brain power. Let the kids for whom spelling doesn't resonate choose another activity like drawing, singing, or playing hockey, that will engage them and enhance their brain activity for their particular positive neural plasticity. Why not update the model and find material that engages children so they thrive? The sooner you can teach gifted/2e students the value of checking a box, the better they can begin to train their minds to adapt their value system. Perhaps offer the yearly spelling be as an optional activity for those who love spelling and spelling out loud.

Anxiety of Reading out Loud

In elementary school, I did everything to get out of reading out loud. I covered my face, made myself as small as possible, and prayed to the gods above that I would not be called on for the next paragraph—and if were, to let it be a short one. Like only one sentence for the love of God. I feared making a mistake because my eyes moved out of sync and I couldn't keep them focused on a single line. The print could sometimes make me dizzy, prompt a visual aura and subsequent headache. When I read out loud, I often jumped ahead trying to read quickly to get it over with. My eyes jumped back and forth over the words and I read and misread in the same way as my eye movements, disjointed and paced all wrong. Anxiety brain networks were in full effect as I read aloud, cortisol pulsing through my veins and flooding my organs. Instinctual fear charged through me. I wanted to get it over with as fast as possible. Because of my visual processing difference, there was an exceedingly large mismatch between my reading performance and my intellectual ability. I felt very strongly that reading out loud was a misrepresentation of me, and that only made the whole experience even more demoralizing.

I detested reading out loud until my son, Spence, was born. The light at the end of my tunnel.

While I was in graduate school, one of my son's and my favorite times together was story time. Spence would sit on my lap every night before bed as I read ten to fourteen books to him. Some books we both had memorized like *Maisy's Fire Engine, Good Night Gorilla,* and *Knuffle Bunny Too: A Case of Mistaken Identity.* Reading to him I learned pacing by pointing to the line I was reading with my finger so he could follow, and laughing with him at myself if I made a mistake. Spence began reading at age three, and soon after, read to me. To this day he teaches me definitions of words. One of my most valued gifts is a thesaurus he made for me when he was in the third grade that replaces ordinary words with extraordinary words for my writing. He is a guide for me. Because of our time, our healing and reading out loud, I now read works out loud, like my poetry at poetry readings, meditations, books, and inspirational quotes throughout my lectures. I love reading out loud; it is a sacred art for me to read written words. There was no accident in how he came to me. We find healing within each other. Spence awakened a reader and writer in me.

Unlocking the 2e Magic Mind and the Butterfly Effect

In high school, I had a transformational experience while attending an all-girls Catholic high school, Alverno Heights Academy. *Academy*, don't be too surprised that I attended an academy. Somehow, in the interview, the director of admissions saw something inside me, a promise. Having daughters, and she herself also not fitting into the nicely packaged female box, she knew there was something working inside of me. She saw a glimmer in me, looked past my previous academic performance, and took a leap of faith. She chose to guide me into my future and let me into Alverno.

At Alverno, I learned that God could be a she, he, or ungendered, I learned evolution, liturgical dance, that you could try anything and everything, how to be a strong woman, how to persevere, to accept and love different cultures, to have gratitude in life, and that asking questions and the pursuit of knowledge was valued. I also had time for my brain to align so that my handwriting developed. I matured to have organizational systems. I found science, literature, art, and sports. Alverno was a haven of enrichment. Education needs to be enrichment. Nestled at the foot of the Angeles Crest Forest where the plush green mountains reached the skies, school felt like a sanctuary.

In a freshman English class, I discovered the butterfly effect. First described by scientist Edward Lorenz, the butterfly effect grew out of his predictions of weather patterns. One day while rerunning a computer simulation of weather predictions he miscopied the original data and deleted the 100th decimal point. This error caused a completely different weather prediction and pattern. The metaphor that he ascribed to the phenomena was that of a "butterfly flapping its wings in Brazil and creating a tornado in Texas."[15] That observation fell in alignment with the theory of chaos that imagines small effects such as that of a butterfly flapping its wings can change the course of weather in a distant location and change the course of events in space and time.

In my freshman English class, Ms. F saw something in me, maybe the flap of a butterfly wing. She read a short story I wrote out loud to the class as an example of telling story through activating one's senses and capturing the reader. I enjoyed writing, but what I didn't know at the time was that I was pretty decent at it. At times when I struggle to write something, I remember that moment when Ms. F saw something in me that I didn't know existed. My moment of insight into the butterfly effect. It changed my internal dialogue to "I can write. I am a writer." The smallest act can change someone's life trajectory. The moment you can unlock a door and reveal a pathway for an unconventional student you teach them they are visible. And with that visibility they can share their magic essence. Teachers and parents help children find their magic. Be a simulation of the butterfly effect and unlock a 2e magic mind.

Imagination is the Upside to Being 2e

According to records, Shakespeare spelled his name as many as fourteen different ways. He is known for his idiosyncratic spellings of words—missing double consonants, omitting the second s in sleepless (sleeples), using y instead of i, and having generally sloppy writing.[16] Does this sound like anyone you know? The art of orthography is the spelling of words correctly. But the mind of a 2e person is disorderly, unconventional, and unbound. The upside of being 2e is imagination. Neural patterns, neural firing, and neural networks are different and divergent thinking is exactly the manifestation that arises from being 2e.

How is it that in our society we have moved from viewing imagination and creative expression as assets to considering those same attributes challenges and obstacles for creativity? Perhaps teaching to the test and developing standard measures for mastery and legitimacy is how we've dampened the importance of creativity. Learning to pass a test requires focusing skills but may not measure intellect, or even imagination. It merely tests what one knows about the subject at hand. The world's greatest playwright spelled similarly to the way our 2e children in the classroom today spell. Shakespeare's irregular spellings are a distinctive signature that has allowed scholars to identify his work.[17]

Being twice exceptional is an imaginative experience. Often in grade school and high school, I struggled with the visual memory of correctly spelled words. On written exams, I knew that spelling errors would be deducted from the total grade. I had, and do have, a rich vocabulary, but I if I didn't know how to spell a word like "cartography," I replaced it with an easier word like "map" so I wouldn't lose points for misspellings. I was compensating and dumbing down my vocabulary. As a result, my exam answers never reflected my full knowledge. I was dumbing down my work to gain access to a higher grade, aiming to earn points instead of expressing myself.

The arbitrariness of English spelling has been illustrated by creatively spelling "fish," as "ghoti," where the "gh" sound from tough is the f, the "o" sound from women as the i, and the "ti" sound from caption as the sh. Sound them out and you have an alternate spelling of fish. In some ways, that blows up the idea of phonics, or perhaps makes a case for it—or perhaps both.

I specifically remember changing my language and the way I said something because I didn't know how to spell specific words. I was dumbing down my language by writing in a much simpler way to avoid being marked down for misspelled words. I was overcompensating in two ways. First, I was creating new spelling, and second I was changing my language to make comprehension easy for my reader. By simplifying my writing this way, my word choices did not accurately reflect my knowledge of the subject and my high-level thinking about it. I was limited by my poor spelling so that my true ability, performance, and potential on the page did not match what was happening in my mind.

Spelling in flow is creative, imaginative, and unfiltered for me. When I write in flow, it is like that moment in a plane when the pilot turns the plane on its side and the earth is suddenly perpendicular and the moon sideways; all the material is still there, but not in its conventional place. Words come to me as automatic connections, creative spelling, an act, a moment, a prayer, an expression of my neuroindividuality. In education, we test a person on their spelling and handwriting but that is not the correct measure for complex thought and intelligence. All we are doing is testing a person's visual memory and fine motor functioning. We are not testing their intellect or creative thinking.

Now we have programs and software that fix handwriting and correct spelling, punctuation, and grammar errors. Teachers, parents, educators, clinicians, health care professionals, and society: please do not judge a person by their spelling. Help them find solutions to improve their spelling but understand their brain wiring is different. And that difference allows for creative spelling and imagination with language. Most important, with creative and imaginative people, is to give them time. Time to imagine. A feature of being 2e is an exceptional gift and an exceptional difficulty (whether it be social interaction, learning memory, sensory processing, or working memory). The brain experience calls on using divergent thinking, which in most cases activates unconventional and nontraditional networks. Build success through a happy child and minimize negative feedback for deficit learning. Being 2e my entire life and not knowing that I was 2e until college was disorienting. I have not completely embraced it until now.

Being twice-exceptional is the range of light, where at any given moment the colors emitted are dependent on the wavelengths and the speed of light. So, 2e, I write this poem for you. You are an exceptional being.

Range of Light

Morning rainbow
Emits from the window
Ray of colors dance on
the tile
the wall
Sneaking into the hall
Never in two mornings has the appearance
   of the rainbow been identical
Unique illumination
Spontaneous beauty
Light
Lite
Light
Lite

Seeing in a New Light Unmasking Neurotypes

"Neurotypical" refers to a normal brain in neuroanatomy, wiring, and perceiving and responding to stimuli from the environment. Often in neuroscience studies, a group that represents the norm is of the neurotypical description, a general description of order of the brain and behaviors. As in all science, the theory of chaos and increasing level of disorder applies also to the mind. A new world order that recognizes unconventional minds includes differential neurotypes with distinctive neurocircuitry, anatomy, and information processing from their environment and autobiographical memories.

"Neurotype" refers to differences in brain volume, network patterns, wiring, and body perceiving that lead to divergent neural, behavioral, emotional, sensory, and motor perceptions and responses. Unique neurotypes are marked by:

○ Atypical nonstandard formation circuitry neural processing

○ Not your neurotypical processing, responsivity, and being

○ A nonstandard brain and body experience

○ Not your ordinary kid

○ Not your ordinary adult

○ Unique gifts masked due to different ways of being present in the world and different way of processing the world

○ Idiosyncratic behaviors, enhanced emotional processing, elevated sensory responsivity, heightened physicality, exceptional imagination, and diverse social engagement.

Approximately 10% of children are identified as gifted,[18] 9.4 % of children have an ADHD identification,[19] 1.69% (1 in 59) of the population are on the autism spectrum,[20] up to 10% of the population are identified as dyslexic,[21] and 4-20 % of the population are estimated to be dysgraphic.[22] Combined, these neurotype identifications cover nearly 40% of the population. Because there are overlaps across these identifications, by a conservative estimate approximately 20% of the population fits into a neurotypes. That means 1 in 5 children in the classroom are neurodiverse. But the number could be even greater, as we see above.

According to National Institute of Mental Health Tracking, about 19.1% of the population has reported suffering from anxiety and 7.1% reported having a major depression episode.[23] Mental health conditions are on the rise. In the home, in the classroom, and in our communities, these individuals may be missed if they do not feel safe to express their states of emotional and mental well-being—verbally, behaviorally, and/or emotionally.

Dr. James T. Webb, founder of the non-profit Supporting Emotional Needs of the Gifted (SENG) and publishing house Great Potential Press, was a world leader and advocate for gifted people, who dedicated his life to raising awareness of the gap in our culture relating to these vulnerable populations. In particular, he found in his private practice and research studies that many of these neurotypes were often misdiagnosed, misunderstood, and misidentified which created greater challenges for them in navigating society and caused them to struggle throughout their lives without the appropriate supports in place that would lead to greater diagnoses of mental health challenges like anxiety and depression.

In a recent study of Mensans, Ruth Karpinski and our team found a 20% increase of anxiety and depression in Mensans compared to the national average, highlighting that this population may be at greater risk for mental health diagnoses and conditions.[24] Specifically, when individuals are misidentified and misdiagnosed they are at a huge risk for not getting proper support and services. This can lead to unnecessary suffering and trauma. We need to address the suffering across these populations to better guide these children and minimize their exposure to mental and emotional health challenges so they are lifted and can thrive.

Across all brain types, centering around neuroindividuality, the brain, body, and whole person does not develop uniformly. From our earlier explorations of Shaw and colleague's work, recall the brain develops in adolescence in its own asynchronous timeline. Recall there is a developmental brain expansion that occurs in the frontal cortex from age eight and a half to 14. The frontal cortex is the control center for executive functioning, planning, completing tasks, emotional saliency, timing, reward, and motivation. It is the motherlode of cognition, working memory, and behavior. In our bright and unusual kids, this development takes longer and it happens with greater expansions. During this period there is a greater brain growth happening. And what is important to remember when we think about neurotypes is to think about the individual that is being taught the information. That in particular, when you have a child, pacing matters, the intention of how and what you are teaching matters, and the emotional connection of the instructor with the material matters. Time and again, studies show that children who continually receive negative reinforcement are hindered in their learning and are much more anxiety prone. And they are much more afraid of taking risks. When one is engaged in any sort of creative process or thinking, negative reinforcement will disrupt any sort of learning and creativity.

It is essential to see the gifts and limitations of each child. When we see a child in class who can read many grade levels ahead but has difficulty writing because of pain in their hand and therefore cannot fully express themselves through written language, there will be a disconnect between their ability and their performance. As guides, we need to reassess what we are teaching and how we are obtaining information from a child. There are alternative ways we can test a child and allow them to share their knowledge that don't require that child to write if it is painful. They can learn to type, do voice recording, answer questions orally, or find other practical solutions. When we have an open mind, children can share their knowledge and thrive. In the educational system we often put kids through preprogrammed lessons that have worked with other kids in the past. It's great to test what else can work. When a bright child is in a classroom that is stuck in traditional teaching and learning techniques that do not address the way the child learns, we need to develop proper alternative accommodations. A great risk in these neurotypes is misidentification and being misunderstood, which can vastly interfere with their self-image, self-esteem, and their true abilities and capabilities in life. If a child is stunted because they've missed using or developing their true gifts and talents, they are at risk for emotional, mental, and behavioral challenges. Thus, if we see a child who appears out of sync and is acting out, it is our job to help them identify where the origin of challenge begins.

With my bright child and nontraditional learner, Spence, it was essential to ask him how to help his particular needs to build maximum engagement for learning academically and non-academically. Understanding where the stops are happening builds knowledge of the source of the incongruities within the child, and helps guide the parents and instructors. Most important for Spence, he needed support for assistance with writing, organization, and time management. Now that he is in high school, he has solid systems in place that have worked in the past through practice and cognitive training to build skills through creating specific behavioral habits. It took many times of hypothesis testing, and trial and error to find the systems that work best for his brain processing, learning, emotional, mental, and behavioral uniqueness. But once we did, his self-perception and understanding of his gifts were able to shine.

When we think about neurotypes going into the classroom, we need to ask what the best way is to let this mind, body, and spirit flourish in their environment. Learning is inherently a rewarding experience. A number of things naturally happen in the brain when we're learning something new, when the material is engaging and motivating. There is an influx of positive neurotransmitters, like dopamine, that reward for positive long-lasting learning. The bottom line is children *want* to learn. Children are naturally motivated and curious. When these children have material that is meaningful, the motivation and learning naturally follows. When we see demotivation or unmotivated behaviors, we know we are getting a look at the effects of trauma. The behavior shows us where we can implement new techniques to facilitate learning and allow our bright kids to express their gifts in a safe environment.

Neurotypes

Unpacking brain types and the origin of behaviors, it can be useful to consider this snapshot view into a variety of neurotypes:

- **Gifted:** the gifted person has expanded processing and cognition related to intellectual, imaginational, creative, emotional, sensory, and/or physical processing and behaviors. This is related to brain volume, processing and networks revealed through MRI, fMRI and other neuroimaging techniques. Brain anatomy and bodily receptivity have implications for neuro-body experiences for ways of being and navigating in the world.

- **Twice-exceptional ("2e"):** Having an extraordinary gift and a challenge that can mask an individual's true ability and performance measures. Often brain anatomy and wiring reveal differences that are expressed in behavioral, social, emotional, mental, physical, and intellectual processing. Often 2e individuals are challenging to identify because standard testing is all over the map and they may appear average across the board. Often observed as asynchronous brain development, asynchronous behaviors and asynchronous performance.

- **Sensory Sensitivity and Processing Enhancements and Differences:** Volume and brain wiring within a single sensory brain region or across all five sensory domains. There can be enhancements within the sensory nervous system across the body and brain for the known sensory systems including hearing, sight, touch, taste, and smell. This enhanced processing can lead to differential sensory experience that can be elevated, altered, and even so overstimulating that ordinary experience verges on ecstasy and/or pain. Differences in sensory processing can appear in identifications and different learning styles such as auditory processing differences, dyslexia, dyscalculia, challenges with reading, writing, spelling, executive functioning, emotional regulation, and body regulation.

○ **Emotional Brain—Anxiety & Depression:** Differences in emotional processing in the brain and differential brain anatomy and circuitry in which circuitry parallels enhancements in behavioral, motor, sensory and emotional responses. Elevated response to perceived and imagined anticipation of fear. There are known functional brain differences in individuals who experience an increase in anxiety and there are often elevated sensory experiences due to brain wiring and processing. Understanding the origin of the anxiety is essential in guiding the individual. A child that appears unmotivated and disengaged can be experiencing anxiety and/or depression.

○ **ADHD active/inactive:** Different modes of attentional focus. Active attention, and hyper-focus, and inactive attention, spaced out. Executive functioning, working memory, long term memory, and managing differences. Brain processing differences that have emotional, behavioral and sensory implications for enhancements and intensities related to attention.

○ **Autism Spectrum Disorder (ASD):** Divergent modes of social and emotional interaction. Processing, neuroanatomy and brain wiring that is different for perceiving the environment and internal states. Wiring and processing the foundation of unconventional being and experiencing the world across sensory, motor, emotional, imaginational, mental, and physical domains. Distinct communication patterns.

○ **Motor Processing Enhancements and Differences:**
Enhancements and/or alterations in fine motor and gross
motor abilities. Delays or advancements in motor processing
can be related to mind-body processing, nervous system
processing, brain network, neuroanatomy and/or whole-body
processing. These psychomotor differences can provide for a
wide array of motor processing differences such as writing,
walking, writing (dysgraphia), reading, playing sports, and
physical navigation in the world (in some cases can be hypo-
or hyper-motor expression).

Features Seen in Neurotypes

Each of these neurotypes can present challenges in traditional
learning environments that miss their neurodiverse way of being in
the world and cannot meet their unique mind and corporeal learning
styles. When it comes to learning and education, individuals need to
be in the right environment for their learning style, and they must
be socially, emotionally, and mentally engaged. When children and
adults are in their element, or "in the zone," their energy flow is
unbounded and they are in a cycle of positive reward, positive brain
wiring and processing and have a surge of positive neurochemicals like
dopamine that enhance learning and motivation. This feeds a positive
loop of learning and engagement. When children have an emotional
connection to the material they are learning, and when they feel safe,
their learning is enhanced and increases. But when children experience
negativity and trauma, their learning is inhibited.[25] It makes sense
that when we are in flow we are engaged and channeling energy easily,
but if we are in an environment that feels threatening we focus our
energy on our basic survival so that our energy is diffuse and directed
toward things other than learning and being in flow. Then our energy
is wasted and we appear disengaged and devoid of interest. We need
to guide these children to harness their energy in the right direction
to share their essence and gifts.

Neurotypes are the continuums and distributions of the bell curve
for human diversity. It is our job to understand guiding outliers and
how to get them best situated in life. Not only in the classroom but

in all areas of their life where their social, emotional, mental, physical, intellectual, sensory, creative/imaginative needs are met on all fronts. These features are common behaviors and indicators that the child who is a non-traditional learner may present.

Common Strengths

- O Eloquent verbal expression
- O Highly imaginative
- O Distinctly creative
- O Innovative problem solver (thinking outside the box)
- O Intense engagement and sustained focus when in the zone
- O Internally motivated
- O High motivation
- O High attention to detail
- O Exceptional ability for multitasking
- O Extraordinarily curious
- O Highly committed
- O Broad sense of interests
- O Advanced sense of humor
- O Strong sense of justice
- O Highly empathetic
- O High emotionality
- O Gifted/special talent

Common Challenges

- O Difficulty in written expression
- O Difficulty in communication
- O Increased risk of anxiety
- O Greater risk of depression
- O Highly empathetic
- O Emotionally intense
- O Sensory differences and enhancements
- O Perfectionism
- O Challenge with organizational skills
- O Challenge with time management
- O Challenge with attention

○ Difficulty with task completion
○ Overstimulation
○ High sense of justice
○ Opinionated
○ Debates and negotiates
○ Difficulty detaching when in flow
○ Uneven academic performance

The flip side of every strength is a challenge, and with every challenge there is strength. It is absolutely necessary to nurture both and find solutions using what is working correctly. Find the ease and the flow of energy in the positive and build bridges, open doors for the challenges. And test all the imagined possibilities, use trial and error, continue to self-test, and build hypotheses and solutions to live a joyous life. Find balance to have a joyful child who is comfortable in their essence. Encouraging the calm is essential with these learners. Because the environment and material and internal states can be overstimulating, it is important to help these non-traditional learners activate their minds in a way that doesn't overtax them and disrupt or interfere with their learning.

Neurotype, learning, and environment need to work in synchrony for optimal engagement and purpose. The right fit for the exceptional brain. That is, where learning matches the mind body spirit, social, and emotional component, and where there is the proper challenge and interest with material. Each individual has their very own brain-print and way of navigating in the world.

Deficit Model in Learning

We live in a culture obsessed with fixing things and looking to the broad areas where we need improvement—massive and miniature—always fine tuning an ever-evading perfection. This deficit learning is something we experience as early as our first words or our first steps. There are checks and balances, and that is all good and well for an ordered society. We are thinking beings from the moment we wake to the moment we close our eyes to sleep. Close to 99% of the day we are caught up in our own thoughts. And a good portion of those thoughts focus on the deficit. Our running thoughts focus on all we are missing, what we are doing wrong, and how we'll never be perfect.

Never be right. This goes beyond the monkey mind of distraction. This is the mind of complete negative and self-critical thinking. And when we look at children in school, we are often too focused on areas needing improvement and miss nurturing all that is going right.

Now, I am not for one second saying we should ignore areas of challenge, but I think that we need to take them for what they are and recognize they are areas that need compassionate guidance. And in some cases, they do not need fixing. We need to balance our thinking so our entire focus is not on our perceived grand deficit. When the mind goes into a deficit model, energy follows and we are apt to hyper-focus on the challenged area and miss the good. All the good. Even the good in the lessons of challenge that can be an opportunity for personal and collective growth.

Especially in bright and 2e children, if they are continually taught that they never measure up because of their unconventional thinking, they will begin to believe it and can be at risk of silencing themselves and their gifts because of low self-image. They can lose confidence in their gifts and hold back from sharing their essence. It is important that we nurture both the areas of challenge and the areas of strength so that our attention to them is balanced. And that we give children the opportunity to embrace their unconventional thinking and allow them moments of success related to their original way of thinking and original way of being. Nurturing both of these in a child will allow for a positive model of self-image and how they see themselves in the world.

We should avoid over-identifying what is wrong and needs fixing and instead focus our attention on what is right. We should aim for a balanced approach for the child, refocus on an approach for what is working in the mind of a bright child, and encourage positive associations for their original thinking. We can cultivate positive thought patterns for personal growth and personal development. This wires the brain for positive neural plasticity of self-image and confidence and allows children to be who they really are.

Risk, Learning, and Trauma

When the system is not working for a child, they can experience stress, various levels of trauma, fear, and anxiety that interfere with learning and motivation. Trauma alters learning and the brain which results in unwarranted physiological reactions, behaviors, and disrupted motivation and these negative experiences dominate the learning process. Learning is halted and the child develops maladaptive behaviors. And when learning becomes even more challenging, the child is at risk of spiraling into a world of demotivation, low self-esteem, learned helplessness, and depression. At this point the child no longer trusts the environment to be a place of curiosity and learning and there is no motivation for learning, thus the child lacks focus because the surroundings are experienced as unsafe.

This rejection of learning directly affects neural plasticity and neural circuitry, shaping their brain and their processing for life. The dominant circuitry is a maladaptive patterning (less efficient, less developed, less productive) where there is lower brain pattern and functioning, while individuals deny themselves the right to their higher thinking and processing. This directly correlates with measures of decreased performance and unsatisfactory behavioral patterning and functioning caused by a reduction in positive neural plasticity.

When we accurately identify the origin of trauma learning, we can implement proper support, strategies, and accommodations that enhance the development of positive neural plasticity, wiring for positive adaptive behaviors, and positive outcomes for the child to be engaged and motivated. When we focus our energy and enhance positive experiences with learning, we encourage the development of positive emotions, behaviors, and relationships, and ignite a mind that is engaged in learning.

Solar Flare and Saving Helen

Helen Keller was locked in radio silence after she suffered the loss of her sight and hearing—until she found a gifted teacher, Anne Sullivan. At one time identified as oppositional, unmanageable, and emotionally dysregulated, Helen Keller was seen and understood by a life-saving and life-changing teacher who found the doorway into discovering Helen's brilliant and beautiful mind. It took a teacher's patience, insight and unconventional teaching strategies to reach someone who seemed like an impossible child. Through adequate nurturing, teaching behavioral expectations, and an individualized learning program, Helen Keller learned how to read, write, and speak.

Anne Sullivan unlocked the mind of Helen Keller. She discovered that Helen could feel the vibrations of syllables and words, and was eventually successful in using a novel teaching method that used sense learning. Anne Sullivan's keen observation was the solar flare—a moment of light, a moment of insight—that freed and unmasked the mind of Helen Keller. She was a powerful and unrelenting teacher who gave instruction and guidance to Helen to be an active participant in society, share her voice, and advocate for human rights. Helen Keller was the first deaf and blind person to graduate from college with a Bachelor of Arts degree. She then went on to become an active advocate for the suffragette movement, a national public speaker, and the author of ten books. This is one example of how a teacher can change the life of a child so that they become an active member in society, help shape culture, and guide people to see the truth of their story and essence. Helen Keller shaped the way society and culture viewed people with disabilities and redirected the future by opening the eyes of society to the value of neurodiverse minds. She created visibility for people with disabilities to be recognized as equals in society.

"Knowledge is love and light and vision."
—Helen Keller

How to Best Support Neurotypes' Learning with Differentiation in Education and Life

1. **Safety**. Provide safety in all learning environments; at home, school and in extracurricular activities.

2. **Determine the origin of the learning difference** and implement appropriate support and guidance for their learning needs and styles. Providing the child with tutors, coaches, enrichment classes, and therapists for mental, physical, emotional, and behavioral needs.

3. **Accommodations**. Get the appropriate accommodations in place for the 2e person so they can thrive in their home, school, or workplace. It may be as simple as replacing all the fluorescent lights with soft light wave lengths, using dictation software, providing a note taker in class, or allowing extra time on exams or projects.

4. **Allow them learn at their own pace**. Remember the mind, brain, and body connection develops asynchronously. Recognize that in some areas they will excel tremendously and in other areas they may struggle due to asynchronous development. Help them and others understand that even though they are good at math they may be challenged with chemistry and that is okay. You don't expect a world record holder for running a mile to also excel at hockey. The same holds true for academics; not all subjects, talents, and abilities are developed and created equal.

5. **Patience.** Processing speed may vary. A child may be rapid in three-dimensional problem solving but find writing simple subtraction and addition problems a challenge. Allow for time and space for the differences in processing speed. In time, the brain development and networks will become less tangled. Give children plenty of time to think, work, and walk their own timeline line for their personal growth.

6. **Encourage and nurture** their divergent thinking. Embrace their uniqueness.

7. **Let children know they are not alone.** There are many incredible people that are 2e: Keanu Reeves (dyslexia); Whoopi Goldberg (dyslexia); Michael Phelps (ADHD); Agatha Christie (dysgraphia); Justin Timberlake (ADD and OCD), and Cher (ADHD, dyslexia), among many others.

8. **Focus on their strengths and help them with their challenged areas.** Beware of being hyper-focused on fixing them. In particular, provide opportunities where they can flourish and experience success for their natural talents.

9. **Watch your language.** With a 2e child it is essential they get the services they need, but also important not to label them as disabled. Being labeled different or disabled can be damaging to a person's confidence and self-esteem. Be mindful of the language you use and focus on their incredible uniqueness that is blended with their 2e-ness.

10. **Encourage them to engage with like minds.** Children need safety in social connections. Center opportunities around their interests that are safe. Most likely, when they are engaged with meaningful activities, naturally meaningful relationships develop.

11. **Compassion.** Model unlimited compassion for their unique way of being, brain wiring, and experiencing. Teach them to practice self-compassion daily.

The Secret of the Side Door for Neuroindividuals to Thrive

In gifted and 2e individuals, finding the secret side door is a critical turning point that can change their life trajectory. A door can be an epicenter for change, growth, and expansion, but if locked, an individual is left on the other side, starved and craving access with no way in.

Remember, there is always a side door. In gifted and 2e kids there needs to be mental flexibility to search for that side door. Much of my life, as I reflect back on it, has been through a side or back door. In some cases, I have broken locks and deadbolts to get inside. One day, when I was struggling with a project, my dear friend, the late Sam Christensen, told me a story about his growing up. His parents always had him enter and exit only through the front door of their house; it was just family protocol. But his house had, in addition to a front door, a side door, a garage door, and a back door. And some of those other doors, were he allowed access to them, would get him where he wanted to go faster or more easily. He suggested that I needed to enter (or approach my problem) through a side door. There is magic in a side door. Gifted, bright, and 2e individuals need a side door for their survival. They use the kitchen door, back door, the attic door, and in some cases crawl through a bedroom window to get inside their home, develop the layout of their mind, and unlock their magic. Help them unlock their essence for being here on Earth with the option of an alternate door or doors.

Some of these children and adults have nontraditional paths. They might be home schooled, need tutors, coaches, need a gap year in their education, or are in some cases unschooled. And some of these kids spend their recess and lunch in the art room painting, in the library reading, or in the music room playing the guitar. It is essential that we properly identify these kids before they have a devastating experience in school where they get all Fs and are lost in the abyss. We need to catch them before the light in their eyes is out. We need to offer them side doors and windows to regain their magic and feel empowered by their unconventional way of being in the world. We need to provide them with meaningful educational opportunities so that their intellect, emotions, and senses are activated in their learning and they are in flow. When they are experiencing flow, it is magic.

"As human beings, our job in life is to help people realize how rare and valuable each one of us really is, that each of us has something that no one else has—or will ever have—something that is unique to all time."

—Fred Rogers

Dear Bright One,

Don't worry, the world will eventually catch up with you. The misunderstood aspects of you are your gold. This doesn't mean that it will be easy. In fact, it may be challenging and painful and life will require you to use your imagination. You will learn the value and beauty of being an iconoclast. This will guide you to the vision and wide lens of human diversity. You are a teacher. Patience is a virtue—your best asset. Prodigy, late bloomer, early riser, daydreamer, wherever they find you, identify you—you are a super-nova, bursting with life. Trust your voice. As faint as it might be, it is your voice, so speak; trust your vision and be free from the ideals of the current world. You see land from a thousand miles away. A land that others cannot imagine. The sunset is yours—a thousand jewels glistening in the ocean. Trust your gifts, share your diversity. We need you to share your gifts with the world. Step onto land, out of the shadows and teach us to be better than we can even dream of. Teach us. We are waiting. We are ready. We are listening. Come out and play.

Love,

Your Big Sister

CHAPTER 3:

The Gifted Brain Rebooted

Wired for Brain Power

Interpreting the gifted brain can be like opening Pandora's box. Every time it's opened, something new stemming from neuroindividuality and asynchronous maturation and existence flies out. The human brain is one way to interpret giftedness, but intelligence expands beyond the brain. Intelligence is a way of interacting and exploring the world.

Gifted individuals possess enhanced intellectual, emotional, sensory, creative, and motor processing—as established by many neuroscience studies. These increased brain volumes and efficiency networks play a critical role in intelligences and intensities in gifted people. Many of these neuroscience studies center around regional brain expansions that correlate to a specific kind of intelligence. I have met a number of individuals in my life who do not express on pen and paper their intelligence or ability, and do not fit into standard achievement measures, but have nevertheless taught me things that cannot be, nor ever will be, found in a book or on an exam. It is an intelligence that is timeless. True intelligence, giftedness, is beyond brain anatomy, it is the how and the why, the intention of how one uses one's gifts. Giftedness surpasses time; gifted people can be years ahead of their time, living many lives of wisdom. One place of humility in my own journey is my son, Spence. He will always have a profoundly greater vocabulary than I do, and every day he teaches me new words and concepts. He has been doing this since he began speaking. He has taught me things that have not come from a textbook or from his environment, but rather were innately known. Where that comes from is something of a mystery and doesn't really matter. Often gifted and 2e children are wired to use greater brain power, and it is our job as a society to help them cultivate their expanded abilities for good. As Sigmund Freud said, "The voice of the intellect is a soft one, but it does not rest until it has gained a hearing."

Advancements in neuroscience have given us a great understanding of the human brain, its wiring, and of the remarkable uniqueness of each brain and the processing and the integration of unique individual experiences. Across all the neuroscience studies to date, gifted individuals show differences in brain maturation in the following eleven domains. They:

1. Develop asynchronous brain maturation where, in particular, the frontal cortex expands extensively in adolescents;

2. Have expansions in brain volume for sensory, motor, visual processing, and executive functioning;

3. Possess more efficient processing at the microstructure of neurons;

4. Have greater myelin fibers; that is, exceptional connectivity across brain areas to transfer information;

5. Demonstrate differences in information processing, either rapid or delayed;

6. Learn information at an accelerated rate;

7. Experience heightened brain activation when provided with greater intellectual challenges and experience considerable flow;

8. Exhibit exceptional sensory receptivity and sensitivity;

9. Have enhanced maturation of brain areas for emotional processing;

10. Show many converging neural networks in the brain "lit up," as seen on MRI brain scans, when in flow;

11. Express flexible and novel thinking to manipulate information.

The rich and diverse brain profile among gifted individuals centers on the principle of exceptional brain power. There is one thing that is undeniable: specialized brain expansions occur in the gifted brain, whether it is a gifted artist, musician, computer programmer, dancer, comedian, *etc*. More important, these brain expansions are unique to the gifted individual, which highlights the importance of our openness to the specialized journey of gifted people in the world.

Another important area to consider is how gifted people use their entire brain, operating in synchrony and asynchronously for differential and specialized processing. The knowledge we have obtained about the human brain in the last 30 years is only scratching the surface of what we can begin to understand about the human range, potential, diversity, and the mind.

Remember, at the bottom of Pandora's box is Hope, through our greater understanding we can hope and imagine ways to guide our bright children through their journey.

Beyond Book Smart

The word "gifted" means many different things to different people, similar to the word "genius." Both are beyond standard testing and book smarts. Giftedness begins in the body, brain, and mind, centered around different neural patterns for observing the world, often unconventionally and with greater openness and awareness across sensory, creative, emotional, physical, and intellectual processing. The curiosity of human intelligence has centered its investigations around the human mind from our earliest times.

The American Psychological Association (APA) explains intelligence as follows: "Individuals differ from one another in their ability to understand complex ideas, to adapt efficiently to the environment, to learn from experience and to engage in forms of reasoning to overcome obstacles by taking thought".[1] Spearman's G is the measurement of general cognitive function and basic processing ability, which is considered intelligence. Intelligence is measured in two forms, testing cognitive ability that includes crystallized and fluid intelligence, which are distinct.[2] Crystallized intelligence is defined as the great knowledge that individuals attain over their lifespan. Crystallized intelligence often increases with age, education, and experience. Fluid intelligence is defined as the ability for analytical reasoning, which is often dependent on the processing speed of information, executive functioning, and memory.[3] Many of these studies that review the brain use IQ tests to measure intelligence.

As discussed in Chapter 2, IQ scores only provide an approximation of intelligence and ability and each test measures a specific and distinct type of intelligence. And IQ is not the only measure of intelligence. For example, creativity is an intelligence.

This broad view of intelligence was best described by Einstein: "The measure of intelligence is the ability to change."

Intelligence is beyond academics, beyond "book smarts." Once a person has been tested and identified as gifted, that person is always gifted. Giftedness does not fade away, it is a life-long journey. Additionally, when someone's intellectual gifts are above the 99th percentile, then their experience in the world is unique: the odds are one in 10,000 that they will find an intellectual peer. It is key that our children that connect with like minds and the best way to encourage connection is through common interests. Even though being in 99th percentile is an individual experience it does not have to be confined to an experience of isolation. Rather it can be an experience of connection and community through nurturing relationships and connection with other people with shared interests and passions. When anyone's intelligence is valued and seen, they are more likely to step into embodiment of their natural gifts and being.

Multiple Intelligences (MI)

In 1983, Howard Gardner proposed his theory of multiple intelligences in his book *Frame of Minds: The Theory of Multiple Intelligences.*[4] In his early accounts he describes intelligence as the process to learn and manipulate information where individuals have abilities in eight specific domains:

1. Musical—rhythmic and harmonic
2. Visual—spatial
3. Verbal—linguistic

4. Logical—mathematical
5. Bodily—kinesthetic
6. Interpersonal
7. Intrapersonal
8. Naturalistic

Later, Gardner proposed the possibility of two additional intelligences, moral-spiritual, and existential, perhaps exploring justice and enlightenment with a goal of attaining self-actualization.[5] Much has been written on the theory of multiple intelligences over the past 20 years, including application of the theory in the area of educational neuroscience.[6] Gardner remains active in the MI community and currently describes multiple intelligences on his website, *Multiple Intelligence Oasis,*[7] as follows:

○ **Spatial intelligence** is the ability to imagine and manipulate large-scale spatial information, or small, local areas of space, like an astronaut, architect, or gamer.

○ **Bodily-kinesthetic intelligence** is the ability to employ one's body—or parts of it—to solve problems or create.

○ **Musical intelligence** is an attunement to the elements of music (rhythm, pitch, tone, melody, *etc.*) that leads to the ability to perform or create music.

○ **Linguistic intelligence** involves sensitivity to the meaning, sound, inflection, and order of words, like that of a poet; the ability to learn language, and/or to use language for rhetorical purposes like a lawyer.

○ **Logical-mathematical intelligence** describes the ability to observe patterns, conceptualize symbolic or logical relationships, and engage in deductive reasoning, like a mathematician, statistician, chemist, or physicist.

○ **Interpersonal intelligence** or "social intelligence," describes the capacity to interact with others with empathy, understanding, and consideration of emotions and motivations, like a teacher, salesperson, mediator, therapist, or counselor.

○ **Intrapersonal intelligence** or "self-intelligence" describes the ability to understand one's own emotions and motivations, as well as the ability to plan and use one's own particular traits. Gardner explains that intrapersonal intelligence is a universal goal, not particular to any subset of people or careers.

○ **Naturalistic intelligence** or "nature intelligence" (not included in Garner's original work, but added later) captures the ability to interact with our environment, to recognize and distinguish features of the natural world, like a farmer, hunter, chef, botanist, or biologist.

A cornerstone of Gardner's theory, as it has been applied to education, is that learners need to be empowered to best understand how they obtain information and are encouraged to explore all learning modalities. Gardner criticized educational institutions for narrowly focusing on verbal and logical-mathematical intelligences to the exclusion of others. No individual is limited to a single intelligence, but has a myriad of learning abilities that can be enhanced through training. This way, understanding one's own natural intelligences allows for greater self-maturation and acceptance. According to his theory, individuals learn to their specific modalities but have the potential to learn across all domains and are encouraged to explore learning in all areas. The foundation is to guide learners to better understand their learning style so they can identify their strengths.

The notion that intelligence is beyond books is that individual development and brain maturation are highly distinctive. An important concept when ascribing to his theory is that the human mind has specific specializations that allow for an individualistic formation based on neuroindividuality centered on special neuroanatomy, wiring, and neural plasticity through interacting with one's environment. An individual's brain will mimic their learning styles and adaptability to manipulate information. Additionally, IQ tests capture a narrow band of abilities within the spectrum of intelligence. Brightness is absolutely beyond book smart. Being able to provide empathy during times of challenge is a higher order level processing that turns knowledge into wisdom. Teaching our children to wisely use their gifts and with appropriate discernment is essential. Academic learning is just a single area to obtain intelligence; a child needs to thrive in all areas of their life including creative, social, emotional, physical, mental, and sensory.

It is important to note that the learning environment contributes to intelligence and brain structure. This is demonstrated by a study where rodents were raised in an enriched environment and flourished compared to rodents whose environment was impoverished. The rodents whose environment was enriched showed an increase in cortical cell density, which is biological evidence of higher intelligence.[8] Not surprisingly, the rodents raised with enrichment were better problem solvers (in a subset of tests) compared to rodents not raised in an enriched environment. And the ability for neural plasticity to wire novel neural networks is a life-long one that is woven in with one's way of learning and interacting with one's environment.[9]

Gifted Brain Maps

Many intelligence measures that test the biological correlates of intelligence use neuroimaging, which is a process of acquiring images of the brain that form into a brain map. The map of the human brain is composed of various regions, many of which are known to have specific functions. Grey matter is composed of neurons and glia cells and brain imaging captures the density of neurons and dendrites in a region of interest. Neurons are the primary cell type we will be referring to because they are the basic computational components of information processing. Neurons provide a network for information to come together so that we can process, interpret, manage, and store that information to use in the present moment and in the future.

Across many studies and paradigms, gifted individuals with elevated intellectual processing have demonstrated regional brain expansions and increased brain activity. Total brain volume, which includes gray and white matter, has also been shown to correlate with intelligence test scores.[10] A study by Thompson and colleagues showed regional brain differences in relationship to intelligence measures.[11] Even though we know there are regional brain differences, network differences, and functioning differences in intelligence measures it is important to study the functionality and differences among individuals in the population. Repeated studies have shown the distinct relationship between gray matter volume and the genetic contributions to brain anatomy.[12]

It is noteworthy that brain volume and IQ are positively correlated because it shows an association for the biological differences in gifted individuals that originates with the neuroanatomy. In a meta-analysis of 37 neuroimaging studies, scientists found that brain volume is positively correlated with intelligence.[13] Honing in on neuroanatomy in gifted individuals provides evidence for a difference in intellectual processing, performance, and functioning. A gifted person is "wired" differently to experience the world differently.

A number of studies show that individuals with higher IQs have greater maturation in the gray matter areas of the frontal cortex, anterior cingulate cortex, temporal cortex, parietal, and occipital cortex.[14]

- **Frontal cortices** are crucial to higher order thinking and intellectual processing such as complex decision-making, motivation, reward, self-control, planning, hypothesis testing, and emotional balance. The frontal cortex has a great expansion in gifted children and adolescents that can account for variability, asynchrony, and enhanced intellectual capacity.[15] It is known that the frontal cortex develops well into our thirties and throughout life[16] and, significantly, there can be developmental delays in a gifted individual related to their frontal cortex maturation.[17]

- The **anterior cingulate cortex** is a brain area involved in executive functioning, decision-making, emotional saliency, trust, and reward. Anterior cingulate cortex is the cornerstone for emotional balance, morality, and justice, which are core behavioral characteristics in gifted people.

- By comparison, the **temporal and parietal lobes** are critical for sensory processing of touch, taste, smell, language interpretation, language formation, and integration of emotional sensation. Often gifted people report greater awareness and receptivity for sensation and often individuals with a higher verbal IQ report greater emotional experience.

○ The **occipital lobe** is the brain region dedicated to visual processing and is key for the way we take in our visual surroundings. Studies of mathematically gifted adolescents show greater expansion of the visual cortices in relation to spatial processing.[18]

Each of these areas are associated with increased brain expansions and intellectual processing that include how gifted individuals respond to and perceive the world with heightened awareness and exploration.

When looking at the brain in action, functional magnetic resonance (fMRI) imaging allows for scientists to see brain activity while an individual is performing a task by measuring the individual's blood oxygenation level dependent (BOLD) signal. Many researchers have been interested in understanding the brain processing of highly gifted children and reviewed their brain activity while they performed cognitive tasks. For example, scientists Geake & Hansen had gifted children and age-matched neurotypical peers solve letter sequence problems while reviewing their brain activation. They found that gifted children with greater verbal abilities showed enhanced activation in the bilateral frontal, parietal, and occipital regions of the brain, as well as bilateral anterior cingulate cortex.[19] Strikingly, there was a linear relationship between verbal IQ and the BOLD signal of the frontal cortices of gifted individuals, pointing to a biological basis and metabolic difference in children with higher verbal IQs.

These studies strongly suggest that gifted individuals have expanded brain regions and heightened brain activation compared to age-matched peers in relation to manipulating verbal information. These studies also provide evidence that the frontal cortex plays a crucial role in cognitive tasks with increased difficulty, and that prefrontal cortical activity may be enhanced in higher IQ individuals. An extremely important implication, when relating to gifted individuals with enhanced intellectual and emotional abilities, is that it helps us to understand the differences that arise from brain anatomy, activity, and increased verbal abilities. It also suggests a higher rate of metabolic activity in the brain in relation to information processing when in flow.

Critical findings such as these strongly suggest that gifted individuals have expanded neuroanatomy networks that relate to their functioning and processing. In addition, gifted individuals have great baseline activation in response to stimuli and information processing. Like an Olympic runner who has a distinct physiology, such as an elevated VO2max, providing a biological foundation for her to become a world-champion gold medalist, gifted individuals also have distinct physiological gifts. They possess greater brain volume and expanded brain networks, and have greater metabolism related to processing information, allowing for enhanced cognitive, mental, emotional, sensorial, and physical processing. Importantly, these studies provide a peek into the brain of gifted individuals and highlight the importance of how the entire brain works together for cognitive abilities. It is not just a single brain area that constitutes the basis for greater abilities and intellectual processing. More important, cognitive performance is highly neuroindividual and sometimes uncharted neural pathways provide the greatest insight.

Is Bigger Better?

There is undeniable evidence that higher IQ individuals have greater brain volume and size, which often correlates with their cognitive abilities. However, the idea that "bigger is better" is an oversimplified explanation of the human brain and human experience. Evolutionarily, it is true across mammals that brain expansions reflect intelligence, but most important, with higher order primates the correlation is specific to regional expansions like that in the frontal cortex—the networks related to higher order cognition and processing account for increased intelligence. Most important, it is how the entire brain works together as a whole to process information and transfer information into knowledge by manipulating concepts that provides for higher intellectual capabilities.

Macrocephaly, or a larger brain, does not necessarily predict greater intelligence. In some cases, a larger brain volume correlates with developmental delays and interferes with proper brain maturation. For example, a subset of individuals with autism, expressing a number of developmental delays, have larger brains.[20] This has long been a puzzling aspect of studying brain development, because in this particular case a larger brain correlates with developmental delays which challenges current thinking that a larger brain volume typically indicates greater cognitive abilities.

Scientists have discovered that in conventional brain development, the cortex develops in six layers of neurons, called minicolumns, that are highly specific in their projection patterns and functioning. Minicolumns are like a community of neurons that have specific firing in relation to function and output within local brain regions and across brain areas, like local streets in a town. When the layers of neurons are disordered there are challenges with development, brain maturation, processing, and functioning. Scientists found, in the subset of individuals with autism and developmental delays, that their greater brain volume was a result of wider and disordered minicolumns and layering which accounted for greater brain volume.[21] Particularly, when there are disruptions in the developmental layer formation of the minicolumns there are challenges with information processing, functioning, and cognitive abilities. Because the cell layers are scrambled due to disrupted cytoarchitecture, the brain wiring is altered through development and thus present notable differences in cognition and behavior.

Scientists recently discovered, when looking at the microstructure in the human brain, that although whole brain volume is consistently a predictor for intelligence, people with higher IQs, had fewer dendrites (the finest structures of a neuron).[22] Dendrites extend their connections to other cells like tree branches, described as dendritic arborizations, and are the communicators between cells. In higher IQ individuals, the dendritic arborization is less dense at the end of neurons. How can this be? Scientists propose that higher intelligence brains run more efficiently at the microstructure of a neuron. Cells communicate across synapses. During development the brain goes through a process known as synaptic pruning where it eliminates the overly abundant synapses. This allows neurons to communicate more efficiently with one another at the microstructure. This is contrary to what we thought in terms of brain maturation, the idea that more is better. By contrast, at the microstructure of a neuron, fewer more well-developed and specific branches allow for more efficient information and energy transfer. It is not the sheer volume of a brain that matters, it is the processing that occurs at the local microstructure and across the brain.

Significantly, the way a brain globally communicates information is dependent on how the whole brain works as a single organ, centering on information and energy transfer at the microstructure that is essential for higher cognitive capacity and abilities. One can have greater brain volume, but if the networks and pathways are not formed properly there will be issues with development, cognition, sensory receptivity and processing, proprioception, emotionality, and behavior. However, if regional expansions develop with cohesive cell layer patterning and proper projection neurons, pathways, and circuitry throughout the brain, then the larger brain volume can contribute to advantaged information processing and cognition. It is much more dependent on connectivity within a region, across brain regions, and how an entire brain works together and adapts to the environment and information.

It is more than the simplistic idea that "bigger is better."

White Matter Paradox

White matter is tissue that makes up the information superhighways by which information is transferred throughout the brain. Energy flow is highly dependent on processing speed and the development of white matter tracts in the brain. Capturing the white matter measurement in the brain reflects axonal projections and thickness, as well as the amount of **myelin** (an insulating sheath that forms around nerve cells) for conductance of energy flow and efficiency. **White matter tracts** are essentially the freeways of the brain. These pathways allow for the exchange of information between brain regions in the same way that freeways allow us to travel between cities. The speed of the information varies based on the attributes of the white matter tracts themselves, such as the abundance, the distance, and the strength of the connections across brain regions. Why is it that some gifted individuals can process some things extraordinarily quickly, while other types of processing seems to take eons? For example, you may have a child that solves a Rubik's cube in six seconds but takes five minutes to write their name. How could the same child have such widely variable processing speeds for different cognitive tasks? This difference may be a result of the way the white matter tracts are developing in the child's brain, as maturation of the white matter tracts happens asynchronously within the individual child. For example, the brain's pathway for solving a Rubik's cube is developed like Elon Musk's underground super-fast Hyperloop highway, a seamless and direct path. By contrast, the pathway developed to write one's name may be like traveling through the Amazon jungle, where a guide bushwhacks a path with a machete to get to the other side, at each step choosing among many possible trails.

Early lines of evidence suggest that intellectual capacity is reliant on white matter tracts and myelin integrity, where greater nerve conduction and speed are related to a larger axon diameter and congruency.[23] Greater prevalence of white matter with increased axon diameter plays a crucial role in cognitive maturation and information processing speed across the entire brain. For example, there is a known reduction of myelination around the fourth decade that is thought to be part of a slowing in cognitive functioning, and the presence of myelin is directly related to cognition throughout life.[24]

Higher IQ individuals have greater overall white matter connectivity and cohesion across the entire brain which would allow for enhanced information processing and manipulation.[25] Specifically, gifted individuals have increased white matter tracts in the brain. Investigators found greater correlation of white matter measures and verbal intellectual ability compared to nonverbal ability where pathways directly influence verbal capabilities. Particularly, projections of white matter connecting Broca's area to Wernike's area, the language areas of the brain, are sensitive to variation among individuals and impact intellectual achievement, such that verbal ability is directly related to white matter tracts in the brain, and thus more eloquent verbal processing was related to better connectivity across brain regions for language processing and production. Gifted individuals often express enhanced processing speed in relation to cognitive tasks and intellectual processing and their neuroanatomy and white matter tracts—information highways that allow information to travel across brain regions.

Penke and team reviewed white matter tracts in the brain and found that brain-wide white matter tracts' integrity is associated with increased processing speed in general intelligence.[26] Particularly, more intact tracts—where the fibers were traveling in the same direction, with congruent pathways—provided for increased information processing. Conversely, when the white matter tracts are more disordered, information processing is slowed and delayed from one region to another.

Gifted individuals often express a combination of rapid and delayed processing speed, dependent on the task at hand. Much of this difference can be related to how the brain develops networks and how the myelin fibers lay down their pathways. In addition, due to asynchronous brain development, it may take some individuals more time to have brain pathways mature for more fluid processing speed. Through practice, one can develop and align pathways to have greater congruency over time resulting in enhanced processing speed.

Another dimension of giftedness is related to having high levels of curiosity and openness. A gifted individual may ponder a so-called "simple" question with a greater level of wonder, resulting a slower response time. For example, one may ask a gifted child the color of a banana: the standard answer is obviously yellow, but a gifted child might respond unexpectedly and say that the banana could be white, cream, yellow, lime green, yellow-green, brown, and even brown-and-yellow spotted. Any or all of these descriptions are accurate and true. In fact, while a banana peel is often yellow, the inside is not. And a banana is never just a single color, and its color changes as it ripens. Instead of delivering the obvious, quick answer, a gifted child might focus on all the endless possibilities of a banana, an exploration which naturally takes much longer to process than a single, simple answer. Thus, we understand that although white matter connectivity and congruency is a predictor for giftedness, it is by no measure limited to white matter development, but rather entire brain maturation and processing.

Often, the processing speed in a gifted child is enriched so that their expanded brain connectivity of white matter tracts allows for greater energy and information flow throughout the brain. But individuals express variation and sometimes the fast-processing white matter paradoxically yields a slower response.

Bright Brain in Flow Lights Up

In flow, bright brains are brimming with activity. They light up with energy because their brain power is fully engaged, much like an engine with all its cylinders firing. In numerous studies, mathematically gifted individuals have shown significant brain activation while solving complex math problems that increase in difficulty, reflecting a state of "flow" where they are fully engaged with a feeling of positive, energetic focus.[27] Notably, gifted individuals can be capable of greater bilateral activation of the parietal lobes, anterior cingulate, and frontal cortex. Their brains light up the fMRI when they are in flow because they are working with engaging material that is at their level. When in flow, an individual's brain activation is bright and full of activity, and the individual experiences greater reward and motivation. This is due to activity of the neurotransmitter dopamine, the neurochemical responsible for reward and motivation, which is active when one is working at their level and their entire brain is engaged.

Recent studies of mathematically precocious youth show that individuals use both left and right frontal cortex with greater activation when solving complex math problems as problems increased in difficulty when compared to age-matched peers.[28] The mathematically-gifted youth showed activation clusters that were always bilateral, and a greater number of regions were recruited, in particular the right hemisphere of the brain, as compared to their neurotypical peers. This highlights that the increased ability to manipulate information in the gifted brain is not only attributable to greater volume, but that greater metabolic processing is also an essential factor. When an individual manipulates information, processing at their full level of engagement, the brain is "glowing" and releasing positive neurochemicals allowing the gifted individual to experience maximal flow. It is as if the gifted brain patterns are meant and built to work at a higher level of activation, suited for their particular abilities, reward, and motivation.

The increased activations in the parietal and frontal regions of mathematically gifted individuals are related to their elevated abilities in visual spatial processing and logic reasoning.

In mathematically gifted individuals, scientists found that IQ had a significant positive correlation with greater volume of the **corpus callosum** (the band of nerve fibers joining the left and right hemispheres of the brain) providing evidence that efficiently transferring information between hemispheres is a critical factor in greater intellectual capabilities.[29] Additionally, mathematically gifted adolescents showed increases in the white matter tracts that connect the frontal regions of the brain with the basal ganglia and parietal regions, which can account for increased fluid reasoning, working memory, and creativity in these gifted youth. The efficiently interconnected brain can account for greater intellectual abilities because information easily travels across hemispheres, provides for greater reward processing, and offers creative ways to interact with information.

Together, these studies provide evidence that to thrive children need to be challenged at their elevated intellectual level. Often when the mind and brain are fully engaged, the gifted brain is able to work joyfully at its highest capacity and ability. When a child experiences an appropriate level of challenge and engagement, there are corresponding reductions in behavioral challenges and other difficulties because the gifted child is engaged in activities that are stimulating. When a brain is fully engaged, an individual experiences greater natural flow, reward, and motivation from a surge of positive neurochemicals like dopamine. Gifted individuals are in their essence and element when their intellectual and cognitive abilities are met. It is essential to point out that this engagement is not just in a single brain region, but rather a reflection of how the entire brain works together in a state of flow. When a child is in flow they are working at their level and experience greater engagement with material that is meaningful to them. Their brains light up and they fully experience the joy that is their flow.

Wired for Greater Empathy and Emotional Currency

Emotional equanimity is a hallmark of emotionally in-tune individuals. Enhanced emotional understanding, empathy, and desire for justice are key emotions and behaviors in emotionally bright individuals. Emotional intelligence is described as having increased empathy, an increased theory of mind, that is, the ability to understand and anticipate what another individual is experiencing or feeling. Emotionally gifted individuals are often considered to have increased emotional understanding of others and themselves and express a wide palate and amplitude of emotions to describe their internal states.

Gardner described, in his theory of multiple intelligences, how persons with greater interpersonal intelligence have a greater ability for empathy. And, we are learning that these individuals have expanded neuroanatomy maturation of regions in the brain dedicated to emotional processing, empathy, and the ability to experience emotions with a greater richness and depth. According to Jim Webb, Susan Daniels, and Linda Silverman, emotionally gifted individuals express emotional intensities such that their levels of emotionality are often misunderstood and dismissed by others that are not as in tune. Brain anatomy, wiring, and behavioral patterning may give us insight into the minds of the most empathetic and emotionally wise individuals. According to a number of studies, emotionally gifted individuals have more brain power dedicated to emotional processing and understanding.

For example, key regions in the brain for emotional processing are reported to have greater volume in individuals with higher IQs.[30] Specifically, scientists studied the relationship between IQ and the higher-order emotional centers in the brain, and found that people with above average IQ scores had increased grey matter volume in the anterior cingulate cortex (ACC) and frontal cortices (FC). Both these areas of the brain are essential for cognitive functioning, emotional processing, decision making, reward, empathy, and bodily homeostasis. Having larger brain volumes for both areas, ACC and FC, suggest a richness in one's awareness and ability to explore the world with greater cognition and emotional aptitude. Thus, emotionally gifted individuals have a deep sense of mission for justice, fairness, and morality. These very brain structures are essential for emotional balance with a greater awareness for morality, self-insight, intuition, enhanced communication skills, better regulation of fear, increased flexible thinking, and the enhanced ability expressing empathy. Having greater brain volume in these areas can account for enhanced ability for emotional processing and emotional knowledge and understanding in bright individuals. This helps us understand that an increase in emotional intelligence and awareness stems from brain wiring and neuroanatomy, where our biological set points are different, stemming from our genetics and enhanced by how our choices develop our neural networks to enhance our emotional awareness. Behavioral practices can cultivate greater emotional balance when our intention and awareness is grounded in our personal emotional thresholds.

Bright individuals often describe feeling things more intensely, more deeply, and having heightened emotional responses compared to those of average intelligence.[31] In a study reviewing white matter networks in relation to IQ, investigators found that high IQ individuals showed an increase in the volume of the right uncinate fasciculus, an area in the brain essential for transferring electrical impulses from the limbic area, the first responder of emotion in the brain, to the frontal cortex, the emotional action and decision maker.[32] Particularly, the right uncinate fasciculus is essential for its role in processing empathy, a key emotion when understanding the feelings, behaviors, and actions of others. A study of military veterans and stroke patients who had a lesion of the right uncinate fasciculus showed impairment in expressing empathy and a decrease in emotional valence and understanding.[33] The connectivity role of the right uncinate fasciculus is critical because it links the orbitofrontal cortex, temporal pole, insula, and the amygdala, all areas that are vital for decoding and conveying emotional information throughout the brain. The right uncinate fasciculus is an essential white matter pathway for relaying emotional information and empathy. Because the right uncinate fasciculus is expanded in gifted individuals, its role in processing emotional information throughout the brain could be one element in understanding the enhanced emotional intelligence and empathy observed in the gifted population.

Neuroscience studies show that the brains of emotionally gifted individuals may be wired for advanced emotional abilities and enhanced empathy. Their brain maturation and innate behaviors can encourage enhanced emotional understanding and elevated emotional processing abilities. Because some individuals are wired for greater emotional capabilities, it is critical to nurture emotionally gifted individuals by helping them understand that the foundation their intense emotional processing is in their nature. Fostering self-compassion based in understanding and supporting an individual to process the full range of complex emotions encourages positive development and promotes self-acceptance for the intensified way they experience the world.

Studies support the connection between high intellectual ability and increased altruism and giving. In an investigation seeking to understand the social and emotional behaviors of mathematically gifted adolescents, researchers used the Ultimatum Game, a game used in economic decision making that measures human economic and cognitive decision-making.[34] The Ultimatum Game is based on economic paradigms that explore how individuals may cooperate or defect based either on sharing or taking a financial reward, allowing researchers to hone in on human altruism.

In the Ultimatum Game, the "proposer" offers a portion of $10 to the "responder," who is free to accept or reject the offer. If the responder accepts the offer, each player receives the amount the proposer offered. If the responder rejects the offer, both players receive nothing. Strategically, the proposer benefits by making small, unfair offers (*e.g.*, $1/$9), and the responder benefits accepting all offers, even small, unfair ones, since the alternative is zero. To succeed and maximize earnings in the Ultimatum Game, players must employ social adaptive mentalizing strategies, such as fairness, cooperation, and reputation.

Although the gifted adolescents were more mathematically strategic than their peers, they were unsuccessful in reading their opponent's behaviors, leading to lower overall earnings. The math-gifted adolescents were unable to employ adaptive strategies. Gifted responders were more reactive to perceived unfairness than their age-matched peers, and rejected proposals at higher than average rates, including "fair" proposals, which led to decreased total earnings.

This intensified focus on fairness and justice, shows how wiring in the brain may directly account for greater rates of altruism in gifted individuals. Brighter individuals appear to be more giving and altruistic, accounting for wider emotional intelligence and prosocial behaviors, where they are wired to give, wired to share, and wired for greater social concern. Importantly, when we give to others, it feels good; it is a long-lasting positive reward and a surge of dopamine flows throughout our brains. This highlights how gifted emotional wisdom is expressed through greater social concern, empathy, and morality and how some individuals are wired for greater emotional concern and justice for the humanity and the planet. Emotional wisdom is a light through challenging times.

Hyper-Brain, Hyper-Body

Gifted individuals report experiencing and processing the world with greater awareness and openness. Bright people use specialized networks and their unique processing and networks are the foundation for how their entire brain operates for deep thinking, feeling, and being. The inner and outer world is different, and the experience of giftedness is far beyond intellectual abilities. Often gifted people are misidentified, misunderstood, and misdiagnosed because of their unconventional behaviors and ways of thinking. As described previously, gifted individuals develop out of sync, where their intellectual and emotional behaviors may fall outside of society's norms, and are interpreted as quirky and idiosyncratic.

Ruth Karpinski, a mother of two gifted boys who expressed unique ways of exploring the world, sought to understand their gifts and challenges in depth. Both her sons were as smart as whips, but struggled in school with social, emotional, and academic success, reflecting dual diagnoses of giftedness and ADHD. Watching her sons navigate the world despite their challenges, Ruth wanted to understand whether what she experienced in her home was common in homes with bright kids across America. In the fourth decade of her life, Ruth decided to go back to college to study psychology. She was a gifted student herself. In her quest to uncover the truth about the challenge and weight that giftedness carried, she conducted a survey study of 3,715 members of American Mensa, Ltd.[35] Mensa is an organization that accepts the top 98th percent of the population who express intellectual giftedness. Because she and her sons were life-long members of

Mensa, Ruth wanted to understand whether bright individuals had an increased prevalence of mental, physical, emotional, and physiological conditions. Many intelligence studies focus their research on enhanced intelligence as a measure for academic, professional, and socioeconomic success, ambitiousness, increased longevity, as well as the relationship between enhanced intellectual capabilities and increased fitness in relation to professional and financial life outcomes. Much of the literature is devoid of studies that explore the mental, physical, and emotional health of bright individuals. Often this view feeds into the stereotypes that if you are bright you are at an advantage, can handle everything, and already have it all.

Ruth and Audrey Kolb, both students at Pitzer College, broke the mold when they designed a questionnaire designed to look into the mental, physical, and emotional health of bright individuals. The foundation of their research studies reviewed the work of James T. Webb, Susan Daniels, and Kazimierz Dąbrowski, and centered around the theory that gifted individuals have potential advanced development in sensory, emotional, mental, physical, and creative expression and these greater abilities allow for extraordinary challenges and gifts across the board. Our study centered on the premise that bright individuals experience the world through elevated processing, a "hyper-brain and hyper-body," where the enhanced experiencing couples with greater psychological and physiological challenges. The questionnaire explored eight specific areas: mood disorders, anxiety disorders, ADHD/ADD, ASD, food allergies, environmental allergies, asthma, and autoimmune disease. In each of these categories, the Mensans reported an increase in prevalence compared to the national average for both psychological and physiological conditions. In this bright population, individuals described close to double the diagnoses of anxiety and mood disorders and approximately three times the national average diagnoses of environmental allergies.

Our study supports the idea that a more excitable brain and body may coincide with an increased incidence of psychological and physiological conditions. For example, we know gifted individuals have increased brain regions related to emotional intelligence and have larger connectivity across emotional brain regions, which can provide for greater awareness of emotional intelligence and empathy. Also, this expanded neuroanatomy can provide for a greater risk of conditions like depression and anxiety. In particular, an elevated mind and body can go into overdrive, leading to greater activation of neuroimmune responses. An elevated neuroimmune response triggers a series of bidirectional processes of the mind and body, where there is a chronic flux of neuroimmune chemicals changing the physical, mental, and emotional processing in an individual such that the activation leads to a hyper-brain and hyper-body receptivity and response.

This original theory breaks the ideals of how the culture and society solely identifies brightness centered on being intellectual. Of course, intellectual engagement is essential for bright individuals to thrive, but there are worlds upon worlds where the social, emotional, physical, mental and sensory needs of a gifted person need to be met to blossom in the world.

Bright people experience their surroundings with greater receptivity and responsiveness, which is an elevated way of being. This study opens doors to exploring the mental and physical well-being of bright individuals so that we can help individuals when they are suffering in relation to their biologically determined set points and engage in positive practices for gifted adults and children. Through our understanding that bright individuals encounter the world with greater awareness and openness, we can guide them with the following:

1. Proper identification

2. Safety within emotional, mental, physical, sensory, and creative areas

3. A safe environment in which to explore and make mistakes

4. Space to experience true engagement, where individuals are given opportunities for more advanced learning and learning that meets their intellectual, emotional, mental, physical, sensory, and imaginative needs

5. Opportunities for individuals' maximal engagement to experience flow

Creative Thinking Unlocks Unique Brain Networks

"Creativity is intelligence having fun."

–Albert Einstein

The creative brain engages unconventional brain networks where manifestation of divergent thinking emerges. A new study found when measuring connectivity within the brains of subjects, researchers could approximate how creative the subject's ideas would be based on connectivity. The researchers found three subnetworks in the brain that are engaged during creative problem solving: the default mode network, the salience network, and the executive functioning network.[36] Interestingly, these subnetworks do not normally engage except when engaged in creative thinking. This finding highlights how an imaginative brain in flow accesses multiple brain regions and both hemispheres. Importantly, for imagination and ingenuity, it is the orchestration across brain regions that produces creative problem solving. The discovery of three subnetworks working in synchrony debunks the age-old myth of "right brained and left brained." It demonstrates how the brain absorbed in creativity uses multiple regions. So, what do these three subnetworks do and why are they in synchrony in creative thinking?

The default mode network is involved in emotions, memories of self and others.[37] It is activated during mind wandering, planning the future, thinking of past events, rest, and meditation. This network is critical for understanding how mind wandering ignites imagination by accessing information at a deep level. The finding may explain the creative behaviors we call being "spaced" or "heady." Perhaps that is exactly what is needed to be in a deep creative thought process.

The salience network sorts through information internally and from the environment.[38] It is hypothesized that the salience network analyzes the thoughts and emotions from the default mode network.[39] It is where the symphony of collecting ideas and memories and sorting through the imagination starts in the brain.

The executive functioning network happens in the frontal lobe (dorsal lateral prefrontal cortex and the orbitofrontal cortex), where essential cognition occurs related to attention, working memory, cognitive inhibitory control like fluid reasoning, problem solving, and cognitive flexibility.[40] These regions may be responsible for taking action on the creative ideas and putting them into play. Testing and working out multiple outcomes based on memories of trial and error is crucial for problem solving.

The incredible value of this study shows that high creativity requires large scale brain networks. Creatives engage a unique brain network for expansive imaginative thinking that allows for creative problem solving and novel solutions. Additionally, there was a strong correlation between respondents' self-reports of creative behaviors and creative thinking.[41] This leads to the next wave: how can we ignite more imagination in our daily lives? By daydreaming, perhaps.

Remember the next time you think your friend, partner, child, or co-worker seems "spaced out" they may be in deep creative thought, developing the latest invention or work of art.

*"Creativity involves breaking out of expected patterns
in order to look at things in a different way."*
—Edward de Bono

Dear 6th Sense,

Does it hurt beyond words to be in your body? Do certain types of clothing feel like pinpricks on your skin? Are people's voices and sounds too loud? Do their voices pound in your eardrums? Do gardening blowers and traffic hurt your body? Does music give you chills at the back of your neck? Do the hairs on your arm rise when you listen to Beethoven's Concerto #5 "The Emperor" 2nd movement? Can bright lights send you into a visual migraine? When reading, is black and white print dizzying? Do stripes give you vertigo? Or escalators? Do certain smells activate your gag reflex? Do tastes and tactile stimulation of things like kiwi or fish skin make you feel nauseated and lose your appetite? Does it sometimes hurt to live in your body? Do they listen? Do they cut the tags from your t-shirts, dim the blinding lights, and lower their voices? Do they hear you? Let's help them understand.

Yours truly,

The Pediatrician You'll Remember All Your Life

CHAPTER 4:

Making Sense of Enhanced Senses

Twenty-First Century of Overstimulation

We live in an unnatural world with continuous stimulation which, more often than not, reaches the point of overstimulation. Artificial sounds, lights, scents, materials, chemicals, sweeteners, and a slew of manufactured sensory experiences that our nervous system, body, and mind have not adapted nor evolved for. We can experience the world with ever-enriching and pleasure-seeking centers in the brain, where entertainment and artificial life (phones, apps, internet, computer programs, video games, TV, radio, etc.) are at our fingertips twenty-four seven. We are not primed for, nor have we developed to handle continuous entertainment, leaving our brain and body with a series of biological mismatches where our sensory system is overloaded. We live in a world as if there is a continuous glitch in our system, short-circuiting our mind and body so that we are on perpetual reboot.

Our overloaded and exhausted nervous system sends signals to our brain and body to retreat, triggering a cascade of stress response neurochemicals, ultimately leading to anxiety, fear, and in severe cases, panic attacks. This, in turn, changes our psychological and physiological behaviors to increased emotionality, disrupted focus, heightened motor feedback, increased perception in pain circuitry, and greater social withdrawal. A person may present with physical manifestations of hyperactivity, trouble focusing, severe irritability, increased pain, and excessive excitement and want to shield their eyes, ears, skin from sensory input because of the enhanced fear and anxiety this environment produces. They may become completely shut down. These behaviors and physiological responses are due to having a highly primed nervous system sensitive to tactile, visual, sound, taste, and odor stimuli. All these behaviors lead a person to express asynchrony in their performance, abilities, and processing. These individuals have a greater challenge in traditional school and work environments where their abilities and natural talents are disrupted because of environmental occurrences that are considered "normal" baseline but that are genuine sensory nervous system insults. These neurotypes can be misidentified with a slew of incorrect diagnoses that including anxiety, depression, ADHD, ADD, OCD, ODD, and other mood disorders and they can manifest stressors experienced as physical, mental, and emotional pain.

These individuals are navigating in the world where sensory experiences disrupt daily flow, activities, relationships, and quality of life. It is as if the person is out of sync with their environment and others and cannot completely express themselves due to the challenges of navigating an overstimulating sensory environment.

Different Brain Wiring for Elevated Sensory Processing

The brains of people with sensory processing differences show distinct neural signatures and exhibit differential neural patterning and circuitry for sensory processing. Specifically, we are discovering that there are in fact biological bases for these heightened sensory processing experiences. Recent findings are unveiling through MRI technology that white matter connectivity and patterning differs in some individuals, and that difference may be central to sensory processing variances. Sensory processing differences and sensory hypersensitivity are found in a number of neurotypes, such as ADHD, autism spectrum disorder, dyslexia, dysgraphia, fragile X, and a number of developmental disorders, but sensory processing differences are often overlooked, misidentified, and misinterpreted because they are not widely known.

Often, children and adults who experience these sensory processing magnifications experience complications in processing what would be considered "normal" stimuli, such as sounds from movie theaters, vacuums, and artificial lights. Even light touch can be experienced as painful. In some of these cases, children with sensitivities retreat from physical contact such as hugs and holding hands. But, the very next day they may pursue those same sensory experiences, called sensory-seeking behaviors. These contradictory behaviors create confusion for parents, clinicians, and educators because identifying the source for the differences in behaviors is not understood nor is how to create safe environments for sensory perceptions and responses. This is where I advise taking it one day at a time and exploring the basis for the sensory-seeking and sensory avoiding experiences.

Many of these children appear to be out of sync in other domains as well, such as with fine motor skills (where activities like holding a pencil or writing are challenging), experiencing increased challenges with proprioception (knowing where one is in three-dimensional space) and equilibrium issues (where one is challenged to remain physically balanced and coordinated). These challenges can cause a child to be labeled clumsy. Many of these physical asynchronies are related to out of sync brain development, which can influence personality, sociability, attention, and temperament.

Sensory hypersensitivity can interfere with social interaction so that these children and adults seem to miss subtle social cues and facial expressions. This can be because their attention is focused on their overwhelming sensory experience. This kind of response can affect a person's behaviors so that they become more socially withdrawn because they are managing their physical and sensory responses and are consumed with regulating their overactive nervous system.

Another area of struggle can include emotional control, equanimity and missing others' emotional cues. The intense sensory experience causes hypervigilance and requires attention, so their baseline reaction is direct limbic (primal) emotion because they are in pain and suffering— their hyper attention is centered on managing sensory insults.

These challenges may have great consequences in social inter-actions for school-aged children, people in the workplace, and for individuals in their familial and peer relationships. Consequentially, these children frequently experience high levels of scrutiny from their peers. They are often left feeling as if they do not fit in, they may experience a great deal of social isolation, and they can be easy targets for victimization and bullying. Their delayed processing and sensory overload can interfere with their social connection and communication. The nervous system is primed for emotions to be woven with sensory information and bodily experiences, as well as perceptions of our environment and our personal memories. Thus, for people with sensory hypersensitivity, their mind and body has developed blueprints for heightened experiences, reactions, and processes. These differences in expanded sensory awareness are in part due to brain wiring, patterns, and sensory imprints, which are developed through one's history of sensing and one's autobiographical memories.

Neuroscience studies of sensory oversensitivities have highlighted how our brain regions are multi-sensory and woven together. While an individual is processing auditory sensory information, there is invisible processing happening across all the sensory domains. Visual stimuli are affected as auditory over-responsivity is happening, and the entire sensory system is on overdrive where there are alternations occurring in working memory and emotional regulation. The brain is not a fixed unit—in fact, the brain is processing information across several domains—and sensory over-responsivity has a distinct foundation in brain pathways that are specific for sensory processing, emotional regulation, and working memory. These differential ways of experiencing and navigating in the world are specific to how the brain developed, how brain networks and pathways relay sensory information, and how heightened sensory processing is directly linked to neuronal patterns where sensory processing is woven with memory and emotional salience.

It is vital to understand how sensory triggers can provide the first steps to guide a child to better understand their own nervous system and brain response to sensory information. Identifying a trigger provides them space to bring in habituation techniques and helps them redirect their mindset so that the stimuli lead to less of an emotional and reactive response, and instead provides pathways to develop positive neural plasticity.

It is estimated that 5-16 % of school aged children have sensory processing differences.[1] Traditional school environments and education systems can impair their unique learning abilities, illuminating how brain development can be out of sync just as much as these children's perceptions, interoception (awareness of internal bodily states), and behaviors. Children suffering from sensory overload may express behaviors that are described and labeled as out of sync, idiosyncratic, and puzzling. It is key that we recognize behavior we tag as "bad" may be a misunderstanding or failure to accurately identify how the child is actually suffering and expressing themselves out of pain. Behavior we might label as acting out is often a symptom and cry for help. We need to be aware and open in order to discover the origin of a behavior. A child may appear tuned out, oppositional, challenging, distracted, and express emotional dysregulation when in fact they are suffering from a hypersensory response. In the classroom, at home, and in our culture, we need to better identify the source of behavior to help guide our children to more adaptive behaviors and positive communication.

Enhanced World Experience and Openness

Kazimierz Dąbrowski, a Polish psychiatrist and psychologist of the early 21st century, is best known for his theory of "positive disintegration." The theory centers around the potential for people to embody advanced development. Particularly, Dąbrowski proposes that greater perception of experience allows one to fully express one's ability for advanced development, which he described as multi-levelness. In this process, a deep psychological transformation occurs. The theory focuses on key aspects where an individual goes through a psychological disintegration only to redefine character through individuality and manifest into wholeness of positive reintegration. Through a deep psychological transformation, an individual can better define their character. He theorized and studied high intelligence and proposed that gifted individuals have a greater probability for going through the process of positive disintegration due to their enriched perception and ability to remain in a state of openness.

A key part of his theory centers on five areas of enhanced processing and perceiving known as overexcitabilities (OEs). These include psychomotor, sensory, intellectual, imaginational, and emotional, and in each of these domains brighter individuals experience enrichments. Researchers, educators, and gifted individuals believe these distinctions greatly help define and explain the inner experience of gifted individuals. Many prominent researchers and psychologist in the field of gifted studies (*e.g.*, Piechowski, Silverman, Webb, Daniels, etc.) suggest that the brighter the individual, the more prominent and influential the enhanced processing can be in a person's life.

○ **Psychomotor OE** is best described by an enhanced excitability of motor function. These individuals are constantly in motion, have elevated energy levels, speak quickly, need vigorous physical activity, and desire constant activity. Many individuals with psychomotor OE find *flow* in physical activities that include sports, dance, and performing.

○ **Sensory OE** is characterized by an elevated experience of sensory input in hearing, smell, touch, taste, and sight that can be incredibly enhanced and felt as ecstasy or pain. The more intense sensory awareness of sensory OE can allow for a deep appreciation of the three-dimensional world, but the sensory processing can at times be overwhelming and can cause them to withdraw and tune out. The sensory intensity can cause pain point of nociception.

○ **Intellectual OE** is defined by a prominent desire to gain knowledge, search for and understand the truth, and to analyze and synthesize information. Gifted individuals who have an intellectual OE have prodigious minds and a drive to take in knowledge about the world. These people may immerse themselves in a book or in thinking for hours, have a keen understanding of the world, and are determined problem solvers.

○ **Imaginational OE** is described as enhanced imaginational play in which the person creates worlds where fantasy and reality blend, have imaginary friends, and are dreamers. Gifted people with great imaginational OE are creative and have an intense desire to remain occupied with their fictional worlds and characters.

○ **Emotional OE** is displayed by sensitivity and increased intense feelings, the ability for complex emotions, a strong ability for empathy, and deep emotional expression. A highly emotionally gifted person has the capacity for deep emotional connection to humans, animals, and the planet. These gifted individuals have an enhanced ability for compassion, empathy, and sensitivity in relationships.

Importantly, a bright individual may possess one, a few, or all five OEs. We should recognize that OEs are not limited to gifted persons, though these characteristics do seem to be far more common in those who are gifted. The brighter the individual, the more likely the OEs are to impact the person's life. Importantly, OEs influence the complexities of the gifted experience and the spectrum of the human experience centered on cognition, behavior, emotion, and neurodiversity.

Making Sense of Our Gifted Senses

A sensory overexcitability can be described as an enhancement in sensory processing that is experienced by the gifted person with a greater intensity. This is found in a subset of bright people who can have enhancement in sensory processing in a single sense, in all five senses, or a combination of the senses. They can experience a very strong sensory sensation from stimuli that is commonly perceived as normal. There can be a number of perceived "normal" triggers such as bright lights, clothing tags, ambulance sirens, food textures, food tastes, and perfumes. This elevated sensory processing in standard settings may range on a scale from 1 to 10 where a person with sensory elevation can sense on a greater magnitude, closer to a scale of 100. This substantial sensory experience can offer remarkable gifts (like those of an athlete, artist, musician, chef, poet, sommelier, or scientist) but that same gift can also create great challenges associated with this enhanced processing. For example, tactile sensitivity may bring joy and flow while building with LEGO bricks, while at the same time make clothing tags feel like pinpricks on the skin, causing an itchy, irritating sensation, even rash, and activate the stress response.

Parents of gifted children reported in a sensory sensitivity questionnaire that their children have a greater sensitivity to their environment and respond with an elevated emotional and behavioral response than children with average intelligence.[2] Gifted children experience and perceive the world at an elevated level that is qualitative and quantitatively different from the norm. These intensified sensory experiences in gifted individuals may include sound (auditory), vision (sight), smell (olfaction), touch (tactile), and taste (gustatory).

Sensory overexcitabilities in relation to giftedness, if they are misunderstood, can be misidentified as oppositional behaviors while missing the root cause of the child's suffering. They can also manifest as stressors such as physical, mental, and emotional pain. Sensory OEs can induce anxiety and a stress response. For example, those with sensory intensities can feel as though they are experiencing more sensory information, where their baseline level of processing is extraordinarily high. Brain drain can result from sensory and cognitive overload, triggering a stress response, chronic low-level cortisol, and reaction to stress that heightens intense sensory processing where a non-harmful stimulus is perceived as threatening.

Sounds and Sensory Processing Enhanced in Gifted Children

Studies show that gifted children had greater brain activity when perceiving a tone of sound, as compared to age-matched peers. Notably, brain scans showed they "heard" the sound prior to it arriving to their ear. Their early brain activity in response to the coming sound meant they anticipated the sound actually reaching their ear. Once the tone was released, gifted children responded to it with earlier and greater brain activation. Once the sound terminated, the gifted children had an extended duration of brain activation, even though the sound was no longer present. These children displayed activity in an enhanced neural network for auditory sensory processing compared to their peer groups, with earlier peak signals, as well as increases in amplitude and duration of the brain signals within the auditory cortex.[3]

In sum, gifted children responded to sound stimulus with three distinct sensory enhancements: the sound was perceived prior to the arrival of sound waves; the brain activation in response to the sound was greater; and brain activation to sound was experienced for a prolonged duration of time even after the sound ended. This evidence supports the notion that gifted individuals experience sensory enhancements for sound, which directly informs us how gifted individuals interact with the world. This evidence of elevated sensory processing is in alignment with both brain expansions and brain activity for sensory processing, offering underlining evidence that gifted individuals have distinctly enhanced sensory experiences which inform their behavior, emotions, sensory imprints, and auto-biographical memories.

This supports the idea that gifted individuals have increased sensory sensitivity and an elevated neural network compared to the general population, at least specific to sound. Moreover, the evidence of an enhanced neural network falls within the line of evidence that gifted individuals' sensory integration differs from the norm and they process external stimuli differently, and at an elevated level.

This and other studies suggest that increased sensory sensitivities may account for an increased emotional and behavioral response in gifted children. In particular, enhanced neural networks dedicated to sensory processing can potentially account for behavioral mani-festations because sensory stressors may case increased symptoms of anxiety and depression and even lead to misdiagnosis and incorrect medication for a variety of disorders, including ADHD, ADD, and Oppositional-Defiant Disorder, within the gifted population. It is of paramount importance that proper assessment of sensory integration and intensities are made in gifted children to avoid misdiagnosis and improper treatment so as to best help a gifted child succeed in all facets of their life.

Along similar lines, studies show that ordinary but unnatural sounds such as traffic, sirens, gardeners' blowers, and sirens increase anxiety and the stress response.[4] Unnatural sounds have incongruent frequencies that are in opposition to one another, which are distracting, overwhelming, and irritating to our auditory and nervous systems. We find ourselves working hard to extinguish these noises as our attentional shifts become highly distracting and challenging. In some instances, it can become impossible to ignore the sound and the auditory insult, even with the best noise-canceling headphones. Once the stress response is activated due to the sympathetic nervous system, a person has an elevated sensory perceiving response. This in turn leads to changes in the mind-body balance, ultimately changing behavior, where the reaction of a highly sensitive person may be misinterpreted as behaviors related to ADD/ADHD. The sensitive person may also experience increased challenges in focusing, greater mood swings due to their attentional shifts, and express more frequent outbursts because their sensory system is on overload, and their ability to control their reaction becomes exhausted.

On the other hand, neuroscientists in the same study found that listening to "green" sounds, sounds of nature, increases relaxation in mind and body by activating the parasympathetic nervous system, reducing the heart rate, stress hormones, and anxiety.[5] Tranquil sounds, like a bird chirping or a running stream are restorative and good for calming your nervous system. This is important to note for an individual with an enhanced sensory processing system for sound that can reach ecstasy or intolerable pain.

Now imagine you are faced with an individual with an enhanced sensory processing system for sound. We know, based on studies tracking brain activation, that gifted children experience sound with greater brain activity, and they experience sound louder and longer. Where there is increased sensitivity, the impact of unnatural or artificial sound on a gifted person's mind and body can be enhanced, so that they experience their environment as extreme and harsh, full of sensory overload and overstimulation. In extreme cases, people's sensory interpretation can verge on a pain level (nociception) such that a person's environment creates continuous signals of distress.

Navigating in the world becomes extremely challenging for highly sensitive people because the evolutionary response of nociception sends warning signals all throughout the brain and body. A person experiences the world as a dangerous place which activates their fear, anxiety, and long-term stress. The cycling stress hormones change both brain wiring and behavioral responses and a person can be viewed as withdrawing from life and daily activities. This perceived withdrawal in turn presents the individual as seemingly socially, mentally, and physically isolated. Their behaviors can be misinterpreted when in fact they are suffering from sensory pain, fear, anxiety, and stress due to uniquely unpleasant sensory surroundings.

It is critical when thinking about a person who has heightened auditory processing that unnatural sounds can active the stress response to the point where it can be debilitating. Identifying the initiating event leading to sensory overload and sensory pain is warranted to discover how to help regulate the person's nervous system and response. Knowledge of one's particular ways of experiencing the world is pivotal when building positive neural circuits, behaviors, and when providing appropriate accommodations for their success and survival, allowing them to thrive with a more balanced nervous system, mind, and body. Encouraging people who have sensory sensitivity to sound to immerse themselves in nature and fill up their soundscape with calming natural sounds can help them cope with stress and anxiety, and can lead to general calming of their mood.

Photosensitivity, Dyslexia, and Seeing the Light

Photosensitivity and visual processing differences in response to light as high intensity in bright children and adults can interfere with their daily life and flow. Photophobia, or light sensitivity, is an intolerance of light, which disrupts the ability to take in our surroundings and environments. Again, when the sensory nervous system is overwhelmed and "normal" activities are experienced as extremely intense, it may in some cases become impossible for an individual to manage. Photosensitivity can be triggered by the type of light, intensity, timing, wavelengths, and flickers in intensity of light. It affects an estimated 5 to 20% of the population with varying degrees.[6] Sources such as sunlight, fluorescent light, and incandescent light can all cause discomfort, along with a need to squint, cover, and close one's eyes to recover and reset their nervous system.

There is a high probability that individuals with light sensitivity will develop visual migraines, headaches, fatigue, and irritation. Everyday living can be challenging because of the chronic tax on the visual system and visual processing. This leads to serious consequences where an individual has intense physical pain that leads to emotional intensities and mental dysregulation. Living at this intense level can cause one to withdraw from personal, social, and community interactions, greatly impacting mental and emotional functioning and processing. This can put an individual at greater risk of social isolation, anxiety, and depression. Eighty percent of people with photosensitivity report having migraines, which are debilitating about 98 percent of the time.[7] Often, light sensitivity goes unrecognized by clinicians because it is not well-researched and lacks the physiological underpinnings of a one's experiences. It is essential to address and treat the symptoms of a person's condition while defining what triggers their light sensitivity.

Often individuals appear highly distracted and even give the appearance of tuning out or being disinterested in their current environments. Both forms of ADHD (to be discussed in Chapter 6) could seem to be present in individuals with light sensitivity. Importantly, tuning out and withdrawing from surroundings is an innate biological protective mechanism for individuals who are experiencing their environment as a noxious sensory experience. Unfortunately, in many cases, high levels of distraction appear to be present when, in fact, a child or adult has sensory overload due to visual input, perception, and interoception. The mind-body's process of interpreting their bodily states are on continuous overdrive.

Children with visual processing differences/disabilities like photosensitivity, dyslexia, and dyscalculia can appear to have high distractibility, mood fluctuations, increased irritation, and chronic fatigue. Environments with artificial lights and sensory feed can cause major challenges for children with visual processing differences and, in extreme cases, interfere with and inhibit learning and interaction with their environment and others. Reading and studying for prolonged periods of time can be visually exhausting and overwhelming. Often, these visually overstimulated children can appear out of sync with their actual level of knowledge and abilities which can impact their production. Unfortunately, their heightened sensory processing interferes with their level of information processing, attention level, and interferes with their potential for achievement. They can be tagged incorrectly with ADHD, social awkwardness, and other deficits when in fact they are struggling to manage their sensory environments.

Fluorescent Lights Activate Inflammation

Artificial fluorescent light was developed in the last 60 years. In a recent study, scientists discovered that fluorescent lights activate inflammation and immune response in vertebrates.[8] To understand the effects of artificial lights on vertebrates' biology, scientists measured the genetic changes in relation to artificial light exposure. What the scientists uncovered was astounding. Across diurnal and nocturnal vertebrate species, there were increases in immune response and inflammatory genes in the skin, brain, and liver after exposure to fluorescent lights, a primarily conserved genetic response across vertebrates that is embedded in the vertebrate genome. It is noteworthy that this occurred in both diurnal and nocturnal vertebrate species, and the increase in both inflammation and immune response was present within all vertebrate species. This test of fluorescent lights is an example of how we are changing and responding to artificial sources and our modern world puts us unknowingly at risk for increased exposures that directly elevate inflammation. This can be another sensory response that activates inflammation in our highly sensitive population, where the nervous system is already overwhelmed, and light is an invisible layer causing a hyper-responsivity of the mind and body. These exposures to inconspicuous triggers from the environment create an undercurrent of inflammation both biologically and genetically. Prolonged exposure to fluorescent lights at home, school, and out in the world can lead an individual with a hyper-aroused nervous state to experience a stress response and anxiety. This is a single artificial trigger that has been identified as activating inflammation and the immune response in vertebrates.

We must recognize that inflammation can be triggered by artificial sources within the world. If an individual has different brain wiring and processing, there can be elevated ways that environmental triggers can activate their inflammation and cause stress within their body and mind. We need to be aware and pay attention to triggers that can be challenging for sensitive individuals to navigate, so when we create spaces that are more natural they are more conducive to working, learning, participating in and being present in the world.

Vision of Dyslexia

Dyslexia is described as a difference in visual processing centered around learning language, reading, writing, spelling, phonics, orthography, visual memory, visual recall, reading comprehension, and communication. In people with dyslexia, reading, printing, writing, spelling, and visual recall are challenging, especially in traditional academic settings. Children and adults with dyslexia may experience a disconnect because their intelligence does not match their academic abilities and performance. The majority of traditional schoolwork is centered around reading skills, so bright children with dyslexia may appear to be out of sync, performing below their level of abilities. Clearly, dyslexia is a learning disability that requires differentiated teaching and an educational environment suited to their learning style.

Estimates are that 15-20% of the population have a learning difference, such as dyslexia, dyscalculia, or dysgraphia. Fifty percent of those individuals with learning differences also have a dual diagnosis of ADD or ADHD. Of the population that receive additional educational services, 70% have a language learning difference. Thus, a majority of children with learning differences experience it within the domains of language and attention.

In dyslexia, visual processing is disrupted by **eye saccades**, where the eyes' fixation of two points jumps between the center of fixation rather than both eyes working in synchrony so that eye movements are smooth. An example is when a child who has dyslexia is reading, their eyes jump from line to line making visual tracking, reading, memory, and comprehension difficult. Because the eyes are out of sync, a shift in attention and focus can follow, and the child's attention span and comprehension are disrupted, impacting visual recall and memorization. Often, reading and studying takes approximately twice the time and effort for an individual with dyslexia because of the challenges with visual processing and resulting attentional shifts. In some cases, this difference appears like ADHD due to the disruptions in focus and concentration.

In a 2018 study, investigators measured children's reading ability, comprehension, and speed with colored lenses, including children with and without dyslexia.[9] Researchers discovered that using green-colored filters vastly improved reading comprehension in the population diagnosed with dyslexia. Scientists measured reading comprehension in children with dyslexia and their age-matched peers and reported that the children with dyslexia retained information they read faster and with greater accuracy when wearing green colored filters compared to their age-matched peers. They explained that the colored filters work in two domains: first, by blocking the light that disrupts reading in dyslexic people; second, by minimizing the number of saccades so that the eyes have a smoother transition from reading word to word and line to line. The scientists proposed that colored lenses most likely facilitate cortical activity and decreased visual distortions.

This neurohack, using filtered lenses, allows the eyes to work in unison, with greater focus, memory recall, and better reading comprehension. It aids in eye movement control so that individuals with dyslexia are able to process and focus reading material, and minimizes the attentional shifts, aiding in sensory control. Individuals wearing these colored filters are able to optimize the differences in their wiring and participate in school activities and study with greater ease and enjoyment because their sensory system is freed from fight, flight, and freeze reactions caused by environmental insults. More important, children with visual processing differences can have improved reading with this novel approach so that wearing colored lenses can allow them to thrive and share their creative minds with society.

An Artist Who Literally Saw the World Differently

Scientists have extrapolated that Leonardo da Vinci may have had strabismus, a binocular vision processing difference described by fragmented or complete incapability to sustain eye alignment on the target of focus, resulting in suppression of the diverging eye that causes 2-dimensional monocular vision. Strabismus is found in 4% of the population and is often corrected with eyeglasses and eye exercises to strengthen the eye muscles and provide for binocular vision. Often gazing with a single eye increases visual, mental, and emotional fatigue, and may cause an individual to need extra time to complete tasks because only a single eye is functioning for visual focus and gaze.

For the study, the methodology used has been validated to extrapolate strabismus in numerous famous artists. In particular, scientists reviewed six self-portraits in which da Vinci revealed that his eye gazed externally at an angle of −10.3° on average.[10] This made it possible for da Vinci to have both binocular and monocular vision, fueling his three-dimensional art. During the Renaissance Period, da Vinci reshaped the progression of drawing human anatomy with precision and accuracy. His strabismus and the way his visual system developed differently created alternate wiring patterns; he literally saw the world differently. He changed the world of art and medicine in history through his vision.

This sheds light on differences: what may have been considered "abnormal" and "atypical" actually contributed to his brilliance and novelty, so that today da Vinci is widely considered one of the greatest artists of all time. Often, what we think is abnormal or divergent may be the exact gift and exact essence one must share with the world to enlighten humanity of its boundless possibilities. There is unlimited creativity and beauty in divergence and the world of art proves that brain wiring and brain divergent patterns provide expansive insight into seeing in different shades and light. Because of da Vinci's uniqueness, he was one of the first artists to create realistic and accurate renditions of human anatomy using both monocular and binocular vision and the distant-depth of landscapes of mountains and hillsides—a true Renaissance human. Twice exceptional and gifted individuals see the world differently and are unique thinkers. In our culture, we need to embrace these divergent pathways to integrate and create a space and time for a new Renaissance.

Selective Food Palate and Diet

We eat with all our five senses. Eating is intended to be a rewarding and highly sensory experience. Food selection in the wild could be a life saver or a life extinguisher. Rejection of food is a life changing instinct because a particular food might be poisonous, cause a fatal allergic reaction, be spoiled, or be full of harmful microorganisms. Everything from color to smell can trigger a response to food.

Enhanced sensory processing in gifted/2e children may encompass all sensory modalities that include sound, vision, smell, touch, and taste. Several case studies have reported that gifted children experience heightened reactions to noise, pain, frustration, and emotional intensity.[11] In particular, gifted children may have an increased sensory response to tags on their clothing, fluorescent lights, odors, foods and additional sounds in their environment.[12] A subset of gifted/2e children have increased responsivity to tactile information, which often reaches the level of nociception, where the stimuli are painful and considered harmful. This increased level of nociception in individuals may induce stress, cause a greater degree of distraction and hyperattention to the perceived harmful stimuli. As explained earlier, parents of gifted children described their children as having a greater sensitivity to their environment along with heightened emotional and behavioral responses, as compared to the children's age-matched peers.[13]

The elevated sensory response carries over to food selection in gifted individuals across all sensory domains. In some instances, specific textures can be unappetizing and even induce the gag reflex. Odors from foods may be another trigger for gifted individuals where specific food scents are avoided and not consumed. Additionally, the heightened sense of taste may cause gifted individuals to have a greater awareness about their food selection and avoid foods that are unappetizing. It is important to note that gifted children are tagged as "picky eaters." It would be kinder to refer to these gifted children as enhanced eaters or as having more selective palates. Often the refusal to eat certain foods is misunderstood. In fact, an elevated response to sight, sound, touch, taste and smell drives particular food selection and eating habits. A healthy diet may also play a role in reducing the effects of sensory sensitivities.[14]

For all these reasons, it is essential to develop a diet that meets a gifted individual's sensory sensitivity and nutritional needs while simultaneously promoting a healthy lifestyle.

Amanda Lives with Highly Intense Senses

Begin to imagine a school day for a child with enhanced sensory processing in a standard learning environment. From earlier chapters, we know that the brain does not develop uniformly nor does the body-mind connection, thus sensory processing fine tuning occurs throughout life, where experience shapes sensing. As a child with heightened sensory receptivity may find a traditional school environment extraordinarily painful and practically impossible to navigate.

Meet Amanda. She is a creative artist and identifies on the autism spectrum. As Amanda walked the hallways of her middle school, the fluorescent lights sent her into visual migraines. The class bells, chatter and the lockers slamming shut triggered her fear so that almost every day she raced to the principal's office crying and begging to have her parents pick her up. For her, walking from class to class felt like being a salmon swimming up-stream on dry land because she experienced a sensory overload to a point of nociception, where pain is experienced throughout the entire body in response to sensory stimuli. With each step, cortisol coursed through her veins and body so that walking across campus sent her into flight, fight, freeze, and finally flop mode in the principal's office. There she was found on the floor, curled into a ball, with all the lights out. Amanda was shut down, playing dead, as if walking in a middle school environment was as deadly as crossing the Serengeti with a pride of lions on her heels. Her mind, body, and brain could not differentiate the "non-harmful" versus "harmful" sensory stimuli, causing her to go into direct panic mode.

After about a month of this new normal, Amanda's parents, Dr. Mike and Julie Postma, had to make a change—a big change. They decided to homeschool Amanda to save her life. Her father explains, "It is physically painful for her to be out in the world and we could no longer see her suffer." As they began to homeschool Amanda, who is a highly creative visual artist, her sensory processing was managed and controlled. But another problem bubbled up: she was all alone in her new school environment. She began to experience deep signs of social isolation, where she struggled with anxiety and depression. She was missing the social engagement that had allowed her to share her passion for art and connect with other people.

The online art community became her lifeline. There she shares art with other artists all over the world. When Amanda is creating a piece, she is in flow, she is alive, felt, and heard through her artistic expression. No longer silenced by depression and anxiety, she is able to create and share her art and her voice, making connections around the world. Her father says that one of her famous sayings is, "Another day I did not use math." Her father describes her as smart as a whip. Amanda currently sells her art online and her father believes that she can make a pretty decent living selling her artwork. Still Amanda struggles with being profoundly gifted and finds it very hard to fit in modern times. The intake is so vast that she feels unsafe. With these profound gifts can come great challenges and struggling to fit into ordinary circumstances.

Her father's mission, being a gifted and 2e educator and advocate, is to correct the misconceptions about gifted/2e people. He says, "A major misconception is that when you are gifted, and particularly twice exceptional, that you are lazy and nonproductive. There is a vast amount of energy that goes into code switching and battling with parameters. They have slower processing speed and it is tougher for them to do things. And when they are given more time they are able and willing to do amazing work. It is essential we take the time to get to know these children and adults and really get to know who they are." Additionally, navigating an environment that feels unsafe uses extraordinary amounts of energy and when things are physically painful it can feel relentless going through the world if there are one to several triggers at a time. Dr. Postma believes the second misconception is that the brain's sensory system is tied up with the limbic brain and this can lead to behavioral issues. Often these children are penalized for being different and it holds a great deal of weight and negativity within their being. These children are also often misdiagnosed, which is another piece of the puzzle because their primary needs and understanding are not correctly identified. He feels from his experience raising children and working with families and 2e children that rumination and fear are huge challenges for these kids and that this develops into obsessive patterns. Fear and worry can be normal for them, and it can be highly difficult for them to let go of that worry pattern because they have a different metaphysical being. He says, "There needs to be greater tolerance and flexibility of differences."

Sense Memory Roadmaps

Sense memory is housed in the limbic cortex of the brain, a region that processes both emotion and sensory information, and they are intertwined. The sensory system is highly integrated with the limbic (emotional center) regions of the brain. The limbic network is responsible for several processes such as motivation, learning, memory, and emotion. Our emotions are intricately braided with our sense memory and that translates to our autobiographical memories where the detailed information carries both emotion and the senses.

Particularly, sense memory of a noxious event, "flashbulb" memory (highly vivid video clip where a memory with highly arousing emotion or negative news was heard) can drive particular neural circuitry. When sense memory triggers an emotional response, the brain and body of a person has an activated limbic region and wiring automatically drives the response and becomes a conditioned response with elevated sensory receptivity and heightened emotions.

A traumatic sensory imprint occurs when the sensation and experience are co-experienced as painful and all levels—physical, emotional, and mental—are on overdrive, activating fear. Because fear overwhelms and floods the system with stress neurochemicals, the memory print is strongly activated and coded as a traumatic sensory experience so that the sensory experience directly activates the stress and fear circuit. Now, this sense memory causes one to withdraw and tune out their environment in hopes of dampening the pain, suffering, and fear related to the stressful sensory event. When an individual encounters a similar sensory experience, the scarred sense memory is activated and present so that the individual may live in continuous fear, anticipating the next encounter with the debilitating sensory experience.

When the sense memory codes, it is as if a lightning bolt in your brain is paired with the noxious sensory experience. Then the emotional centers start to overrun the brain. The limbic cortex houses our emotional processing and aids in our behavior related to motivation, long term memory, and our emotions. In particular, the limbic system is connected with negative, potentially life-saving, emotions. If it is chronically activated and coded with negative experiences, then only negative and maladaptive responses occur, which manifest as negative behavior. For our senses and sensory memory, emotional processing intertwined with our autobiographical memories directs and dictates our specific behaviors related to our experiences. If the senses are on overdrive, particularly fear, the personal memory is embedded deep in the brain, where fear has the evolutionary responsibility for our protection and safety. But, if the sense memory is overwhelming the system, it can create a looping fear circuit in the brain and the sensory imprint is elevated leading to greater resistance and withdrawal.

If sense memory is coded as a traumatic experience, the limbic cortex takes over the experience and higher order processing in our brain is off-line. The information flow in the limbic cortex begins with the amygdala where the amygdala processes our emotional response to fear. Then, the trauma of the sensory print is stored in the hippocampus for long-term memory. Finally, information about the sensory trauma travels to the the orbital frontal cortex (OFC) where decision making and valence of the emotional context is processed. When the brain is in fear, the higher order processing of the OFC is not engaged and the brain, body, and mind are overrun with fear that drives the experience.

When sense memory is encoded in a trauma pathway, sensory processing, learning, and emotional memory have trauma patterning that is embedded with sensory responsivity. Thus, the sense memory centers are overwhelmed, overtaxed, and stimulated with emotional memory. The emotion drives the experience and environment and experience is felt as threatening and unsafe. When the sensory imprint is entangled with activating the limbic cortex, then a person will withdraw from any environments that have produced the sensory experience and will live a life in fear and avoidance.[15]

The Looping of Sensory Overload, Anxiety and Fear

Studies show that when a person's sensory system for visual and auditory stimuli is continuously overtaxed for three to five hours, a subset of subjects reported having hallucination-like experiences.[16] Due to sensory overload a person's natural baseline and reset for their sensory processing is derailed and runs on overdrive. The person is deprived of recovery sensory reset, and their system goes haywire. Their entire mind and body experience feels as if they are living hyperaware on pins and needles. This hyperaroused state causes the noradrenaline (NE) sensory processing heightened awareness.

In a recent study, researchers manipulated the levels of noradrenaline in subjects while processing visual information. Subjects with a decrease in their NE had reductions in their arousal state and a decrease in their processing of visual information.[17] Thus, adequate levels of NE are necessary for sensory processing and maintaining a state of arousal. Additionally, NE is secreted by the locus coeruleus located in the midbrain. NE is necessary for proper sleep and wake cycles, and is necessary for arousal.

Conversely, when the stress response is continuously, or "tonically," activated, in a continuous state of tension due to anxiety, neurohormones are elevated and the body goes into fight, flight, freeze, or flop mode. Having high level stress hormones tonically activated in turn alters other systems including the NE system and sleep. Because NE is necessary for arousal, altered levels of NE in individuals with enhanced sensory processing can lead to a state of hypervigilance. This chronic state further enhances sensory receptivity, activating a neurochemical loop for enhanced arousal and sensitivity to their surroundings. Thus, a person who has enhanced sensory processing has an enhanced neurochemical and physiological response to sensory feedback.

Expanded brain regions can explain sensory enhancements ranging from ecstasy to pain. Where overstimulated senses trigger or activate nociception, this leads to social and environmental withdrawal, tuning out of the environment, and interaction due to a reaction of stress and pain. An individual who is in fear and pain goes into basic instinctual survival mode. This can occur across all the sensory domains or only in a single domain, but it is important to understand that these avoiding behaviors can be associated with the elevated processing that can be misidentified, and are more often than not misinterpreted.

In a subset of bright people, sensory processing is enhanced, experienced in a deeper way and woven in emotions more intricately. We experience based on the way our body and mind are fine tuned for reward processing. Elevated experiencing parallels reward and aversion—aversion to a stimulus that is experienced as painful or harmful. It is necessary to guide the individual with enhanced sensory processing to safety when their environment is overstimulating. It is critical to teach them ways to navigate securely throughout the world.

Senses and Behaviors Indicating Enhanced/ Differential Sensory Processing

Hearing (Auditory)

- Covers ears and crouches in response to sounds
- Easily startles
- High level of irritability to sounds that others find within "normal" range
- Behavioral and emotional outbursts to sounds
- Sound is highly distracting and focus with sound is disrupted
- Challenges in listening and response
- Challenges in auditory processing
- Delayed auditory processing
- Challenges in communication
- Challenges in auditory memory
- Auditory fatigue
- Fatigue in general
- Equilibrium differences
- Clumsiness
- Attentional shifts

- Greater chances of nociception
- Mood shifts
- Emotional outbursts
- Higher risk of social withdrawal

Visual (Visual)

- Challenges in visual processing
- Altered visual memory of visual processing
- Challenges in writing
- Challenges in reading
- Unnatural lights may trigger photosensitivity
- Imaginative spelling
- Outbursts to lights or visual patterns
- Emotional irritability
- Increased chance of visual migraines, dizziness, and motion sickness
- Visual fatigue
- Visual auras
- Frustration with visual information
- Proprioception differences
- Clumsiness
- Attentional shifts
- Higher chances of nociception
- Greater risk for fatigue in general
- Changes in mood
- Emotional outbursts
- Higher risk of social withdrawal

Touch (Tactile)

- Highly irritated with fabrics and tags on clothing to the point where skin irritations or rashes may develop
- May seek high sensory touch
- May withdraw from any sensory touch
- May avoid hugs or other forms of affection
- Sensitive to touch
- Texture of food may cause gag reflex
- High reaction to touch that activates a pain response

○ General sensory exhaustion
○ Mood swings
○ Easily overwhelmed
○ Proprioception differences
○ Differences in equilibrium
○ Attentional shifts
○ Mood fluctuations
○ Emotional outburst
○ Higher rate of nociception
○ Clumsiness
○ Higher risk of social withdrawal

Taste (Gustation)
○ Highly particular diet selection
○ Food avoidance
○ Limited ability to test "new" foods
○ Sensory taste triggers can cause reaction of disgust
○ Easily activated gag response
○ Greater possibility to be a sommelier
○ Higher risk of social withdrawal

Smell (Olfaction)
○ Intense smell related to memory and especially emotional memories
○ Sensory scents can cause reaction of disgust
○ Odor avoidance
○ Highly reactive to smells where they can trigger migraines
○ Odor sensitivity to trigger the gag reflex
○ Greater possibility to be a sommelier
○ Higher risk of social withdrawal

Space-Time Continuum of Sensory Roadmaps

Can a person outgrow sensory processing enhancements and overload? Yes and no. It is highly individual and neurodiverse and dependent on environment, genetics, brain wiring, brain adaptability, practice, and neural plasticity. More often than not, these intensified sensory experiences will be continued processes one will have to navigate throughout life. Over time, a person can identify the triggers for their sensory stressors and learn to avoid them and/or habituate (lessen one's reaction) to the sensory trigger. It takes time, attention, intention, focus, practice, and patience to manage these skills to dampen and determine the challenges.

For example, as I mentioned earlier, loud unnatural sounds and fluorescent lights and wavelengths give me visual migraines, headaches, disrupt my focus, and in some cases make it entirely impossible to focus. I still have these sensory experiences as triggers, but I also have the knowledge that I have photosensitivity. I wear specific glasses to minimize the wavelengths with blue color filters and prisms that aid in blocking out the distinctive and disruptive wavelengths. Additionally, I take noise canceling headphones with me everywhere to block out unnecessary sounds that can initiate a stress and anxiety reaction in me. Thus, blocking out the stimuli, I am protecting my nervous system from being overloaded and experiencing my surroundings as painfully unpleasant. Although the environment and my surroundings may have many triggers at once, I can better identify the initiating event and help myself avoid stimuli that can provide a great amount of distraction, as well as physical, mental, and emotional dysregulation and pain. This helps calm my nervous system.

Practical Steps to Detangling Your Sensory Experience and Identifying Your Sensory Limits

Individuals with great sensory experience and responsivity can begin to unpack their sensory triggers and emotions related to their heightened sensory and emotional responsivity. I describe this method as "survey and scale." Studies show that simply identifying and labeling the trigger with verbal or written expression helps mitigate the level of challenge associated with an unpleasant experience and emotions.

The first step is surveying the environment. By surveying the environment an individual becomes aware of their surroundings. With this awareness, one can evaluate their experience based on their sensory experience, emotions, bodily sensations, and their running thoughts or stories.

Second, one can scale their environment from a one to ten (ten being the most challenging, down to one being noninvasive) based on their scaling of their experience to better identify the level of intensity of their experience. This allows for greater understanding in identifying and determining the emotional response and the autobiographical narrative that makes up our sense memory. Importantly, when we can identify the primary challenge, we can better address how we can manage the experience, whether it be to block out the sensory insult right at the start or begin to habituate to the stimuli that is perceived as harmful.

Careful attention and consideration of the sensory experience can begin to help a child navigate more smoothly and effectively through the various landscapes and natural environments with a compassionate understanding of their personal limits and their ability to share verbally and nonverbally with others their experience of roaming the world.[18]

Earth's Magnetic Sense and Our Internal Compass

Scientists Joseph Kirschvink and Shin Shimojo are uncovering that humans are magnetically sensitive organisms. It is widely known that honeybees, whales, bats, cows, dogs, fish, and other vertebrates can sense the magnetic pull of the earth. There has been great debate about whether humans can sense and experience the earth's gravitational properties. Scientists now have evidence that humans perceive the earth's geomagnetic pull. Perhaps, humans may experience a 6th sense, perceiving gravitational shifts, pulls, and properties.

In a Caltech laboratory in Pasadena, California, a team measured peoples' brain waves using an electrocephlagraph (EEG) that measures brain activity during an activity. Participants wear a skull cap with electrodes that measure brain waves that are visible on a computer program. After placing participants in gravitational neutral chamber corrected for 60 degrees gravity to make it gravity free, the researchers emitted a gravitational wave into the chamber. The team reported that when they emitted an electromagnetic wave, individuals' brain activity for sensory perception was activated.[19] A number of the human participants sensed geomagnetic pull as a sensory component. Now we have evidence that humans along with other species experience and perceive the Earth's geomagnetic waves. It is conceivable that people experience the geomagnetic pull in varying levels and degrees. This is another area where we are learning about humans' rich experience in perceiving their surroundings.

We are still uncovering the magic of the mind, the magic of the universe, and how it is all intertwined. We need to be aware and listen to each individual experience and guide these unique children and adults to live unbound and free. High sensory processing is a lifelong journey, so understanding our personal thresholds and levels of response is critical for navigating this world with equanimity.

The amazing finding of this sixth sense study is its demonstration that we are still uncovering the endless possibilities of how humans interact with our world and our environment. When we continue to question, we continue to uncover, and we continue to rise above our expectations and raise awareness of the vast uniqueness and diversity that we experience in this world. We each have an internal compass for navigating uniquely in the world and we need to trust that internal compass to lead us to better share with others how we experience the world. Parents naturally know and have an understanding of how their children are. Seeing a child's unique gifts, they can help shine a light on their child's optimal way of being in the world. Each of us has our own geomagnetic pull, and our own internal compass for exploring the universe.

"Beliefs are our foundation and our guiding compass,
navigating us through life."
—Kim Ha Campbell

Dear Heart-Mind,

You've been told you are "too sensitive." You just you need to get over it. You hold onto things way too much. You're dramatic. A drama queen, a drama king.

It was just a joke. Don't get so upset, I'm only kidding.

The people who say that to you do not understand emotions are carried in your body like knotted, microscopic little fists that rage, pulse, and weigh on your heart and soul. You see, you hear, you feel, you carry others' suffering and pain. You are the vast ocean of emotion. These emotions are beyond the water's surface, beyond the visible waves, beyond the baby waves. They are invisible energies brewing in the alchemy of the deep thermal vents—extremophiles living in you. You feel and your body aches. Although the temptation to is a beast, do not numb these feelings. I promise you, they are your gold. With practice, you will learn to burn, repair, restore, reclaim, and rebirth.

Let me tell you, Heart-Mind, you do not have to hold it. Let's learn how together we navigate the space time of emotion, how we shed and release all that is not ours and give it to the sharks. They'll happily feast. First, swim with us in the shallow waters and tell us about the range of emotions living within you. Speak, and let us understand the waves, the winds, the tides, the knots, and we will bathe in the depths of the ocean, the blue and black waters of the deep, where we will ride those waves, tides, knots, and emotions together.

Ready to swim with you,

Deep Sea Diver

CHAPTER 5:

Emotion—Joy, Empathy, Anxiety & Everything on the Spectrum

The Full Range of Emotion

We live in a culture of feel-good tricks, popular science that touts a "happiness gene," and people living in a state devoid of emotion thanks to a multitude of numbing vices. We are glued to our scrolling screens, addicted to shopping, alcohol, and a slew of other substances. You name it, our culture plays into *not feeling* even while it sells us stuff based on our feeling bad about ourselves—a feeling that it promotes.

As a little girl, I was told by others that I was too sensitive. That I didn't need to take things so seriously. That I needed to get over my emotions and get over them quickly. Although I ascribe to the idea that we should not take ourselves too seriously, that we can and should laugh at ourselves, I also believe that people need to be able to talk and share their emotions. Emotions give us information that can be self-protective, that can be useful for knowing how we feel about something, and that can give us insight so that we can adjust our behavior and take an action. I am not talking about swimming in our emotions and letting them run the show, but I will say this: we all feel in varying degrees and our emotions essentially make us human.

When someone shares their feelings with you, they are conveying information about their experience. In particular, it is respectful to listen to a child when they share their emotional state. It diminishes a person to tell them they are too sensitive at that moment of vulnerability; the emotion they are experiencing *is* their reality. Specifically, their emotion is how *they* are experiencing the world and each person's brain is wired differently, giving them unique and varying ways of processing and understanding their emotion.

If you are highly in tune with your emotions, it is okay to feel their entire range. I'm not saying you should wallow in an emotion. Rather, I am saying that it is okay to allow an emotion to be what it is—without judgment and without trying to change it. But let it be exactly what it is at the moment. Let the emotion flow through you like a wave without getting swept up in its current. This is *allowing* the emotion, not *attaching* to it. You acknowledge that there is an emotion, but you don't allow your mind to focus on changing that emotion if it is undesired, or attaching to it if it is pleasurable. Just let it be what it is. Allowing an emotion without trying to dismiss or change its undercurrent lets it move through you. In contrast, *attaching* to an emotion centers on the how and why of the emotion and the impulse to manipulate it. Simple acknowledgement provides insight into your internal state, set points, and present condition.

We especially need to give ourselves time and space to feel the spectrum of our emotions and ride the waves as a skilled body surfer would, catching and releasing each wave with the current. With children, we need to listen to their emotional states. Children need safety when they share their emotions. Train children to acknowledge their feelings, and not to attach or detach, or get swept away; to be wise riders and recognize that the emotion is just that. Bringing this into practice is invaluable for their development and growth into greater self-awareness and actualization.

This is the first act of compassion for yourself and for others: to allow the feeling to exist within you and within others. Emotions are woven into our bodies, hearts, and minds. Our mind, our bodily states, and our emotions are interconnected like a web that make us neuroindividuals. We perceive our surroundings through our unique senses, memories, stories, and running thoughts to evaluate our surroundings. Our emotions inform how we feel about the current state. Our emotions are essential in conveying information about our environment, about the people around us, and whether we feel safe or not. Emotions provide information for learning, development, and are one way we communicate through our actions. Our thoughts can activate an emotion, just as an emotion can activate our memory or a sensation. Our emotions, sensations, and thoughts influence each other and prompt us to take an action through our behavior.

Deepak Chopra has said we have approximately 60,000 to 80,000 thoughts per day.[1] Although the basis for this claim is not certain, it seems this figure is extrapolated from research done in the 1970s by Nobel laureate Daniel Kahneman that involved measuring pupil dilation as an indication of mental effort.[2] Assuming we average about one thought per second, during a sixteen to eighteen hour day of wakefulness, each of us might have between 57,000 and 64,000 thoughts.

Although this estimate might seem remarkably high, it's hard to dispute that our thoughts are incessant. We are often engaged with many thoughts at once. For example, we might be making a mental shopping list on our way to the market while listening to a story our child is telling about his day at school, and all the while keeping an ear to the news on the car radio. We are primed in our DNA, minds, and culture to be able to think this way for our safety and survival. Our thinking mind allows us to understand our world and our environment.

Is having a racing mind filled with more than 50,000 thoughts a day good for us? Healthy? Do we need to have more? While we're awake, can we prime our mind for the kind of thinking that is most beneficial to us? This accounts for thoughts during consciousness, but what about when a person is dreaming? Are they having thoughts then, too? A thought every second? Or how about several thoughts in a second? And what constitutes a thought anyway? A single word? A sentence? A chain of thoughts? A series of day dreams? What about simultaneous conflicting thoughts? And how about meditation? True meditation, when the mind is focused and free of thoughts? Does the actual *number* of thoughts per day matter when in truth our thoughts are incessant?

How we manage our thoughts is what is at the heart of this thought experiment. Directing our mind to focus attention on the nature of the thoughts so that ultimately we can understand the underlying story. Shaping our reactions and behaviors as they relate to our thoughts and stories is how we can begin to activate alternative neural networks to focus our attention on thoughts that cultivate positive neural patterns and behaviors in relation to our thinking. Thoughts are not the enemy, it is our reactions to our thoughts, our beliefs, and the stories we tell ourselves that shape our mindset. How can we work to redirect our mind to create positive neural patterns and rewire our brain for the better good? We can, if we understand our experience is a manifestation of our continuous thoughts and is our reaction to our thoughts.

For example, in a brain imaging study, people were tested on their reactions to imagined fears compared to their experienced fears. In the scanner, people's brains showed the same neural activation while viewing video clips that prompted actual fear as they did when simply asked to *imagine* a fearful scene.[3] The brain cannot distinguish between real and imagined fear; the emotion elicits the same neural activation whether real or fake. That is why Hollywood is so good at playing with our emotions. The thoughts and the stories we tell ourselves are powerful and can change our neural patterns, physiology, and mental well-being. We have the power to change our imaginative stories and emotional associations to shape our reaction patterns and our mindset.

Thoughts, feelings, emotions are all an interconnected continuum and loop of circling patterning where emotions are felt in our body and mind. And because our stories are attached to emotions and bodily sensations, our sensations activate our emotions and thought patterns. In her book, *Stroke of Insight,* Jill Bolte Taylor tells of a personal experience of perceiving an emotion and having it take close to 90 seconds for that emotion's chemical reaction to register in her brain so that she could take an action.[4] Although this has not been scientifically validated, the important takeaway here is that there is a timeframe for our experience of an emotion based on chemical and neural patterns that cause a physiological reaction and motivate us to take an action. Jill Bolte Taylor points out that by being aware, we can choose to first acknowledge an emotion and then influence how that emotion affects our thoughts.

A foundational principle of emotional biochemistry is that our emotions are at the first level perceived in the limbic cortex then in secondary structures in higher order brain areas to take an action in relation to the emotion and are driven by neuropeptides that provide chemical signals to convey information. If we were to really encounter a predator in the wild, let's hope that we would react much more quickly than in 90 seconds. Perhaps emotions have varying reaction times, depending on the immediate need to take an action and adjust our behavior to meet the circumstance at hand with the higher thinking portion of our brain. I imagine that with our autobiographical memory and our particular neural wiring (along with our unique and various emotions and triggers of varying degrees and lengths according to our individual physiological baseline), our reactions to an emotion will depend on our individual behavioral patterning. For example, if one has conditioned one's mind to continually experience an emotion, that emotion may have a faster reaction time because there are more neural pathways, plasticity, and circuits dedicated to the response to that particular emotion.

Although we are continually flooded with emotions, we experience a delay in our processing which should allow us to change our behavior and modify our action to appropriately meet the emotional currency we are picking up from our environment.

Can we experience two, three, four, even five emotions simultaneously? Say, for example, you walk into your sixteenth birthday surprise party—can you be feeling surprise, joy, amusement, confusion, excitement, and embarrassment all at once? Most likely, yes. We receive multiple emotional cues, sensory perceptions, and reaction patterns that are instinctual to our survival for interpreting a situation.

Emotions are powerful for teaching us who we are and they are entwined with our mood, personality, motivation, and temperament. Originally, scientists centered their work around studying emotion by identifying six universal core emotions across cultures: anger, happiness, surprise, disgust, sadness, and fear.[5] In 1980, Robert Plutchik proposed a "wheel" of eight core emotions in opposite "poles": joy versus sadness; anger versus fear; trust versus disgust; and surprise versus anticipation.[6]

In 2017, investigators Alan S. Cowen and Dacher Keltner, at UC Berkeley classified twenty-seven universal emotions in participants viewing video clips and identifying their emotions through facial expressions, sound, and tone. The universal twenty-seven are: "admiration, adoration, aesthetic appreciation, amusement, anger, anxiety, awe, awkwardness, boredom, calmness, confusion, craving, disgust, empathic pain, entrancement, excitement, fear, horror, interest, joy, nostalgia, relief, romance, sadness, satisfaction, sexual desire, and surprise."[7] This impressive classification helps us identify our emotions with greater accuracy and consciousness because we all feel in varying degrees. It is noteworthy that our emotions have an overlap, so having greater and more accurate language with which to classify one's emotional state lends voice to better communication.

Having the language to pinpoint emotions and be able to communicate them with greater accuracy is invaluable when teaching children how to share their feelings. We need to ask children what they're feeling, then help them share and explain their internal states with accurate language about emotions so they can feel safe when they make themselves vulnerable by sharing their emotions.

Scientists have found that not all emotions last for the same length of time. A team of researchers at KU Leuven, Belgium conducted a survey study in which college students identified their emotions and described the duration of the emotion from its initial onset to the time it extinguished.[8] Participants used the universal twenty-seven emotions to identify their emotional state. In addition, the participants answered questions about the strategies they used to cope with their emotions. Some emotions last longer while other emotions have a shorter duration. For example, sadness lasted the longest by returning to baseline after 120 hours; anxiety lasted twenty-four hours; fear and shame only thirty minutes; gratitude five hours; and the good news is joy lasted thirty-five hours.

Why would sadness last over 120 hours?

With emotions, we are continually writing our stories. Sadness is, in our minds, a loss representing something we desired and perceived in our imagination but did not manifest in reality. We work to rewrite new stories and patterns and that can hurt. It takes a good deal of mental energy to revise our story and our expectation. Thus, understanding the formation of the story-emotion connection is invaluable when working through our emotions in our daily lives. It is also important to note that in the study, sadness lasted 120 hours *on average,* but that length of time varies with each person and depends on their particular emotionally. Some people can get over sadness quickly, others need more time to process their emotions. And as I keep noting, our experiences are highly neuroindividual.

All these emotions live inside us simultaneously and there are times when certain ones are turned up and we mold a story for ourselves from that emotion, letting our mind run wild. But we have a choice about whether or not to attach to the emotion or recognize the pattern we are engaging in. Our mindful choice can help guide our relationship with the avoidance, the attachment, and the igno-rance in relation to our emotions. It is essential that we first identify an emotion, its underlying story, and then not attach or repress our emotion but rather have compassion for ourselves and our emotional vulnerability.

Research shows that when you can acknowledge your feelings and name them, you can better regulate your emotions. Having the right words to accurately describe your emotions frees you from being dominated by them. Think of it this way: our cell phone's emojis for texting have more emotional context than what we allow ourselves. Can you give yourself more than an emoji to express what you feel? In a recent study, where scientists used expressive writing as a tool to work though the emotion of fear, it actually helped the participants when they wrote about their fear as compared to participants who did not.[9] Specifically, therapeutic journaling is a valuable tool to help people work through their emotions and have greater insight into their emotional workings. The value in understanding our emotions nurtures us in all aspects of our lives, where the mind, body, and heart connection are fully alive.

Cartography of Pain in the Brain

When people are taught and trained to deny their identity, they become disillusioned by the loss of self and their personal story, just as if they do not see anyone else like them in society. Silencing one's own voice and story, and the suppression of true self, causes deep suffering within and can lead to a feeling of loss of belonging in society. Without space to integrate into the population, people silently suffer due to a lack of visibility or appreciation from others, and they can often be dismissed and excluded. The authentic self of any person is multifaceted, conveyed through thoughts, senses, emotions, values, and behaviors. Our authentic self has a great deal of plasticity and fluidity, and through expression of our core values, the true self becomes visible. In neurodiverse individuals, the self is typically complex, often does not seem to fit with what others expect of them, and may camouflage itself in an attempt to "fit in." Their external representation of self becomes incongruent with their internal state, and the true individuality is hidden.

In mammals, social isolation and exclusion activate the pain centers in the brain in a way that is similar to the patterns seen in brain activation because of physical pain.[10] Pain, regardless of whether it is triggered by psychological or physical stimuli, has a distinct signature in the brain, among brain regions of the anterior cingulate cortex (ACC), prefrontal cortex (PFC), and insular cortex. Each of these regions have critical interconnected networks that are woven with many systems involving not only emotion but cognition, decision making, autonomic responses related to mental states, personality, and health outcomes.

ACC has several significant roles in cognition including influencing decision making, error detection, anticipation of reward, and emotional regulation. It also regulates autonomic physiological states such as blood pressure and heart rate.[11] ACC is highly interconnected throughout the brain with connections to the PFC, parietal lobe, motor cortices, and visual cortex. Importantly, ACC is critical to high-level cognition, detecting incongruent outcomes, and emotional regulation. Chronic activation of the ACC due to social isolation therefore has long term consequences on mental health and well-being.

The brain regions that are activated by social exclusion and pain are the exact same regions that are essential for compassion, personality, cognition, anticipation for future outcomes, awareness, social appropriateness, and decision making. It is not surprising that these states and functions have a significant overlap. Antonio Damasio, a world leader in studying emotions in biological organisms, especially humans, describes these as "mental experiences of body states," meaning that the brain's interpretations of our emotions are physical states that emerge when an individual responds to stimuli.[12] Emotional information is woven and multilayered in our body through memories, primitive survival instincts, neurochemical release via the endocrine system, and serial brain activation for responding to and processing emotional content of information. The hub of all this brain activity is in the insular cortex.

Chronic emotional pain shapes mental health, well-being, brain networks, and thought patterns over time and can lead to many negative health consequences. The effects of chronic emotional pain may include psychological conditions such as anxiety, depression, anger, and physiological conditions. Stress hormones can also trigger a cascade of events leading to physical pain, alterations in digestive health, and immune functions.

Can we, as a society, curb the consequences of long-term social exclusion of a person's mental and physical health? What happens to the brain circuitry and the drive in an individual that continually denies who they are?

If an individual experiences long-term social exclusion, are ACC, PFC and insular cortex chronically activated, and are negative emotional patterns hard-wired? How does this chronic state of social isolation change the brain's wiring? What does social exclusion do to long-term well-being and survival? How can we help neurodiverse individuals in our society remain seen and minimize the consequences of social exclusion and isolation?

It is damaging when individuals deny their life stories, diminish a sense of self, or experience exclusion from society, resulting in mental health risks. We need to open our minds as a culture to make space for neuroindividual stories to be heard. Is there a way that we as a society can use positive thought processes and social inclusion to accept one another for our diversity and open the doors and neural networks of compassion and social inclusion? Perhaps it begins with compassion, tuning in to the unique differences and diversity among humans. Social inclusion can activate the compassionate networks in the brain where we are all seen, accepted, and reflected in society.

Mirror, Mirror

We see one another, ourselves, reflected in each other's smiles, frowns, eye rollings—in all that we do we mirror one another. In our minds, we imagine and mirror each other's actions and our brains light up as if we made the action ourselves. Humans have a biological mechanism, through neural pathways, to experience one another in our minds. When someone is observing someone else's action, the observer's brain mirrors the electrical impulses. This is neuronal synchrony in its most exquisite form. Humans and other primates have an intricate circuitry dedicated to understanding, interpreting, and imagining each other's emotions and actions through the mirror neuron system found in cerebral cortices and higher-order brain areas. Primates are primed to see others as they see themselves, through cognitive congruency, reflecting one another, imagining one another to gain a greater understanding.

The mirror neuron system was first discovered in the monkey's premotor cortex. A monkey lifted a piece of food, and an observing monkey's premotor cortex lit up at the exact moment it was viewing the action, as though the observing monkey had lifted the food itself. The two monkeys' brains were like mirrors, showing the same activation in both brains, experiencing the same action at the same time, as if they were both doing the same task.[13] More intriguingly, it was discovered that the mirror system is also activated in relation to facial expression and facial cues.[14] Microfacial expressions are woven into our evolutionary behaviors to build trust, and humans mirror one another's body language and facial expressions to elicit safety, openness, and oneness.[15] Centered on this principle, when we are in unison, not only do our physical bodies mirror one another, our brains mirror one another, and we create a mutual neural map of our mind-body connection in that moment.

One of the greatest discoveries of the mirror neuron system is our decoding of an intention of another through their actions.[16] It is an evolutionary advantage to understand what action is being performed, but it is even more important to understand the motivation for an action, the true intention of another. This can be a life-saving form of mirroring and forms the basis for intuition, developed through seeing one's vulnerability and invulnerability through our ability to identify the intention of another, happening through the electrical signals in our brains.[17] In the experiment, participants viewed hand signals without information about the purpose of the action, but they were able to intuitively understand the motivation and the signal communicated by the hand action, through the activity of mirror networks in the frontal cortex coding the experience. Developing our intuitions in relation to one another's intentions provides us greater awareness. The mirroring network signals to us whether someone is trustworthy by decoding the intention of their action. If there is a glitch or alarm in the mirror system, your survival instinct is telling you to get the heck out of there.

The plot thickens for the mirror neuron system. Mirror networks are at play in our emotional understanding and in communicating to and with others. Mirror activation is elicited by empathy for others so that we can view emotions through reflective experience.[18] The mirror neuron system is known to activate when observing and experiencing others' disgust and observing when others are facing pain.[19] Importantly, when people are experiencing strong emotions revealed through bodily action and facial expressions our brains perceive what others are experiencing in their brains so we can better develop and understand social cues, emotional communication, and our connection.

The mirror neuron network activates our imagination to see life through the eyes of another, provide synchronistic brain firing between humans, and involves an energetic exchange where vibrational frequencies of oneness are mapped through pathways within the mind. Humans evolved for an emotional, imaginational, and physiological exchange, mirror to mirror, face to face, through elusive and grounded poles of the greater mind.

Emotionally Gifted and Navigating the World

High emotional capacity is a blessing and a curse. Without high emotional intelligence individuals like Mother Teresa would have not impacted our world so profoundly. We need these individuals to open our eyes to be more empathetic, caring, and to develop creative solutions to better society. Even with all of Mother Teresa's massive progress, she suffered silently with her faith, doubt, and the vunerability of the human condition. Gifted individuals with a high emotional intelligence are told they are too sensitive, that they just need to get over it, and that they take too much to heart.[20] In reality, highly gifted emotional individuals can't get over it or stop being too sensitive easily; their brain is wired differently.

Gifted individuals have expanded brain regions and networks for emotional processing, in the insula, and cingulate cortex,[21] allowing them to feel all dimensions of emotions (fear, anger, sadness, disgust, surprise, anticipation, joy, and trust, as identified by Robert Plutchik)[22] and ponder the deep emotional complexities. Sensory information (touch, taste, smell, tactile, hearing, and seeing), along with memories, are coded and decoded in the expanded regions for emotional processing. Thus, a heightened sensory response can elevate emotional content of an experience or memory. We know that gifted individuals experience the world with an elevated intensity[23] and their brain wiring and neuroanatomy are the core of their expanded ability for processing information. It is paramount that we embrace the range of human neurodiversity.[24]

Gifted individuals with a high verbal IQ self-reported increased worry and rumination compared to age-matched individuals.[25] At a glance, a gifted individual with an expanded vocabulary evaluates words, language, and meaning in a more complex manner which can amplify their thought process, emotions, and experiences. A gifted individual may have all 464 meanings of a word right at their fingertips, may ruminate on the beauty of language, and create poetry like Maya Angelou.

Many emotionally gifted individuals have a profound commitment to make the world better which may exacerbate their emotions and intensity. Social justice is a core value that weighs on an emotionally gifted individual. When the justice balances seem uneven, the emotionally gifted child may become highly argumentative, persevere, and find themselves unable to release the perceived unfairness.[26] For example, a gifted child on the playground who experiences a classmate cheating in a game of dodge ball may cause a rage of fury if the cheater is not disciplined. The injustice on the playground may stay with them throughout the day and they may have difficulty letting it go because the gifted individual is prone to worry and rumination.

An increase in anxiety and depression was self-reported by gifted individuals compared to the national average.[27] It is hypothesized that their increased emotional ability may be a precursor for increased accounts of anxiety and depression. Gifted expansive empathy is seeing, feeling, and embodying things more deeply and is at the center of the gifted experience. In a recent study, individuals who experienced social exclusion activated anterior cingulate cortex and anterior insula, indicating that physical and emotional pain elicit similar neural networks.[28] Is too much empathy a bad thing? In a recent study, researchers found that too much empathy can actually be disadvantageous because it can hinder processing other information and be linked to negative emotions.[29]

On the flip side, individuals must experience the broad range of emotions and in our society we over-emphasize that individuals need to be joyous and happy all the time. In reality emotions, thoughts and, bodily sensations fluctuate moment to moment. The moment, feeling, experience, or situation need to be evaluated for what it actually is rather than what it is expected to be. A gifted individual can find peace in the truth of the moment rather than what is expected. Tuning into the moment mindfully can aid in their understanding and self-healing. Specifically, when individuals practiced a mindfulness meditation while watching other's pain, it allowed for an adaptive mechanism for suffering.[30] Here are ways to help support an emotionally gifted individual and strategies to navigate the complex world.

1. **Listen to their needs and feelings.** A profoundly gifted individual needs to be heard and the act of listening and acknowledging their stories, feelings, and bodily needs is the first step in understanding the depths of their emotions.

2. **Understand that language for a gifted child has a million meanings.** Gifted individuals with an elevated emotional processing have profound verbal ability. Choose your words carefully and make sure when you use a word, you both understand the same meaning.

3. **Have patience when they respond, and let them ponder the why.** Allowing the individual to respond within their own time frame and being patient is crucial. No two brains are alike, and processing speed of emotional information is unique to every individual.

4. **De-identify as only their problem.** Get them engaged with like-minded individuals to help them understand they are not alone. Being part of a tribe or group that holds similar beliefs and values guides them to understand they are part of a collective that is bigger than themselves.

5. **Empower them and cultivate in them a belief that they can make a difference.** Give them hope that they can make a difference. It is through our difficulties and suffering that great change happens.

6. **Start small and grow.** Making a small change is better than no change at all. My son, Spence, is increasingly worried about global warming and the state of our planet and he decided to reduce his carbon footprint by becoming a vegetarian.

7. **Help them establish things that are out of their control.** Guide them to understand that they can only be responsible for themselves and that they can bring about change by their own behavior and actions.

8. **Help them recognize that each day is different and that some are better than others.** Model behaviors that help them embrace the unpredictability and the impermanence of life.[31]

9. **Reality check.** Sometimes life sucks and it really sucks. Like the fact that the Arctic is melting and as a society we need to come together to aid in solving the problems of global warming.

10. **Have them practice loving-kindness meditation for self-compassion.** Cultivation of self-compassion is good for healing and wellness.

11. **Don't go at it alone.** Remember the words of Mother Teresa: "Do not wait for leaders, do it alone, person to person."

Unraveling the Strings of Anxiety

Anxiety is an adaptive emotional response that can be life-saving. Anxiety's evolutionary purpose is to induce immediate self-protective action when one is facing an environmental and existential threat, say like a mountain lion. It produces transient anxiety to induce fight, flight, freeze, and flop, by activating the sympathetic nervous system for an instinctual response intended for you to get the heck away from that lion and out of harm's way, as fast as you can. It makes sense that if we were in the wild and facing a mountain lion that we would have a greater state of arousal and awareness, providing us with an acute attention to self-preserve, flee, and seek refuge. In our daily life, our encounters with mountain lions are limited and more often the imagined mountain lions and lionesses are the ones really wreaking havoc on our mental, emotional, and physical health.

Transient anxiety is a normal part of life and it can be healthy in small doses when it stimulates us to take positive action. Normal stress-producing situations like project deadlines, coffee-spill accidents, commuting in traffic, and disciplining a strong-willed teenager can all induce some level of anxiety. Here, the importance and perspective of the story we associate with feelings of anxiety becomes pivotal because our way of thinking can cause us to be overrun with anxiety. Anxiety is fear of future fear, fear of the unknown. Whether we follow our fears and anxiety down the rabbit hole is dependent on our thinking and our relationship with our own emotions. According to a recent study that surveyed college students to measure the duration of their emotions, anxiety lasted an average of approximately twenty-four hours from the initiation of the triggering event.[32] We know that anxiety can be experienced in degrees and different durations, but most important it is the weight of the emotion and the story we feed ourselves that determines how we manage around our anxieties.

As Søren Kierkegaard wrote: "Anxiety is the dizziness of freedom." We have endless possibilities for free choice to define our own experiences, and if we can release our fear of the unknown and tame the unseen threat of a lioness that exists in our imaginations, we can live free of anxiety.

General Disorder of Anxiety

What is the difference between normal anxiety and anxiety disorder? Anxiety is a feeling of worry, nervousness, or unease, typically about an imminent event or something with an uncertain outcome. Occasionally, anxiety occurs in our daily life with job stress, the academic stress test taking, driving in traffic, making a decision that impacts one's life, and in our relationships. Anxiety is a protective process developed by our body to maintain homeostasis and to motivate us to take action. But what happens when our anxiety response is amped up, excessive, and continuous, so that we feel chronically anxious?

Generalized Anxiety Disorder (GAD) describes the experience of an individual who excessively worries and that worry lasts for six months or longer.[33] In GAD, the homeostatic imbalance is disrupted so that the individual suffers immensely and their quality of life is directly impacted. An individual that suffers from anxiety disorder is at great risk for their condition to worsen over time unless they get professional help and support. The symptoms of GAD interfere with daily life activities, including school, work, home, social interactions, relationships, sleep, and practically every other aspect of life. Anxiety can take hold of everything.

According to a 2001-2003 National Institutes of Mental Health (NIMH) survey, 19% of adults had experienced anxiety disorder.[34]

Females reported higher instances of anxiety (24%) compared to males (14%). Survey participants classified their level of anxiety: mild (33%), moderate (28%), and severe (43%). Importantly, of the population reporting anxiety, 43% described symptoms at a level that was severe, meaning anxiety was taking away their freedoms in life, as Kierkegaard indicates. Strikingly, Harvard medical school reports that 31% of adults in the U.S. have experienced anxiety disorder at some time in their life.[35] In adolescents, based on a self-reported survey of adolescents from ages 13-18 from National Comorbidity Survey, 31.9% report they experienced anxiety disorder, and 8.9% described their anxiety as a severe disability. Of the adolescent population, 38% of females reported having experienced anxiety disorder, an alarming rate, while anxiety was reported by 26% of males surveyed. Based on these data, it appears that females experience anxiety at greater rates.[36]

Anxiety disorder is a serious condition that can severely impair one's life. Anxiety disorder can present in a number of ways in the population, including general anxiety disorder, social anxiety disorder (social anxiety), separation anxiety disorder, panic disorder, obsessive compulsive disorder (OCD), post-traumatic stress disorder (PTSD), phobias, agoraphobia, specific phobia, and selective mutism. In all of these sub-categories of anxiety, the person suffers the mental, emotional, and physical consequences and symptoms of anxiety.[37]

The physiological manifestations of anxiety present in an individual where the heart races, blood pressure rises, the pulse quickens, breath shallows to the chest, adrenaline courses through the veins, muscles tense, and the emotional brain runs the show. The frontal cortex and higher order thinking is temporarily off-line. An individual experiencing an episode of anxiety is a shadow of their real self. In the body, anxiety presents as exhaustion, uneasiness, rapid heart rate, headaches, nausea, stomach ache, change in appetite, shakiness, muscle tension, digestive dysfunction—ulcerative colitis and irritable bowel syndrome and altered gut bacteria—all of which cause a general sense of malaise. In the mind, an individual experiences difficulty concentrating and has a "monkey mind" of uncontrolled thoughts; a racing mind that cycles through unwanted thoughts, emotions, bodily sensations, stories (imagined and perceived). The mind can blank out of its present reality so that the anxious person may have difficulty concentrating and appears to be highly distractible. Behaviorally, an anxious individual has heightened awareness and arousal where their sensory receptivity is increased, verging on being overstimulated, and a person may appear irritable, withdrawn, socially isolated, have altered sleep patterns—insomnia, restlessness, unsettled sleep, and hypervigilance where rest seems impossible. Individuals cycle through many emotions that are mostly reactive, originating in the amygdala, such as fear, terror, vigilance, anticipation, anger, rage, and sadness. Each of these emotions increase doubt and distrust.

What is happening in the brain when anxiety is ruling imagination and reality? When anxiety overruns our mind and body we are caught in our emotion—it carries into everything we do. Chronic anxiety changes one's brain, body, and physiology. It is unhealthy for us. Anxiety can have debilitating effects on one's life because uncontrolled anxiety interferes with an individual's ability to engage in everyday activities, affecting relationships, work, personal motivation, satisfaction of life, and meaning. An individual suffering with high levels of anxiety could lose out on meaningful relationships, suffer from low self-esteem, and experience isolation.

Out of control thoughts rooted in anxiety disrupt one's ability to be in the present moment. Anxiety becomes the living story and dominates the thought process. It is like getting stuck in a loop, an energetic black hole where anxiety, the mind's running story, and obsessive thinking overtake the brain and body. One becomes a hostage of one's anxiety, flooded with stress hormones being pumped into the body and the amygdala and a fear cycle take over while the executive functioning and decision making get thrown out the door. The baby and the bath water are thrown overboard and lost in the vast ocean of emotion. The emotional brain invades the mind and body where an individual flows into their default reactional states of anxiety—fight, flight, freeze, and flop.

Fighters and fleers primarily center on escaping from danger, motivated by fear to physically move the energy of anxiety through them, whereas, freezers and floppers stop dead in in their tracks and the energy of anxiety is stuck in their body until it drains out. Across all reactional types, stress hormones are circulating throughout the mind and body. Chronic exposure to cortisol, the stress hormone, can have devastating consequences for the physical and psychological aspects of an individual's health. Cortisol is a neurotransmitter that activates the sympathetic nervous system and effectively puts an individual on high alert. In chronic anxiety, the brain circuitry, hormonal stress response, and bodily reactions to stress can become hard-wired so that an individual can get stuck in a negative cycle. Effectively elevated levels of cortisol rewire brain circuits where the emotional networks cycle, the prefrontal cortex (responsible for decision-making) is temporarily off-line, inhibiting effective decision-making, and an individual is paralyzed. A persistently activated low-level stress response causes an individual to navigate in the world in a fog. All that causes a great amount of physiological, psychological, emotional, and sensory wreckage.

Chronic neuroinflammation may present a number of symptoms ranging from GI symptoms, ADHD like behaviors, heightened sensory responsivity, chronic headaches, body aches, physical manifestations of pain, social withdrawal, and isolation. In addition, one can become hypersensitive to their environment through enhanced awareness across all sensory domains where the sensory processing is overactivated and can cause a sensory overload. Chronic stress response induces global inflammation where there is a chemical change throughout the entire body's systems for inflammation and immunity. When an individual experiences global inflammation, immunity is compromised in all bodily organs and systems, leaving an individual more prone to exposure to illness and disease. Chronic inflammation and altered immunity present as joint and muscle pain, digestive issues, headaches, migraines, and alarmingly an increase in autoimmune activation and allergies. The entire mind and body become dysregulated and illness takes over. When anxiety reaches this level, the main challenge is determining that anxiety origin of the bodily dysregulation because many of these physiological symptoms induce anxiety as well, where there is a loop feeding into the anxiety manifestation.

With neuroindividuality, there are different set points for the anxiety response. We tend to look at our different set points as physiological, neurobiological differences, and our anxiety response is highly individual, meaning we are each hard-wired differently for our individualized responses and reactions in relation to anxiety. We each must learn to understand and identify the circumstances that induce anxiety in us to help navigate our emotions and honor our personal thresholds, while also being cognizant that others may have different triggers and thresholds. Anxiety is a personal and individual relationship that we can learn to dump.

Are we doomed if we are anxious beings? Not at all, but it will take an activated awareness to transform our thought patterns, behaviors, and relationships from devolving into anxiety. It begins with de-identifying our language that anxiety is just part of us. We each have the ability to rewire our mindset and create new patterns in response to anxiety-producing events through our attention and awareness, recapturing our mind. Anxiety is a transient experience. Do not let it take you hostage. You have the power at any time, any moment, to change your experience and circumstance. It begins with your mindset.

Here are some simple steps to transform your anxiety and step into the full you:

1. **First, talk with someone, anyone, about your experience with anxiety.** Getting help is the first sign you are on track to becoming aware that you are suffering from anxiety.

2. **Name it, label it, and identify what is causing the anxiety.** Determine in the moment if there is anything that can be done to eliminate your anxious feelings. Understand your thoughts and the story around the anxiety and begin to reframe your story, knowing that you are not a victim of your anxiety.

3. **Notice your language around anxiety and de-identify with anxiety—it is not you. Anxiety is an experience.** We often say, "I am anxious," identifying ourselves with the experience we are having, rather than describing the circumstance that is causing the experience of anxiety. There is no reason we need to use language that states anxiety is within us. Break up with anxiety. It is not your friend, trust me. Anyone that takes your freedom is not your friend.

4. **Breathe.** Often when anxiety arises we breathe shallow and so we struggle to get enough oxygen to our brain and body. When you take three deep diaphragmic breaths you rebalance your nervous system, activating the parasympathetic nervous system known as the rest and digest relaxation system. Three deep breaths induce the vagus nerve that releases the trust neurochemicals oxytocin and vasopressin, which are the neurotransmitters responsible for pair bonding in both mate and infant pair bonding.

5. **Exercise.** One feature of stress is that the neurochemicals get trapped in the body like many cars stuck in traffic on the interstate highway. First and foremost, when you exercise you activate natural endorphins and release the impurities in the body and excess energies that cause tension and inflammation. Exercise in fact counteracts inflammation by increasing the ability of the body to clear out toxins through sweat and boost immunity.

6. **Meditate.** Meditation and mindfulness have known benefits to rewire the mind and neural patterns related to emotions. Mediation practices build resilience in being aware of your present moment. Mindfulness and meditation help us make complex decisions from a rational standpoint. When we drop into or tune into our body and experience we are able to better evaluate real and perceived dangers and develop emotional equanimity.

7. **Sleep.** Sleep and mood are directly related. Sleep allows your brain to recover and restore while your subconscious works through your problems.

8. **Write**. Writing your feelings and managing them can help you with identifying triggers of your anxiety. Putting your worries on paper therapeutically releases them by acknowledging your fear.

9. **Talk to a therapist.** Talk therapy is one of the best therapies to help an individual work through their breakup with anxiety.

10. **Exposure therapy** to the "anxiety triggers" can help reframe one's relationship with anxiety and should be practiced under the supervision of a licensed health care provider.

11. **Medication.** There are medications that target anxiety systems. With proper dosing and under the care of a professional you can lessen your symptoms and anxiety.

12. **You have the power to be anxiety free.**

Wired for Anxiety—Anxious People Flee Danger the Quickest

Some people's brains are primed for anxiety and people who are more anxious flee danger more quickly.[38] Scientists at Caltech measured people's reaction time in response to danger using a computer simulation. People who self-reported higher levels of anxiety had a quicker response time evading a predator and dangerous situations. In general, people that are more anxious have a greater baseline arousal state because they have, on average, more NE and cortisol that enhance the sensory nervous system. The activation of the sensory nervous system allows for greater receptivity of sensory systems to fine tune into one's surroundings.

Some people are naturally more anxious because their brains makes them predisposed to being anxious. In a recent study, scientists evaluated the anxiety response and the neuroanatomy of more anxious people and found their brains were "wired" in a way that increased their level of anxiety.[39]

Anterior cingulate cortex (ACC) is a brain region that wraps like a glove around the corpus callosum, the region that connects both hemispheres of the brain. It is essential for autonomic functions like heart rate and blood pressure. Cognitively, ACC is essential for reward, anticipation, impulse control, and emotion. This area is highly related to anxiety. What happens with anxiety physiologically? Again, we know that there is increased heart rate, blood pressure, and sweaty palms. Cognitively, the ACC is implicated in reward (related to validation), anticipation (mentalizing future events), a sense of implied control, and emotion (where it interprets emotions from the limbic region). So, the ACC is a pretty important anxiety-related structure in the brain. For individuals wired for a greater anxiety response they tend to flee unsafe environments quickly, which may be adaptive for one's survival. Perhaps they were the evolutionary alarmists.

Neuroscience of Anxiety in the Bright Brain

William Shakespeare wrote, "Present fears are less than horrible imaginings." It is important to remember that when one's mind tends to drift, imagining can be positive, negative, or neutral. It is the state of our reactions to our emotions and bodily sensations that matter, whether we attach or detach to our fears and anxiety. Ultimately, the stories we tell ourselves can dictate our state of mind and well-being.

Psychologist Kazimierz Dąbrowski proposed that bright individuals have greater imaginations and intensities in five domains (intellectual, emotional, sensory, psychomotor, and imaginative), and elevated experiences in the world.[40] Bright individuals may be more prone to disabling and destructive elements of anxiety because they typically have expanded emotional brain networks, increased sensory processing, and elevated physiological responses to stressors, both real and imagined. Intelligent people report 25% greater rates of anxiety compared to the national average.[41] In particular, the brain circuitry, hormonal stress response, and bodily reactions to stress can become hard-wired and bright individuals can get stuck in a negative cycle. When the sympathetic nervous system is activated, elevated levels of cortisol rewire brain circuits where the emotional networks cycle, the prefrontal cortex (responsible for decision-making) is temporarily off-line, inhibiting effective decision-making. Effectively, the body moves into four states—fight, flight, freeze, or flop—where the inflammatory response is elevated. In turn, a low-level stress response is continuously activated, causing the individual to experience the world on "pins and needles."

Consider a child who has been tagged with slow processing speed, which can be related to numerous learning differences, asynchronous brain development, sensory integration, metabolic processing, attention, executive functioning, or emotional development. Parents and teachers may comprehend that it takes the child longer to their work, even providing accommodations such as more time to take tests. From the child's point of view, extra time can create more anxiety because they cannot engage in other school activities such as recess and lunch which are connection times with peers. As a result, the bright child may experience greater feelings of social isolation. Higher IQ individuals have increased brain regions responsible for emotional processing, which is a gift and a curse, leading to intensified experiences of happiness and sadness.[42] The exact brain regions identified for emotional intelligence and processing, anterior cingulate cortex and orbitofrontal cortex, have altered functional connectivity in individuals with greater anxiety.[43] These studies support the idea that some individuals may be more prone to anxiety due to their neuroanatomy.

Commonly, these children are unlikely to be identified as suffering from anxiety because of an absence of obvious symptoms and the child's inability to verbalize their experience as anxiety. As a result, these children may suffer negative physiological, psychological, and neurological effects due to absence of treatment, misdiagnosis, and misidentification. Their increased stress hormones and overactivated stress networks can cause elevated levels of inflammation and, eventually, the entire mind-body connection is disrupted. Bright children may present with a number of symptoms ranging from gastrointestinal (GI) symptoms, "ADHD" behaviors, heightened sensory sensitivity (touch, taste, hearing, smelling, seeing), chronic headaches, and social withdrawal.[44]

A child with anxiety may complain of physical symptoms, such as stomachaches, headaches, and physical pain, which in turn can lead to a diagnosis of a GI issue or other physiological diagnosis rather than the actual anxiety. While most professionals and parents acknowledge that anxiety plays a role in these symptoms, the fact that the child is not identifying their emotional state as anxiety makes it difficult to judge the how anxiety factors into the manifestation of physical symptoms and vice versa. It is important to pay attention and identify the source of the symptoms and how they are woven in with experience of anxiety. Guiding the child to recognize the trigger is the first step.

Professionals and parents need to be aware of the possible long-term consequences of anxiety. Because each person has a unique brain and physiology, the approaches must be individualized to manage their anxiety.[45] There is a wealth of evidence that supports the effectiveness of holistic interventions. Teaching a child to notice the initiating experience of anxiety from physiological, psychological, and emotional perspectives is key in guiding a child. The interplay of the mind and body requires an approach incorporating the interactions among these systems.

Keep in mind, the label of being "gifted" carries a great weight of expectation for success, so guiding a child to balance expectations is paramount. Provide safety and compassion for failure, mistakes, and mishaps, which are the key components of a growth mindset and resilience. Communicate about anxiety and fears and listen to what your child has to say. Breaking the silence reduces social isolation and minimizes the stigma associated with anxiety.

As Fred Rogers ("Mr. Rogers") said, "I'm convinced that when we help our children find healthy ways of dealing with their feelings, ways that don't hurt them or anyone else, we're helping to make our world a safer, better place."

Cognitive behavioral therapy is an effective remedy, especially when focused on integrating the mind-body connection. Mindfulness practices focused on self-compassion can lead to reduced symptoms of anxiety and greater understanding of self and others.[46] Breathing exercises to calm the nervous system are effective by activating the parasympathetic nervous system, and releasing positive neurochemicals that reduce the stress response.[47]

"Anxiety is fear of fear held in our imagination," as my dear friend, the late Sam Christensen, said.

A recent study found that positive imagination reduces fear.[48] Guiding a child to activate their positive imagination may help them cope with their anxiety. Regular exercise of twenty minutes a day, healthy sleep routines, and mindful eating habits can rewire healthy mind and body patterns and circuitry. When we support the mind, body, and spirit of the child, the child is unbound and thrives.

Free Solo

Individuals have different set points for emotional responses including fear, risk-taking, and thrill seeking. Novelty is arousing for the brain, activating the pleasure and reward centers and releasing dopamine. Risk-taking activates brain areas involved in fear and anticipation of reward and anxiety. The documentary film, *Free Solo*, chronicles the story of Alex Honnold, the first free solo climber of El Capitan who completed the 3,000-foot climb alone, without ropes or safety equipment.[49] Honnold showed reduced brain activity in response to standard fear paradigms. Being a free solo climber is most likely the highest level of thrill seeking that one can take where acute attention, motivation, and focus are all life-saving.

To better understand Alex's brain and fear insensitivity, scientists studied his brain anatomy and activity. While in an MRI scanner, Honnold viewed clips of "normal" fear-inducing situations. His brain showed less activity in the amygdala, the brain area responsible for our fear response to threats from our surroundings. As shown in the documentary, neuroscientist Jane E. Joseph Ph.D. at the Medical University of South Carolina compared Honnold's brain to a same age climber while they viewed fear-triggering images. While the age-matched climber's brain radiated activation of the amygdala, Honnold's brain was devoid of any activity, and on a risk assessment test, he scored twice as sensation-seeking as the average person and 20% higher than the average high sensation seeker while also registering unusually high levels of conscientiousness.[50] This finding illustrates the neuroindividuality that provided for his extraordinary gift as a free solo climber. With his incredible physical and mental training and stamina he primed his brain to memorize the layout of the face of El Capitan, and he had each of his moves mapped in his mind prior to his ascent of a mountain, a feat that requires incredible skill for spatial, tactile, motor, and memory coordination. His divergent brain circuitry, mind, and body gave him the amazing gift needed to ascend the face of El Cap without ropes—a skill that he trained for over and over again, hundreds of times over more than seven years. Honnold enhanced his neural plasticity with small steps in the beginning, with simple climbs without ropes that allowed him to train and take the risk for greater challenges of climbing without ropes. He trained his mind *and* body, which enhanced his ability to be one of the very best climbers in our lifetime. Through training and exposure to novel situations, we can change our relationship with our preset levels of fear, anxiety and risk-taking. Alex Honnold shows us in new ways how neuroindividuals carry a key to unique ways of navigating in the world and provides inspiration to honor our own ways of navigating while working to enhance our particular neural plasticity for greater emotional, mental, physical, and sensory well-being and meaning. Each of us has our very own set points of emotional response and we have the power to nurture positive mental and neural patterns to live life free solo climbing mountains in our very own ways with ropes, guides, safety nets—ascending in our own terms and on our own timeline.

Imposter Monster

Have you ever felt like a fraud? Where a haunting voice that brews from within saying, *it is only a matter of time before they find me out.* Telling yourself that you are *just lucky* and have gotten where you are *by sheer luck.* The voice of the imposter monster feeds a negativity wheel spinning through thoughts, stories, and messages of uncertainty telling you that you are a fake, phony, and a fraud—undeserving of your success, undeserving of your accomplishments, undeserving of being the full expression of yourself, and minimizing your essence. Over time, this monster brainwashes you that *you are an imposter.* The monster causes chaos and confusion in your mind, body, and heart, where that loud shouting opinion, that feeling of being an imposter is evaluated as fact.

Our thoughts are powerful. As I described earlier, it has been estimated that we have approximately 60,000 thoughts a day. If our pattern of thoughts becomes an uncontrolled snowball of negative thinking, and a lack of self-trust is at the nucleus of our attention, we are frozen and unable to build positive intentions and actions. If we wallow in our self-doubt, we miss ourselves, we miss the opportunity, we miss out on life.

William Shakespeare wrote, "Our doubts are traitors, and make us lose the good we oft might win, by fearing to attempt."

You are not alone in feeling like an imposter. In some popular accounts, approximately 70% of the population has had experienced imposter syndrome, while a recent literature review found wide variations in prevalence of imposter syndrome from 9 to 82% of the tested population, depending on the diagnostic tool.[51] I believe the number is most likely closer to 100% of the population: at some point each of us has felt like an imposter. The difference is that people experience imposterism in varying degrees, and the imposter experience can be transient so that a person can feel like an imposter at any time, depending on the circumstances.

In the original research studies by Pauline Clance and Suzanne Imes in 1978, they identified imposter syndrome in high-achieving females. Many of these highly successful women were bright undergraduate students, PhD doctoral candidates, women with advanced degrees such as doctors, lawyers, and academics. Many of these women believed they were not intelligent and felt that people overevaluated them. These highly accomplished women discounted their success as luck or no big deal. Strikingly, these women had a common feature where they feared being found out as frauds and felt guilty about their success.[52] Early studies suggested that the imposter experience was only found in women but more recent findings suggest both men and women experience imposter syndrome to an equal degree. However, studies show that gender may impact how imposter syndrome affects the individual.[53] Another complexity for men who experienced imposter syndrome was that they did not talk about it with family, friends, peers, or colleagues due to stereotypes, and men who suffer from imposter syndrome tend to react more negatively to feedback and accountability. The silence and gendered expectations caused men with imposter syndrome to feel even more stressed and isolated.

Professor Amy J.C. Cuddy, in *Presence*, summarizes the prevalence this way: "Imposter syndrome is found in many demographic groups that include but are not limited to teachers, doctors, physician assistants, nurses, engineering students, dental students, medical students, law students, African Americans, Koreans, Japanese, Canadians, disturbed adolescents, "normal" adolescents, preadolescents, old people, adult children of alcoholics, adult children of high achievers, people with and without eating disorders, people with new success, people who have failed."[54] So basically everyone.

Numerous famous people have experienced imposter syndrome: Tom Hanks, Sonia Sotomayor, Chris Martin, and Denzel Washington. For example, Jody Foster said, "When I won the Oscar, I thought it was a fluke. I thought everybody would find out, and they'd take it back. They'd come to my house, knocking on the door, 'Excuse me, we meant to give that to someone else. That was going to Meryl Streep.'" And when Meryl Streep won the Oscar she said, "You think, 'Why would anyone want to see me again in a movie? And I don't know how to act anyway, so why am I doing this?'" Imposter syndrome takes away our confidence, self-trust, our power, and clouds our essence and existence to share all the very best parts of ourselves. We all can understand that imposter syndrome does not discriminate—it is in every gender, profession, home, community, and can attack anyone at any time and any place. Why is this so prevalent in our society?

It appears that the most prevalent cause for imposter syndrome is fear of failure.[55] In Amy Cuddy's book *Presence*, she points out that people who are actually trying something and trying something with meaning and purpose that requires them to put themselves on the line are not frauds at all. Striving for something that is bigger and more profound than yourself is frightening and that is where the imposter monster can come into the mind and body, feeding into insecurity and doubts that interfere with putting oneself on the line. When a person fears that they are unsafe, they lack trust in others and themselves. For example, Maya Angelou, one of the greatest poets and authors of our time, wrote, "I have written eleven books, but each time I think, 'Uh oh, they're going to find out now. I've run a game on everybody, and they're going to find me out.'" In her writing and wisdom, she bares a level of humanity and vulnerability that is transformational for humans. Being vulnerable is at the heart of the how and why the imposter monster clouds our thinking, judgment, and self-identity.

Often, people become swept away in the imposter experience, like a runaway racehorse circling through thoughts around a racetrack such as *I must not fail, I feel like a fake, I just got lucky.* Frequent feelings of imposter syndrome are fear, anxiety, guilt, and shame, all of which can lead to low self-esteem, anxiety, and depression. There are a number of risks associated with imposter syndrome that include mental, emotional, and behavioral challenges. Often, a person struggling with imposter syndrome has vast amounts of self-doubt and they lack the foundation to develop and nurture their self-trust. An individual is missing the neural patterning, thinking, emotional regulation and behavioral responses that one has for self-confidence and self-esteem. The most common signs of imposter syndrome are perfectionism, overworking, undermining one's achievements, discounting praise, and fear of failure.[56]

Dr. Valerie Young further researched bright and high-achieving women and defined that they classified into five main types that experienced imposter syndrome; the perfectionist, the expert, the natural genius, the soloist, and the superwoman/superman. In her book, *Secret Thoughts of Successful Women,* Dr. Young describes these five subgroups in depth and how these different types manifest imposter syndrome.[57] The perfectionist, who has to get 100/100 all the time and who often beats themselves up when they miss a point. The expert, who never feels as if they will know everything and constantly doubts themselves, feeling that they do not know enough. The natural genius, who struggles to master a new skill set if it doesn't come naturally, and gives up or burns out quickly if they do not master the skill with ease. The soloist, who feels they must do everything alone and cannot depend on others for their support or help. The superman/ superwoman, who feels they must excel across all areas and domains in their life. Each of these subgroups manages their anxiety and their feelings in a way that causes them to fly under the radar in an effort not to be judged or found out.

The varying degrees of imposter syndrome within bright individuals can be overwhelming. Commonly, bright people experience little compassion in society because our culture promotes the narrative that success is easy for bright people. Over time, it is a daunting expectation to feel the pressure that, as a bright person, one *should* achieve greatness. There is a disconnect about how much it takes for a bright person to create, produce, and make a vision come to fruition. Many can struggle with varying degrees of perfectionism, both healthy and unhealthy behavioral and mental patterning which can cloud their self-vision and expectation. They might tell themselves stories like *I have all this I want to give and share, why am I not operating at the level I should be? I should be doing better. I should be doing more. I should work harder.* Often, people experience high levels of self-judgment, are hypercritical, and place a great deal of pressure on themselves to be the very best.

Additionally, bright people are masters of illusion, chameleons at hiding who they truly are. They can blend into almost any crowd and, because of their intelligence, get lost in the experience of who they actually are and what they can provide. Bright people are exceptionally intuitive. Intuition is innate knowledge without any proof, evidence, or conscious reasoning of how the knowledge is produced. Intuition is unconscious reasoning, which without proof can be a great source of struggle and doubt. Intuition can be disconcerting for bright people. Innately knowing how things work, without study or an external source from which information is acquired, can be unsettling.

It is as if a bright person has the map of the Rocky Mountains downloaded in their brain where others need a map or GPS. A bright person may have incredible spatial navigation without needing modern technology. Since a gifted person cannot explain their ability for spatial navigation, this experience is foreign to others and can be seen as cognitive dissonance. The gifted individual may hide their gifts to blend in, or may withdraw from the intellectual stimulation so as not to be tagged as a know-it-all. Importantly, the ways that they hide their gifts to not be ridiculed is a survival instinct. An aspect of imposter syndrome that is not as well studied or mentioned is the gift of intuitively knowing about life and how this divergent experience plays into imposter syndrome.

Divergent thinking, breaking the mold, generating and expanding on new ideas that no one has expressed before can be intimidating and frightening. Synthesizing information in a unique and original manner can fill one with doubt. It can be a lonely experience. At times, this drive and way of thinking can be intimidating to others.

This can cause a bright person to hide, or quiet their voice and they can become filled with self-doubt and have a good amount of self-distrust. The voice of self-doubt can be a very loud one, a beast with an overwhelming roar. This is the epicenter of fear that builds the negativity bias. Life can feel like a continued state of cognitive dissonance. Wanting, striving, needing to have happiness but with the negative voice churning all around, hijacking your happiness and draining you so that your dreams are frozen.

I had the honor to speak with the late Jim Webb, a world leader in gifted and 2e behaviors, mental, emotionality, and psychology, to understand the ways the imposter monster overtakes the mind of a gifted child. An important point Jim made is that people don't feel like an imposter 24/7, it comes and goes with the waves of life and it isn't clear when or how it will manifest. It doesn't happen all the time, and even though a gifted person does something a thousand times there are the extrinsic and intrinsic aspects that feed into the voice of self-doubt. It could be experienced at deeper levels in gifted individuals because of an intense self-evaluative aspect about what others think, an imaginary audience of criticism, and a deep metacognition. And the higher the aspirations, the more one puts oneself out there. Then there are the "hiders" who do not take risks and come across as low aspirational. But it is the fear of believing their voice and story. Jim explained that the huge defining feature is how you were raised, that is, criticism versus nurturing. This plays into the experience of feeling things more intensely, and of having more sensitivity about how they are falling short. It is essential that there be an absence of criticism when a bright individual is testing something out early on. That when a bright person is trying new ideas, they are in a safe and supportive environment and they have confidence that they can connect with others and talk about their ideas without our criticism or judgment. They must be able to cultivate positive patterns and thinking as they travel through the forest of not knowing the final destination by weeding out negative voices and distractions. And developing a focused intention to hush the voice of self-doubt, and squash the imposter monster.

Amy Cuddy describes how power posing works to minimize the imposter monster and nurture one's authentic self and nature because the practice is centered on building positive behavioral, mental, and emotional patterns. Power posing sets the action of an intention to positively guide your brain, mind, and body to nurture positive neural pathways, similar to that of a meditation. A meditation practice, yoga practice, power posing practice, focuses an individual's intention to take action and turn their attention toward a deeper awareness of their nature in the world. Positive practices build positive neural and behavioral patterns, which grow positive thinking. Remember, it has been presumed our minds are flooded with approximately 60,000 thoughts per day.[58] If we center our mind to positive thinking and give ourselves the space to make mistakes, we become more self-actualized. Understanding and accepting who you are in all dimensions of the good, the challenge, the positive, negative, neutral provides a greater balance of the spectrum of light. Power posing sheds a light precisely on the mind-body connection where fear, anxiety and doubt occur. The simple process is a neurohack, to be in the presence of yourself with greater intention awareness; attention is empowerment. It is flipping the neural patterns and introducing positive neural pathways, replacing the negative and maladaptive patterns and behaviors. Cuddy's power posing and setting an intention to make a commitment for positive growth, greater self-awareness, and actualization to accept one's true nature is essential.

Create space for greater self-compassion, treat yourself as you would treat your most beloved friend. Practice self-compassion, and talk to yourself from a place of love and understanding. For your beloved friend, you imagine yourself in their place in order to understand what they are feeling or experiencing. Do the same for yourself. Compassion facilitates prosocial (helping) behaviors that come from within, rather than being forced, so that we behave in a more compassionate manner. The action of understanding, being aware of, being sensitive to, and vicariously experiencing the feelings, thoughts, and experience of ourselves. Employ positive thinking to cultivate positive neural pathways and promote thinking that results in positive action and personal development to set the intention that when you greet the world with love and peace, the world is a safe place. And tell that imposter monster to get lost!

Here are some ways to nurture yourself and redirect your mind when the imposter monster shows up[59]:

- ○ **Develop self-compassion** for your experience of imposter syndrome. Talk to yourself as a beloved friend and tell the imposter monster to take a hike.

- ○ **Normalize imposter syndrome**, recognize that it exists in a good number of the population, indeed 70 to 100% of people, and you are not alone in your feeling.

- ○ **Seek support and guidance.** Talk to people about feeling like an imposter so that you are not suffering in silence and you can gain insights into others' experience with the imposter monster.

- ○ **Remember that "perfect is the enemy of good."** (Voltaire) Identify the healthy and unhealthy aspects of making things perfect and have compassion for your process as you work to release the unhealthy habits and patterns of perfectionism.

- ○ **Remove the words "just" and "only" when talking about yourself.** Both words are minimizing language. I understand that often we do not want to brag but it is not humble speech when using "just" and "only" in reference to yourself or your accomplishments. In fact, these words are reducing and unnecessary words when describing yourself.

- ○ **Honor your truth, voice, and story.** Give yourself a ton of space to grow and make mistakes.

- ○ **Reframe expectations for competence and ability.** Know that across all domains you will have variation. Some things may be very easy for you whereas other areas may be much more challenging. Create proper expectations for your natural gifts and abilities and for things that take greater effort. Effort is not equal across all domains.

○ **Recognize that success, failure, and everything in between is a part of life.** All of it. And much of failure leads to the greatest breakthroughs.

○ **Always try your best.** No matter what, even if it leads to failure.

○ **Accept failure**—it builds knowledge and awareness.

○ **No one, not anyone can make you feel inferior unless you give them consent,** as Eleanor Roosevelt said, and that includes the voices in your head. Tell the imposter monsters they are no longer welcome in your mind.

○ **You can generate positive thought processes** that enhance positive patterns, behaviors, and emotions. Simply through your thinking, attention, and intention you can change your feelings and your mindset to move up, forward, and ahead into dreams.

Imperfectly Perfect

In my early years documenting my experiments in the laboratory, I wrote my notes with a Sharpie® pen, only to find that when I knocked over a jar of 70% alcohol onto my lab book, my notes bled a sea of blue across the pages. Months of documenting experiments, wiped out in seconds. Dazed and confused by the alcohol fumes, I learned that permanent marker is not permanent. A solvent dissolves another substance. And in the blink of an eye, the alcohol solution erased my progress. My efforts and knowledge were suddenly undocumented. I also learned that Sharpie˙ pens were soluble in water as well as in alcohol, so the trick was to keep things that could spill away from my lab notes and perhaps reconsider my choice of writing instrument. My proprioception had a mind of its own and from time to time, I spilled. When I made mistakes, *silly, stupid mistakes*—I made up a story and filled my mind with thoughts about what a failure, and how stupid, I was. I judged and criticized myself even though I was learning new things. My lab brain was still growing, testing, and hypothesizing.

For example, by age two, infants develop the concept of object permanence, the principle that objects exist even though they cannot be perceived through their five senses. To experience object permanence, someone can close their eyes and recognize the book they were just reading is still in front of their face, even though they can no longer see it. The book exists regardless of whether your eyes are open or closed. Over time, infants develop that same understanding and recognize that even though they cannot directly perceive all objects in their surroundings, those objects do exist. There are many developmental behavioral patterns, brain wiring, and memories involved to develop and understand object permanence. And there are many errors a bright, malleable brain makes as it learns object permanence. My brain was wide open as I explored in the lab. I made errors, miscalculations, mistakes. I spilled things. On my notes.

Spilling is a part of life. Soggy lab notes happen. Humans make mistakes. When I made a mistake, I had a distorted view of myself; I saw myself as reflected in a carnival fun house mirror. My self-expectation of perfection was an altered reality. As if I should have known better, done better, been better, been smarter, as though I had impossible powers to not fail, to make mistakes. I set myself up with the idea that I should not make mistakes. A wet and ruined lab book is disaster, and if I cause that, I am a failure. But the reality is that I am human, I am imperfect, I make mistakes, and I fail. I will continue to fail. I do fail. And I will fail in the future. I fed myself impossible stories and minimized what I'd learned from being imperfect. That day in the lab, I learned that nothing is permanent, nothing is fixed in space and time, mistakes happen. And also, I learned not to write my notes with a Sharpie®. I learned a mistake does not mean failure. I learned that there is always another way.

From that day on, I learned to write in pencil in my lab book. I learned lead pencil is highly resistant to many solvents, can withstand a range of chemicals, and has a handy eraser attached on the end to fix mistakes. Still to this day as I journal and write, I use pencil.

I learned that our thoughts can shape our reality. At that particular time, I was devastated and frustrated and I worked diligently to rewrite and remember the series of steps I'd followed in my experiments. I learned that many of those steps were committed to my memory, my growing lab brain. The steps in my mind were like that of object permanence. I actually did not need the lab notes. I thought I had derailed myself from moving ahead. But when I look back on it, my emotion attached to making a mistake and the story I told myself about being perfect fed into the error about myself.

Importantly, I learned our thoughts and ideas shape our reality and our emotions, our perspectives and how we think, feel, and react to situations. We can change our thoughts, patterns, and our minds to change our perspectives and change our reality and our life stories. When we feel stuck in a pattern, we have the power to change. A failure can be a momentary setback that contains the values and lessons for what to do next, how to move forward with wisdom. We *will* make mistakes because as humans we are imperfect.

> *"No one is perfect... that's why pencils have erasers."*
> —Wolfgang Riebe

Perfectionism, the Good, Bad...Truth

In 1978, Don Hamachek described two types of perfectionism, "neurotic perfectionism," which centers on the negative and unhealthy attributes, and "normal perfectionism," which focuses on the potential positive and healthy attributes of perfectionism.[60] Perfectionism is centered on the characteristics of striving to obtain what is perfect without flaw, of having extremely high standards, behaviors, thought processes, concerns, and mental states that are hypercritical of one's own accomplishments. For many years there has been a great body of research centered on the negative aspects of perfectionism, to the point of psychopathological mental, emotional, and behavioral patterns. But can some features of perfectionism be considered positive?

According to many researchers who focus on the positive attributes of perfectionism, distinguishing healthy perfectionism versus unhealthy perfectionism centers on whether the perfectionism is related to perfectionistic strivings versus perfectionistic concerns.[61]

Perfectionistic strivings can be considered a positive, healthy attribute when individuals enjoy their strivings for perfectionism. At the core of unhealthy perfectionism is when people suffer from mental, emotional, and behavioral consequences related to their perfectionistic strivings and concerns. Is there a fine line? Absolutely. But if we can identify, perhaps in ourselves and in our children's mindset, story and emotionality at the core of the perfectionistic tendencies we can decipher the positives and the negatives of perfectionistic strivings and concerns. Perfectionism is multifaceted with many layers and degrees of social, emotional, mental, individual, and societal concerns that are at play with the behaviors and mindset of perfectionism.

Perfectionism is multidimensional and its tendencies and experiences can be identified, such as: personal standards, organization, focus on mistakes, self-doubt, parental expectations, and parental criticism.[62] Hewitt and Flett report perfectionism as multifaceted including self-perfectionism, socially directed perfectionism, and other-assigned perfectionism.[63] More important, unhealthy perfectionists focus a great deal on their parents, past and current evaluations from their parents, rather than on their personal strivings and expectations. It is essential to make the distinction that individuals who suffer from unhealthy perfectionism have a greater concern when it comes to others' expectations.

Healthy Perfectionism

"Healthy" perfectionism is identified as high-level striving and low-level concern, that is, striving to one's highest level with little to no attachment to outcome. In particular, healthy perfectionism revolves around positive perfectionistic aims that include self-driven perfectionism and elevated individual standards, but does not include undue concern for the outcome of one's efforts. And, healthy perfectionism allows for mistakes and disparity between expectation and the actual level of achievement.[64] The cornerstone of healthy perfectionism is an attitude of striving for one's best, but with a balanced and realistic outlook regarding outcome and a recognition that one's goal of excellence and perfectionism is internally generated and not externally imposed. Focusing on doing one's best without undue attachment to the outcome has positive implications for one's mindset.[65]

In the words of Michelangelo, "The true work of art is but a shadow of the divine perfection."

Unhealthy Perfectionism

The cornerstone of unhealthy perfectionism is high-level striving and high-level concern about outcome in relation to their perfectionistic strivings. In unhealthy perfectionism, negative habits and behaviors are driven by maladaptive thoughts and emotions about not meeting one's personal standards, the standards of others, and over-focusing on one's mistakes, self-doubt, and the difference between high-level expectations and the actual level of achievement outcomes. Historically, the idea of perfectionism has centered on the negative features of perfectionism where individuals have greater diagnoses of anxiety, depression, obsessive-compulsive disorder, and eating disorders.[66] These mental health diagnoses can have a great impact on one's mental, emotional, and physical well-being and are a serious risk and consequence of unhealthy perfectionism. Additionally, there are several negative consequences for an individual who suffers from unhealthy perfectionism that include mind-body dysregulation, increased worry and rumination, and elevated levels of mental, physical, and emotional overload. The health risks associated with perfectionism include higher levels of stress, sleep disturbances, inflammation throughout the body, weight loss or weight gain, higher levels of stress hormones where this interferes with quality of life, joy, and relationships. Due to the challenges brought about by unhealthy perfectionism, research investigators and our culture have centered their attention on understanding the underpinnings of the mindset of unhealthy perfectionism.

In the mind of a person who struggles with unhealthy perfectionism, nothing they do is ever good enough, and they inevitably come up short. In that mindset, a person never measures up, things are never done right or on time, and they live in a persistent state of fear, anxiety, depression, rumination, self-doubt, obsessing, and suffer physically, mentally, and emotionally. When a person fears making mistakes and has intense fears and anxiety about failing—at any level, small, large, or in between—they are often overly concerned with others' evaluation of them. Often, these individuals overcompensate, trying to be perfect but can never, ever measure up. An individual manifests chronic self-criticism which leads to self-doubt and constant questioning of their personal actions and decisions. There is a disconnect between their actual level of ability and what is perceived as good or something they can achieve. They overcompensate to live up to an imaginary expectation of themselves, overwork, are high achieving, highly focused on achievements, and yet feel continuously inadequate. Self-doubt can lead to low self-esteem and feeling like a fraud who must hide their true self because they cannot live up to their own or others' expectations.

Perfectionists drive themselves to exhaustion and self-harm; they may live in a state of perpetual fear, and that fear bleeds into chronic states of feeling anxious. This can have crippling consequences resulting in a complete inability to even begin a task or project. These individuals are at greater risk for anxiety, depression, OCD and incessant negative thoughts and concerns. An individual can become locked in negative self-talk and self-ridicule. Perfectionists stuck in this cycle of great concern about an outcome determined and measured by external sources but never satisfied can often appear self-indulgent, obsessed, and experience challenges in connecting with others and with social interactions.

Perfection Pressure Leads to Perfection Paralysis

Perfection is a state or object that is without defect, flawless. Paralysis is the loss of ability to move, think, or take any action of either mind or body. Combined, perfection paralysis happens when a person feels an overwhelming pressure to create a state that is perfect and disallows any possibility for error or mistake. The main drivers of emotion are fear and anxiety (anticipation of fear, imagining the worst of a scenario). Anxiety leads to stress in the mind and body and manifests as physical, mental, and emotional pain. For example, heaviness in the chest and difficulty breathing; thoughts and feelings of being overwhelmed, defeated, unattached, sad, and of always being behind.

Perfectionistic pressure related to perfectionistic concerns leads to serious consequences where one is paralyzed and unable to manage the anxieties and fears surrounding their strivings. A person is an ice sculpture, frozen in space and time, without the energy to move. Suffering from perfection pressure and perfection paralysis is a self-defeating cycle that hijacks confidence, motivation, disrupts completion of tasks, and leads to major stress that is manifested in the mind and body. A person suffering from perfection paralysis has major stress and feelings of being overwhelmed, exhaustion, detachment, anger, sadness, frustration, and is disconnected from their essence and being their authentic self. Aspects of unhealthy perfectionism are the consequences that include greater risk of mental health issues such as anxiety, depression, and obsessive-compulsive disorder, all of which can feed into the cycle of perfectionistic pressure and paralysis.

The neurobiological and physiological symptoms manifest in the brain and body where the fear circuit is cycling, which leads to prolonged feelings of anxiety. There are then shifts in the neurochemicals causing whole-body inflammation which leads to exhaustion, brain fog, and malaise. The mind is lost in a primal state of fear, unable to access thinking and higher cognitive processes like creativity, decision making, analysis, imagination, and fluidity. Finally the person ends up feeling defeated and unmotivated which leads to rigidity and the feeling of stuckness; they live in a loop of negative self-talk focused on failure and fear of making mistakes.

When they do not meet their standard of perfection and excellence they feel like a failure. They commonly have challenges where they procrastinate and are immobile, frozen, and caught in perfection purgatory. In some cases, the project or idea is never even started and exists only in their imagination. Feelings of failure are momentous due to the incomplete and so-called failure. In this cycle of perfection paralysis, emotions of fear, anxiety, guilt, and shame fuel experience of failure. A person is stuck in emotion. They are not truly in their essence and cannot share who they are.

For example, if a gifted/2e person continually works and feels they cannot express themselves at their level of ability because of the challenges associated with being gifted/2e, they will make mistakes and then place exaggerated negative judgment on themselves. They want to do their best, but the challenges of being gifted/2e get in the way, masking their greatness. As a result, they can inflict added pressure on themselves to strive for perfection. These individuals become risk averse, basically shut down, and do not try for fear they will never be successful. Often, they appear unmotivated and withdrawn. They live in an ice age of immobilization.

In perfection paralysis, the negativity bias is active and one is primed for suffering because of their focus on their pain identity. Too often we focus on the negative story, emotions, experiences, and processing of our environment and we forget the good. We miss the good. We are buried under a negativity avalanche, out of control, with unrealistic expectations of excellence.

Perfection paralysis is a common tendency when the overwhelming thought patterns of seeking perfection alter one's ability to begin, continue, and complete a task. An individual suffers the consequences through a cycle of an unfulfilled prophecy and lives in a story and thought pattern that does not meet reality. It is important to acknowledge feelings, stories, thoughts and stressors happening in the mind. Help the child or adult understand the stressors of perfectionism that lead to paralysis. Start small. It begins with breaking a thought pattern that is centered on imagined fear. Learn to scale the stressor related to perfectionism. Assigning a reasonable expectation helps build greater awareness between the imagined perfect and the reality of the imperfect. This can work in the mind to better decode the challenges and guide you to aim small, with intention, and revise your perfectionistic strivings. Know that these are goals and measures that are just approximations and not the limit or the ceiling. When mistakes are welcomed into the equation, then the fear of the unbound unlocks and you can begin to unfreeze and melt the ice, freeing yourself of your fears and anxieties.

To escape perfectionistic paralysis, we need to be comfortable with messiness and imperfection.

> *"Perfectionism is a mean, frozen form of idealism, while messes are the artist's true friend. What people somehow (inadvertently, I'm sure) forgot to mention when we were*

children was that we need to make messes in order to find out who we are and why we are here."

—Anne Lamott

Signs of Perfection Paralysis

○ Challenge with getting started

○ Challenge with time or completion

○ High level of self-doubt

○ Altered self-perception and low self-esteem relating to perfectionistic concerns and strivings

○ High risk for feelings of fear, shame, and anger

○ High risk for mental conditions of anxiety, depression, and obsessive-compulsive disorder

○ High risk for emotional outbursts and tantrums

○ Mental stuckness due to high-level strivings

○ Perfectionistic qualities that tend to interfere with relationships

Rewire the Mind and Build from the Imperfect

The balance and drive of nurturing healthy aspects of perfectionism are centered on detachment from the outcome, release of criticism related to mistakes and actions, ability to have a healthy response to "others'" expectations, self-expectations, quieting the mind and negative self-talk and understanding the difference between the imagined perfect and the reality of one's actual achievements. In the words of Margaret Atwood, "If I waited for perfection... I would never write a word."

The negative imagination can play a large role in what one can actually achieve and strive for when centering one's attention. Unpacking where the perfectionistic tendencies come from is the beginning of better identifying the underlying motivation, whether it be centered on one's individual striving versus one's drive based on others' expectations and/or their concerns related to their strivings. Focusing solely on doing their best so they can build an awareness of their reality and strivings, and where the two converge, is essential. Particularly, adjust the mindset, language, and feelings around perfectionism and high-level perfectionistic strivings to one of a detached attitude and behavior toward a perfect outcome. It is absolutely healthy to strive for high levels and it drives ambition and progress.

Perfectionism is a spectrum, and personal behaviors, mentalities, and mindsets related to strivings can be healthy for personal and societal growth and progress. By contrast, overidentification with the negatives is the source of our pain and concern. Perfectionism is multifaceted and includes behaviors, conditions, and thinking related to both positive and negative tendencies of perfections centered on strivings and concerns which lead to both healthy and unhealthy tendencies.

Best Practices for Supporting a Perfectionist

1. Work with them to set realistic expectations.

2. Help them identify their mental patterns and stories in relation to their perfectionistic tendencies and concerns.

3. Provide safety for them to share their feelings about their perfectionistic ambition and concerns.

4. Set up a safety net for them to fail. Allow them know it is more than okay to make mistakes.

5. Give them compassion when they struggle with perfectionism.

6. Train them to mentally engage in their positive imagination and outcomes.

7. Have patience and compassion, working through perfectionism is a process.

8. Teach them to complete a project rather than trying to make the project be perfect and therefore never done. Remind them that "Done is better than perfect."

9. Remove any parental expectations of perfectionism.

In truth, we will all make all kinds of mistakes, so many they are not even quantifiable. The beauty is that each mistake allows for learning, growing, and rebirthing, and gives rise to an individual becoming more aware of their special unique human condition.

We can rewire the mind for positivity circuitry. It is essential that we understand how to use the positive aspects of striving for perfectionism with detachment from concerns about the actual outcome of our strivings; that always trying our best is the optimal way of going about things.

My Mother Always Told Me, Try Your Best

In my earliest memories of my mother, she always said, "Nikki, try your best." Being a kid that was 2e and not knowing it, I had a grand imagination of how things *should* be, and that was perfect. Often, the expectation of what I built in my mind was far ahead of me in years and I felt that I came up short. I searched for the flaw, and engaged in a story that I was a failure. I was young and my brain, fresh and germinating, needed time for its very own botanical growth.

My mother, with her mirror neurons and her exceptional empathy, recognized my pain when I was stuck. She'd ask, "Nikki, did you try your best?" And that was it, I was always trying my best. I have, for as long as I can remember, put in the maximum, 100%, into everything I do. Even knowing I have tried my best, it is still an effort to let go of the negative self-talk and stories that circle around any perceived fault, failure, or setback on my part. I do believe that it is important to come back to one of my mother's earliest questions, *Did you try your best?* If the answer is yes, then I should move on. Really move on and let it go. The practice is to let go of the illusion of perfection and embrace imperfect. Let go. There is finite time in this earthly body and the more time we can live in our flow—among all the beautiful and messy imperfections—the better we are. That is living life. Human beings have their very own neuroindividuality, asynchronous mind and body, and we all arrive in our own spectacularly thorny botanical time.

The second lesson was from the wise one, Sam Christensen, where he saw this tiny misshapen woman-girl fighting with the devils of imperfection, and he taught me to orbit my thoughts in the universe of joy with this one simple question: "Was that fun?" He asked this every time I performed in his class. Every time, I responded, *yes, yes, yes!* I did have fun. Even though I'd stuck my neck and chest out so far that I teetered on the edge of a mountain cliff with a hundred-foot drop. Fun because it required my full attention, full presence of myself. Not even a drop of sweat trickling down my forehead could cause me to blink. I was having fun. Real fun. And Sam, with his Santa Claus smile, cradling this newborn little girl, told me, "You looked like you were having fun." We are here to share, share ourselves, as frightening as that seems, with all our demons and voices, we are gifts to one another. Ask yourself: *Are you having fun?* Living in your essence is fun, where you can embrace the flaws and flawless, the spectrum of imperfection. When you get past the fear and orbit your mind to try your best and have fun, that is freedom.

Depression, More Than Feeling Blue

According to NIMH, depression is the most common mental health challenge among the United States' population. Depression can take hold of anyone's life at any time, it does not discriminate. Depression is a condition that interferes with every aspect of life and is a serious condition that requires one to get immediate help. Depression falls into a number of mood disorders: persistent depressive disorder occurs when an individual has depression lasting longer than two years and episodes and symptoms can fluctuate; postpartum depression is a form of depression that some women experience after giving birth; psychotic depression is a form of depression that causes one to experience delusions and have hallucinations; and bipolar disorder episodes which can cause major symptoms of depression alternating with periods of elated mood known as mania. The symptoms vary and an individual may have one, all, or a combination of symptoms and the symptoms can fluctuate. "Symptoms and signs are persistent sad, anxious, or "empty" mood, feelings of hopelessness or pessimism, irritability, feelings of guilt, worthlessness, or helplessness, loss of interest or pleasure in hobbies and activities, decreased energy or fatigue, moving or talking more slowly, feeling restless or having trouble sitting still, difficulty concentrating, remembering, or making decisions, difficulty sleeping, early-morning awakening, or oversleeping, appetite and/or weight changes, thoughts of death or suicide, or suicide attempts, aches or pains, headaches, cramps, or digestive problems without a clear physical cause and/or that do not ease even with treatment."[67] Individuals may have a combination of symptoms that change over time. More recently, there is evidence that the gut microbiota is altered in individuals who experience major depression.[68] Depression affects the entire mind and body and consumes one's life. Depression usually develops in adulthood. But depression is identified in adolescents and children too.

Deception of Depression

Depression is insidious. For people suffering from depression joy is elusive. Depression is not only a general feeling of sadness or being down and out. It is a serious condition and needs attention. People suffering from depression cannot just get over it and move on. They need support, healing, and to discover the epicenter of their pain. It is estimated that 6.7% of the US population has had an episode of depression. That's 16.2 million Americans. Of that population, 63% describe their depression as a major hindrance in their life.[69] Depression can be debilitating. It is a serious condition.

One of the most tragic aspects of depression is suffering in silence. Lack of connection and social isolation is a major factor in depression. The pain areas in the brain for social isolation are triggered as physical pain.[70] Pain is activated and represented in the brain for both social and physical pain and are experienced without distinction. The difference is that when we see an individual with a physical aliment like a broken leg, we have a natural protective and generalized way to empathize with them by imagining the pain with the help of the empathy circuit and mirror neurons in our brain. But when an individual suffers from depression, it is masked, manifests from the great abyss, and may be hidden to us, leaving the person to suffer in isolation.

A recent study in *Nature* found that 36% of graduate students reported having depression, approximately six times the national average.[71] Why is depression escalated in graduate students? It is not clear whether it is due to the deep study of human existence, continued failure, persistence of feeling like an imposter, or striving for the impossible. In our recent study, conducted by Ruth Karpinski, we found that individuals with greater intelligence reported an increase in depression.[72] People with higher verbal IQ tend to worry and ruminate and have an association with more depression and anxiety. A more active and engaged mind may have the challenge with an imagination of more possibilities of the worst case, bad, and ugly, while that same mind can imagine a best outcome, good, and beauty. Being aware and tuning into the source of the depressed thoughts and how the imagination can play a role in depression. Understanding the relationship with the thoughts and storytelling around depression is the first step toward grounding a person struggling with depression.

More alarmingly, teen depression has been on the rise since 2005. It is hypothesized that our society is becoming more disconnected, and despite connections through technology we are missing in person real-time social interactions. More and more studies are pointing to the fact that addiction to screens, social media, and video games are on the rise. Is this leading us all to being so disconnected? Encouraging face-to-face connection is essential for wellness in our developing minds and really teaching kids healthy habits when engaging with social media.

The most common signs of depression are feelings of chronic sadness, depletion, or anxious mood, low energy, sleep disturbances, weight fluctuations, feelings of powerlessness, defeat, hopelessness, unworthiness, suicidal thoughts, physical pain, and gastrointestinal disturbances. An individual can have one or a combination of these symptoms. It is essential, if you or someone you know is experiencing any of these symptoms, that you or they get help. Depression can be treated with a number of therapies for healing, including talk therapy, meditation, and medications.

If you are dealing with depression, here are some strategies so you are not alone:

1. **Reach out to family and friends and share what you are experiencing**. People who care for you want to support and

lift you. When you share your pain with others, you give them a chance to embrace and care for you.

2. **Find a support group for your specific challenges and needs.** When you understand that other people encounter painful experiences, emotions, and situations in all walks of life, this aids you in not feeling alone. Here are websites for national support groups: http://www.mentalhealthamerica. net/find-support-groups http://www.pbs.org/inthebalance/ archives/whocares/resources.html

3. **Seek support from a professional.** Talk therapy is proven to be one of the best therapies for depression, anxiety, trauma, and mood disorders. Here is more information from National Institute of Mental Health (NIMH) to find the best approach for you: https://www.nimh.nih.gov/health/topics/psychother-apies/index.shtml

4. **Practice a loving-kindness meditation.** This cultivates your self-compassion.

5. **Write about your pain.** Studies show that writing about your pain has been proven to aid in healing and reduce suffering.[73]

6. **Connect with a crisis hotline.** If you are alone and feel that there is no one you can reach out to. https://suicideprevention lifeline.org

7. **Helpers need help, too.** If you are supporting others through a challenging time and need advice on the right words, join the Option B support group. https://optionb.org/groups

Bullied Brain

Anyone who tells a child that has been bullied to "develop thick skin," is wrong, dead wrong. A child that has been the victim of bullying suffers from trauma. Their brain processing, body, and physiology is altered. It is essential to express compassion for the child, listen to their experience, validate their feelings, and provide them with safety. Neuroscience and psychological research are now illuminating the detrimental effects bullying has on the emotional, physical, and mental health of a victim. Bullying is different than someone just being mean or making a mean comment. With greater social consciousness of bullying, and social media as new platforms for communication, bullying is at the forefront of our societal fabric. The distinction between whether someone is simply being mean, versus inflicting abuse and bullying is a fine line. Bullying is defined as recurrent and intentional actions, words, or behaviors by an individual or group to harm another person or group.[74] Often there is a power dynamic at play where the abuser has power over the victim. Biff Tanner, in the film *Back to the Future,* is a classic example of a bully. He and his gang cause harm verbally and physically and intimidate their classmates to obtain power and dominance to get what he wants, for example, having George McFly do his homework as Biff steers insults his way and slaps him around.[75]

Victims often cave in due to fear and intimidation. They feel powerless and carry the scars of trauma and emotional wreckage. The victim of a bully lives in a persistent state of anxiety and fear with elevated cortisol, and chronic inflammation, which alters social interactions and interferes with relationships. Victims become a shell of themselves, masking who they are. They feel unnoticed, withdraw socially, and hide. When a bullying victim socially withdraws, their negative self-perception increases, causing low self-esteem and, in many cases, depression. Biological changes occur in the brain and bodies of bullied victims, which may be the genesis of many of their behavioral, mental, and emotional challenges.

Studies show that there are devastating consequences of bullying for the mind, body, mental, and physical well-being. The principal brain and mental shifts for a victim of bullying include chronic stress that triggers trauma networks and changes circuitry in the brain, where the brain is primed for heightened levels of anxiety. A victim of bullying lives in a constant state of fear leading to alterations in brain and body biochemistry with elevated levels of cortisol, the response to stress hormone. Both boys and girls who are victims of chronic bullying have elevated levels of cortisol surging in their body.[76] High levels of cortisol circulating in the blood can affect homeostatic balance for immune response, increase inflammation throughout the body and brain, and cause degeneration of neurons (kill brain cells), which alter brain networks and functioning. All this leads to a disruption in learning and memory, harming the ability to form new memories in the area of the brain known as the hippocampus.

In a study looking at the effects of bullying on learning and memory, teens who were bullied performed lower on memory tests compared to non-bullied peers.[77] It is conceivable that the elevated levels of cortisol in the bullied teens plays a distinct role in the disruption of forming new memories. Bullied victims' brains and bodies are in a primal state flooded with emotions of shame, fear, and anxiety. Physiologically, the body is overtaxed due to the stress of worry, which causes inflammation and a general feeling of malaise. Behaviorally they are in a mode of self-defense and self-preservation where their attentional focus is to seek refuge and safety. In their heightened stress level and alertness, victims focus on their present surroundings and potential dangers from the bullies, which interferes with learning new information that does relate to their immediate safety. And, when the mind is spinning and ruminating in a trauma circuit, the higher centers of the brain for cognition and intellectual processing, such as the frontal cortex, are muted and interfere with processing new information. A bullied victim's brain power, attention, and all their resources are centered on protecting themselves from insults and navigating in an unsafe environment.

On top of that, elevated levels of cortisol in the brain and body disrupt biochemical changes and block attention and working memory, and also alter brain function and information processing. In effect, their higher processing brain and body are temporarily shut down disrupting their cognitive and thinking abilities. Behaviorally, these children appear to be tuned out, in a daze, and disengaged because they are navigating emotions of shame, fear, and anxiety. Often victims of bullying appear meek, antisocial, and quiet in in their effort to hide and veil themselves from future attacks. In the classroom, at home, and in life, they may be living in a constant state of fear, where they are shell-shocked and appear withdrawn, emotionally hollow, and devoid of social and personal engagement. This lack of engagement disrupts their self-image and causes a massive blow to their self-esteem. A victim of bullying has a greater risk for mood disorders and mental health conditions.

Teens faced with continuous bullying have alterations in their brain circuitry, which puts them at a greater risk for mental health issues like anxiety and depression. Peer victimization during adolescence directly impacts mental health and functioning by changing brain wiring during critical developmental stages, causing anatomy and circuitry for emotional processing to be altered, wiring maladaptive networks and patterning. A 2018 study by Erin Burke Quinlan and her team of researchers reviewed questionnaires on bullying and acquired brain maps of 682 adolescents aged 14 to 19 to decipher how bullying altered brain anatomy.[78] Thirty-six of the 682 teens experienced continuous bullying. In the brains of bullied victims there were reductions in the caudate and putamen, and victims reported increased levels of anxiety and depression. The caudate and putamen are brain areas involved in a number of activities and behaviors such as attention, motivation, reward, conditioning, and emotional understanding. This could be an explanation of why individuals who are bullied have challenges with working memory due to the reductions in both the caudate and putamen—circuitry essential for memory formation. Additionally, the attentional shift to seeking safety and refuge from unsafe encounters with bullies may lead to greater emotional dysregulation. Because bullied victims experience more fear, anxiety, and depression.

The famous Stanford Prison Experiment explored the impact of abuse and power dynamics on randomly selected "prisoners" and "guards" in an experimental prison setting, where "prisoners" experienced mental suffering due to negative reinforcement from the "guards."[78] Despite its questionable ethics, this experiment exposed the mental, physical, and emotional distress that results from a perceived power dominance dynamic, highlighting the loss of freedom, loss of voice, and the painful experience of disempowerment, i.e., the heart of bullying. In this dynamic, participants who were the guards had domineering behaviors and mentally and verbally abused prisoners. The power dominance and struggle for the prisoners turned into devastating consequences where one of the experimental prisoners called the experiment off due to the mental and emotional dysregulation they experienced being a powerless prisoner.

This highlights that in a short amount of time, just 12 hours, individuals are at risk for disordered mental and emotional regulation when exposed to verbal and emotional abuse centered on disempowerment. And when an individual is subjected to powerlessness and social distress they suffer emotional and mental pain. Importantly, this study was conducted with students who had no known previous mental health concerns demonstrating that disempowerment directly affects mental and emotional processing.

In a study where scientists explored the biochemical mechanisms for aggression and power dynamics in hamsters, subjects of aggression exhibited stress and alterations in neurotransmitters.[80] Notably, vasopressin, a hormone essential for mate and infant pair bonding, was altered in the hamsters who had suffered from the aggression. Vasopressin is known as the trust molecule. An alteration in the neurobiochemistry of trust has consequences for brain, body, emotional, and mental development. This revealed that subjects targeted with chronic aggression by litter mates have differences in their stress level and trust neurochemicals that interferes with pair bonding, socialization, and navigating in their environment. It also pointed to the biochemical consequences of bullying that lead to differences in brain, behavior, and emotional processing that disrupt the development of trust circuitry, leading to long-term ramifications that induce maladaptive behaviors and emotional functioning related to stress and trust.

Sibling bullying is no joke. A study finds that children who are bullied at home are three times more likely to develop mental illnesses like depression and engage in self-harm.[81] In a longitudinal study of 3600 children, parents were surveyed about bullying in the home and the mental health of their children. Researchers found that children who had experienced bullying from siblings had increased incidents of mental health issues. Bullying and trauma in early social relationships dictate whether a person develops mental health complications throughout life which demonstrates that in the home, siblings shape each other's mental health. Safety at home is required for the natural balance of emotional and mental health development. Parents, educators and health care professionals must be aware of long-term consequences of bullying in the home; it is a form of trauma and stress that can cause the victim of bullying considerable risk for mental health issues throughout life.

Individuals who experience bullying have physiological and physical changes in the body that shift mental, physical, and emotional health and well-being. These changes in behavior and brain wiring incline an individual to be more prone to maladaptive patterns and behaviors. Chronic bullying leads to acute stress where individuals are at a greater risk for conditions such as anxiety and depression. Individuals who are bullied early in life have increased incidents in activating trauma circuits in the brain which set in motion hormonal, biochemical, and epigenetic events that reorganize the brain and body's response to fear and stress. This reshapes emotional processing, interferes with learning, and derails a person's self-image and esteem.

Negative reinforcement and trauma interfere with learning, neurogenesis, and neural plasticity. Bullying has detrimental effects on the emotional, physical, and mental health of victims. Victims of trauma and bullying may acquire maladaptive behaviors and coping strategies. Persistent fear intensifies stress hormones, distrust, and mental illness where victims spiral into a deepening sense of suffering and alienation.

Social isolation and exclusion alter brain circuitry, functioning, and behavior. Social isolation is common in mental health disorders like depression and anxiety. The experience of social isolation activates the pain centers in the brain—the same areas in the brain associated with physical pain.[82] Pain, whatever the source, triggers a psychological and physiological response to retreat and, as a result, the individual becomes even more socially isolated. Bullied victims suffer isolation from a loss of belonging in society. Victims can experience separation from family, friends, and communities.

"No one sits alone" is the founding principle for the phone app *Sit With Us*. Natalie Hampton, a high school student, developed this app to provide connection for individuals suffering from social isolation. Natalie had been a victim of violent and verbal peer bullying in her high school. She describes in her TEDex talk how her classmates socially isolated her to the point that she ate lunch alone every day. A girl in her class threatened her life with a pair of scissors. That was when she left her school. Natalie describes that she suffered a great deal of trauma but did not verbalize her suffering to her parents or teachers. The school staff and faculty often turned a blind eye, adding insult to the injury. Often victims of bullying internalize the abuse and believe they are deserving of mistreatment. Frozen in suffering, many victims silently absorb the abuse and pain. Her suffering sparked a determination in her that that no one, not one person, suffer the consequences of bullying as she did. Her app, *Sit With Us,* has a founding principle that you take an oath to never allow someone to sit alone during lunch. Users of the app login and report whether they are sitting alone and other users in the vicinity invite them to join them for lunch. It is a win-win where one day a person can be sitting alone and find a group or person to have lunch with and another day that same person can be the one who extends an invitation to someone else so that no one sits alone. The app now has over 100,000 subscribers and is being used in eight different countries. Natalie Hampton was named by *People* magazine as one of the 25 most influential women of 2017. She is a light who speaks and spreads brightness through all the shadows and suffering. She has found a way to guide future generations to combat bullying before it even begins.

It is essential that we work to teach, train, and reduce bullying before the damage occurs. Though education, safety, trust, and communication, we can begin to protect the natural mental, emotional, physical, and behavioral development of children who are free from oppression of the psychological, physiological, and physical consequences of bullying. Children need guidance to thrive and be free to develop safely at home, in school, and in their community. It is time we stand together and stop bullying before it begins. It is time we teach children how to communicate with compassion and respect. It is time we are a united voice that stands up to bullies. It is time that no one suffer alone and we end the harmful effects on the brains of bullying victims.

A Smile can Lift the Veil of Social Isolation

In college, I read an article in the *San Francisco Chronicle* that forever changed the way I interact with humanity. If I could tell the author thank you a million times I would, but sadly I don't know the author and the article clipping is packed away somewhere. The reporter told the story of a man who committed suicide by jumping off the Golden Gate Bridge. Stunningly, in the suicide note the man left, he said that his note would not be found at all if at least one person smiled at him as he walked to the Golden Gate Bridge. The man lived a mile and a half away from the bridge. To give you an idea, the entire city of San Francisco is seven miles across, and has a population of 896,047 people (as of August 2020), the 4th largest population of any city in California.

This story hit me. This took place in the time before cell phones, social media, and our twenty-four-hour connectedness—a time when we could be perhaps more in tune and present. That was not the case for the man in this story; he felt so socially isolated he took his life. In his mind there was a huge gap. He was disconnected from himself, from others, from life. Often people who suffer from social isolation feel as if they live at the edges of existence and fitting in and connecting with others is a challenge.

Social isolation and exclusion are the greatest components for mental health disorders such as depression and anxiety. Both anxiety and depression can fuel and intensify social isolation. The feelings of loneliness spiral and worsen as the individual reacts by further closing themself off from family, friends, and their community. Commonly, people do not talk about their feelings of social isolation, depression, and anxiety. People suffer behind a veil of silence and pain.

Social isolation feels like pain in the brain and when we are in pain we have a psychological and physiological response to retreat and become even more socially isolated. When the root of the pain is not addressed an individual is at greater risk for mental, physical, social, and emotional damage.

In the original article, the man who committed suicide was looking for a smile, a connection. A place to feel rooted in humanity and in his existence. He wanted not to feel alone. Mostly, people want to be told that they are okay. Just okay. That in all of the shadow and light of a person, it is universal to our nature that we just want to hear we are okay. I tell you this. You are okay. You are more than okay.

I know that the cure for mental illness is greater than just a smile shared with a stranger, but a smile could be the difference that sparks a person to get the help they need. Ever since reading that article in college, I smile at strangers. And I get all sorts of reactions, some good, some not so much. But, I smile anyway. For someone, a smile tells them you are okay and you are here. If you can find be the bridge that lets someone know they are not alone, that is a gift.

When we mirror one another's behavior, we activate mirror neurons in our brains and model one another. A mirror of a smile in the brain generates a smile within, a connection, and a pulse of neurons firing electrical signals. You radiate light and they radiate the light back. A mirror lets us know we are part of something bigger than we can ever imagine. And a simple reminder that life begins with a smile.

The Golden Equation

I learned an equation in a meditation class that transformed my relationship with pain and suffering. Originally the principal equation stems from the Four Noble Truths, where the first noble truth identifies and acknowledges the presence of suffering, the second noble truth searches for the cause of suffering, the third is the end of suffering (or that all suffering is finite), and the fourth is the process that ends suffering.[83] Shinzen Young, an author of many books and dharma teacher, summarizes the Four Noble Truths into an equation: Suffering = Pain x Resistance.[84] One does not reject the existence of pain but also does not add resistance to the pain. The equation points out that when we add resistance to the pain we amplify our suffering.

Where has this equation been all my life? Pain in life is inevitable. All humans experience pain. It may be physical, something as simple as stubbing your toe, or emotional, such as the pain of losing someone you love, of being abused or oppressed, feeling injustice, violence, voicelessness, or powerlessness. Emotional pain and physical pain activate the same brain regions, insular cortex and anterior cingulate cortex, buried in the frontal lobe. When we feel pain, regardless of the source, it has same neural pathway in our brain. The neural pathway has evolved to protect us from danger. What we do with the information matters and informs how we can access our higher wisdom and learn to acknowledge and live with the pain. Shinzen Young's equation brought to light my own patterns and habits of holding onto suffering and showed me how I can identify my attachment to my suffering and reframe my patterns and thinking related to my pain.

According to the equation, our resistance to pain directly affects our suffering. The more we resist, according to the equation, the more we suffer. When we loosen our resistance to pain our actual suffering decreases. For example, say we have a negative emotion such as anger or sadness and we force ourselves to repress it. What happens to our physical, mental, and emotional body? The emotion is carried in our thoughts, body, and mind. Repressing an emotion does not make it go away. We carry an underlying feeling of anger or sadness in all that we do. Repressing the emotion may cause us to act in ways that are not authentic to our true being.

Now, what happens if we acknowledge we are experiencing anger or sadness and say, YES, I acknowledge I am experiencing anger, sadness, fear? We gain insight and tune into our being. Even though the emotion may remain, our relationship to the emotion changes. We begin to discover the origin of the emotion. We gain knowledge about the source of the pain. When we define the source of our emotion, we can release our resistance and transform our relationship with suffering. We can work with our resistance to lessen its grip and release into what actually is by acknowledging our pain, emotions, and fears. This in turn frees us of the burden of suffering by identifying our human limits. A moment of grace and humility arises for what actually is.

Acknowledging our emotions, mental states, and thought patterns ignites our understanding of our emotionality, the stories we tell ourselves, the patterns and attachments of our pain, and our ability to release our attachments and move through our suffering in a balanced manner. As the poet Rumi says, "The wound is the place where the Light enters you." This understanding of the origin of suffering is the first step to find healing and peace in times of great mental and emotional turbulence. Know that you have the power to ease your suffering by releasing your resistance to pain. Whether that is a story you tell yourself, emotional avoidance or attachment, or the denial of pain, you have all that you need inside of you to ride the waves and keep your balance through a raging storm. Allow the light and the lesson to come into you. Although there is pain, realize that you are stronger than you will ever know.

Neurohack Attitude of Gratitude

Practicing gratitude is a rapid reboot for your mood and state of mind. Be thankful. It's good for your brain, body, health, and for everyone around you. In our emotional spectrum, gratitude lasts five hours and can change your mind and thinking, so why not rewire your mind to take in the good? Here are some simple reasons to start giving thanks and rewire your mind toward the good.[85]

Researchers found that keeping a daily gratitude journal increases your positive outlook on life.[86] Additionally, this cultivates an attitude of abundance rather than lack, so you are able to see more of what you have rather than focusing on what you perceive as missing in your life. This simple life hack of gratitude raises your level of happiness.

Studies show that practicing gratitude releases positive neuro-chemicals, like dopamine, and engages the reward system in the brain.[87] Your attitude of gratitude builds long-lasting reward circuits that are coupled with positive behavior and thought patterns developed through meaning and intention. The simple act of gratitude strengthens positive brain circuits, allowing for greater brain power and prosperity.

Engaging in gratitude has major health benefits like lessening symptoms of depression and anxiety, reducing heart rate, as well as decreasing physical ailments and reducing physical pain.[88] This highlights how a positive thought process actually improves your physical and mental health. Giving thanks can actually increase your longevity!

Gratitude builds positive relationships with people around you and enhances prosocial behavior.[89] Because the act of gratitude recognizes goodness within and outside yourself, whether it is as simple as someone opening a door for you, or your spouse making dinner, your mind is opened to compassion for others by magnifying your behavior to be giving and altruistic. Build the practice of paying it forward. People with more gratitude have more positive social and family relationships.

Gratitude is a building block for an optimistic attitude. A person who sees light at the end of the tunnel, or a glass half full, has a more optimistic outlook and is grateful. An optimistic attitude is correlated with meaningfulness, greater social bonds, and longevity.

My words of gratitude: thank you, Mom, for teaching me to have courage; thank you Dad, for supporting me to do what I love; Spencer, thank you for making me laugh and see the light; Billy, thank you for your endless devotion; Coco and Star, my spirit animals, thank you.

Thank you, dear reader, for catching me on the other side of the page.

"If the only prayer you ever say in your entire life
is thank you, it will be enough."

—Meister Eckhart

Dear Original,

You are misunderstood, to say the least. You are the odd one. The underdog. The other. Made of things to make bullying easy. The bookworm. The oversensitive zealous one. You are too sensitive, take things too much to heart. Too emotional and take everything way too seriously. You are neglected. You are alone. Alien. Quirky. Last one to be picked. Refuge for you is to hide. You hide all the time, casting shadow on your true existence. On your true nature. Guard your heart with chicken wire and torches. You recoil from violence. You are alone sitting at the lunch table. Laughed at. Picked on. Threatened. Devoured. You are everything they wish to be. They are afraid. Tell us your sorrows. Share your stories of violence, your stories of neglect, squashing. Remember this, you have more than every right to exist. You are like a tree, glorious, weathered, changing with the seasons. Tree of the land, trunk filled with bone and osteoclasts, roots of the under gods and branches and leaves reaching for the sun's rays. Always reach. Take your space like a tree. You are valid. You are glorious. You are safe now. Show us your beauty. You are free from the violence and neglect. We see you, we hear you, we feel you. We are not afraid. Grow your branches, the rings of life in your trunk under the starlit sky.

Yours forever in the quiet of the wind,

Quaking Aspen

CHAPTER 6:

The Deconstructed Mind of Attention

Assembling the Puzzle Pieces of Attention

Attention is one of the main ways we can control our mind's plasticity and growth. How, what, when, and with whom we focus our attention builds our mind, temperament, and mindset. Our attention and awareness directly impact how we interpret the world. Attention and tuning in to the present moment are not as simple as we make it out to seem, though. Attention is complicated because there are numerous conflicting pieces melding together. For example, we have the current conditioning of our mind and maturation, which is filled with our stories and memories, which are continuously evolving. As we learned, thoughts flow like a river with up to 60,000 thoughts a day.[1] From nanosecond to nanosecond we perceive our environment filled with conflicting information where we need to weed out unnecessary information. On top of it, our emotional valence contributes to our running thoughts, stories and responses to our environment where we need to decipher the best way to maintain our focus. The mind can slowly be deconstructed as our observation shifts from the most arousing stimuli that captivates our attention. Attention is braided into the fabric of our level of safety where we survey our surroundings as we climb the ladder of security.

When an individual experiences elevated processing in any domain, such as physical, mental, sensory, or emotional, that can cause infinite attentional shifts. Some unique minds have the ability to hold many thoughts, processing, and analyses at once, where their attentional focus and processing are different than the norm. Especially if one has differential wiring, their attention follows uncharted paths of the psyche, where the possibilities are endless.

Attention is our ability to focus our mind on specific information while accessing what information is relevant or is not. For purposes of this discussion, we will consider our processing of our attention as divided into six main styles[2]:

○ *Focused*—the ability to center one's mind and respond directly to a single input, such as a sensory, intellectual, physical, emotional, or social stimulus. Listening to Queen's "Bohemian Rhapsody" is an example of focused attention. "Bohemian Rhapsody" is an incredible, iconic song to focus your mind with rich and complex musical arrangements.

○ *Sustained*—this is the ability to continuously focus on a single task without distraction, like a child who plays LEGO for hours with no interruption, building imaginary objects, kingdoms, universes. LEGO provided endless entertainment, sustained attention, and opened imagination for my son. Without LEGO, I'm not sure this book would have been written.

○ *Selective*—the ability to focus one's attention on a single area with many simultaneous environmental distractions and the ability to tune them out. For example, this can be where a child in the classroom ignores the flickering bright lights, the noise of their teacher typing on their keyboard, the tapping of their neighbor's pencil on their desk, and can maintain selective attention on filling in their U.S. history facts sheet.

○ *Alternating*—this is the ability to shift one's attention between different cognitive tasks. Driving through Los Angeles requires alternating attention where you are switching your focus from Waze directions, the road ahead where you are suddenly cut off by another car, potholes in the road, changing traffic signals, lane changes, and traffic flow.

Alternating attention is what allows you to safely arrive at your destination.

○ *Divided*—this is the ability to process two types of information simultaneously, often referred to as multitasking. Divided attention is, for example, when one can listen to music and write at the same time. Their brain is processing different kinds of information at the same time. Some individuals have the gift to multitask and in other people multitasking can be nurtured through practice and maturation.

○ *Social*—the mode of attention that centers on socially relevant information includes facial cues, gaze direction, and microexpressions. An example of social attention is how one is tuned into the experience of another individual. For example, if someone falls and expresses pain and the observer experiences empathy for the individual who fell. That felt, sympathetic pain is centered in humans' mirror neuron systems.[3]

So how does this all play out in life and in the classroom? Attention is messy, tricky, sticky, and unpredictable with all the competing factors, asynchronous development, attention hogs, and different modes of attention. Throughout a person's life, one can experiment with the different styles of attention in order to identify the proper mode of attention that will match the cognitive task at hand. Different actions require different styles of attention. For example, while you are out to dinner with friends and telling a story about your trek in Nepal, and how your entire group was attacked by leeches, you want the social attention working in your listeners' brains to allow them to alternate between listening to your story and noticing what's being offered on the dessert tray.

Teachers have their work cut out for them when it comes to capturing the attention of a class packed with a myriad of individuals. Never mind that each student is going through their very own asynchronous brain and body development, coming into their own on their own botanical timeline. In some people, their attention networks develop differently with alternative brain wiring that produces unfamiliar attention styles and out of the ordinary behaviors. As we know, the frontal cortex develops and matures into our midlife and is the motherlode for all styles of attention.[4]

The heavy lifting of our brain processing happens in our frontal cortex, which is crucial to our attention, focus, and executive functioning. It is the control center for saliency in our decision making, regulates our emotionality, guides our motivation, centers our focus for task completion, allows for reward and incentive, is essential for our working memory, and holds the upper and lower bounds of our cognitive load. Often our executive functioning efforts revolve on cognitive and emotional control where actions and behaviors are executed in response to one's surroundings. Executive functioning is influenced by one's ability to manage their cognitive load (how much brain power is being used for a task) and is bound by one's working memory. The process of storing temporary information in the present moment is reliant on working memory, for example, storing a five-item grocery list for the ingredients for apple pie: apples, brown sugar, nutmeg, ginger, and pie crust. Cognitive load is defined as the quantity of mental energy being utilized by working memory while performing a task, much like getting all the ingredients. As you walk the isles of the grocery store collecting the five items, the cognitive load is the amount of mental energy your mind uses to stay on task and to accurately collect all the ingredients for apple pie. You can't make apple pie without the apples. For some people, walking through the store collecting items is a breeze while for others the lights, smells, temperature, items in the aisles, provide many mental and attentional shifts and collecting all the ingredients for the apple pie becomes taxing, even overwhelming.

Because of our neuroindividuality, each of us has our very own set points for our working memory, cognitive load, and the ability of our brain to manipulate information in the past, present, and future. Attention for each person is highly preferential due to their genetic predisposition, level of nurturing, experience, acquired knowledge, motivation, emotional processing, mental flexibility, adaptability within their environment, and their internal states.

Information overload is another component to our attentional shift and regulation, so that each of us has a different ability to process information to a point where our cognitive ability is maxed out. In some environments or experiences, working memory can be over-taxed, causing a mental tune out, where we are dazed and confused. In other instances, attentional shifts can ignite overexcitabilities, where the brain, body, and mind are in overdrive and we are wired with all cylinders firing. Think for a moment about a child who has insisted on remaining awake an hour past their bedtime. The mind and body compensate for tiredness, where the body is given a nice dose of noradrenaline to remain awake, causing the child to be wired with a surge of energy rather than sleepiness. On another day, the same child can be taxed out completely an hour before their bedtime, too exhausted to even brush their teeth, cranky and highly emotional. Our thoughts, emotions, and senses go where our brain flows with our attention, behaviors, and actions. If we are drained, then our mind cannot function at its highest ability, causing us to have greater challenges with our attention, cognition, actions, and behaviors. We can be out of sync with our surroundings.

Attention is deeply rooted in our memory skills, and particularly, executive functioning is highly reliant on the ability of our senses to take in the environment, our working memory, and long-term memory for reference. There are three modes of memory—sense memory, working memory, and long-term memory. Our *sense memory* is where we build memories through our sensory perception and encompass mind-body information processing. An example of sense memory is to visualize walking through the grocery store to process seeing the aisles for the apple pie ingredients. Our *working memory* (short-term memory) is essential to our attention and is constricted to our individual cognitive load ceiling. Our working memory is the memory centered on the list of ingredients needed for the apple pie. It lasts 18-30 seconds. Do you remember the list of ingredients for an apple pie? That is your working memory and your sense memory working in synchrony. Let's test your memory, name them in your head. The ingredients are apples, brown sugar, nutmeg, ginger, and pie crust. *Long-term memory* is the memory in which we store our autobiographical memories and is the hub of our knowledge, using sense memory and working memory to access the information, like a personal memory of smelling your grandmother's brown sugar apple on Christmas morning. Long-term memory can last for minutes, hours, days, years, and through our lifetime. When attention and memory are in sync, executive functioning is at its peak. When they are out of sync, executive functioning may be at its limit and a person may express more unconventional behaviors and thinking. Essentially, we need to have an open mind and be aware that because of our uniqueness there are many ways that individuals process information. The more engaged someone is with the material, activity, and learning, the greater positive neural plasticity matures with attention and memory. When a person is not engaged with the activity or material, their attention will wane and they may look for outlets to occupy their cognitive, emotional, physical, sensorial, and imaginative desires and interests. We need to develop and find positive solutions and practices where attention, imagination, and the entire person is in synchrony to flourish in all aspects of their life.

Where does the line of attention, inattention, and daydreaming flow? And what are the divisions? Or is it in fact that these intersect one another, orbiting in our life where it is dependent on our situation, attentional type, task, our focus, and awareness? Attention and focus are highly dependent on our very own biorhythms, ways of perceiving our environment, our particular brain processing and behavioral patterns, attentional histories, and being in the world. What we deem as acceptable, unacceptable, or okay in our society for attentional focus is dependent on our lives, our circumstances, and our attention. We need ways in which neurodiverse attentional differences are developed, trained, nurtured and encouraged for people to reach their boundless potential. Different attentional styles provide insights for how and where we can focus to develop the natural gifts and talents a person has to offer. Attentional set points are great guides for helping a person grow naturally into their essence and ways to show them for greater meaning. First, we have to understand the different set points and identifications for attention variances to better guide our children and adults with differential attentional processing, original thinking, and out-of-the-box behaviors.

Mysterious Mind of ADHD and ADD

In recent years ADHD diagnoses have been on the rise. Reports by the Center for Disease Control (CDC) state that 9.4% of children ranging from 2 to 17 years have been diagnosed with ADHD. Boys are more than twice as likely to be diagnosed with ADHD compared to girls, with 12.9% boys and 5.6% of girls identified.[5] Common signs of ADHD include challenges paying attention, verbal and physical hyperactivity, and difficulty with impulse control. Inattentive-type ADHD presents as being "spaced out"; these individuals have challenges paying attention to a specific form of directed attention. They are the daydreamers. Hyperactive individuals need to be constantly moving and speak rapidly. These are your movers, talkers, and shakers. These are the ones who are full of unbounded imagination, your firecrackers. For ADHD, many of these cognitive processes are hardwired and controlled by the frontal cortex woven with the different attentional styles and bounded by one's personal set points for cognitive load and working memory.

Common signs and behaviors of ADD/ADHD
Inattention

- Misses the fine details, such as putting their name and date on their homework

- Difficulty with focused attention for long periods of time

- Appears to be daydreaming, caught up in their imagination

- Easily shifts between attentional modes and gets sidetracked

- Misplaces and loses items such as homework, reading glasses, keys, earbuds, wallets

- Attention appears to others as unfocused and as mind wandering

- Daily routines and activities fall off the radar

Hyperactivity and Impulse Control

- O Constantly moving
- O Talks rapidly
- O Fidgets and has trouble sitting still (squirms a lot)
- O High energy, runs, moves climbs; constantly in motion
- O Has difficulty waiting their turn
- O Interrupts and blurts out
- O Finishes people's sentences

Children diagnosed with ADHD are often set up for living in a world in which they are required to check the box and, nine times out of ten, they will not. We need to change the paradigm so they are not forced into a standard of living within a box but rather are encouraged to use their creative thinking to find solutions which will set them up to strive and thrive at being exactly who they actually are. People with ADHD are out-of-the-box thinkers and have more unconventional behaviors with more twist and turns. ADHD identification is no longer a diagnosis of doom but rather an identification of multipotentiality. Mysteries of the ADHD mind center on different brain wiring, development, and maturation of the brain, and variations in neurotransmitters that help regulate attention, motivation, and reward processing. The way we teach and interact with an ADHD person requires full attention on learning how to revise our traditional teaching to meet their mind. I am not saying that teachers need to live in a classroom overrun with mayhem and chaos. Classes need structure and order. Rather, we should break through old educational patterns that do not meet the attention of an ADHD person and find ways to engage their uniquely wired mind. Science reveals that the ADHD mind is its own land of possibility with differential maturation and processing.

In an ADHD person, the brain takes more time to mature in some key regions, particularly the prefrontal cortex, the area for executive functioning.[6] The prefrontal cortex is the master center for attention, emotional processing, planning, motivation, impulse control, and reward and is the core brain area that has differential development in ADHD. These differences in brain development in

ADHD people are seen in as early as preschool age children.[7] More recently, researchers discovered that there are delays in brain maturation in the amygdala, the control center for emotions and the first order processor of instinctive emotions.[8]

By contrast, in ADHD the area for motor processing and movement tends to develop more rapidly than normal, and is divergent from the delays in maturation.[9] For motor processing there tends to be a decrease in inhibition in the motor cortex that parallels the hyperactive behaviors seen in ADHD.[10] In pictures of an ADHD brain, it is asynchronous. Due to inattention, hyperactivity, or impulsivity, an ADHD brain is out of sync with developmental milestones and expectations. ADHD people literally have differential developmental baselines that account for their varying behaviors and their unbound attention shifts. ADHD persons need more time for their brains to mature to catch up with cognitive abilities. Fundamentally, individuals with ADHD meet developmental milestones out of synchrony. Due to their differential brain development, standard measures are not appropriate for their abilities and true capacity. ADHD brains develop is on their own timeline. They may appear all over the place and can change from day to day.

One of the earliest studies measuring cortical thickness in children with ADHD showed the key player in executive functioning, the frontal cortex, had delayed development in children with ADHD. But, their frontal cortex thickness caught up to their peers in their teen years.[11] This highlights that development is differential and asynchronous in children who have ADHD; they need more time for their behaviors relating to controlling their attention, inattention, activity and impulsivity to mature. Their timeline is individual and perhaps our practices and strategies for teaching ADHD people need to be revised to meet their developmental needs. An integral piece of the puzzle is that the increase in the cortical thickness in ADHD adolescents in their teen years allows for marked improvement in their cognitive abilities related to ADHD. These results highlight the value of understanding how neurodevelopment of the brain is asynchronous across neuroindividuals and that people with ADHD have unique brain growth and patterns that mask their true abilities and potential. In ADHD people, their particular brain development catches up with their peers in their teen years showing a clear pattern for a differential timeline. We need to change our measures for ADHD people's development because their personal timeline is different, and relates to the genetics of their brain maturation, neurotransmitter systems development, and behavioral practices and teachings to ensure positive neurodevelopment.

People with ADHD have differences in their neurotransmitter systems and the brain development related to their neurotransmitter systems. Neurotransmitters are the way that brain cells communicate with each other. Alterations and variances in the neurotransmitter systems can create changes in receptivity to stimuli, attention, brain processing, and behavior. In an early study to understand the relationship between the brain development and neurotransmitter systems, scientists found that individuals with ADHD had alterations in the gene responsible for dopamine function.[12] The group found that brain regions that were most influenced by the different genotype for the dopamine receptor were the frontal and parietal cortices where both of these brain areas are delayed in development in children with ADHD. Dopamine is the jack-of-all-trades when it comes to a neurotransmitter function. Dopamine is essential for working memory, executive functioning, motivation, decision making, attention, sleep-wake cycle, reward, and impulse control. Fundamentally, these studies provide the evidence that people with ADHD have differential brain wiring, patterns of development, and unique set points for receptivity and processing that lead to idiosyncratic behaviors. These differences in brain development are at the core of the one-of-a-kind way in which ADHD people explore the world.

Impulse control is highly related to frontal cortex wiring, processing related to inhibition, excitation, and the neurotransmitter systems in the frontal cortex that provide for cellular communication. Neurotransmitters like dopamine and norepinephrine have differential expression in ADHD persons. Alterations in norepinephrine neurotransmitter systems can cause a hyperarousal state, where the person's system is hypervigilant, on overdrive, causing them to be continuously aware of their environment and take in their surroundings with an elevated receptivity that relates to greater attentional shifts. Because their mind-body receptivity is in overdrive, their imagination runs free as it considers all the responses to their environment and has greater physicality in relation to their motor output, meaning their system is primed to move in case there is any danger. Specifically, children with ADHD have greater environmental perception that shifts their attention into many different modes where the required attention in the classroom does not meet their baseline level of interest for attention. For a kid with ADHD external stimuli are more interesting. Engaging within their own mind and thinking about the inner workings of many systems captures their imagination.

There are several key considerations in addressing concerns about attention and inattention in a person with ADHD. The first concern is identifying whether the child is bored. Not any child or adult's attention will focus if they are bored, they will lose interest and will automatically tune out the information and wander into the land of their imagination. When it comes to inattention, we need to address the internal imagination of persons with ADHD, where it may appear they are not paying attention when they are in their imagination. When a person is wrapped up in their imagination, their default mode network is activated. This is the imaginary dream state network in the brain, where the brain is actively firing in many brain regions. The mind is captivated and activated and deep in thought in their imagination.

Second, a child with ADHD may have very different thresholds for cognitive load. They may reach cognitive overload sooner. That is a culprit of the continuous attentional shifts. For example, if a child has greater awareness and processing of their environment they may reach the level of cognitive overload more rapidly. They may appear to have greater inattention when in fact their environment causes multiple system overload for their sensory, mental, emotional, imaginative, and physical processing. The differences in inhibition and development of the brain relate to how one processes their experiences and surroundings. A person with ADHD may be overstimulated in a way that interferes with their ability to harness their attention and focus.

Differences in Girl and Boy ADHD

Because boys are two times more often diagnosed with ADHD, many of the ADHD identifications may be skewed toward "male" behaviors. In some cases, we can be missing the ADHD diagnoses in girls.[13] Many of the diagnoses and identifications for boys fall within the criteria for hyperactivity and impulsivity. By contrast, girls' identifications tend to be more in the nature of inattentive ADHD. Could it be that we are missing the girls' diagnoses due to the gender bias of the symptoms for identifying ADHD?

ADHD presents in girls more often as the inattentive identification of ADHD, where they are daydreamers, caught up in their imagination. Generally, when a child appears as inattentive they are passive and tend not to disrupt class, whereas hyperactive ADHD presents with greater outbursts and class disruptions in a traditional school environment. Inattentive ADHD may not show up until the child is falling behind in school. In general, girls with inattentive ADHD may be more difficult to identify in a traditional class system because they are zoned out. In a classroom of thirty to forty kids, the loudest tend to consume a good amount of the attention. In a recent experiment where educators were assessed for their ability to identify girls with ADHD, the educators missed altogether the identification of inattentive ADHD in all the girls.[14] This is a critical problem facing our children and educators since inattentive ADHD does not present with the "classroom problem child." To the contrary, these girls tend to be the invisibles because inattentive ADHD is obviously more challenging to identify and blends with gendered stereotypes and societal expectations that persist. Unfortunately, the lack of identification puts girls at risk for underachievement, higher rates of drop out, other mental health concerns, and restricts their ability to get proper services and support their needs both in and out of school. Educators, parents, clinicians, and professionals serving children need to have greater education and clearer guidelines to better identify all children with ADHD, comprising both inattentive and hyperactive ADHD, and need support themselves to grow their awareness and understanding of the many faces of ADHD. More accurate identification allows children to receive greater understanding, acceptance, support, and practices to succeed in ways that match their true gifts and abilities.

Misunderstood, Misidentified, Misdiagnosed Misfits

In our culture, we often center our attention on the differences associated with ADHD as something to cull, fix, and manipulate into behaviors deemed acceptable to align within the values of our society. But perhaps the mind of a person with ADHD has a different set of values and order. We need to bend our perspective to nurture individual variations for individuals to thrive in the world for exactly who and what they are. With ADHD identification, we focus on behaviors we desire to change to force a person with ADHD to fit into a mold of a quiet, good, and obedient child. That may not be something we can expect from them. Setting people up to be different from who they are is setting them up for failure and unnecessary suffering. When we design a paradigm to be met when one's inherent way of being is treated as lacking or fails to fit within the extremes of a defined "normal," we send a message that to be normal they must be different than who they are. But what is "normal" anyway? More often than not, children and adults with ADHD are pushed into apologizing for who they are.

Debbie Reber, founder of Tilt Parenting, activist, and author of *Differently Wired*, shares the challenges she faced with our culture and rigid educational models when her son was identified with a trifecta of learning differences. Her son Asher is incredibly gifted, is identified on the autism spectrum and has an ADHD diagnosis. One of the most awakening and heartbreaking stories in her book is when she describes how her son apologized at lunchtime while homeschooling. When Debbie asked about this, he said that he was conditioned to apologize all the time at school for his ADHD, for his fidgeting, or forgetting to raise his hand. The distressing point of this story is that Asher felt as if he had to continually apologize for who he was. Apologizing, for Asher, was his default mode. Basically, he was getting signals from society that who he was wasn't acceptable. Debbie writes, "People apologize for the things they've done wrong. Things they regret. My son apologized for who he is." This is heartbreaking. This needs to stop. We are failing our children if we are sending them the message that they need to apologize for who they are at their core. This is a call to action to change our cultural conditioning that says if you fall out of the bell curve of "normal," navigate differently, process differently, that if your brain is different, you need to apologize.

Children and adults with ADHD are often misunderstand and shamed for their nonconventional behaviors because others are uncomfortable with their hyperactive and multifocused minds, big personalities, excitable behaviors, and ways of expressing themselves. Children and adults are given signals and messages that they are bad, difficult, and need to be different from who they are. But we must remember that children and adults who act out are not intending to be bad or problematic, rather they are informing us that they are wired and process differently.

When people are conditioned to believe they are problematic it leads to isolation and suffering and sometimes, even to them, the roots of their suffering are unknown to them. They hide who they are because who they are is being erased right before their eyes. Neurodiverse people are fed false stories. If these stories aren't rewritten, we will lose their core narratives and insights. I hold these words from Lidia Yuknavitch's *The Misfit's Manifesto* close to my heart: "If there is a phrase that I should probably tattoo on my forehead it is this: *I am not the story you made of me.*" And she goes on to write, "We can always reject the story placed on us, and we can always revise and destroy one story and restore another."[15] These are such powerful words when it comes to the stories that are placed on individuals who navigate and process differently. That others cannot see how you process does not invalidate your processing. You are inventing your tribe. Your tribe is out there. Your tribe is within you. Your tribe will reflect and accept who you are. Earlier, I wrote about mirror neurons and how through our mirror neurons we experience actions and empathy for others, but being unconventional, there will be a point that not everyone can keep up with your brain and ways of experiencing the world. That does not mean, however, that the how, where, and why of what you experience does not exist. It means that you are leading the way for others to see new stories—stories that to them are unimaginable.

In Christmas of 2019, I learned that one of my family members was identified and tested for ADHD. As we began to talk about their symptoms, I suggested that because they were identified as gifted, they were in fact 2e. "What is 2e?" they asked. I explained that 2e is when you are identified as gifted and have a learning difference. They said, "Thank you for saying I am 2e, being 2e is much better than being told you have a comorbidity." I was stunned. I couldn't believe the tester had said they had comorbidity. How can we be telling the brightest and most innovative people that they are flawed at the core for the way they process the world? One of my least favorite words, or overuses of a word, is "comorbidity." I first learned of the word when my mother was diagnosed with Parkinson's disease. The neurologist pointed out all the comorbidities of Parkinson's disease—anxiety, depression, the list goes on. Hands down, we need to stop using the word whose origin is of death when a person is living with many conditions and identifications. The language that we use in terms of diagnoses are a game of mental Tetris; we think we have a handle with a single identification and then the mental landscape shifts and we are told things like "there are comorbidities." This does not set someone up with the best outlook and acceptance of who they are. They are being told that their way of processing is problematic. This terminology adds insult to injury and is harmful for a person's mental and emotional health. Using this kind of language does not help a person deal with having multiple conditions. In fact, it leads to feeling defeated and conditioned with a story that something is wrong with them. Where in fact, the proper identification of being 2e means highly gifted and having ADHD. Replacing "comorbidity" with "co-occurrence" is more inclusive. Language is just as important as identification because language shapes our narratives and stories. We want neurodiverse people thriving, so we need to engender compassionate and accurate language to identify their extraordinary ways of processing the world, not use language that limits, stifles, and minimizes the way they are in the world. Being neurodiverse, gifted and ADHD, in this case, is exceptional.

Scientists Gomez and colleagues investigated whether an ADHD diagnosis was valid in gifted persons and uncovered that gifted ADHD differs from standard ADHD.[16] In their findings, gifted ADHD generally has less frequent diagnosis of the inattentive nature than non-gifted ADHD children. As we have learned, gifted people are wired for greater brain power and enhanced emotional, sensorial, mental, and physical abilities, and it is essential that gifted people are not misidentified and misdiagnosed. Remember, overexcitabilities are part of gifted enhanced receptivity and pinpointing the origin of behaviors seen in a gifted person is critical for their development and maturation. For example, Gomez and colleagues found when comparing gifted and non-gifted ADHD that non-gifted ADHD had higher occurrences of inattentive ADHD and gifted ADHD had more incidences of hyperactive ADHD, specifically, in motor processing and verbal expression. The elevated hyperactivity can be related to overexcitabilities and greater brain and body power to take in the world with elevated open-mindedness, enhanced processing, and reveal as behaviors with greater magnitude. To think about different developmental growth, gifted ADHD children could have greater brain power for motor and verbal activities that lead to bigger physical and verbal abilities. Thus, we can embrace practices that harness their gifted brain power and support the whole child so that there is safety and support for their uniqueness of being gifted-ADHD.

Essentially, gifted-ADHD people are wired for greater mental, physical and verbal abilities and their educational and general attention needs to reflect their abilities. For example, a profoundly gifted child with ADHD may experience unmet needs for engagement in their education and begin searching for stimulating material in their environment. Their curiosity is their intelligence sparked, and the search is fun and engaging, but to others it may appear that they are being disruptive. Due to their high intellect, they may easily understand the material and become disengaged. A gifted child rapidly works through their schoolwork with their enhanced verbal processing and cognition but, in the rush, may miss details and fail to carry over a decimal point or take time to proofread. In some cases, their true abilities are masked. Understand and recognize the highly individual triggers that spark an

ADHD attentional shift. Essentially, we can identify triggers on a case by case basis. Guiding a child to identify the things in their environment that are overstimulating and understimulating is essential if we hope to guide a child's attention and learning. Consider, as mentioned earlier, whether the material is disengaging. Has your gifted-ADHD child escaped to the freedom of their imagination so they can enjoy being engaged at their intellectual level? Particularly, being 2e in this case can prevent one from working at their level because the symptoms of ADHD can overshadow their giftedness.

Many of these children are at risk of having their gifts to go unidentified because of overwhelming differential processing and experiencing. It is our responsibility to help them identify their core features and allow them to express entirely who they are, embody their full essence, unbound, and unlock their shackled mind and set points. In a traditional school environment, children are often praised and encouraged for being quiet, orderly, and punctual. These hallmarks of conformity are not the most sought out characteristics for an individual to be innovative. Often in traditional school environments students suffer a stigma and exclusion for being different, for providing nonconventional responses to conventional questions, and for their specific and unique way of thinking and being. Often these children have differential learning, brain processing and maturation styles. Developmentally, a gifted and ADHD individual is likely to be out of sync with standard measures. In some areas they may be highly skillful and mature for their age. In other areas they are working to catch up to developmental markers and mature standards. It is essential that we create safety for each of these children to be authentic, innovators, influencers, hyperactive multitaskers, trail blazers, movers and shakers.

Wired for Greater Mobilization

Some people are wired for more, bigger, louder, and enhanced mental and physical activity. As we know, children with ADHD have brain maturation where motor cortex develops more quickly than other brain areas such as the frontal cortex. This asynchrony can account for enhanced physicality and motor processing. In other studies, scientists found that the motor cortex in ADHD has 40% less inhibition, which accounts for greater physical movement, activity, and ADHD hyperactivity.[17] Children and adults with ADHD are built and wired for greater physical activity and need much more movement throughout the day than the average person. ADHD children's nature requires greater movement and physical activity and they are often tagged for their differences with judgment and over time become highly self-critical, judging of themselves, and over focused on working to inhibit hyperactivity. In fact, they need to have more outlets and natural environments that encourage their greater movement, embrace their hyperphysicality, where they can safely move their bodies.

ADHD people are innately wired for greater motor and physical input and output, their minds and bodies are often more open, have greater awareness and flexibility and they survey their environment with rapid attentional shifts to their environment. Their reactions and behaviors can be out of the norm, and may take others by surprise. Much of the time, these children and adults are met with negative feedback, shamed and commanded to slow down and be quiet to fit into what society deems acceptable. Because children possess different abilities with elevated baselines and set points for motor processing, it is often challenging to communicate expectations. These children can be met with misunderstanding, which in turn leads to resistance from the child. The child can be tagged as a problem child, told they are disobedient, shamed for acting out, and met with harsh commands like, "*You need to get control of yourself!*"

Imagine for a moment (or for some readers, remember) that for most of your life you have been met with the message that your inherent way of being is problematic, that you make others uncomfortable, and because you do, you should stop being you. Imagine (or recall) you are told to sit still, be quiet, and stop being distracting, but your set point is one where you need to run, you need to explore; you are an innate hunter, you are a mover and shaker. You are searching for the next big idea. For you to do your searching, for your brain and body to process right, you need to move and be in your body. Imagine (or recall) being peppered with negativity and criticism for being nothing more or less than the person you naturally are.

Highly active and physical kids are especially challenged by a common school expectation that they should be sitting for extended periods of time. Each individual has their very own unique biorhythm, so for some, sitting still can be quite painful. This is a challenge of our time in that physical activity and movement is not nurtured by our modern technologies and devices and our sedentary society can impede our natural level of motor movement. This is even more true for our most energetic, gifted kids, whose spirits can be crushed when they are ordered to sit down and be quiet.

Mind-Body Disconnect

According to most recent reports, 80% of American adults and adolescents do not get adequate physical activity.[18] Americans sit way too much, physical activity is way down, and lack of mobility is leading to a slew of medical problems. We live in a world that is not nurturing natural movement. We are members of the animal kingdom and not meant to remain seated for hours on end. We are meant to move. Movement is part of meeting our natural physiological needs. It is not natural for us to sit for extended periods without physical activity. The most recent report determined that preschool aged children need to be active throughout the day to enhance and ensure proper development and maturation. Adolescents (6 to 17 years) need at least sixty minutes of physical activity a day. Adults are recommended to have seventy-five minutes a day of intense physical activity, as prescribed by the *Physical Activity Guidelines for Americans in 2018*. "Sitting is the new smoking," some say. In recent reports, sitting is identified as an occupational hazard. Over the last fifty years, humans have decreased their daily physical activity by 100 calories, which is one of the major causes of obesity.[19]

Could it be that our society is suffering due to inadequate physical activity? Maybe children and adults are conditioned to suffer from hyperactivity because we are missing our time to be in our bodies. We are missing physical activity and have gone too far into mentalizing everything. Is it that children are wound up because they spend fewer hours with free time? Because they are glued to their screens and have fewer opportunities for physical activity? And is it possible that our children who have challenges need to be in their bodies every day, but the movement comes out at "inconvenient" times?

Think for a moment about how a child who has great physical potential in psychomotor and physical domain can be misidentified and written off as a kid with ADHD. In fact, the child is more physical than their peers and needs to express themselves through movement, because, as a bodily-kinesthetic learner, it's the way they approach and solve problems. Being highly active can be interpreted as distracted in the classroom, but that child may actually have enhanced physical and psychomotor processing such that they require a high level of physical outlets. Individuals have various biorhythms of the body and different kinds of motor processing, which is highly individual. For some, sitting still for several minutes can be challenging and cause distress to their internal states, forcing them to repress their natural way of being in the world. This mismatch causes unnecessary pain and discomfort because it ignores their natural way of processing. Requiring children to conform to standard settings is inherently problematic for everyone, especially when their development is asynchronous, which creates challenges, resistance, and confusion for everyone. We need to meet and guide children where they are developmentally, emotionally, physically and mentally. Perhaps these movers, our kinesthetic learners, are telling the rest of us to get out of our seats, get off the couch, get away from our screens, and go outside and get moving. Maybe they are on to something, telling us to move. Moving can improve your life, and there is plenty of scientific evidence that being physical and spending time in your body can even save your life.

Ryan's Hyperfocus and Exceptional Motor Enhancement

Mary, a profoundly gifted adult, found school boring. Knowing her, that is no surprise. But she learned how to navigate out of harm's way by keeping her head down and getting her work done. Being invisible was a better option than being a problem in the in-and-out of the classroom. Much of her childhood was spent caring for others. She did not allow herself the space to be in her body. She described that as a child she really shut down because things were overwhelming and there was a mix of trauma. Mary describes having a truly intense emotional sensitivity and reaction in her body: "I've always had sensitivity to energy. I can feel energy. I can feel emotions. I've always done that, but I didn't know what I was doing. I could look at somebody and talk to them and I could feel what they were feeling, and I didn't know why, and I didn't realize it was theirs. I just knew I felt it." Once she became pregnant and gave birth all that changed and she came into feeling in her body. Prior to the birth of her firstborn daughter, Brianna, Mary had a nine-to-five desk job. That all changed after becoming a mother. She took her first yoga class, and in that yoga class realized the power of her body, being in her body, expressing herself through her body, and guiding others and healing through the mind-body connection. Mary spent much of her early life intellectualizing, being a math whiz, but she was meant to be in her body, a kinesthetic being. Being in her body allowed her to understand her emotions, regulate her thinking, and come into greater self-awareness and presence. Now Mary says, "I'm a yoga teacher, but I have all these different modalities that I'm learning, and I'm creating my own thing with all of these different practices."

Mary's story is an example of how a person who has a great physical gift and awareness breaks the nine-to-five mold and comes into living, being, and traveling a non-traditional path.

Through her greater awareness, Mary has come to realize that she wants things to be different for herself and for her children who are gifted and experience being in the world with an elevated processing and wiring. She is mother to two profoundly gifted children who are nothing alike. There is Brianna, the performer and chemistry master, and Ryan, a natural athlete. Aware of this, Mary made sure that the school system met the needs of her children so they could reach their full potential. She describes her son Ryan as highly active. He never stopped moving as a child. He ran all over the place, climbed trees, and everything he did was centered on being physical and moving his body. Ryan was constantly in motion and never stopped moving. In his youth, people cleared the path to make way for him. His engine was always roaring and he was non-stop. Mary remembers holding Ryan, "Oh my gosh, the first time I ever held him I felt like he wanted to get out and he wanted to crawl everywhere. He was like that. I remember we took him to T-ball, and one of the moms went up to me and she's like, 'Oh my, he looks like a cartoon character!' He wouldn't stop moving around, he couldn't sit still. I thought, oh my gosh, what am I going to do with him? Because he's never going to survive sitting in a classroom." Mary was talking with a friend and mentioned that Ryan would never sit still and was concerned about sending him to school. Her wise friend advised that Mary put him in taekwondo to help channel his energy. Mary thought, "I don't know, he's only five, I don't think he can do that." But as it turned out, he was able to hyperfocus. Socially, Ryan is more reserved, at times feels socially overwhelmed, and prefers to keep his thoughts to himself. In contrast, his sister, Brianna, is outgoing, highly verbal, and a social butterfly.

Ryan, much to Mary's surprise, managed fine in the classroom because he was able to channel is physical energy with taekwondo. By the time he was 11, he'd earned a second-degree black belt in taekwondo. Mary was amazed with his ability to become a second-degree black belt when he was so young. When he practiced taekwondo, Ryan could completely focus. She describes observing his test: "I was amazed, because when they do those tests they have to learn all the forms, from white to black belt. Then they had to learn the black belt forms, and that was the whole test. It blew my mind that he knew that much. There is an intelligence for learning how to move your body that way." A kinesthetic intelligence. At the time he was 11 and needed to adjust his schedule because he was playing three sports—soccer, baseball and taekwondo—and he needed to release participating in taekwondo. Baseball is his favorite and that is the sport he now channels all his energy into. In high school, he is on varsity baseball and Mary remarks that he is one of the youngest and smallest players, but a gifted athlete. Mary feels lucky that they found sports for Ryan to channel all his energy and that his athletics is a gift that needs nurturing.

Essentially, Ryan is a child that is wired for greater physical activity and needs to be in his body, which is a way he channels his energy and connects with the world. This highlights that for active, even hyperactive children, being in their body through sports and a physical outlet allows them to center their attention, focus, and meet their greater need for physical activity. Ryan needed physical activity for his increased motor processing and not medication for ADHD. It is highly important that we are aware in our culture that Ryan could have been misidentified as ADHD for his hyperactivity, but in his case he needed to have at least two hours of physical activity a day for his specific body rhythm. This provides us with the awareness that increasing an ADHD child's physical activity can help with general attention, focus, hyperactivity, and impulsivity. And that in some cases, the most simplistic solution is to get a highly active child involved in sports, dancing, and other activities where they can express themselves by being physical. Although Ryan is more socially reserved, through sports he has developed meaningful connections with peers while doing something he loves. Mary tells her kids, "The best thing I can do for you is to help you find your passion, and once you have that, then yeah, there might be things you're doing in your job that you don't like, but you'll love, hopefully, most of it because of that. It's just figuring out who are you, what you love, and then building from there."

Billy Sit Down or Run Around the Playground

My husband insists that all his friends call him Billy, a kid's name that embodies his essence of being a bit of a troublemaker. He's an attorney, and he knows all the rules, and he'll sure let you know what they are, but he also doesn't mind breaking them a little when he thinks there's a better way. A voracious reader and an intensely curious child, Billy would often finish his assignments well ahead of his classmates, which gave him plenty of extra time to disrupt the rest of the class. His teachers told his parents that even when he seemed "spaced out" counting the knotholes in the wood ceiling of the classroom, he'd recite the lesson word for word when the teacher tried calling him out for inattention. Billy was paying attention with half his brain, and in the second grade, that's all he needed to do.

A formative experience was in third grade where Billy was incapable of sitting still in class. His teacher, Mrs. H., a wise, experienced, and loving instructor, knew what to do with a bright, energetic kid who had learned all he needed for the hour. She sent him outside to run laps on the playground. After 10 laps he'd return, out of breath and sweaty, but calmer. Sort of like a Golden Retriever who's had a most excellent game of "catch." This elegant solution let Mrs. H. keep control of her class, let Billy burn off some of that abundant energy, and let the rest of the class catch up, amused by the unusual solution. Some kids like Billy would have been prescribed ADHD medication, but for him, physical activity, involvement, and creative outlets were almost enough to occupy his mind. It might not surprise you that we met in a marathon training group, raising funds for the Leukemia Society.

Boredom and excessive energy still sometimes make it difficult for my husband to stay on task. As it was in grade school, distractibility and his enthusiasm to take on everything has been a lifelong challenge for him. Knowing that he needs to keep busy, he takes on lots of projects and ideas, keeps himself busy, and feeds the clown inside him by taking improv comedy classes, and yes, he occasionally gets distracted.

And when he does, I admit, we send him outside to run laps.

Social, Unsocial Media, Devices, Addiction, and Our Mental Health

We live in a culture where attention and focus are often interrupted and we face cognitive drain and overload, unable to be present in our current environment and live in the moment. For attention to be directed, one must experience alertness, have a wide attention span, maintain attentional control, cognitive control, have the ability for attentional shift, and remain mindful of one's attentional focus. Because of the number of electronic devices available to us, we are constantly refocusing our attention and draining our cognitive battery. According to the latest research, adolescents experience continuous cognitive shifts, moving through different media platforms up to 27 times per hour, which can effectively reduce cognitive ability up to 15 IQ points.[20] This cognitive overload leads us into information brain drain.

The Chainsmokers' song, "Sick Boy," sums it up in a line: *How many likes is my life worth?* Constant interruption, the desire to be entertained twenty-four seven, and continued connectedness are taking a toll on our mental, physical, and emotional health.

There is now a wide body of evidence showing that heavy use of smartphones, the internet, and many social media platforms can have debilitating effects on our neural processing, cognitive performance, and behavior. On average, smartphone users check their phone close to 85 times a day and interact with their phone about five hours a day. Increasing evidence is pointing to the fact that our smartphones are not making us so smart after all but *are* leading us to increased unhappiness.

Sean Parker, one of the developers of Facebook, has publicly admitted they designed the program to monopolize our time and attention as much as possible.[21] Specifically exploiting the principles of psychology, Facebook triggers the social validation loop and activates insecurity so that people are searching for continued validation and reward. When this happens, we fall into a pattern of a hedonic reward cycle, pleasure seeking, for social validation. Much like Pavlov's dogs salivating at the sound of the dinner bell, we are conditioned to check our phone for our satiety of social approval, wondering if we got enough "likes."[22]

A novel study by Adrian F. Ward and colleagues found that the mere presence of a smartphone induces a "brain drain," a distraction that limits one's ability to participate in the present moment.[23] This reduces cognitive capacity for the task at hand by increasing an attentional shift toward the smartphone. This process is exhausting, and that is exactly how our brain feels as it wastes energy. So, when you are at a lunch date, dinner, business meeting, or engaged in a conversation, have your phone out of sight so you can focus on the present moment. Engage your attention in a single task and pay attention to the person there in front of you.

Not only do smartphones hog our attention but they impair our learning and memory. Interestingly, a study found that too much media multitasking causes a cognitive overload, which interferes with learning.[24] Heavy multimedia users were more distracted and did not perform attentional tasks as well compared to light multimedia users. Unfortunately, more often than not, the loudest thing gets our attention. Our smartphones can create infinite distractions that can alter our cognition, behavior, and performance.

Heavy smartphone users experience greater impulsivity, hyperactivity, and negative social concern, as reported in a study conducted by Aviad Hadar and colleagues.[25] Additionally, heavy smartphone users showed greater difficulty with number processing and reported greater inattention. This could explain why many of us feel depleted and have difficulty remaining on task. Unfortunately, people who use many social media platforms feel increased anxiety and depression. And a poll has found that most people (73% of respondents) do not want to see their "friends'" vacation photos posted on social media.[26] So, what is happening? Connectedness and being social is getting lost in translation. We have entered the new divine age of keeping up with the Jetsons. Basically, following friends on social media creates increased envy, depression, and negative mood in college students.[27] When social validation does not happen, or we are rejected on social media, our brain hurts, we experience emotional pain, and this affects our mental health and well-being. Overuse of smartphones has major consequences for health, life satisfaction, meaning, and happiness.

Is all social media and the things we do on our smartphones bad? No. Like so many things, it's about balance: when and how often we use our devices and how we interact with them. A smartphone, the internet, or social media can all lead to negative consequences. It is our responsibility to use and interact with them wisely. If we condition our mind and behavior toward constant validation through social media and smartphone use we may suffer from anxiety, depression, and negative mood. But we have a choice in how we interact with our smartphones and social media.

Here are a few guidelines to use your smarts when using your smartphone and connecting.

1. Every day, reduce your screen time 10 minutes and shift those minutes to engage in your surroundings. Mindfully detach from your smartphone. See what happens.

2. Shut down your smartphone when you are not using it and keep it out of sight.

3. Keep your phone silenced and out of sight when you are in a meeting. Give the meeting your full attention.

4. No phones at the dinner table.

5. Try a phone-free Friday.

6. If you cannot control shutting your phone and need some support, try a cell phone lock box.

7. Kindness matters on social media. Practice the "Golden Rule" when posting. Treat others with compassion and respect as you would like to be treated. Be a Charter for Compassion (https://charterforcompassion.org/).

8. Develop positive promotion of others and yourself. Learn the rules of Humblebrags[28] and avoid them when possible.

9. Social media is for sharing and being social. So, share your great ideas and share others' great ideas.

10. Recognize if you get trapped in the social validation reward cycle and step back. You can always check your number of likes later and bank the reward. This is the practice of delayed gratification.

11. You are in control of your smartphone. It does not own you. You are the smart one!

Tick Tock, the ADHD Sleep Clock

Attention, cognitive load, and processing are highly related to how well a mind is open to work with new information and to melding our acquired knowledge. Science points to how a rested and relaxed mind processes better and with higher efficiency because during our dreaming state, the brain recovers. More and more evidence reveals that the key piece when it comes to attention is sleep. Dreaming, sleep, recovery, and attention are interconnected. Many vital cognitive tasks are dependent on sleep, such as working memory, cognitive load, long-term memory, alertness, and attention. Studies show that in people with ADHD, there are alterations in this cycle.[29] Circadian rhythms and attention are intertwined and studying the relationship between

ADHD and sleep reveals there are key challenges in ADHD related lack of sleep. Altered circadian rhythms related to issues with lack of sleep affect hormone systems such as norepinephrine and dopamine, affect cognition, attention, mood, motivation, focus, restraint, level of activity, metabolism, digestion, and emotional reactions. For 75% of people with ADHD, their physiological bedtime clock is delayed by an hour to transition into sleep phase.[30] These delays include essential systems like the release of the hormone melatonin, body temperature adjustments, and reduced movement. In ADHD people, there are a number of sleep-related conditions that interfere with their getting their ZZZ's such as sleep apnea, restless leg syndrome, and being more alert in the evening. In addition, light throughout the day can alter their sleep-wake cycle because they can be more sensitive to artificial lights that keep their system running and awake.

Dream time is delayed and their natural biorhythm is actually that of a night owl. Perhaps night owls were evolutionarily meant to keep the night watch for their tribe, their people. From an evolutionary standpoint, it was not until more recently that humans adopted practices that are diurnal in nature. In fact, across all humans, there is great diversity for peak alertness and wake cycle. Perhaps people who prefer to be more active at night are conforming to a diurnal society and way of life that is inherently in opposition to their natural biology. For people with ADHD, living in a 9-5 world forces them into an unnatural biorhythm. Their issues with cognition and attention are connected to being out of sync with their innate clock. Being out of sync and having to live in an unnatural sleep-wake cycle creates a multitude of issues for an individual living with ADHD.

When introducing routine sleep practices in children with ADHD, those aged five to eleven showed improved sleep, increase in cognition, and a reduction in ADHD symptoms.[31] Having consistency and routine practices that center on priming oneself for sleep helps the child with motivation, relaxation, executive functioning, decision making, and recovery during sleep. Another study, called the Eight Hour Challenge, observed sleep practices in college students at Baylor University and encouraged them to get proper sleep before their final exams. Students reported their clocked sleep hours prior to their exams and investigators reviewed the raw score of their finals. Students who had slept at least eight hours the night before did better on their exams as compared to their peers who stayed up all night cramming for the exams.[32] Having more sleep allows for improved recovery, memory consolidation and clearing of junk from the brain. More sleep equates with better abilities for taking college exams. Basically, a good night's sleep allows the brain to work better and primes it for complex thinking with all cylinders firing.

Your brain works better when you've had restful ZZZs, because while you're sleeping your brain is cleaning and clearing out toxins such as proteins and chemicals that can be harmful for your brain's performance. Imagine for a moment being in your brain during sleep as it clears the unnecessary cobwebs from the day. For example, it is known that in diseases of neurodegeneration like Parkinson's and Alzheimer's, patients have excess proteins in their brains not unlike blockages in roadways. These blockages occur in brain pathways and interfere with information flow, memory, movement, and cognitive processing. A study conducted at the University of Rochester found that the deeper you sleep the better your brain can remove toxins and garbage from your brain and recover.

Because children with ADHD have altered sleep cycles, it's possible that they are not getting adequate sleep for their brain to develop and recover. Inadequate sleep is one of the factors that could be contributing to their delayed brain development and create greater asynchrony because during sleep is when the brain to replenishes and clears toxins. Excess toxins potentially interfere with natural brain development, delaying brain growth and neural circuitry. If a child seems spacey or caught in a dream state, it may be related to a lack of sleep and their attempt to catch more ZZZs through daydreaming. I highly encourage developing a standard routine practice for good sleep hygiene of at least eight hours is crucial for the brain to recover and work at its best ability. Thus, guiding yourself and children through an effective sleep routine ensures improved cognition, mood, aging, metabolism, gut motility, and a decrease in inflammation.

Adult ADHDing and Ken's Superpower

The first time I met Ken, I was struck by his blue eyes, the bluest I have ever seen, like the Maldives sea. His smile was equally radiant, the warmth of your favorite cup of tea. Ken is a master of multitasking. Talk about attention, he can shift rapidly from focused attention to sustained attention, to social attention, to selective and alternating attention the in blink of an eye all while riding a unicycle, juggling three balls, and brandishing a huge smile. He ran all the behind-the-scenes for Sam Christensen Studios and ensured that every class was smooth sailing, and students were met at the door with a beam of positive light. No matter where you had come from or what walk of life you lived, when you walked in the door, you were safe and embraced to be fully you, and who you were meant to be. Walking into class, I learned one of the most important lessons in my life, to live in my essence and that my essence is my light and right.

Ken's gift of making all the heavy lifting seem breezy allowed Sam the freedom for Sam to be Sam. I once asked Sam Christensen, "How do you decide to collaborate with people?" He said, "You have to work with people who are equal partners, where you each bring something to the table and you lift one another." Sam and Ken were undoubtedly equal partners. The life of the studio would not exist without Ken.

As I got to learn more about Ken, I learned he had navigated with ADHD. To him, his ADHD is his superpower. His unique brain wiring gives him the gift to see what others cannot. The way Ken describes ADHD is that there are different kinds of people in the world, harvesters and hunters. The harvesters are methodical and learn to plant, grow, and develop through experience. Then there are the hunters. He says people with ADHD are hunters. "We get our focus by responding to an outside need. We have to do something about it and it is the outside stimulus that focuses an ADHD person." He describes how everything he does falls under his having ADHD, that he goes where his instincts take him. It has taken him directly to his work and he describes his calling as, "a love for the uniqueness that every person possesses, and making people aware that they can step into themselves 100% and use fully that which is God given—their unique humanity."

He discovered in 1998, as an adult, that he had ADHD when a friend pointed out that he processed differently in his brain. He was identified as ADHD through testing at the Amen clinic. When he was identified with ADHD, it helped him realize how his original thinking could be empowering because he now understood how he saw the world. One of the great positives of having ADHD for Ken is that he is highly spontaneous, and says, "Sometimes I am a sharp left turn that has everyone mystified." His unconventional thinking allows him to be an extraordinary problem solver and allows for great freedom in thinking about deconstructing things and reassembling them. Where other people are perplexed, he comes at a problem in a unique way. His mind goes through a cyclone of twists and turns. Much of the time his way of getting there is baffling to others, but in his mind, he follows all the winding roads.

Ken takes Adderall, one of the main medications for treating ADHD symptoms. For him, it is important that he takes half the prescribed dosage. Even though Adderall is a known stimulant and makes his engine purr, he feels completely focused, balanced, and capable. For him, a half-dose makes him feel free to be himself and feel highly functional. These stimulants are working on the brain in the areas responsible for reward processing and executive functioning, the frontal cortex, and are centered on balancing the neurotransmitters for dopamine and norepinephrine.[33] It is proposed that in ADHD there are alterations in reward processing and the key brain area and systems that have differential processing revolve around the frontal cortex.[34] Pharmaceutical interventions can greatly improve the lives of individuals struggling with the challenges of ADHD. When we consider medication and treatment for ADHD, though, regular monitoring by the prescribing doctor is essential, so that dosing is adjusted as needed, especially when treating children. Keen awareness of a child's asynchronous brain maturation can be essential in making key adjustments to the treatment plan to encourage healthy growth of the child's mind and body for their life.

Importantly, not everyone with ADHD needs medication or experiences benefits from medications. The decision to use medication can be highly challenging in children that are asynchronous. We must ask whether their challenges in relation with their executive functioning will be something they grow into, or could they be better treated with coaching and holistic interventions. One consideration is whether the child is experiencing massive challenges in life: if they cannot function a single day and every other measure has been attempted through repeated trial and error, then the child may benefit from a biochemical intervention. Medicine can help them process their environment with greater ease, rather than difficulty.

As a neuroscientist, people have asked me to take a stand for or against medication for ADD and ADHD. I believe we are each neuroindividuals and ADD/ADHD have moving targets and differential baselines. In my opinion, if we can find holistic approaches for a child and adult that are effective, then we should go for it. But some people need more than a holistic intervention. That said, I also believe that we tend to approach too many behavioral challenges and health difficulties from the perspective of medication before we look at the entire picture. In some cases, behavior we tag as "bad" is a symptom of a child who at their core is in pain and is acting out. If we can find the source of their suffering, and help them manage the root cause, then they may not need medication after all. For example, a child may have enhanced sensory receptivity and processing that lead to ADHD-like symptoms and may be acting out due to sensory processing rather than true ADHD. In that case, removing the over-stimulating sensory stimuli could eliminate the symptoms. In such a case, the child never needed medication. What they actually needed was a sensory-safe environment. I believe it is essential to treat the whole child (or the whole adult) and not just their symptoms. More important, we can identify the underlying triggers and causes of behavioral challenges. Humans are highly dynamic and have great fluidity and receptivity to rewire for positive neural plasticity when their environment is safe.

The solution to the debate of whether to medicate or not medicate is individual and is found through trial and error. Specifically, finding an accurate dosage is critical. For example, a recent study found, in the context of anesthesia, that the necessary dosage is highly variable across patients, and many people could receive actually a much lower dose than previously thought.[35] Lead author, Dr. Ana Ferreira, explains that these practices need to be carefully monitored and that there needs to be a move toward more personal care, where weight and gender, and the dosage recommended by the manufacturer, are not accurate measures for proper anesthesia dosage. In the study, scientists measured the brain waves of patients under anesthesia and found that dosing was highly variable among patients, independent of gender, weight, and height, and any recommended measures used to prescribe the dosing. Across the 126 patients, the team found that administering a slow rate of infusion, carefully observing the patient, and monitoring the response was essential to ensure they were not overmedicated. In all cases, weight, age, height and gender were not good markers for prescribing the accurate dose. In fact, much less medication was needed to achieve proper levels of anesthesia, and typically patients only needed about 2/3 the recommended dose. This points to the fact that medications in general are developed under limited criteria, centered on weight, age, gender, and height, which do not always correlate with an individual's metabolism in relation to their brain and body processes.

Additionally, as I mentioned earlier, there are neurons in the heart, the gut, the CNS, and PNS. All these systems can be affected when one takes a medication. Understanding individual metabolism is essential to determine how one will respond and react to a medication. Ken mentioned that for his ADHD he takes a half-dose of Adderall and that does the trick to keep him balanced. With any new medications, work with a doctor and begin with the smallest dose that might be effective to ensure the safety and development of each individual. Medication is highly individual and each person's response to dosing is individual, based on a person's metabolism, activity, brain processing, and receptivity to the medication. Ken's insight into himself, that a half-dose is sufficient, gives us a glimpse into the features and variability within the human population.

Ken also reminds us that one of his superpowers is *gestalt*—where he envisions the whole picture of what he is doing, how the pieces fit together into a whole, without getting into the fine details. Ken admits he easily loses patience for fine details. This type of self-awareness is key to understanding one's personal information flow, creative thinking, and innate biorhythms. Often people with ADHD are shamed for missing the fine details. Mindless and senseless points are shaved off exams and homework for missing fine details, even if some of those fine details might be entirely irrelevant to the subject at hand. Continued criticisms for missing the fine details can cause people to feel as though what they do is never good enough, creating a complex where the negative talk of others turns into repeated negative self-talk and shatters their self-esteem and self-image. Fine details are great jobs for the harvesters, perfecting the new visions of the hunters. This duality is one of the many reasons Sam and Ken worked magically together. Sam, a harvester, Ken, a hunter, together a balance of the yin and yang, equally matched, building on one another to share their gifts.

For my son, one of his greatest challenges in his younger school years was writing his name on his worksheets and homework. He would get right to work on his math sheet, solving all the problems correctly. But frequently, he turned in work that was missing his name, the date, etc.—the fine details. Handwriting was also challenging for him. Handwriting hurt his hand, and his writing was so distinctive that all the teachers knew the unnamed worksheet was his. Much of his challenge was related to his growing frontal cortex. He was excited to get to the heart of the material, the math problems. He was engaged with the material to the point that the fine details could not compete for his attention. The work was the heart of the activity for him. Unfortunately, children and adults are shamed by detail-oriented people for not following the directions exactly. Shaming leads them to feel they are failures because they do not meet certain arbitrary measures of success. More often than not, in time their brain and body will balance, the yin and yang. It takes time for them to catch up with the ordinary day-to-day tasks and measures. Kids with ADHD are the kids who skip coloring. They turn the page over and draw, or they make paper origami characters, or airplanes, or confetti, while the harvesters are methodically going through their worksheets. The hunter's brain is fixated on something different, based on their different brain wiring, based on their different receptivity and their different way of processing their environment. All the while they are playing in their imagination and creating something far beyond their years. When hunters are captivated by their own imagination they may lose track of time and miss the fine details.

Ken shared with me one of the best pieces of advice he'd gotten from a friend: "God does not have a wrist watch." Often individuals with ADHD are judged based on standard measures and the conventional ways that society runs. Hunters' brains are fascinated with the workings of the world. They live in their own time, in their own way. People with ADHD are often highly imaginative and creative people. When you are in your own imagination, it takes you to portals within yourself and in the universe. The concept of time impedes creation. Creation is timeless and needs no bounds. It is the inner vision of the harvester and hunter to make, see, and strive for the better, to be better, do better, and live better. As Mary Oliver writes, "Creative work requires a loyalty as complete as the loyalty of water to the force of gravity." Many hunters are driven by their inner vision, a force beyond themselves where there is a gravitational pull that will not relent until their curiosity is satisfied.

Ken has a message for his younger self, too: "Trust. Breathe deeply and trust." Trust is the foundation of coming into yourself and coming into what will be. Trust requires us to believe and have faith in the endless possibilities that will arise. Trust counters our fears and allows for a centering in positivity of outlook. Studies consistently show that more optimistic people live longer and have more social connections. Both optimism and connection are key for longevity and well-being. Breathe, deep breathe, for anyone can center the mind and reset the nervous system. Deep breathing calms and soothes the nervous system because the breath can help alter one's mood and outlook. Studies show that three deep breaths focus and center the mind, while providing oxygen-rich molecules throughout your mind and body.[36] Deep breathing rewires the stress patterns and induces calming patterns so that positive neurohormones are released to soothe and relax the nervous system, mind, and body.

Ken encourages a routine for parents with kids who have ADHD. "It is so important to create a home environment where everything is the same every day. Where there is routine and a consistency that enables the ADHD kid to rely on that consistency. So their minds can do what comes naturally." Individuals with ADHD need practices and routine to train their brain and body for positive mind body practices. Much of their routine, rituals, and repeated activity provide safety and consistency. Ken pointed out that ADHD persons are stimulated by their environment, thus the more stable their external environment to more it will create a more balanced mind and allow them to work at their highest cognitive, intellectual, emotional, mental, sensorial, and imaginative abilities. Having positive practices helps the mind rewire for positive processing, cognition, and behaviors because they learn repeated measures that create a positive self-image and allow for success, both big and small. Importantly, allow your kid to be who they are whether they are a kid who struggles to remember to write their name on their work, or a kid who spends a lot of time daydreaming, have patience and help them create systems that fit within the fine details. Maybe get them a stamp. Think about neurohacks that can help manage the expectations of those who value fine details, help develop your child for positive thought processes, self-perception, and promote self-acceptance so they embrace who and where they are in relation to the world.

As Ken said, his mission is to help people see their divinity and what is their God-given essence—no one else will ever be them throughout all of time.

"The privilege of life is to be who you are."
—Joseph Campbell

Dear Silent Wisdom,

Where has your voice gone? Is it dormant somewhere in your body? Are you tired of others speaking for you? Telling you how you feel, how they imagine it is to be in your body? Telling you that you lack empathy? Or are too sensitive? Or that you are awkward? Telling you socializing is not in your blood. That you lack appropriate language. Timing. Have no voice. Where is your voice in your body? Where are the many voices? Stories. Imagined. Real. Where is your truth? Are you tired of your body aching with pain? Aching voice, stuck in the space between tongue and teeth. Lost communication. Where is your voice, my dear gifted one? Do you need others to stop talking and listen instead? Where shall we listen from? Heart, perhaps. Unfiltered mind without prejudice, without prior knowledge. It is a voice of a songbird. Tell me, dear one, where is your voice in your body? Your throat, right hip, left ankle, space between your shoulder blades, fire in your belly, looping in your hippocampus like a film, inhibited frontal cortex paused. Tell us to be quiet, tell us to be patient, tell us to listen. Only then will we stop with all the misinformation and imaginings of what it is to be you. Only then will we begin to hear your voice. Your truth, your home.

Yours, ready and waiting to hear your voice like a lion's roar,

Bold as a Lioness

CHAPTER 7:

Beyond Autism Spectrum Disorder

There is someone beautiful, imaginative, profound and perfect inside the mind of every individual with autism. We just have to be awake, be aware, and have patience as they tell us their story. As Leo Kanner, the child psychiatrist who authored foundational studies in autism, would say, individuals on the autism spectrum possess *a silent wisdom.*[1] In graduate school, I entered the world of studying autism to better understand the range of human diversity. My project explored neuroanatomy of autism. I scanned brain tissue under the microscope, carefully counting, cataloging, and photographing neurons and glial cells. As I viewed tissue across all the subjects, I quickly began to understand that no tissue section, no brain region, was exactly alike across the brains of individuals with autism or even in their age-matched peers. Every brain was distinct.

Concurrently, my mother was in the later stages of the progression of Parkinson's disease (PD) and she slowly stopped speaking. First from anxiety and depression, and later from motor impairments of PD. She completely lost her voice. I knew in my mother's case that her inability to communicate did not reflect a fraction of what was going on in her mind. In addition, as I read the patient reports for my research, I quickly realized that what I was reading was not the entire picture of the person with autism. I began to read work from Temple Grandin, the legendary advocate for people with autism and neurodiversity, and I discovered there was a gaping hole between the clinical research and the humanness of an individual on autism spectrum. I firmly believe there is much more that meets the eye for the abilities, functioning, and intelligence of an individual with autism spectrum disorder (ASD).

ASD is a spectrum, exactly, and no two individuals on the spectrum are alike. It is the core of neurodiversity. Autism spectrum disorder is heterogeneous clinically and etiologically where the diagnosis is entirely based on the behavioral phenotype.[2] According to the DSM-5, autism is a neurodevelopmental disorder described by two core features (often diagnosed by age three): a lack in social communication and restricted repetitive behaviors.[3] The diagnosis of the disorder is at present entirely clinical, based on differing aspects of behavior and its developmental time course. In addition, ASD people can have additional diagnoses in the clinic that can include attention deficit hyperactivity disorder, Rett syndrome, seizures, and other disorders and neurological symptoms that occur with autism.

As of March 2020, about one in 54 children in the United States—nearly 2%—are diagnosed with autism or autism spectrum disorder (up from one in 59 in 2014 and one in 150 in the early 2000s).[4] This continuous increase in the prevalence of ASD diagnoses has raised tremendous concern among parents, clinicians, and the scientific community and has led to the suggestion that environmental factors may contribute to the increase of autism diagnoses.[5] Because the diagnosis is strictly a behavioral phenotype, and verbal expression and communication is typically lacking, a true understanding of an ASD person's ability and function can be masked by symptoms. True ability can be missing from the assessment of an ASD person because they may lack verbal expression and may have differential processing that can interfere with their reaching developmental milestones. Because autism spectrum disorder is a heterogeneous disorder, it may involve additional symptoms, including seizures, sensory enhancements such as hypersensitivity, motor deficits, and gastrointestinal alterations.[6] Seizures occur in 38% of individuals with autism, and the frequency of seizures has great impact on the individuals' lives.[7]

Sensory intensities have often been described in autism spectrum disorder. These include pain insensitivity and hypersensitivity to tactile, auditory, and visual stimuli, which can be debilitating.[8] Gustatory and olfactory sensitivities can interfere with adequate nutrition. Over 90% of individuals with autism have sensory enhancements in multiple domains, and the sensory disabilities are extensive, multimodal, and continuous across age and ability in individuals with autism. In addition, individuals with autism experience a number of motor differences.[9] These may include gait differences, various postural instabilities, greater imbalance, and altered motor coordination.[10] Sensory sensitivity and motor processing can hugely interfere with an ASD person's ability to navigate in the world. Often, being highly receptive can cause sensory overload so that a person on the spectrum can become debilitated by a world too intense for them to process.

Intense World Theory

Intense World Syndrome was first described by the Markram group at the École Polytechnique Fédérale de Lausanne research institute in 2007, where they sought to explore the neurobiological basis of autism using a valproic acid rat model of autism.[11] The theory proposes a bottom-up model for autism, where at the molecular, cellular, network, and behavioral levels there is a hyper-receptivity and hyper-plasticity, which accounts for the different processing, wiring, and behaviors seen in autism. Importantly, there is no single known cause for autism and much of the behavioral phenotypes are heterogeneous and highly individual. The team further adapted the model for humans with autism as Intense World Theory, explaining that there is a hyper-perception, hyper-synaptic plasticity, hyper-attention, and hyper-memory in the neocortex and there is hyper-emotionality rooted in the limbic brain creating enhanced and intense experiences that overwhelm the mind and body of an individual on the spectrum.[12] Moreover, they hypothesize that the intense experiences of hyper-perception are rooted in the trauma circuitry of the limbic system where navigating through the world is extremely painful and challenging. The Intense World Theory attempts to collectively unify the complexities of autism to best nurture the individual by addressing the sensory sensitivities, hyper-focus, repetitive behaviors, eccentricities, withdrawal, and the extraordinary talents brought forth by different brain wiring that leads to more intense experiencing.

An individual with hyper-perception can experience overstimulation from their environment or experience, where their brain, body, and collective nervous system become overtaxed. When a nervous system is overwhelmed, this leads to an innate protective response such that the individual withdraws from their environment or experience to ensure their safety. This natural response to overstimulation can appear as if the individual is disengaged, where at the core of hyper-receptivity they experience hyper-arousal and hyper-pain that lead to an activation of the limbic centers in the brain. When the limbic centers attempt to rescue an overtaxed nervous system, it pushes the brain and body's response into sympathetic activation of fight, flight, freeze, and/or flop. As the limbic system aims to center the mind-body experience, the nervous system is caught in a loop of hyper-plasticity and firing, where trauma circuits are engaged, leading the mind and body into sympathetic overdrive. When an individual is experiencing sympathetic overdrive of the fight/flight response, they can express repetitive behaviors, respond with hyper-emotionality observed as tantrums, or express hyper-focus. Whereas, when an individual is experiencing freeze/flop, they can seem withdrawn or disengaged and lack emotional expression, appearing as unemotional.

The Intense World Theory provides a neurobiological framework based on hyper-plasticity, meaning different brain wiring and synaptic connections (the way neurons communicate with one another) in the brain are the cornerstone for the hyper-perception and hyper-emotionality experienced in ASD. The hyper-plasticity is founded on having different cytoarchitecture (cellular and network formation) leading to greater neuronal activation and firing in relation to having a hyper-receptivity across sensory (sight, taste, smell, sound, and tactile) perceptions. This can be related to differential connectivity and hyper-plasticity across brain networks for sensory and emotional perception. In addition, this hyper-plasticity can lead to differences in learning. They can develop differential networks for learning where the cortical layers in the brain for learning, memory, attention, and working memory have differential neurocircuitry leading to differences in learning, described as hyper-learning. Importantly, hyper-emotionality is linked to the elevated receptivity in the limbic cortex, where the activation is related to the expanded neurodevelopment of trauma circuits linked to core perceptions of the world, where the behaviors and reactions are embedded in the fear, anxiety, and the stress response and circuitry. Intense World Theory proposes that the overall expression of hyper-connection can lead to hyper-functionality in the brains of people with ASD so they experience the world with heighted intensity.

Take a moment to imagine feeling as if you have several pinpricks across your body. And now imagine the pain increases to the point where dizziness consumes you, igniting a shooting pain through your head activating a migraine. Your stomach turns and churns from acid, and anxiety takes over, flooding your blood with stress hormones. Would you feel like talking or interacting with anyone? What would you do if you were in this kind of extreme pain? Scream, curl up in a ball, cry, express repetitive behaviors to calm and sooth your nervous system?

When an individual is suffering from sensory overload, their mind, body and the whole individual goes into stress and panic and they cannot think, let alone communicate. They express behaviors that aim to soothe and calm their nervous system such as social withdrawal, having less mental flexibility, and exhibiting repetitive behaviors to relax their internal state. In addition, when an individual has anxiety and/or experiences physical pain their natural response is to withdraw from their surroundings and gain refuge for safety, which can be seen as antisocial. Often, what we see when an individual suffers from a sensory overload is their attempt to regulate a hyper-sensitive and intense nervous system. That is the foundation of the Intense World Theory, that individuals with autism have a hyper-experience of the world and, more often than not, they seek ways to calm their nervous systems. Finding solutions to build awareness, effective communication, and compassion to help guide them to safety and mitigate the loop of hyper-sensitivity is crucial. Fundamentally, we need to understand that people who are intensely experiencing the world may express heightened or withdrawal behaviors, but these are centered on regulating an immensely intense experiences.

A Silent Wisdom—Intelligence in Autism

There is longstanding evidence of the link between intelligence and ASD beginning with the earliest descriptions by Leo Kanner. In the late 1930s, Kanner evaluated twelve children in depth, including parent reports of behaviors and uniqueness within this population. Kanner described high intelligence as a core feature of autism, remarking many times that there appeared to be a *silent wisdom* among those children.[13] Kanner's foundational narrative accounts of autism shaped the language and awareness of the extraordinary thinking and processing in the mind of someone with autism. He observed common behaviors across the children and noted that all the children possessed a high level of intelligence, observed by both their doctors and family members. The children also expressed challenges in social behavior and engagement and had difficulty with language such as the proper use of pronouns. They tended to mimic language, expressing routine language patterns in response to environmental cues. Further, the children were highly sensitive to touch and demonstrated repetitive behaviors and restrictive behaviors within their environment. And they were highly self-contained, sufficient, and engaged in imaginative play.

The original analysis highlighted the fact that each of these children were highly intelligent. For example, he writes about one subject named Donald, "He quickly learned to read fluently and to play simple tunes on the piano." And he goes on to note, "[Donald] expressed puzzlement about the inconsistencies of spelling: 'bite' should be spelled 'bight' to correspond with 'light.' He could spend hours writing on the blackboard. His play became more imaginative and varied though still quite ritualistic." These observations indicated that there is a great deal going on in the mind of a child on the spectrum. Personal intelligence is driven by personal interests centered on what one finds rewarding and engaging and this ignites a person's curiosity. He further describes how Donald's answers showed he thought in pictures, "When asked to subtract 4 from 10, he answered: 'I'll draw a hexagon.'" Donald expresses himself through pictures and his answers use metaphor—a complex form of communication. The answer shows a high level of intelligence and thinking behind Donald's response. When we give children the ability to express themselves creatively, they can communicate their complex thoughts and ideas.

Richard was a young boy with a number of repetitive behaviors, described by Kanner as quite self-sufficient. Richard had an imaginative way of storytelling, and was identified as quite intelligent. Kanner notes that his mother wrote, "He gave the impression of *silent wisdom* to me..." In another case, a young girl named Virginia scored a below-average IQ of 94 on a Binet test. The psychologist wrote in response, "Her intelligence is superior to this. She is quiet, solemn, and composed." An important subjective note, the psychologist observed the scored test did not reflect Virginia's intellect. In general, children on the autism spectrum are at a disadvantage when taking standard intelligence tests because the tests do not capture their particular type of intellect. Their thinking, beyond measure, does not fit into a standard educational paradigm. Kanner writes, "Even though most of these children were at one time or another looked upon as feebleminded they are unquestionably endowed with good *cognitive potentialities.* They all have strikingly intelligent physiognomies." In Kanner's original observations there was a wider view of intelligence, a human view of intelligence that permitted the complexities of the mind. In another remarkable note, Kanner observed, "There is one other very interesting common denominator in the background of these children. *They all came of highly intelligent families.* Four fathers are psychiatrists, one is a brilliant lawyer, one a chemist, one a law school graduate, one a plant pathologist, one a professor of forestry, one an advertising copy writer who has a degree in law and studied at three universities, one is a mining engineer and one a successful business man. Nine of the eleven mothers were all college graduates." He goes on to describe that all the children's mothers worked prior to marriage, and some after marriage, where the women included a freelance writer, a physician, a psychologist, and a graduate nurse. Kanner further observed the children came from a long line of intelligent people, tracing back to the grandparents and additional family members.

Kanner's early instincts were on track: high intelligence is a core feature across families where individuals are on the spectrum.

Importantly, individuals who obtain higher education and degrees are often internally driven in pursuit of knowledge. They are often self-sufficient, spending hours, days, weeks, and years studying and working independently with a high level of focus to meet their mind's level of intellectual engagement. In addition, people on the autism spectrum are internally driven, intensely focused, and highly self-motivated. They can work independently while their mind is completely engaged in their imagination and intellectual areas of interest. Any individual who is in flow may demonstrate reserved behaviors, have an intense focus, and desire aloneness. These are all behaviors that people on the autism spectrum commonly express while they are actively and mentally engaged. Kanner's original observations shed light on the important observation that individuals on the spectrum have a unique intelligence. Their intelligence is embedded in their brain's processing, wiring, and output centered around their intellectual interests. In the case of the autism spectrum, perhaps we are looking at a rare form of intelligence, an intelligence liberated from social constraints, social cues, and socializing, where in autism, the essence of intelligence stems from the purest form of curiosity.

In recent years, Simon Baron-Cohen, a researcher at University of Cambridge, found in an anonymous university survey that individuals in the field of physics, engineering, and math have greater incidence of family members with ASD than do individuals in the humanities disciplines.[14] To pursue an education in the field of math, physics, or engineering requires great brain maturity and mental processing specific to visual and spatial capabilities. It is well documented that individuals on the autism spectrum have greater visual processing and functioning that lead to expertise and enhanced visual skills.[15] In fact, ASD individuals have increased spatial processing abilities and can manage mental image mapping with greater accuracy and speed. They have been shown to have heightened abilities to perform mental rotation, which is the ability to visualize and mentally rotate two-dimensional and three-dimensional objects in the mind.[16] Individuals with ASD may have brain wiring that leads to enhanced abilities and performance for visual and spatial tasks while creating mental images and maps in their mind.[17] In another study, researchers found that parents of children with autism were more capable of solving visual puzzles, highlighting that these abilities for enhanced three-dimensional visual and mental processing are often found within the family.[18] It appears that these elevated cognitive abilities to solve puzzles with greater fluidity that exist in individuals with autism originate from familial characteristics, and these differences in cognitive abilities are due to brain development and maturation for specific visual processing. This evidence points to a different intelligence and cognitive type where the core nature of mental processing revolves around enhanced visual processing, greater visual accuracy, higher capabilities for building mental maps, advanced abilities for decoding puzzles, and greater creative problem solving. The minds of individuals on the spectrum are unique.

In the field of autism research there has been a debate about whether individuals on the spectrum can experience theory of mind (TOM), which is the ability to anticipate the emotions, desires, intentions, thoughts, and knowledge of others. Early studies used a test to measure the mentalizing of another individual, such as the false belief test in which individuals can identify that others may have false beliefs by how they convey their emotions. The ability to identify a false belief is found in children. In the earliest studies, individuals on the autism spectrum failed the false belief test; they could not mentalize that people could have a false belief.[19] There have been numerous studies that report that individuals on the spectrum lack theory of mind. But, more recently, Morton Ann Gernsbacher, professor at University of Wisconsin, proposed that the evidence fails to prove that individuals with autism lack theory of mind and focuses on detangling these misconceptions.[20] Professor Gernsbacher challenges the assertions that ASD people lack a theory of mind, or that they are unable to comprehend that other people have a mind, as harmful misconceptions that are unfair to people with ASD. In her in-depth analysis, she and her team find that the original studies claiming that people with ASD lack theory of mind fail to replicate. She explores how a number of TOM measures are not related to TOM at all, and that they specifically negate autistic characteristics, such as socialization and empathy. Her study finds that research outside the TOM measures fails to replicate inside the TOM measures. She concludes that the prior claims that ASD people lack theory of mind are harmful to the population and to our society as a whole. In particular, those who would make a broad—and erroneous—assertion that ASD people lack theory of mind do disservice to the population because that purported deficit is not empirically found in every individual on the spectrum. Second, because there is a language delay in autism, people on the spectrum may experience greater challenges in communicating their abilities to perceive TOM and may be disadvantaged in identifying or describing their emotions, thoughts, intentions, and actions. It is imperative that we emphasize nurturing an individual through proper guidance to communicate their mindset and to practice mentalizing others' mindsets. Through guidance, training, and improved communication, individuals on the spectrum can better identify and convey their own mindset and that of others. More important, individually nurturing the cognitive, emotional and mental development of an individual with ASD is essential. There is more than meets the eye in the mind of an individual on the spectrum. To make broad claims about the population, claiming a deficit, is harmful to their mental, emotional, and cognitive development. Instead, we can shift our language and thinking to become more inclusive, to view differences as identity instead of disorder, and to have a flexible view that allows room for the positive characteristics of people with ASD.[21]

Perhaps, Kanner's words, that these children "are not feeble-minded" but rather possess good cognitive potentialities, were aimed to teach us to look beyond the autism spectrum diagnosis and embrace the individual, embrace their singular intelligence and empower and encourage these individuals to explore their minds beyond any label. These are stories that look beyond ASD, where trailblazers invite promise with their warrior spirits, senses of humor, and out-of-the-box thinking. Our society needs cognitive diversity for creative innovation and divergent thinking.

These are our nonconformists, our iconoclasts with unique minds fueling neurodiversity.

Mother Warrior

Harri O'Kelley, a lioness in her own right, wears a silver mane and a free-flowing smile of optimism. She is the mother of three 2e children: Jordan, her oldest, age 15, and her twin girls, age 14, Rachel and Macey. All three are 2e. She runs The O'Kelley Lab in her home where she tailors her children's education to meet their individual needs and maturity, all while working on set in Hollywood. As I sit across from her in her home laboratory, I tell her I would describe her as a *mother warrior*. She replies, "Some days I am a mother warrior and others I am a mother worrier," and chuckles. Humor is a saving grace and a motivating element in their home. Harri says, "The O'Kelley family aims to create innovative therapies to empower parents and children who are twice exceptional (2e)— gifted, with some form of disability. Our ideas and therapies are geared toward improving the lives of people on the autistic spectrum." Harri herself is 2e and was self-identified with dyslexia later in life. She describes that she lived most of her life with dyslexia, unaware of her disability so that it shadowed her gifts and her strengths. The unwavering resilience that Harri expresses is contagious. She says, "I am an intuitive problem solver, and if there is an intervention out there to help my kids, I will try it."

Harri is as well-versed in 2e as any PhD. She has taken numerous courses and workshops on 2e education with experts in the field like Susan Baum, Debbie Reber, and many others, to ensure that her children receive proper safety, support, and engagement for their unique minds. She tells me, "All three kids are 2e, and are in that amazing time of brain development that you and Dr. Daniel Siegel talk about. Rachel is gifted and on the autistic spectrum. With the help of a therapy called 'Floor Time' that was created by Stanley Greenspan, I have been educated in the ways of 'following my child's lead' as a way to connect and support their individual differences." For example, when Rachel was nine, by following her lead, stand-up comedy was a great way to help her develop her sense of self, point of view, and humor. In her first stand-up comedy class, Rachel described herself as, "I'm kinda like Amelia Bedelia meets Dorie from the movie *Finding Nemo*." Harri explains how Rachel is a very literal thinker and has working memory challenges. Even though she faces challenges with communication and working memory, Rachel continuously comes up using creative humor to share her unique perspective on the world. Rachel found that stand-up comedy was a great way to organize her thoughts and ideas into writing and creating jokes. Diving further into the brain and psychology behind this, humor and creativity are innately connected to reward and motivation. When Rachel is in her natural state of thinking and creatively exploring ways to communicate, humor is a rewarding way for her to communicate. Using humor to communicate is one of the many innovative educational approaches that come from The O'Kelley Lab.

Macey, Rachel's twin sister has challenges related to her physical developmental health. Harri says, "Macey is gifted, but is medically fragile and has developmental delays as a result of being born with Biliary Atresia, a liver condition where bile ducts malfunction. Macey had challenges post a liver transplant and suffered from medical trauma due to serial hospital stays. Macey has spent her time advocating to bring awareness about medical trauma through different organizations. She has been a Liver Ambassador and Liver Champion for the American Liver Foundation, and she has also done fundraising for the American Liver Foundation and The Painted Turtle Camps." Macey's elevated awareness and desire to share her story with others is an example of a profound emotional intelligence that can be overlooked in a child who is 2e, and in some cases can even be missed completely. Macey's emotional drive to be an advocate and promote greater awareness for people suffering from liver issues is an act of great emotional saliency and compassion. She is 2e and goes beyond the expectations and delineations society has created for her, expressing high emotional ability. More often than not, due to labeling and lack of identification of different modes of emotional intelligence, children on the spectrum or that are 2e get tagged as "devoid of emotions," or are misrepresented as lacking emotional ability due to their challenges and differences in communication styles. This is an important misidentification and misconception, that children on the spectrum lack empathy. For persons with ASD or autistic-like traits, there is a difference in their emotional maturity and the way they convey their emotions, but it is not accurate to say they are lacking empathy.

Understanding the science behind the behaviors of her children are very helpful for Harri's family. She recalls, "There were plenty of heartbreaking and funny moments my husband and I went through as parents. You can laugh or cry over something on any given day when you're raising 2e kids. Your perspective on anything and everything is very important and an opportunity to build resilience by embracing a situation and staying in the present. I found Daniel Siegel's books, his philosophy on parenting, and basic education about how the brain works and affects the body, very helpful in understanding the why of why my kids behave the way they do. We had a poster of the brain in our kitchen and referred to it or used our hands as a brain model. This understanding brings healing and cohesiveness to a family that can seem out of sync or different." Because both she and her husband are filmmakers, they have many developmental moments they can share with their children. Reviewing the videos with the children is healing for them because she has greater compassion for what she didn't know while at the same time she can point out to them how far they've come and how advanced they were without even knowing it. For example, Jordan was a highly verbal child and had difficulties with his motor control. So, on video they have him saying his first word, *cat,* while he is struggling with his motor control.

In The O'Kelley Lab, having support is a key component. Early on, Harri sought help from coaches, tutors, and occupational therapists. Harri reflects on having a particularly insightful OT, Heather, who helped their family with communication and safety, teaching each child how to clearly share and express their needs. "Early intervention and supports are so important to the whole family's well-being and safety, especially when you are a family in crises like we were, in those early years of overwhelm and when siblings are so at risk for falling behind. Importantly, it was during the OT's home visits that I was made aware of Jordan's ADHD and autism," she says. Increasingly, as schools failed to offer proper support for her children's unique educational needs, she found herself and her son, Jordan, at four different schools in four years. She was quoted in her children's IEPs because she advocated for her children relentlessly when they were misidentified and misunderstood. Macey suffered a great deal of educational trauma from improper placement and engagement. Finally, Harri and her husband remortgaged their house to afford a private school, Bridges Academy, that specialized in 2e education. Harri says, "I refer to Bridges Academy as a sanctuary, not just a non-public school. There is a healing process for the family and for the student that occurs once the educational environment stops assaulting the child and embraces their strengths. Starting from the shadow day, my kids could feel the difference in this 2e education model and wondered why this model isn't the standard. Bridges Academy saved my kids."

Her statement highlights how all her educational training and understanding culminated when her children began at Bridges. In her early years, she was navigating the trauma and stress of having children that fit outside of the educational box. Many of her efforts had been centered on the deficits and on the challenges of 2e kids and not focused on the innate strengths of having different brain wiring. She says, "As I look back, I have a few memories that were glimpses of giftedness in each of my children, but it wasn't until later that I became more educated about giftedness. You only know what you know, and once the kids were identified as autistic, that's the education that I was mostly interested in and exposed to." Now, she understands that her children are gifted and ASD, and she employs the strength-based model. Harri builds each of her children's strengths while providing support to areas that need more attention. The strength-based approach is empowering for both the child and parent to develop safely and explore things that come with ease, and are enjoyable and natural to them. When we employ the strength-based model, we encourage the natural growth of a child's innate gifts and guide them to where they naturally flow and are motivated because their minds and bodies are engaged and so they can thrive.

Father Warrior

Mike Postma, Ed. D, founder of Gifted & Thriving, LLC, former executive director of Supporting the Emotional Needs of the Gifted (SENG), has dedicated the last two decades to leading efforts to address the holistic development of both gifted and 2e children and adults.

Mike is a father of four children, three of them are 2e. Not only is he the author of numerous articles and books, including *The Inconvenient Student,*[22] he was the architect of the Minnetonka Navigator Program, a magnet school specifically designed for highly gifted and 2e students. His educational strategies and techniques seek to ensure safety and engagement for 2e and gifted children and have been implemented nationally and globally. His philosophy emphasizes the development of social and emotional skills within the gifted/2e population to help support academic endeavors. Indeed, without these essential skills, gifted/2e children will continue to struggle to adapt to the world around them. Much of his work centers on building resiliency and adaptation based on neuroscience research. For him and his wife, Julie Postma, having three 2e children who do not fit into the mold makes this a family matter. They are family warriors. They have created numerous support groups and work to guide families to deep dive into education and understanding unconventional thinkers with humor and honesty.

As I chatted with Mike, he told me that this is personal to him: the livelihood and safety of his children are his driving force. One of the greatest challenges he sees his kids face is social isolation because of being misunderstood. It breaks your heart as a parent seeing your child experience intense loneliness. Both his son, Sean, and daughter, Amanda, have sensory processing disorder that makes it challenging for them to be out in the world. Sounds, lights, and scents can send their sensory system into overdrive where they experience intense anxiety and panic. What seem like "normal" activities on the outside can be emotionally, physically, and mentally draining for Sean and Amanda. They experience immense anxiety and Mike and Julie have developed family routines to ensure their safety and health. In the brain, when someone experiences painful neurosignals from their sensory processing, the sympathetic nervous system is activated, the primary stress response takes over and the emotional cortex sorts through information and responds to interpreted insults and higher brain areas are off-line. Over time, when the brain has multiple repeats of painful sensory information the person develops memory imprints that create an overactivated nervous system so that being out in the world is perceived as threatening and unsafe. Often, when an individual's nervous system is overwhelmed they tend to express certain behaviors to calm their nervous system, such as repetitive movements, covering their eyes or ears to reduce the magnitude of the sensory stimuli, and withdrawal from the outside world to seek refuge. When an individual routinely withdraws from the outside world they tend to experience greater social isolation which leads to greater mental and emotional difficulties. For example, Sean was homeschooled beginning in 9th grade because the sensory input at school from classroom activity, hallway lights, and the sounds of students moving from class to class—talking, footsteps, lockers banging—was overwhelming. Standard school sounds became unbearable for Sean to navigate. His nervous system was overwhelmed. Mike and Julie's techniques focus on calming the overactivated nervous system and retraining the brain to be more adaptable to the outside world. They worked on techniques to help Sean manage and now he can be out in the world through practice and setting practical expectations that do not overwhelm his nervous system. For Mike, it is essential that gifted/2e children do not merely survive their environment, but thrive.

Another challenge is that our society has little patience and acceptance of quirky behaviors. Mike describes how Sean's core challenges center on a slow processing speed and difficulties with his working memory, both of which are artificially slow. There is not a clear origin of his delayed processing, rather there is entanglement with his working memory and processing speed which interferes with his being able to complete tasks in a timely manner. As Mike says, "Things take him longer to process." Now, at age 19, Sean took the general education exam (GED) and scored a perfect 25/25 but he took forty minutes longer than the standard testing time. Even though Sean achieved a score of 100 percent accuracy, he technically did not pass because his individualized education plan (IEP) test report had expired, so he was not allowed the standard double time for the exam. This artifact of education technocracy resulted in his failing the general education exam. The challenge he now faces is that he will not be allocated the extra time until he is retested and qualifies for accommodations. His father says, "He clearly has a processing speed difference and he will not be rewarded with a GED even though got everything right because he took double the time and his IEP is not up to date, so he has failed."

Unfortunately, this dilemma leads to greater difficulty; the family cannot currently afford another battery of assessments for Sean to meet the measures of double time. A standard assessment costs between two and five thousand dollars. Thus, Sean's life is held up and he is left in limbo waiting to complete his GED because his accommodation measures have expired. Not meeting the standard measures for accommodations leaves Sean caught in an educational stranglehold where he cannot progress to college full time. It is important that we understand the financial strain families face educating 2e/gifted children and how the educational system lacks flexibility for non-traditional thinkers and test takers. This is where standardized tests do a disservice to non-traditional thinkers and processors so that their lives are held up in bureaucratic limbo. Even though Sean has a slower processing speed, we need to recognize that simply with more time he can complete tasks with one-hundred percent accuracy. Luckily, Sean has a father warrior and a mother warrior, so Sean is now taking college classes at the local community college to progress toward his dream of working in the U.S. Forestry Service. And, it is only a matter of time before he will get a GED completion slip in his hands. They are not stopping, they will continue to pass GO.

One of the most devastating parts of the story that Mike shares with me is that Sean experiences a great deal of social isolation and rejection because he does not fit into the "normal" framework in society. Sean's in-person interactions are limited because people often misunderstand him. Experiencing extreme social isolation has been a setback in Sean's life because he has not developed social and emotional connections and is missing acceptance and safety. More recently he has begun to develop friendships online, through online platforms where he shares his photographs and his passion for photography. Sean is making friends.

Sean is a gifted photographer and is able to remain undetected and capture images of wild animals in their natural habitats. Sean can sense the flow and energy of an animal and calms in their presence. He is at home in nature. Mike tells me, "Sean can get within a foot of a deer and photograph it without startling or disturbing the animal." Sean possesses naturalistic intelligence. He is comfortable in the presence of wild animals. He has images of a snake in a rearing pose and a faun sleeping. Animals have an unspoken language, and have instinctive levels of trust. Sean can tune in and connect with an animal to build a deep connection. Sean plans to join the forest reserve and become a park ranger so he can combine his natural gifts and his passion. Mike reports that Sean is studying to be an animal biologist with a specialty in cryptozoology— the study of animals whose existence or survival is disputed, like yeti (Bigfoot). He spends a great deal of time out in the wild (usually by himself) and reads maps very well because he has a gift for spatial navigation. From an evolutionary standpoint, even though Sean has challenges with the elements of our artificial world, when he is in the wild and in a natural setting with animals, he thrives.

It is important that we explore whether individuals on the spectrum have potential opportunities in careers and life paths where they can work in more naturalistic environments and therefore have greater life satisfaction and nervous system balance. When we work to find the right fit for our children, build from their natural gifts and let them lead the way, there is no stopping what they can do.

Kid Wonder Kid Warrior

Meet Jordan O'Kelley, a kid warrior like no other. At age five he designed a positivity chart that was implemented in three schools and that received a first-place award from an organization that recognizes inventions by kids who have special abilities. He wrote his first book in 5th grade, his second book in 8th grade, and entered college at age fourteen. These are only a few accomplishments of this now fifteen-year-old. Jordan is 2e, on the autism spectrum, and gifted. As I get to know this kid wonder, kid warrior, I learn he has a huge heart and compassion, a feature that is often left off the list of attributes of kids and adults on the autism spectrum. He tells me that he created a positivity chart because his friend Graham was constantly getting negative behavior reports sent home. Jordan said to himself, *no, no mas,* and he made a positivity chart. The premise of his positivity chart is that when you do a favorable act you are rewarded with a key. When you have accumulated ten keys you get a small prize—like a pencil or an eraser. When you reach one hundred keys, you get a big prize—like a LEGO. When a child receives one hundred keys they get their picture taken with their prize and it is displayed in the classroom. This process builds a circle of positivity, where each key builds on rewarding positive actions and behaviors by focusing the mind on positivity. This creates a positive association between the behavior and action in the child's mind. And this sets a platform for children with learning challenges to focus their mind on what is going right.

Let me remind you that Jordan was five when he designed this particular positivity chart that uses a foundational concept for developing a positive growth mindset that is used in positive psychology today. I tell him, "You are forward thinker, already teaching yourself and others to build positive neural networks, patterns, and behaviors, and you were only five!" He says, "All I knew is that I didn't like getting yellow back then." Yellow was the color used to indicate "bad" behavior. Jordan recalls that often the kids deemed with "bad" behavior were missing out on recess which caused them more stress and anxiety because recess was the time they would blow off steam. As punishment for their "bad" behavior, the kids were stuck in the classroom at recess–a time when they most needed a mind and body break—and their punishment only fueled more "bad" behavior. I often explain to people that children whom we deem as behaving badly are usually acting out because of an unmet need and that at their core they are suffering and searching for safety and connection. And too often they are met with opposition and disapproval, which reinforces a negative cycle. So, five-year-old Jordan decided to create a positivity chart to change classroom behaviors, improve attitudes, and promote overall well-being for the students and teachers because they all worked toward the common goal of positive behavior. Jordan received his 100th key and he purchased a purple and orange lava lamp. Once he and his classmates reached their 100th key, they took a photo together with their rewards as a reminder for their success of positive behaviors. Jordan was then interviewed by local newspapers and received a 1st place award.

At that time Jordan was not yet identified as gifted, he'd only been labeled as being on the autism spectrum. Somehow, the schools were missing that Jordan was (and is) gifted. For years, Jordan was not engaged in school and was not at all working to his level and ability. Jordan's mother, Harri, knew that Jordan was gifted, but the schools refused to acknowledge that and ignored her instinct. Often Harri was labeled as a problem mother, but she persisted, knowing that her son was being mislabeled and misidentified. She was set on unlocking and discovering his gifts. Finally, Jordan was tested for giftedness in third grade. He was reading five grade levels above his actual level—an indication that he should be identified as gifted. Or what we call "crazy smart."

Jordan tells me that elementary school was incredibly boring for him and he felt that he did not learn anything. Because he was not tested for giftedness at the time, he was not stimulated, and that was torture. This is not an uncommon occurrence. Harri sees a number of students and families that are struggling with a school's lack of awareness and understanding of a 2e child. Too often 2e children are tagged as special needs and the schools miss the gifted piece so that a child is locked out of getting an education that meets their level of ability. Harri explains, "That's another example of teachers who are not educated about what gifted is and do not realize it's good to have a child called twice-exceptional. They should be tested and they need to be given different things. It was the beginning of our education with that. In fourth grade, the homework didn't match up with where he was, and once again in IEP assessments he was five years ahead, but no one told us as parents that he was five years ahead in reading. And we were still looking at him through the eyes of, oh, he's special needs, he's autistic. We still hadn't gotten that clarification that he was in fact also gifted. Until you have all those pieces, you really don't know what you should be doing as a parent, so it's really important. Then in the fifth grade is when his world really crashed and burned. He was just frustrated, mostly because of the teachers' style of trying to toughen the kids up and get them ready for middle school." Unfortunately, when a 2e child is labeled as Special Ed, they have a huge challenges because there is a disconnect in their ability because the focus can be on the areas where they struggle and not the areas where they thrive. Over time, removing the label of special needs and special ed is almost impossible. Often this experience is traumatic for the child and the family.

Jordan's spark was ignited in 3rd grade when he was able to start typing on a computer at a STEAM magnet. He learned how using technology helped his gifts and strengths flourish. Typing was a game-changer that allowed all the intensity and brightness in his mind to come to life on the page. His mother, Harri, describes, "One intervention that made a huge difference was his 3rd grade typing. His teacher was able to see what he was capable of so that's I think why we went from teachers saying, 'No, no, he's autistic, he has an aide, he can't be tested for gifted' to having a teacher say, 'Have you ever tested him for being gifted?' I was like, 'No, I know I can't because he's autistic,' and she looked at me like I was crazy." His mother Harri explains further, "He went from not being able to do homework, where they were cutting his homework in half, to being able to catch up to his classmates. In addition to ASD, Jordan has dysgraphia, and typing made it much faster, easier, and less painful to express himself." This simple step unlocked Jordan's mind and allowed for communication. This is critical to think about. When a 2e child is given proper support and has a tool to communicate, the sky is the limit. And in Jordan's case, he wrote his first book a year after he was introduced to typing.

Jordan recounts, "My first book, *O'Kelley Legendary LEGENDS of LEGEND or 'How I Got Out of Homework in 4th Grade'* was essentially an excuse to get out of writing summaries of books. I was running out of books due to the fact that my reading level was above *Geronimo Stilton* and I could read it in one night. I was essentially just doing *Harold and the Purple Crayon* and stuff. Because Ms. M. is awesome we made a deal where instead of doing summaries I would write a book, and I wrote a book, and I finished the book, and I published the book two years later after essentially everything had been set into place." His book is a narrative about his and his family's wild adventures. Jordan says, "I couldn't write one page in my previous school without a computer, but I wrote a whole book with the use of a computer at my new school."

Jordan's humor, insight and passion to excel comes through his storytelling. On the back of his book, Jordan wisely advises that "if you have a kid that hates doing homework then maybe let them do something they want to do." When given the proper support, tools, and guidance, Jordan went way beyond what his teachers and even his mother thought he could do. Jordan teaches us that we need to provide creative solutions when working with unconventional thinkers. His transformation from a mi-matched Special Ed experience, to writing an entire book, offers us a lesson. When we choose alternative educational solutions for alternative minds, their true ability and capability shines through. Jordan describes, "It went from horrible to amazing. The teachers were all very nice, like we got to call them by their first names and we would talk to them out of class. There were breaks between every class. Just better in every single way. It's an amazing feat, but yes. The teachers actually were able to teach me, unlike the previous year. I learned more that year than I would've if I was stuck in that same year for like three years." And when he attended Bridges Academy, everything got better. He describes that the teachers were able to meet his intellectual capabilities and did wonders with it. It was the first time he felt completely academically engaged. And in 8th grade he wrote his second book, *O'Kelley Legendary MONOLOGUES or How I Got Out of Homework in 8th Grade.* His training in improv, mime, and acting funneled him into writing the monologues.

Jordan describes his ability to communicate through writing as similar to the film, *LIFE Animated,* where a child with autism, Owen Suskind, learns to speak through the Disney characters from watching Disney films.[23] In the film, this is a light bulb moment for Owen's parents because they begin to speak to him in Disney speak and they are able to communicate and connect with him. Owen Suskind went on to complete high school, college, and receive an Oscar nomination for his film, *LIFE Animated.* This is another powerful story, showing how technology unlocked a child's voice so his mind could freely communicate. Owen's parents' astute awareness and willingness to follow his lead provided for a dynamic change in his life outcome because he was given the tools to communicate. Jordan, the kid warrior, is a world leader and example of neurodiversity and neuroindividuality. He broke out of the standard educational system and is now fourteen years old and in college. When neuroindividuality is embraced and nurtured, we experience outcomes that exceed our wildest imaginations.

Mime as Therapy

Terry Hart is no ordinary mime. Terry uses mime, improv, and acting to teach individuals with autism and 2e kids ways to communicate and tell stories through movement. For Terry, mime is an ancient art form for storytelling. Sam Christensen once told me that we are all storytellers, we just need ways to express our voices and essence, and Sam's joy and place is to help people find their essence. That is exactly what Terry does, he is an essence detective who teaches 2e kids to be comfortable in their natural way and to express themselves. Terry is a multi-talented artist, and expresses himself in many forms—as a writer, actor, improvisor, and a mime, all of which give him unbounded creativity to work with neurodiverse thinkers. Terry tells me, "I started doing mime back in 1976. Back then, Shields and Yarnell were on television and I studied with the America's foremost mime, Richmond Shepard, who studied with Marcel Marceau." Marcel Marceau, the French actor famously known for his "Bip the Clown," called mime the "art of silence."

Terry explains, "When I started to do improv about 25 years ago, part of improv is using space work. Creating a world out of nothing. So, mime came back in." Mime tells stories and creates worlds without spoken language through the use of gestures, movement, and space. Terry began his first classes and instructional videos to teach mime to children and saw the impact on their ability to communicate. When Terry met Harri at their kids' school (Terry also has two gifted daughters), Terry's wife disclosed he was a mime. Inspired to help her kids communicate, Harri couldn't resist recruiting him to work with young storytellers, 2e kids, and kids on the spectrum. Terry's experience observing different kinds of gifted kids and seeing how their behaviors and social styles are very different, gave him deep understanding and insight to work with differential learning types.

Terry describes his instructional style as being specific to the child and the child's needs. He relies on going into his senses and body to imagine how to help the child access their own senses and body with greater awareness and accuracy. Common physical characteristics in children on the autism spectrum are challenges with motor processing, motor timing, and proprioception, which is understanding their body in three-dimensional space.[24] Often behaviorally there are delays in physical actions and body mechanics where children not only have delay in speech, but in motor activity as well. Additionally, children who have a mismatch between their bodies and where they are in three-dimensional space tend to bump into things and appear clumsy. Occupational therapy is a known to aid in eye, hand, mind, and body coordination, which helps build networks for planning physical movement. Occupational therapy works with training the brain through repetitive physical and verbal instruction and the child builds behaviors and networks based on that training. Similarly, scientists found that teaching pantomime can potentially activate the mirror neuron system in the brain to teach and model motor behavior.[25] Mirror neurons, as we discussed in Chapter Five, are responsible for an internal representation of observing an action in another individual.[26] Mime can teach a person to activate these networks through observing the action/movement and repeating the movement/action to build a brain pattern for the physical action.

Terry describes a student, Quincy, who had major motor challenges. "I created an exercise for Quincy to pick up an imaginary glasses using mime. Quincy raps. He's a 26-year-old guy and he could rap like crazy. But he has no motor skills at all. So, we drew up an exercise where I have them notice something, then share with the audience that they've noticed it. It's a glass. I have them reach out, hold the glass, pick it up, drink, put it back down, let it go, take their hand away, think something about it, and walk off. And all the kids did it. But Quincy had no idea...so, I worked more methodically with him. I put a real glass inside his hand, so he could try to feel the grip. His father was like, 'Oh my gosh.' He didn't perfect the grip, because it takes a long time to learn. But his father is now getting him to do dishes. Teaching him how to do dishes and stuff like that, learning to work with space and objects and movement. It's all a learning process." For Terry, each class is different. He focuses on the group dynamic and tailors it to their behaviors and receptivity. He pays attention and starts at the most basic element, then moves up. He applies aspects of the Social Thinking model developed by Michelle Garcia Winner and her team, which dovetails beautifully with "Mime as Therapy."

Terry developed "Mime as Therapy" with the O'Kelley Lab over the last few years, sharing the art of mime for neurodiverse kids through an online video series. He was recognized at the Autistic Network for Community Achievement (ANCA) World Festival for his novel mime therapy and community service for individuals with autism. ANCA's mission is to see and understand "how" the autistic mind processes information. They are focused on the "the Autistic Paradigm—from the inside out—a mental/cognitive processing map unique and distinct to all autistic people, children, teens, and adults."[27] At the international festival where individuals with autism from around the world gather, Terry performed "Mime as Therapy" workshops. "It was interesting, because when we went to Canada, I had kids who didn't speak English that were from all these different countries, but I was able to do these same exercises because they transferred over. The kids were able to get them through mime." This highlights how that art in particular translates across all languages, nationalities, and cultures and that communication through movement is universal to human beings.

At one training session in particular, he tells the story of the butterfly. "The founders of ANCA have a son who is severely handicapped. He is in a wheelchair and has no body function at all. I was showing everybody how to do the butterfly. It's all about eye gaze and transferring movement." He explains how, as a mime, he can imagine and depict a butterfly fluttering through space, "seeing" the imagined creature in one place, then another and another. "I was showing everybody how to do the butterfly and these kids…and these are not kid-kids, but these are late teenager and adult kids, that were doing this and and their son in a wheelchair started to do the butterfly movements by transferring his gaze. I said, 'Oh my gosh.' Often, we don't know if he's paying attention or not, because it appears he is in his own world. But he is listening. He is in there. Due to his brain damage he has tremendous challenge with his body, but he did the butterfly gaze and transferred the movements with his head and gaze. His mother and father were so amazed." By participating in the butterfly exercise, this young man let us know that he has much more going on in his mind. Because his body lacks specific mobility, this young man has been misunderstood and miscategorized as having low overall cognitive ability. Clearly we can too readily misinterpret different behaviors and ways of being because we do not fully understand what's going on. Too often we miss individuals on the autism spectrum because they lack the ability of motor timing to mirror us, and we incorrectly assume they lack ability to completely process rather than seeing what is actually going on in their minds. Terry's example of this young man's transformation through the butterfly exercise shows us that training to communicate with physical actions, like mime, may be better than with verbal cues so that individuals can express their comprehension with physical action. And it is a lesson to all of us that there is much more going on inside than meets the eyes. Terry saw how "Mime as Therapy" can transform the mind-body connection, and Terry and the O'Kelley Lab have refined exercises for neurodiverse populations to help build networks and pathways for communication, even in the silence.

"The art of silence" may be the key to why mime works for children on the spectrum. Mime requires a laser focus of attention of the body in three-dimensional space. One connects to their body in silence when in the process of mime and there is a peacefulness in silence. Not only can mime serve as occupational therapy to train the brain and potentially activate the mirror neuron system, it can be a therapy that actually addresses challenges with sensory overload by eliminating the interaction of multiple sensations. In silence, the mind can center and focus on the task at hand. For children with enhanced sensory processing who are easily overstimulated, mime can be a path that removes all other stimuli so they can safely explore their body-mind connection. Mime slows down the mind by centering awareness on physical movement which offers a way for people to communicate and express themselves through movement.

Terry is quick to acknowledge that people often underestimate mime and misunderstand its value. In his early years as an actor he was pigeonholed as a mime. He says, "Because people think being a mime is like being a clown, you get labeled as the mime guy. People have this weird feeling about mime. I must say, just like clowns, mimes freak some people out." So, Richmond, his mentor, advised him to keep his passion for mime a secret.

But Terry cannot resist the art, loves the silence, the space work, and conveying stories with movement. For Terry, mime connects the minds of individuals who are often left out in our society, the ones who are pigeonholed as disconnected and different. Through mime he teaches people to see themselves and others beyond a label, to see their essence as a human being.

Yes And...

Improvisation, the live theatrical art, uses the power of imagination, mirroring, and tuning in to the present moment. An improv group collaboratively creates a scene on the spot, without a script. Viola Spolin, the "mother" of modern improvisation taught and coached actors how to be presently aware and make choices through improvisation that modeled real life.[28] The catchphrase, basic rule, and best-known game of improv, is *"Yes, And..."* Improv players accept the information given by another person ("*Yes,*"), then build on or add to the content ("*and...*") so that each person works with the others to collectively build a scene. This basic principle of improv, accepting other people's offers of creative ideas, then building on those ideas and avoiding judgment, fosters trust and cooperation so participants become dynamically in tune with one another.[29] In this safe environment without judgment, lowered inhibitions lead to more flexible thinking and increased creativity.[30] In middle school music classrooms, theatrical improvisation has been shown to increase flexible thinking.[31]

Recent neuroscience studies have treated improvisation—particularly musical improvisation—as a useful window to understand the neuroscience of spontaneous creativity, observing that jazz and blues musicians and freestyle rappers use the brain's executive function networks in the prefrontal cortex[32] and increase connectivity among different areas of the brain, activating positive feelings associated with creativity and openness.[33] Theatrical improvisation requires no musical training, yet its playful, collaborative nature builds brain patterns and connectivity for flexible thinking by tapping into the collective consciousness where thoughts, ideas, and emotions are shared among the improvisers to improve social connection and happiness.[34]

Improv enhances flexible thinking in a safe environment where improvisers are free to explore and invent a scene without having an end result in mind. The quick-paced thinking and adaptability of improv nurtures the spirit through humor, where individuals experiment with their intuition of human behavior. The goal of enhancing one's ability to become tuned in to one's emotions and perceptions is at the nucleus of sound storytelling. Laughter, especially social laughter, the key component and goal of theatrical improv comedy, releases natural endorphins which reduces stress and enhances joy.[35] Improvisers learn how to perceive and read the reactions and behaviors of others while directing their own behaviors to match the mood of the stage. More recently, improv has been used as a tool to help guide individuals on the autism spectrum to identify their emotions and tell stories. The different perspectives of unique thinkers can be a fit for the element of created humor that is based on a combination of recognition, pain, and distance—turning incongruous experience into joy.[36] Top notch theater companies, like The Second City, offer classes to kids, teens, as well as adult actors, and professionals in other careers to support creativity and flexible thinking.

Terry Hart uses improv as one of the many creative ways he enriches the lives of 2e children. For Terry, it is all about connection and meeting the child exactly where they are and helping them build awareness of being in their body so they learn to read themselves and begin to read and interpret others. "I always think, how many ways can I use this to communicate what it is? This is the whole thing that I have to break down. I have to come up with some key models. I'm teaching these guys to know their body. Because they can't read people's expressions and they have challenges identifying other people's emotions." He captures their attention and helps them focus their mind to connect into the present moment by breaking things down to the microscopic level. This level of detail helps children better understand and unpack human behavior and emotions by using archetypes and language. Terry explains, "I say to them, 'Tell me what a pirate looks like. Show me what a superhero looks like.' We'll go through a bunch of archetypes. From the archetypes, I make them realize that a small action like leaning in, or leaning away can mean many things. I am teaching them to be aware of their body, aware of how they walk. Walk like a superhero. Walk like somebody who's lost. I teach them to perceive how their body comes off, how they're communicating, and how others are communicating with their body. Or how to read another's body language." When Terry familiarizes children with their body-mind connection it automatically builds a sharper awareness of their body in three-dimensional space. "Improv is secondary to just perceiving their body. This all helps with their motor skills, balance, strength, and coordination."

Another powerful gateway of improv is tapping into the foundations of emotional and social connection, where participants read one another's emotional and social cues to build a story. Terry harnesses the power of archetypes to teach emotional and social cues by having the children express exaggerated emotions. He thinks of cartoon characters and has them express the character's big emotions. "First of all, they love cartoons and I have a series of characters where we play with expressing the emotion. I say, 'Show me angry. Show me sad.' Then we walk around the room in the characters and they learn that they are conveying emotion through their actions," Terry says.

Harri O'Kelley describes how reading emotions and body language is challenging for her children. Terry's improv exercises help them identify and mimic the process of an emotion's expression in the body. A parent with a child on the spectrum may faces challenges because the child may be inflexible in their thinking. Improv helps get out of rigid patterns. Improv breaks up rigid thinking and brings in more fluidity—in a safe and fun environment. And recent studies show that theatrical play within a peer group, mediated by supportive role models like Terry, decreases anxiety and increases social engagement in young people with autism.[37]

Harri's experience echoes that research. She says that improv teaches her kids the cultural norms of human interaction. For example, she says, "You teach them to be flexible and notice where someone's standing and if they come too close to you, then you move a bit away. Or in an elevator, you look to them to see if they're going to push the button, or are you going to push the button? Is it a man or a woman that's getting in the elevator? What are the rules? Do men let women go by first? The improvisers can explore in that space. But with the physical connection, not just standing rigid, you can use improv to expand and explore the space for them."

Improv serves as a vehicle for activating mirroring between individuals, which in turn builds theory of mind, the mental process of anticipating and visualizing what another is thinking. Improv can be an essential tool when guiding children with different learning styles and cues for social behavior. Improv playfully teaches the rules of engagement and allows children to learn how their minds work in relation to mentalizing, or conceptulizing what another individual is thinking. In addition, the brain mirroring patterns created by improv's cardinal rule of "*Yes, and*" helps build greater social awareness and understanding of internal and external behavioral styles. When people are in sync, there is a release of positive neurotransmitters: oxytocin (the neurohormone of trust and pair bonding), dopamine (the neurotransmitter for reward and motivation), endorphins (which, during laughter, boost one's mood), and serotonin (a neurochemical essential for social engagement). Not only does improv activate theory of mind to help understand what others are thinking or feeling, but also the connection and social laughter can boost one's mood with surges of positive neurotransmitters. By activating positive neurochemical and neuropathways, improv improves social connection and communication. Comedic creative expression builds mental and behavioral flexibility by opening a person's imagination into the mindset of another human being and increases their social, mental, and emotional connection to the other person.

Humor uncovers another piece of social thinking—the laughter mindset. When one is laughing, one is activating all different parts of the body and is aware and present in the experience. Humor is a huge release, and when someone is laughing they are having fun. Through laughter, one is more flexible in their thinking, more receptive to taking risks, and less afraid of failing. Through humor, where the risk is relatively low, one can better understand their behavior patterns. The beauty of improv taps into the collective; everyone participates through the live experience. Everyone is included in the experience, playing the group mind game, thinking: *What will we do next?* As Terry describes, "I point out their strengths. You want to encourage them, you want to get them to laugh. I laugh even if it is mildly funny. People in the audience laugh at improv shows not because something was so particularly funny, but because they think, 'They said exactly what I would have said.'" That's what makes it funny, the parallel thinking among the improvisers and the audience. The vulnerability of humor, of human nature, where we collectively think things but are afraid to say them. Improv is on the spot and in the present moment and it gets people away from critical thinking and monkey mind. Terry says, "When someone's talking to you, you're thinking, 'What am I going to say that's funny?' You miss everything because you're in your own head." By contrast, when you are in the scene and you naturally say the next thing you are engaged and in the present moment. Being tuned in and allowing the scene to naturally unfold dampens the discomfort and uncertainty. Actively playing the improv game, the mind has no time for rumination or self-criticism.

Scientists at University of Michigan and Stonybrook University have discovered that twenty minutes a day of improvisation allows people to feel more at ease and more tolerant of uncertainty.[38] Researchers reported that the improvisation participants had enhanced positive emotions and expressed greater happiness compared to participants who performed scripted tasks. Scientists believe that the practice of improv lets participants reap benefits beyond the classroom or stage—it can improve social interactions in their everyday lives.

They went on to report that improv improves mental health without negative consequences. It can be a valuable therapeutic practice, without associated stigma. Another key finding is that improv can lead to greater creative and divergent thinking compared to individuals performing from a script. This study shows the invaluable outcomes of participating in improv—participants engage in creative thinking and curiosity, have enhanced positive mood, and their discomfort and uncertainty is eased. These positive benefits open the mind to greater flexible thinking so that engaging in the present moment precludes an individual from overthinking and allows them to become activated in participating in life with the response to "*Yes, and...*"

Terry explains: "It's the collective. Everybody's part of the collective. In mime, in improv, you're in the collective. When people engage in improv, everybody understands the story because of the collective mind." It's a positive, flexible mindset that we all explore together when we say "*Yes, and ...*" to each other.

Thinking Outside the Box

Unconventional thinking is a hallmark of people on the autism spectrum. Individuals on the spectrum possess unique thinking that demonstrates enhanced creativity. They express behaviors that can set them apart from the crowd. But often, their originality is misinterpreted. Children on the spectrum are frequently misunderstood and missed entirely as creative beings. These children are often highly imaginative, but they may struggle to verbally express their ability and complex thinking. Additionally, individuals on the spectrum often challenge traditional conventions of creativity: in other words, they think outside the box. To better uncover creative thinking, we need to know what is going on in the brain.

For many years we have been misinformed about the creative mind. The notion has persisted that the right hemisphere of the brain is the control center for creative thinking and the left hemisphere is where logic lives. This "right brain, left brain" story is a myth. In fact, for creative thinking, it takes two hemispheres to tango. Creative expression ignites electric signals across both hemispheres. Creative expression uses logic to communicate ideas and logic depends on creativity to process the endless possibilities. Creativity and logic are on a continuum. For some activities, for example, navigating in the woods, you need both creativity *and* logic to spatially orient yourself. And if you're painting a forest, you need both precision (to accurately place your strokes) and imagination (to make the scene come alive on the canvas).

Scientists at the University of Southern California (USC), measured the brain activity in highly creative visual individuals—architects—in the MRI scanner.[39] Researchers asked the participants to review images of letters and numbers and then examined their ability to imagine rearranging the images in their mind. When the participants visualized rearranging the objects, both the right and left hemispheres lit up, demonstrating how creative processing requires both the right and left hemispheres. In fact, the left hemisphere is critical to supporting creative thinking. Many other studies have shown that creative thinking is not limited to a single brain region or network, but rather involves the orchestration of the entire brain specific to the type of creative thinking and processing. Thus, when we think creatively, our mind engages in our very own patterns, uniquely firing electrical impulses.

Many individuals on the autism spectrum communicate and express themselves creatively and have active imaginations. A survey study, conducted by Catherine Best and colleagues, measured divergent thinking, a hallmark of creativity, along with autistic traits. They found that individuals with greater autistic traits expressed more original ideas, although they expressed fewer ideas overall.[40] In the analysis, seventy-five percent of the participants were on the autism spectrum and participants had varying degrees of autism traits. Best and her team asked questions such as, *How many ways can you think to use a paper clip?* Individuals who had more autistic traits skipped the more obvious ideas and went directly to the more creative ones, highlighting that individuals with greater autistic traits may automatically pass over evident solutions and directly tackle problem-solving with greater engagement and innovation. In this study, these individuals preferred more complex thinking solutions. This result particularly sheds light on the positives of autism, reflecting a tendency toward creative thinking for individuals on the spectrum, contrary to the view that individuals with autism are more inflexible in their thinking. In this case, their expression is much more creative, pointing to our society's biases about what we consider creative. We often tend to value volume or number of ideas and set parameters for creativity. We expect people to follow the obvious checklist. In the case of our unbound thinkers, they may provide perhaps a single more original, divergent idea. That form of creativity can get missed if we are prejudging what creativity is meant to look like and focusing on the value of a large quantity of ideas rather than on the originality of a single idea.

Scientists have explored visual processing in autism and found that people with autism process visual information more rapidly, leading to greater visual processing and fluid visual reasoning.[41] The team at Harvard Medical School investigated the relationship between the brain activity and the Raven's Standard Progressive Matrices (RSPM) where people with ASD displayed brain activity indicating that they could better decode visual information. Both accuracy and response time revealed that individuals with autism responded similarly to the control group, but for the visual matching tasks, found that individuals with ASD responded more quickly than neurotypical individuals. When the researchers compared brain activity, the participants with autism showed an increase in brain activity in the visual areas and expressed a reduction in brain activity in the prefrontal cortex. This finding led the scientists to conclude that people with autism have a greater ability to decode visual information based on their prominent brain activity. In fact, people with ASD often report enhanced visual processing which aids in their reasoning and overall thinking. It appears that the brain matures so that patterns dedicated to visual processing are enhanced in autism. The origin for the novel and different thinking is embedded in a different neurocircuitry. From these studies we can better understand how people on the spectrum think differently based on how their brain processes information.

Dr. Temple Grandin, a world leader in autism advocacy who is on the autism spectrum herself, describes how she "thinks in pictures." She sees the universe through visual images, like movie clips.[42] She is the mother of the neurodiversity movement, author of several books, professor of animal science at the University of Colorado, and spokesperson for people with autism. She did not speak until she was fifteen years old. Temple Grandin was one of the first people to describe what it felt like to live with autism. Her personal account matches the brain research in that she thinks in pictures and movie clips run in her brain, providing insight about her creative and diverse thinking.

As an advocate, Temple Grandin highlights the importance of helping kids diagnosed with autism find meaning in what they do and find a community where they can share their passions. When a person with ASD finds their passion and meaning, social bonds grow within a community of those with parallel interests. She spotlights how individuals on the spectrum have unique ways of thinking, which is an enhancement, not a deficit and necessary for human advancement in the world.

Thinking outside the box comes naturally to individuals on the autism spectrum. They skip the obvious ideas and elevate their minds to imagine the unimaginable, coming up with novel ideas. Studies show that people with ASD often see the world with greater visual processing, leading to them to have visual enhancements for perceiving their environment. This directly informs how they interact with the world. Their creativity and originality is grounded in how their brain is wired, and understanding their brain processing can provide a foundation to better guide and encourage different types of creative thinking. Brain science lends hope that when we open our minds and begin to unpack ASD originality we learn how individuals on the spectrum can be our leaders and visionaries with non-conventional solutions for humanity's greatest challenges.

As Temple Grandin says, "I don't want my thoughts to die with me, I want to have done something. I'm not interested in power, or piles of money. I want to leave something behind. I want to make a positive contribution—know that my life has meaning."

Dear Butterflies in your Belly,

It is difficult to explain, but your stomach hurts. Your entire GI hurts most of the time and it feels like it will never stop aching. The physical pain pulls you out of your skin, out of your body, and out of your mind. Engaging with others is taxing and overwhelming. It's exhausting when your stomach aches.

Eating is challenging. It can be painful, dangerous, distracting, debilitating. Your mood follows your food, your aching belly. It seems few things can settle you. It is aching, burning, and churning in your body. You tire easily. It is painful to be in your body. Your GI holds the key to your joy, your life, your wellness. You need to feel settled in your GI, grounded in your body, peaceful in your mind.

Everyone has the answers—prebiotics, probiotics, dairy-free, wheat-free, vegan, paleo, low fat, high fat, fish oil, folic acid, supplements—your head dizzies with all the noise.

Come here and rest among the next pages, listen to the facts, non-advice that is free from the nonsense of marketing. Choose the steps for you, your mindful eating, your mindful being.

Happy gut, happy brain, and peace of mind. Let's discover possible solutions together.

Truly yours with a rock-solid stomach,

Good Belly

CHAPTER 8:
The Supreme Gut Brain Connection

Mighty Gut, Microbiome and Our Ever-Changing Behavior

Now more than ever there is increasing evidence that the inter-connectedness between the gut, brain, and our microbes affects our physical, mental, and emotional health. Since the Industrial Revolution, there has been an introduction of over 70,000 synthetic products made from converting raw materials such as natural gas, oil, metals, water, minerals, and other gasses.[1] The production of unnatural materials emits a vast range of chemicals that trigger numerous chemical reactions and alter human physiology. Many consequences from this environmental shift are the yet-unknown effects these new chemical compounds have on our physiology, behavior, and genetics. In addition, alterations to the environment affect organisms such as plants, microbes, and the balance of natural chemicals. All this has ramifications for our livelihoods and well-being.

Globally we have adopted clean hygiene practices that can alter both good and negative microbes (a microscopic living organism, including bacteria, viruses, protozoa, and some fungi and parasites) that are exogenous (outside) and indigenous (within), ultimately changing our relationship with organisms in our environment. In particular, the clean hypothesis proposes that we are interfering with the relationship we have with our microbes by eliminating the positive/good (symbiotic) microbes from our environment, causing us to be more susceptible to the consequences of bad/negative (parasitic) microbes. Negative consequences may lead to more sickness related to allergies, autoimmune disease, mental health, physical wellbeing, and even cause behavioral changes.[2]

Cesarean sections comprise 32% of births in the United States and have been on the rise over the last number of decades with a sharp upturn in the 1970s.[3] This change in birthing practices has implications for newborns' health and immunity. Newborns from cesarean sections have altered microbiomes. Another way in which we are altering our relationship with microbes is with the overuse of antibiotics. Chronic use of antibiotics can disrupt the symbiotic relationship in the human GI by suppressing the "good bacteria" that aid in digestion and nutrient absorption and permitting an increase in the "negative bacteria," thereby increasing GI difficulties, altering mood, and physical health.[4] It is not clear to what degree or how we are adjusting our relationships with microbes, but this happens to be one of the greatest explorations of our time.

Our Microscopic Buddies

"Microbiome" is the latest science buzz word. It has made its way into major news, dedicated book selections at Barnes and Noble, and TED talks. But the most exciting element is that we are on a new frontier of science. The microbiome is the makeup of microorganisms in a specific environment like that of the gastrointestinal tract, and other parts of the body. Each of us has our very own distinctive and specialized microbiome.[5] So here is the lowdown on our microscopic buddies. We live in a microbial world. Humans are 90% bacteria and 10% human, that is, bacterial genes outnumber human genes by approximately 150:1. And there are more than 10,000 different species of bacteria.[6] At birth, every person develops their own unique microbe fingerprint based on birth mode, geographical location, diet, allergies, and genetic makeup.

As mentioned, 32% of human births in the United States are by cesarean section and that number is increasing.[7] Scientists now know that infants born via cesarean section have a different microbiome.

Cesarean-born infants' microbiome is similar to skin cells from their mother, whereas infants born through the vaginal canal have a microbiome similar to that of their mother's vagina.[8] An essential bacteria for gut flora, *lactobacillus*, is transferred from mother to infant during passage through the birth canal and populates the infant's gut lining. This difference matters because *lactobacillus* aids in immune interactions and GI functioning. At six months, infants born by cesarean section begin to have a microbiome profile similar to infants born via vaginal delivery. But although they catch up, for the first six months of life, their gut flora is delayed in maturing, and that delay is tightly woven with immunity. The relationship between an infant's microbiome and the infant's development during the first six months of life is not clear, nor is it certain whether birth by cesarean section influences neural networks, emotional and intellectual development, immune interactions, or the relationship of neuroimmune interactions. It has been shown, however, that children born by cesarean section have a five times greater chance of developing allergies.[9] Another study found that even seven years after birth, the microbiome in children born via cesarean differs from those born via vaginal delivery.[10] The way we have adjusted our human delivery practices is a clear example of how we are interfering with Mother Nature and impacting our natural health and development. One simple adjustment to this mechanism is that if a child must be born via cesarean section, a process called "vaginal seeding," currently the subject of clinical trials, involves simply placing the vaginal secretions (bacteria) from the mother's vagina on the infant right after birth.[11] This may allow for the more natural microflora population of the infant's gastrointestinal tract. It is worth considering after a mother so carefully tends to her infant in the nine-month haul of pregnancy. This practice could enhance the symbiotic relationship between microbes and infant development. It is still not clear what happens in the first six months of the infant's immune development, and how the mode of delivery affects immune and neural development. This leaves mothers, clinicians, and scientists with a puzzle to solve on how to best develop the infant's gut, immunity, and brain functioning. We know that the microbiome has many important roles in immunity,

GI functioning, brain function, and behavior. Greater evidence is emerging on the vast importance of microbiome, gut, immune and neuroimmune interactions.

Here is more evidence about how our microscopic buddies influence human organs, systems, and our health:

- ○ Microbiota have a direct role in development of the immune system

- ○ Stress alters the microbial composition of the gut causing increased "bad" bacteria

- ○ "Leaky gut" is a condition where gut microbes are altered and "good" bacteria is depressed and "bad" bacteria overruns the gut

- ○ Fermented milk products build good bacteria and elevate mood and reduce anxiety

- ○ Prebiotics and probiotics work differently in the gut

- ○ Prebiotics feed indigenous (our original and natural populations) microbes

- ○ Probiotics populate new colonies of good microbes in the gut

- ○ Diet directly alters gut microbiota

- ○ Gut microbiota have been found to alter the expression levels of drug metabolizing enzymes and transporters, where the microbiota may be helpful or harmful to the individual in obtaining the optimal dosing of medication

- ○ In mice, probiotics change behavior, gut pathology, and inflammatory molecules in the body.

Human GI 101, Our Second Brain

The enteric nervous system (ENS) regulates gastrointestinal functioning and is composed of a web of neurons extending from the esophagus to the anus.[12] Approximately 500 million neurons compose the human ENS, roughly the size of a cat brain. In comparison, the average human brain has approximately 100 billion neurons and the spinal cord has 100 million neurons.[13] The ENS has five times more neurons than the spinal cord. The ENS is our second, little brain. Fundamental features of the enteric nervous system are the intricate neural circuits for motor functions of the gut, blood flow, secretion, and transport of nutrients from the mucosa, immune functioning, and endocrine functioning.[14] The ENS utilizes and produces more than 30 neurotransmitters, which are often identical to the neurotransmitters of the central nervous system (CNS) such as serotonin, dopamine, GABA, and acetylcholine. There are approximately 100 identified neurotransmitters, the communicating molecules that transfer information across neurons, throughout the body and brain. For example, the luminal cells of the gut generate 90% of the body's serotonin and 50% of the body's dopamine.[15] Both of these neurotransmitters are essential for gut motility, and they are also vital for mental functioning, attention, motivation, reward, mood, physical movement, and sleep-wake cycle.

Listen to Your Gut, Gut Cells Make Hormones that Can Affect Mood

Your brain, gut, microbiome, behavior, and emotions are connected like a web. Consider the phrase, "Listen to your gut, it tells the truth." Have you ever had a gut feeling? Your gut may be a more reliable source of information that we previously thought. Its connection to the brain is essential for survival. We know that gut feelings, known as intuition, are processed in the brain areas of the frontal cortex, which help us navigate emotional reactions, process decision making, and avoid dangerous situations. Now there is a wide body of evidence emerging that the gut has a role in emotions, behavior, and mental and physical health.

Remember, your gut lumen is responsible for producing 90% of your body's serotonin. Serotonin is essential for mood, sleep-wake cycle, depression, sensitivity to light and noise, gut motility, and digestion. Serotonin converts to melatonin, the hormone that regulates the sleep-wake cycle, and serotonin is a common target for a class of antidepressants classified as SSRIs (selective serotonin re-uptake inhibitors). More recent evidence supports that alterations in the microbiome filled with "bad" bacteria can alter the gut luminal cells and interfere with serotonin production.

Because the luminal cells of the digestive tract produce almost all our body's serotonin, gut health has great implications relating to behavior, mood, and mental health. Specifically, serotonin is implicated in behaviors related to depression and a general feeling of malaise or being unwell. It is essential to understand the many functions of serotonin in the digestive system and in the brain. SSRI antidepressants target the serotonin system to balance neurotransmitter regulation in the brain and body. Serotonin is essential for our sleep-wake cycle because it is a precursor to melatonin. Altered levels of serotonin in the brain can directly alter the production of melatonin and in turn cause a disruption in the sleep-wake cycles. It is not clear whether differences of serotonin in the digestive tract and brain trigger differences in the sleep-wake cycle of gifted individuals.

Serotonin imbalances have been reported to increase inflammation in the gut and trigger global inflammation throughout the body. It is known that diet and gut bacteria have a complex interaction with respect to the production of serotonin, and certain individuals could have a greater susceptibility to altering gut microflora (gut bacteria), which in turn can cause a series of reactions including global inflammation.

It is essential to understand the functions of serotonin for digestive health and for mental health in order to better serve individuals with increased susceptibilities for serotonin dysregulation through diet and by developing a more balanced gut microflora with commensal "good" bacteria. A study of subjects that ingested probiotic yogurt for a month reported an increase in mood and outlook on life compared to subjects who did not eat probiotic yogurt.[16] This study, supported by other studies with similar results, shows promise that healthy diet and "good" gut bacteria could improve the mood of individuals suffering from mood disorders and gut sensitivities.[17]

It's in the Gut: Greater GI Issues Exist in Gifted, ADHD/ADD, and ASD Populations

A wide body of evidence finds higher rates of gut issues, sensitivities, allergies, mood disorders, reaction to medications, appetite restrictions, autoimmune disorders, and anxiety in ASD, ADHD, and gifted populations.[18] Our survey study revealed that members of Mensa, a subset of the gifted population, describe higher rates of autoimmune diseases, mood disorders, and both environmental and food allergies, compared to the U.S. national average. All of these systems are directly related to physical, mental, and emotional health.[19] Across all groups of gifted people, evidence shows there are intensified experiences among neuroanatomically gifted people who are hard-wired differently. Across all neurotypes there is differential brain and body processing that accounts for differential experiencing, where physiological systems may differ in relation to hormone release, baseline bodily states, and chemical signals throughout the brain and body. Gifted people have expanded and developed brain regions. Each of these unique brain patterns lead to differential body processing: there are parallels happening throughout the brain and body. It is not clear how physiological manifestations or differences within neurotypes specific to the gut-brain connection develop over time, or to what degree there are differences between gifted people and the general population. The puzzle of the gut-brain relationship is a novel area, ripe for scientific exploration among the 2e and gifted population. These populations are vulnerable because the mechanisms that influence the increased incidence of gut sensitivities is unknown. Understanding the mechanisms and pathways for gastrointestinal dysfunction in neurodiverse people is essential for both physical and mental health, overall well-being, and life outcomes.

My Stomach Hurts: GI Issues in Autism Spectrum Disorder

There is compounding evidence that individuals on the autism spectrum have an array of gastrointestinal issues. Identifying the core of GI issues is more challenging for those on the autism spectrum because they have reduced verbal communication. In one report, 43% of individuals on the spectrum had altered intestinal permeability compared to age-matched peers who had none.[20] An increase in intestinal permeability causes a series of challenges, ranging from increased global inflammation, where a person generally feels unwell, to suffering a variety of GI-related symptoms including greater GI pain, more irregular bodily elimination schedules, greater distractibility, higher risk for emotional outbursts, challenges with body metabolism, and altered neurohormone and neurotransmitter release. Of these gastrointestinal disturbances, the most severe symptoms include constipation and diarrhea. Constipation is associated with severity of language and social impairment in individuals with autism.[21] Emerging evidence of increased autoantibodies may indicate an inflammatory state of the intestines that may alter the mucosal barrier and integrity, which may lead to gastrointestinal issues in individuals with ASD.[22]

Are gut issues are caused by or correlated with ASD? In a survey of parent evaluations from pediatric gastroenterologists, diagnosis of autism was consistent with a clinical diagnosis of any gastrointestinal disorder (95%), most commonly constipation (85%), and was associated with younger age of diagnosis and greater challenges in verbal expression.[23] It has been hypothesized that individuals with autism have a "leaky gut," or high intestinal permeability, caused by a disruption in the tight junctions of the gut that have their origin during infancy.[24] The gut, like the blood-brain barrier, has tight junctions, which when disrupted could allow for absorption of substances that could adversely affect brain function.[25] A subset of individuals with autism (36.7%) and their first degree relatives (21.2%) show increased intestinal permeability.[26] In addition, individuals with autism who have gastrointestinal problems exhibit elevated levels of autoantibodies that bind to the intestinal mucosa on the basement membranes of epithelial cells.[27] These autoantibodies may indicate an inflammatory state of the intestines and could in turn alter the mucosal barrier and integrity leading to gastrointestinal problems.[28] This is another line of evidence pointing to systemic infection and chronic inflammation in individuals with ASD, suggesting that the gut and brain together are susceptible to systemic inflammation.

For this reason, scientists like Buie and colleagues are describing and promoting as standard practice a set of recommended diagnostics for individuals with ASD, such as guidelines for routine pediatric testing of abdominal pain, chronic constipation, and gastroesophageal reflux disease.[29] Understanding the gut-brain and microbiome interaction is paramount to promote quality of life and healing for individuals with autism who also suffer from gastrointestinal challenges.

It's Not a Myth– Increased Allergies, Food Sensitives, Autoimmune Disease in the 21st Century

It almost goes without saying that the allergy table at school is usually filled with the smartest and most neurodiverse kids. A lunch club in the making. It is a fact, not a myth, that there are higher incidences of allergies, autoimmune disorders, and GI issues in gifted and 2e kids. A vast body of evidence is unveiling the gut-brain connection where the GI, our second brain, has many operations essential to mental functioning, mood, and behavior. Bright and 2e people report an increase of autoimmune disorders, elevated reports of both environmental and food allergies, and increases in asthma.[30] High IQ individuals report a 25% greater rate of autoimmune disorders and food and environmental allergies compared to the national average.[31] More important, bright and 2e children are at risk for misdiagnoses because they have increased allergic responses and exhibit behaviors such as distraction, high activity levels, temper tantrums, and/ or impulsivity.[32] Teasing out the origin of the reaction is necessary because many of these behaviors mimic behaviors that overlap with those found in ADD/ADHD, oppositional defiant disorder, ASD, and other behavioral disorders. And some of these behaviors have dual origins, for example, a person might have allergies and ADHD, causing simultaneous combined reactions.

Many investigators have noted that gifted individuals have increased incidence of allergies.[33] Reports of allergies in gifted people date back all the way to 1966, when children enrolled in a gifted school reported increases in allergies and asthma.[34] In the mid-80s, the trend continued: highly gifted adolescents reported an increased prevalence of allergies and more than 60% of the highly gifted adolescents had mood issues, twice the rate of their age-matched peers.[35] Gifted people have consistently reported experiences of allergies and autoimmune disease, indicating that this prevalence is not a sudden rise or peak but rather part of the gifted diversity. In the early 2000s, Silverman and colleagues conducted a survey in highly gifted children and found that 44% of children with an IQ score over 160 suffered from allergies, whereas only 20% of age-matched peers reported having allergies. Ten percent of gifted children reported having asthma.[36] Clearly allergies are inherent in the biology of gifted people. Their seats at the allergy table is a real one and may not change anytime soon. What are the causes of these allergies? According to Dr. Webb, 30 to 40% of gifted children experience allergies related to food or common chemicals in the environment.[37] A twenty-year clinical evaluation found the most common food allergies in gifted individuals were dairy, eggs, wheat, corn, chocolate, caffeine, and red food dye.[38] These happen to also be the most abundant allergies in all populations.

There are reports of increase in food and environmental allergies in children with ASD.[39] Children on the autism spectrum were more likely to have food, skin, and respiratory allergies than children without autism. Diet and allergies are a common target for ameliorating behavioral issues in children with ADHD. Children with ADHD commonly have increases in both environmental and food allergies. There are numerous resources that offer dedicated nutritional guides for ADHD households. Scientists have developed elimination guidelines for foods that are potential triggers for ADHD.[40] For example, avoiding sugar, foods with artificial dyes, mercury, chocolate, caffeine, and energy drinks, all of which can exacerbate ADHD symptoms. Because allergic reactions can mimic behavioral problems, it is critical to understand whether an allergy might be a cause of, or a factor in, attention-related behavior issues.

Allergies and Behavioral Issues

Allergies have been associated with an increase in mental health conditions like anxiety and depression. Allergy sufferers develop patterns and internalize their allergic experiences. They do not share their suffering with others.[41] Allergic people tend to experience low level insults so that their body is out of homeostatic balance. In a longitudinal survey study where parents reported on the symptoms of allergies and emotional states, children who had allergies had greater depression and anxiety scores than children who did not have allergies.[42] Importantly, this study clearly shows that allergies could cause increased incidences of anxiety and depression. In fact, allergies may cause negative emotional states and mental health conditions where individuals express more reactive behaviors and have emotional outbursts related to their allergies. Specifically, individuals with allergies are more susceptible to emotional and mental health conditions that can lead to behavioral issues. More often than not, these behavioral issues are misidentified and misdiagnosed. Surprisingly, allergies are significantly associated with panic attacks and anxiety disorders.[43] All these issues are related to a baseline homeostasis, where the center of the dysregulation begins. Allergic symptoms activate the stress response in the body and set off reactive emotional and behavioral patterns. Understanding the relationship underlying the mechanism of allergies and autoimmune reaction in neurodiverse people is pivotal to understanding the behavioral response and to ensuring that these individuals are identified with the proper diagnosis. For all of you stuck at the allergy table in elementary school, know this: the superhero Wolverine's origin story begins with him having allergies, too.[44]

Industrial Revolution—Rise of Autoimmunity, Food Sensitivities, Allergies, and Leaky Gut

Since the Second World War, autoimmune diseases have increased at an alarming rate.[45] It is hypothesized that the increase in unnatural chemicals and plastics plays a vital role in altering our biology and genetics, making us more susceptible to environmental toxins and increasing autoimmune diseases. In autoimmunity, an individual's own body attacks normal healthy tissue. In many types of autoimmunity there is a cycle of inflammation that leads to the physical, mental, and emotional distress of a person suffering from an autoimmune condition. The most common autoimmune diseases of the 21st century include celiac disease, inflammatory bowel disease, Hashimoto's disease, Graves' disease, pernicious anemia, rheumatoid arthritis, psoriasis, and systemic lupus. Across all autoimmune diseases the body's natural immune system attacks on its own tissue and organs cause an increase in inflammation throughout the body and the brain.

Inflammation is our body's natural wound healing response. An increase in cytokines, proteins signal to immune cells to fight infection. In usual inflammation, cytokine production often subsides and standard immune functioning resumes. But in chronic inflammation, there is a continuous production of cytokines, damaging tissue and interfering with tissue repair and function. The persistent elevation of cytokines causes an increase of blood cells to rush to the site of inflammation, raising the rate of blood clots, the pain response, and tissue damage. Often, people who have persistent, low grade inflammation experience high levels of pain that interferes with their daily life, relationships, work/school, and with overall life satisfaction. Chronic inflammation over time can develop into an autoimmune condition, where the body attacks its own tissue and organs and interferes with the body's normal functioning. Chronic inflammation causes global immune dysregulation, where the immune system is out of balance.

Seventy percent of the immune system is located in the gastrointestinal tract, which makes our gut a hub for immune functioning and regulation.[46] The gastrointestinal system plays a vital role in immunity and homeostasis. A number of gastrointestinal diseases originate from immune dysfunction localized in the gut. Autoimmunity and GI dysfunction play key roles in a number of diseases and disorders and an interaction between the two may explain the recent rise in the incidence in GI dysfunction and autoimmunity.

In the gifted, ASD, and ADHD populations there are reports of increases in allergies, gastrointestinal dysfunction, and autoimmune disease.[47] Particularly, food allergies are known triggers for immune activation in the gut and can be responsible for systemic inflammation and increased incidence in autoimmune disorders. More recently, food sensitivities have been found to trigger inflammation, which alter normal gut functioning. In particular, the gut microbiome is sensitive to changes in the host's immunity and can even alter immune functioning of the host. Several lines of evidence have shown that gut dysbiosis (more "bad" gut bacteria) plays a vital role in the development of autoimmune disease.[48] In both inflammatory bowel disease and celiac disease, there are alterations in the host's gut microbiota where there are elevated pathogenic microbes that induce inflammation and increase the progression of disease.[49] Autoimmune types of colitis include inflammatory bowel disease (IBD) and ulcerative colitis (a chronic colitis that affects the large intestine), where the body's own immune system attacks the gastrointestinal tract, possibly though a microbial dysbiosis.[50]

Gut microbiome alterations play a critical role in the pathology of the small intestine, including an increase of inflammation of the gastrointestinal tract and systemic inflammation.[51] Gut dysbiosis, or the decrease of healthy "good" bacteria, has a series of consequences in the colon that include localized gut inflammation, systemic inflammation, altered productions of neurotransmitters, increased intestinal permeability, more chronic infections, impaired metabolism, and higher rates of autoimmunity.[52] Damage to the small intestine does not allow for proper nutrient absorption and the microvilli of the small intestine separate, causing an increase in permeability across the intestinal wall. An altered intestinal barrier intensifies the symptoms of "leaky" gut, where toxic molecules and metabolites pass through the intestinal barrier, increasing systemic inflammation that may contribute to autoimmune disease. Systemic infection may result from chronic global inflammation and immune activation.

An example of a systemic infection is "sickness behavior." In sickness behavior, inflammation raises signals to the brain that slow metabolism, suppress appetite, increase social withdrawal behaviors, and cause an ill feeling. The rise in cytokines (interleukin-1 beta and tumor necrosis factor alpha) changes basic physiology and behavior. As a result, the person feels unwell due to a dysregulation of their immune system and experiences sickness behavior due to inflammation.[53] Sickness behavior is another example of how systemic infection and inflammation can alter immune function, the brain, and behavior. There are a number of parallels between sickness behavior and major depression, such as the somatic features of fatigue, loss of appetite, sleep disturbances, and depressed mood.[54] It is important to note that each of these mental illnesses are associated with neuroinflammation and immune dysregulation, which may originate from the gastrointestinal (GI) tract. It is critical to understand the role the GI plays in systemic inflammation, neuroinflammation, autoimmune disease, mood disorders, mental health, and behaviors associated with mental illness, as well as healthy practices to encourage mental well-being.

Microbiome and Mood

Humans have a unique fingerprint of microbiota based on birth history, geographical location, ingestion of specific foods, food sensitivities, food allergies and autoimmune disease. For example, as previously discussed, individuals born by natural birth have a micro-biome (community of microbes in the gut) composition typical of the gastrointestinal tract whereas individuals born by C-section have a microbiome more similar to that of the skin.[55] Evidence over the last decade has provided insight into the complex interaction between microbiota (gut bacteria) and human health, behavior, and neurological functioning. For example, the commensal "good bacteria" are essential for proper development and immune functioning in mammals.[56] There is growing evidence that indigenous microbes can influence behav-iors and neuronal functioning during development and disease states specific to behaviors of anxiety, depression, and social behavior.[57] More recently it has been proposed that the complex microbiome requires a balanced level of the indigenous bacteria throughout life for proper health and mental functioning. There are increased findings of GI sensitivities related to the microbiome in a number of neurological disorders, including ASD, ADHD, ADD, anxiety, depression, as well as neurodegenerative disorders such as Parkinson's disease (PD) and Alzheimer's disease (AD).[58]

It is not clear how these increases occur, or why there is greater GI dysfunction, allergies, and autoimmune malfunctions in these populations. It *is* clear, however, that the relationship between the gut and brain plays a pivotal role in immunity, mental functioning, and well-being. Specifically, in our Mensa survey study, high IQ participants had a remarkable overlap with increased reports of ASD, OCD, anxiety, depression, environmental and food allergies, and autoimmune reactions compared to the national average.[59] Gifted individuals report an increase incidence of anxiety, depression, and worry compared to those with general intelligence.[60] In addition, intelligence was a unique positive predictor for worry and rumination severity.[61] It has been reported that gifted individuals have increased diagnoses for gut sensitivities, allergies, mood disorders, reaction to medications, appetite sensitivities, autoimmune disorders, anxiety, and depression.[62] There is a greater susceptibility for increases in allergies, GI dysfunction, and autoimmune reactions in these populations. This increased susceptibility contributes to overall changes in the microbiome because there are direct influences in metabolism specific to the biochemical and hormonal production and regulation, protein and fat synthesis, and absorption of nutrients.

The connections between and among mood disorders, gastrointestinal dysfunction, allergies, and microbiome differences is not clear across these populations, including individuals with ASD, ADHD, ADD, anxiety, depression, and neurodegenerative disorders such as PD and AD. The different physiology involving the genetic and environmental interaction may cause these vulnerable populations to have greater susceptibility to fluctuations in their microbiome, GI, allergy, and autoimmune reactions triggering greater mood disorders, stress, and emotional and behavioral disorders/reactions. Unfortunately, children who suffer from GI dysfunction, allergies, and GI sensitivities are misunderstood and are frequently misdiagnosed with ADHD and ADD, due to a failure to properly identify their symptoms. Because stress and GI dysfunction are bidirectional, accurately detecting the origin of the symptoms of stress that induces physiological changes can be essential to addressing behaviors and challenges associated with stress and related GI dysfunction. No wonder we talk about a "gut feeling"!

When working with, teaching, or parenting an individual with greater sensitivity and increased allergies, GI dysfunction, and autoimmunity, it is imperative to understand the origin of the behaviors related to GI dysfunction, whether it begins in the GI or brain or is a combination of both. Compassionate awareness allows for accurate understanding to provide the proper treatment for the triggers causing illness.

Stress: It's in Our Mind, Gut, and Microbiome

Recent findings show that proper diet is the primary driver for a healthy balance of the GI and intestinal microbiota. A happy and flourishing microbiome in the GI supports a robust gut-brain connection. Diet is directly related to positive mood, behavior, and mental functioning, and diet nourishes the gut bacteria.[63] What you choose to put into your body builds the foundation for your entire body's energy—and that includes your mind. The old saying goes, "What you put in is what you get out." Diet literally feeds the microbiota, thus when our guts are fed junk and foods that increase inflammation, negative bacteria take over and cause a multitude of problems. On the other hand, nourishing our bodies with healthy nutrition feeds the good bacteria and supports good health across all the body's systems. When the gut microbiota is imbalanced, elevated amounts of "bad" bacteria cause issues with normal GI functioning, interfere with emotional balance by inducing stress, increased body pain, and jumbling brain function, resulting in a brain fog. In contrast, a diet that supports the growth of "good" bacteria aids in proper GI function, enhances emotional balance, and reduces anxiety, physical pain, and emotional distress. Diet directly nourishes the population of the bacteria in the GI, which can affect one's overall wellbeing and outlook on life. Recall, stress is bidirectional between your brain and GI, meaning when the mind is in a stress state, it can drive a physiological response, such as an upset stomach and impaired GI functioning. Likewise, an unbalanced GI can trigger a negative mood by increasing physical pain from GI distress and induce inflammation that creates an imbalance in the microbiota and hormone release, causing a disrupted gut-brain connection.

Stress alters intestinal microbiota, increases digestive dysfunction and discomfort, and alters mood.[64] In studies of humans ingesting probiotics containing "good bacteria," the participants showed increased digestive health, brain functioning, elevated mood, and had a more positive emotional state. In one of the pioneering studies, subjects who consumed probiotics (*L. heretics* R0052 and *B. lonfum* R0175) reported a reduction of anxiety.[65] Feeding the body good bacteria increases mental and physical health. Another study independently found that subjects treated with probiotics self-reported decreased depression and aggression.[66] In all these cases, probiotics support enhanced health and balance.

The effects of probiotics are short-term, though. Fermented milk, soy and rice products aid in populating the GI with good bacteria, but the duration is transitory. Scientists report that when one consumes these probiotic food products, good bacteria remain in the GI for up to a week. Thus, regular ingestion of these products is necessary to build the harmonious GI balance.

A bounty of evidence supports the notion that probiotics are important in building positive mental states and greater emotional balance. In a study where individuals reviewed clips of negative emotional content, participants that ingested a probiotic exhibited a reduced emotional reaction to the clips compared to individuals who did not consume a probiotic.[67] Particularly, in this account we see how probiotics balance the microbiota in the GI, which in turn ensures a greater state of emotional equanimity. Having a healthy microbiome flora enriches mood, mental functioning, and overall wellbeing. Microbiota play a central role in the gut-brain axis because having symbiosis of the microbiota means there are more good bacteria allowing for improved health and mental functioning.

Absorption of nutrients is a main function of the GI. Microbes in the GI are responsible for aiding in nutrient absorption. Greater gut imbalance impedes nutrient absorption, causing body and mind to operate closer to empty because vital nutrients are not being absorbed in the body. Improper nutrient balance interferes with proper mental and physical functioning. Nutrition feeds into all the systems and organs of the body. When there is an imbalance in nutrition, the systems and organs of the body have issues with normal functioning. For example, a study found that intestinal microbiota directly interacted with the absorption of medications.[68] Specifically, gut bacteria influence drug absorption and metabolism, so drug effectiveness is reliant on the activity of gut bacteria. In addition, the gut microbiota have been found to alter the expression levels of drug metabolizing enzymes and transporters, where the microbiota may be helpful or harmful to the individual in obtaining the optimal dosing of medication.[69] In particular, individuals who have a very limited food selection may have an altered microbiome that may directly affect their digestive health, nutrient absorption, medication absorption, and mental health.

Greater Brain Power—Higher Risk for Reactive Hypoglycemia

A subset of highly gifted children express the symptoms and behaviors of reactive hypoglycemia.[70] Reactive hypoglycemia is caused by sudden decrease in blood glucose a few hours after a meal.[71] Glucose is the essential energy source for the brain and body and it is derived from what we eat and drink. Glucose is regulated by insulin, a key hormone produced in the pancreas and distributed throughout the body and brain. However, the underlying mechanisms for reactive hypoglycemia are not completely understood or well-researched. Reactive hypoglycemia has a sudden onset and its symptoms and behaviors are the first signs that a person is struggling.

Reactive hypoglycemia presents as hunger, shakiness, fatigue, sweating, dizziness, headaches, muscle twitch, irritability, tremors, craving for sweets, nausea, vomiting, and numbness or coldness in extremities. An untreated episode can even lead to a coma.[72] Behavioral symptoms include difficulty speaking, depression, nervousness, panic attacks, irrationality, bad temper, and disorientation. The behavioral symptoms of reactive hypoglycemia may mimic mental health conditions, so identifying the trigger can be tricky.

Webb and colleagues found, among the 5-7 % of gifted children who report symptoms of reactive hypoglycemia, half of those children have food allergies, often sleep only 4 to 5 hours per night, and have greater sensory receptivity to things like sounds, tags, and smells.[73] These same children frequently suffer from allergies and, based on sensory processing, most likely experience their environment and the world with greater receptivity and reactivity. More often than not, children who suffer from reactive hypoglycemia are mislabeled and misdiagnosed for disorders such as ADD/ADHD, bipolar disorder, and are even labeled as emotionally immature. But in fact, they experience their world with greater intensity and openness.

Webb and others noted that gifted children who have reactive hypoglycemia mimic misunderstood behavioral disorders. Webb writes, "Though there is little formal study of giftedness and hypoglycemia, anecdotal evidence suggests that the two are related. These are children—usually slender—who function quite well in school until mid-morning. Then they have a meltdown; they are highly emotional, distractible, irritable, impulsive, and have difficulty concentrating. About 30 minutes after lunch they once again function well and pleasantly until about mid-afternoon, at which time another meltdown occurs. The intensity [of gifted children's behavior] appears to be related to running out of fuel, where glucose metabolism occurs rapidly and these children need to have healthy snacks that are high in protein with moderate carbohydrates."[74] Parents report their children have both the physiological and behavioral symptoms of reactive hypoglycemia. They find the behaviors challenging and their children's physiological reaction alarming. Unfortunately, there has been little to no research on reactive hypoglycemia in gifted children, and its cause is not clear.

One explanation may be that gifted individuals have an increased sensitivity to the body's regular release of the hormone, epinephrine, which causes a decrease in blood glucose levels. Epinephrine is essential for the flight-or-fight response and is produced in the adrenal glands by neurons in response to stress. In fact, elevated levels of epinephrine can cause hypoglycemia and hypoxia.

An emotional response has three components: (1) behavior produced by the brain; (2) reaction of the autonomic nervous system (sympathetic nervous system) to the stimuli; and (3) hormonal regulation through epinephrine directing us to take action through behaviors such as speech or physical movement. Fear is the main emotion linked to epinephrine. In a study, when human subjects were injected with epinephrine and reviewed neutral film clips, individuals with the injection reported an increase in fear, negative emotions, and remembered the film clips in greater detail than the control group.[75] The physiological response of the subjects injected with epinephrine included a heart rate and lower limb shaking and can be linked to the fear response. An increase in epinephrine can be related to an increase in the fear response, which can cause individuals to have increased anxiety levels in response to the biological process of fight, flight, freeze, or flop.

Brain functioning accelerates with intellectual challenge in gifted individuals, which means gifted individuals use more energy, that is more glucose.[76] Mathematically gifted adolescents have larger areas of the brain that are responsible for executive function (right ACC), interpretation of sensory information (left parietal lobe), and motor function (left premotor area).[77] In addition, they show an increased number of white matter tracts that connect frontal regions with the basal ganglia (the part of the brain that is highly sensitive to reward and decision making) and parietal regions (which account for increased fluid reasoning, working memory, and creativity).[78] This means that gifted students have brains that may be consuming more energy in order to manage information more efficiently. The gifted brain is further activated (as seen by measuring the glucose level in the brain) when presented with increased challenge. It is not just the brain size or the activation that ultimately accounts for the differences seen in approaches to challenge and problem solving, but rather the ability of the brain to utilize these parts in qualitatively unique and more complex ways. Thus, gifted individuals could be at greater risk for reactive hypoglycemia when in flow because they are using more glucose and more areas of their brain for complex problem solving. Understanding glucose consumption in the gifted brain is required to better serve the population and enable them to work at their highest and best potential. And to prevent outbursts and crashing because of energy drain.

There are ways to mindfully prevent or reduce the episodes of reactive hypoglycemia. These simple interventions include eating small meals and snacks every 2-3 hours, limiting or avoiding sugar intake, and regular exercise to keep insulin levels consistent thereby helping keep blood glucose steady. Dietary choices matter. Choose a diet high in fiber. Choose a varied diet that includes proteins, whole grains, vegetables, fruit (watch the fructose level), and dairy products. Reduce or avoid foods high in sugar, especially on an empty stomach. There is hope. With mindful eating practices and increased awareness, gifted individuals can avoid the consequences of reactive hypoglycemia.

Flight, Fight Food Reactions

Nutritionist and dietitian Wendy Crump has been specializing in holistic eating practices for more than fifteen years. A mother of four children herself, she experiences first-hand her children's varying food selections and eating practices. In her dietary guidance practice, she has noticed a rise in food sensitivities and allergies in her clients, especially in twice-exceptional children. The source of these increases in food sensitivities and allergies is not completely clear among the population. Often, identifying the origin of these food reactions can require a lengthy process of experimenting with foods and trigger identification through trial and error, a process that can be a nerve-wracking and frustrating. Moreover, it can be challenging to identify the source of food reactions, especially if they are food sensitivities or food intolerances.

A *food sensitivity* is when a person's body adversely responds to a particular food, triggering an immune response. Symptoms present throughout the entire body, such as headaches and muscle fatigue. A *food intolerance* is when a person's body lacks a particular enzyme to break down a food and cannot absorb the nutrients. An example would be the inability to break down milk that happens when someone is lactose intolerant. A *food allergy* is when the body's immune response mistakes food for a harmful substance and releases the antibody Immunoglobin E. In extreme cases, an allergy can be life threatening. Common food allergies may include shellfish, dairy, and nuts.

Wendy further explains that food allergy causes an immediate reaction—a flare-up in response to the allergen—whereas a food sensitivity has a delayed response, is dose dependent, and is challenging to identify due to the unexpected symptoms. She explains, "An example would be somebody with a food allergy to milk. If milk just touched their skin, they would just flare up immediately. They don't necessarily need to ingest the milk to have a reaction." When someone experiences an allergy to food the reactions can include:

○ Tingling in the mouth or tongue
○ Itchy skin appearing as hives or eczema
○ Facial swelling of the lips, tongue, throat, nose, or chest
○ Nasal irritation or runny nose

○ Trouble breathing, coughing, or wheezing
○ GI irritation including nausea, vomiting, abdominal pain, or diarrhea
○ Blurred vision, lightheadedness, or fainting

In some extreme cases a food allergy can be life-threatening. Identification of a food allergy is essential because it can interfere with adequate nutrition and quality of life. Food sensitivities, on the other hand, are more insidious by nature because there is a delay in the appearance of symptoms and the symptoms are not obvious. Often there is an entire mind-body reaction in response to a food sensitivity. This is due to the inflammatory response that happens across the entire body and causes multiple symptoms. Pinpointing the food sensitivity takes time and elimination strategies. Symptoms of food sensitivities include:

○ GI irritation presenting as nausea, vomiting, gas, bloating, abdominal pain, diarrhea, or constipation
○ Heartburn
○ Body aches, muscle or joint pain
○ Headaches or migraines
○ Irritability, nervousness
○ Challenge with concentration, ADHD-like symptoms
○ Mood fluctuations
○ Brain fog

The thing is, food sensitivities are not always in the gut. Symptoms manifest in the body, such as in the joints, or may cause headaches or challenges with concentration. A food sensitivity occurs as a cascade of inflammatory and immune reactions that trigger global inflammation and induce stress throughout the mind and body. The key thing is that food allergies, food intolerances, and sensitivities cause homeostatic imbalances. On top of it all, people who suffer from food reactions may experience inadequate nutrition resulting in their entire mind-body and well-being becoming out of whack. Identifying the problematic food source is essential in calming the GI, nervous system, and the body's immune response, and for regaining homeostatic balance. When homeostasis is imbalanced in a child or adult, a slew of symptoms present as behavioral, emotional, and mental issues that impact relationships, daily activities, life engagement, overall life satisfaction, and well-being.

Using her son as an example, Wendy describes in detail how this works. "My son used to have complete melt downs, and it was directly related to diet. But the minute I tested him for food sensitivities and we took everything out of his diet that he was reacting to, his whole personality changed. He even noticed it himself—he wasn't having meltdowns. When he had meltdowns, he felt like they were completely out of his control." The food sensitivity test Wendy refers to is the Mediator Release Test (MRT)***, which specifically tests the inflammatory immune response released by the mediator and reacting cells in response to food sensitivities in the GI. The MRT has about 93.6% accuracy rate.[79]

Wendy's son was 10 years old and struggling with emotional regulation. He could not control his emotions, had frequent outbursts, and suffered chronic migraines and nausea. Wendy says, "Basically, the reason I tested him is because he was getting horrible, horrible headaches and I was thinking a child at ten years old shouldn't get migraines. I mean, this is not normal. We did a brain MRI, had an entire work-up, and everything was totally normal. I'm like, No, no, no. Something's wrong. This is not right. A child does not get like severe headaches, where they're just scowling in pain, severe pain." When Wendy tested her son for food sensitivities, they found that a number of foods he regularly ate were setting him off. She describes, "At the time he was doing baseball four days a week and my husband would take him to eat with all his teammates. He would drink Gatorade with all those food dyes, eat hot dogs with all the nitrates, and have Doritos with all the artificial flavors. Inevitably, he has sensitivity to pork, nitrates, and food dyes. Everything he was consuming was setting him off." Wendy says they had no idea that all

---

***MRT points out that the mediator release is the pivotal element that causes suffering for individuals with food sensitivities: "MRT is a functional measurement of diet-induced sensitivity pathways." The MRT method focuses on identifying foods that trigger mediator inflammation response and eliminating the identified foods with individualized accuracy to ensure a healthy mind, body and GI.

the foods he was eating after baseball practice and games were triggers for entire body inflammation, expressed as behavioral outburst, horrible headaches, and his stomach feeling like it was in knots. It is important to point out that her son's food sensitivities changed his entire body physiology to such a degree that he experienced chronic flight and flight response.

How can food sensitivities send the entire body into to fight and flight? It all begins with having an imbalanced GI that activates a persistent low-level immune reaction and causes global inflammation. Global inflammation that begins in the GI activates the stress response throughout the body so that the nervous system becomes overtaxed due to the chronic sympathetic activation. This leads to an overwhelmed nervous system which causes a rise in behavioral issues and physical, mental, and emotional pain. At the center of the reaction, cognitive abilities are disrupted, attention is divided as the mind attends to suffering, and there is higher emotional reactivity because the nervous system is responding from more primal states. Basically, the body is consumed in the reactive stress response due to GI inflammation. Chronic inflammation increases emotional imbalance and mood disorders, and inhibits proper mental functioning. The main way to regain homeostatic balance is to eliminate the foods that trigger this reactivity. As Wendy points out, when her son eliminated the foods that were causing headaches and emotional outbursts, his symptoms waned. Her son's emotional balance and health increased once the triggering foods had been eliminated. Basically, his behavioral outbursts were related to inflammatory trauma, and he had no idea what was happening to him. Importantly, Wendy's experience provides us with insight into why her son was having a great deal of behavioral issues and felt out of control. When they eliminated foods he was reacting to, he was able to recover emotional regulation and his behavior changed.

Wendy has also seen in her practice that the parents of children who experience emotional outbursts have a challenging time working with adjusting their child's diet. She describes how, for parents of "a child who has outbursts, you're going to tiptoe around it. I mean, you have to learn how to deal with their emotions and their outbursts, so that making drastic changes to the diet are scary because you don't know, because they don't get to eat what they want then they're going to have the outbursts again. It's sort of scary a lot of times for parents to make drastic changes." The key here is patience for the process while guiding your child to eat foods that are not triggering and that provide nutrition.

Wendy also sees food sensitivities increase during puberty and college. In her practice, she finds that if a child has been struggling with food sensitivities, by the time they are in adolescence it can increase by tenfold. Addressing the food sensitivities earlier rather than later is paramount. There is a stark rise in food challenges in college age students. She explains, "I see people a lot when their child goes college and then they're really having a challenging time. They realize, 'we've got to make some changes.' Now, because they're not college age, they're more inclined to making some changes, however the challenge comes in because now they're in a dorm and they don't get to make their own food and you have to deal with what's offered, but do the best you can with foods that are prepared." She points out that when people cannot prepare their own food, it is especially challenging to avoid food reactions. It is important to be able to empower individuals to make foods that are good for their particular dietary needs.

Another cautionary point from Wendy is that often, when people are struggling with behavioral issues like emotional regulation, we tend to focus on medicating them rather than regulating their diet. In her practice, she urges that we look at diet before we medicate a person. Particularly, diet can affect the absorption rate of medications and their efficacy. Practicing a more holistic approach to guide a child with ADHD, ADD, and ASD by working with their diet can yield significant positive changes in their behavior. She recommends that if we simultaneously work on diet along with medication for a child struggling with emotional regulation, it could help reduce their symptoms as well as decrease their medication usage. Dietary adjustments may not completely replace medication usage, but a focus on diet can possibly curb the necessity for medication. As a mother, she has experienced firsthand that changing her son's diet changed his behavior and increased his emotional balance. And in her practice she has seen similar effects.

Mindful diet and eating practices can build greater awareness and resilience and empower an individual to feed themselves for their unique gut, brain, and body. Understanding one's particular nutritional needs allows an individual to be better nourished and to participate in a more meaningful life.

Food Rules

Clearly, diet directly affects behavior, and healthy eating habits are critical for proper organ and brain functioning. The numerous consequences of GI inflammation can impair our mental functioning, emotional regulation, physical health, and overall well-being. The science of diet is illuminating how, when it comes to our gut and brain functioning, a low-inflammatory diet is best for maintaining optimal cognition and whole-body functioning. There is an entire industry focused on obtaining our cash for the promised diet that can "help us." Wendy Crump points out that there are a number of fad diets our culture becomes obsessed with, but moderation is the key component for best health. She explains, "Diets are generational, so they change. The Atkins was a big high-protein diet and was huge in the '80s. Then everybody was into low-fat or non-fat diets. Everything had to be non-fat, and then we recognize, no. We actually need fat because good fat is something that we need for our brains and our skin. Everything lasts around ten years or so and then it's something new. It changes, and so now the no carb high protein is what everybody's aiming for. But really, eating whole foods is actually the best way you can go in terms of any diet." Wendy's advice centers on the fact that we need to eat foods that are balanced in nutrition and that do not cause inflammation in our GI.

Another point Wendy makes is how packaged and processed foods have limited to no nutritional value, and often contain ingredients that trigger inflammation. The more foods you eat that do not have a label, the better. She advocates skipping those foods whose labels list ingredients you don't recognize (or that don't even sound like food) and opting instead for foods in their natural form. The more you can consume whole foods, the better you can absorb a greater number of nutrients. If you have the time and enjoy cooking, you can have greater control over what ingredients you consume.

A low-inflammatory diet is the most effective one for positive outcomes relating to GI and brain functioning. It is paramount to develop a low-inflammatory diet specific to your body's metabolism, microbiome, allergies, autoimmune function, and your particular palate. There is no promise here about any specific diet plan to follow for your GI health and well-being, but rather a few guidelines for mindful eating practices.

From my own experience I have learned I have a number of food sensitivities. If I don't follow mindful eating practices, I can trigger IBS simply by consuming one of my activating foods. For me, being mindful means not consuming foods that trigger inflammation. When I have a misstep and consume one of the foods that trigger inflammation, I can experience difficulties. My energy wanes, and my mood worsens, and even my cognition is disrupted. Mindful eating is essential for my mental health and functioning. Tuning in, paying attention to what I eat, and intention setting prior to meals and snacking helps me have more balance in my eating practices.

Eating with intention builds mindful and healthy eating practices. Pay attention to your natural biorhythm: the times during the day you feel your energy drop and the other times you feel your energy at its peak. Each of us has our own brain-body connection, microbiome, and foods that provide positive nutrition.

As they say, you are what you eat—so be mindful.

Mindful Eating Practices

1. **Begin your meal with gratitude.** Have awareness of, and gratitude for, the food you eat. Start by thinking about where the food came from and how it was prepared. Recognizing the steps it takes to bring food to your table opens your mind to a greater awareness that you are sharing your meal with the world.

2. **Experience your food with all your senses.** Smell, taste, see, and notice the texture of your food. Even listen to your food—how pasta makes a swooshing sound, how nuts crunch and crackle.

3. **Describe your food to center your mind so you can savor the flavor and experience.** Between our first bite of something and our last, the flavor of the food loses its magic with our satiation and the habituation of eating. When we describe our food, it prolongs our enjoyment of nourishing both our body and our mind.

4. **Slow down your eating.** When we sit and gobble quickly on automatic pilot, we tend not to notice the amount of food we are eating. When we carefully chew each bite, about 10-20 times, we more fully digest it, and derive more nutrients. Also, chewing slowly helps regulate the amount of food we eat.

5. **Take a mindful pause.** Pay keen attention to the moment you begin to feel full. Notice the moment you shift your attention from hunger to, "I am not sure I want another bite." That moment is when you can take a mindful pause to reflect on whether you have had enough to eat.

6. **Guilt is a useless emotion with anything, but especially with food.** Do not feel guilty if you happen to overeat or you eat something that is deemed "not good" for you. Recognize you are human and desire to eat is a basic and primal mechanism for our survival. Food is essential for our energy and for our health, and it can also be enjoyable. Being hungry is a normal process, so overeating happens from time to time because eating is built into our basic biology as a rewarding experience. So, lighten up and recognize that to be human is to eat.

7. **Pay attention to bidirectional signals from your body to your mind and mind to body.** If something seems displeasing and you do not want to eat it, listen to your gut. Humans have basic survival skills when it comes to ingesting things and if something does not seem appetizing, skip it.

8. **You do not need to finish everything on your plate.** I know many people that have been taught to eat until their plate is clean, and so they may tend to overeat. Listen to when your

body is full. Let go of the food on your plate. Either way, the food will end up as waste. If you are full, don't eat the extras.

9. **Know what foods trigger sensitivities and allergies for you and avoid these foods whenever you can.** Careful choices help maintain a healthy GI, reduce inflammation and feed the "good" microbes. As mentioned above, the MRT can measure food sensitivities and abundance of food reactions. This test informs you of the particular foods you need to avoid to reduce inflammation and support a healthy GI. A food log is a good way to track triggering and non-triggering foods. Also, a food log helps you identify foods that give you energy and enjoyment, helping to make the connection between what you eat and how you feel afterward.

10. **Complete your meal with words of gratitude and abundance for the nourishment you received from the food.** Gratitude boosts your mood and general sense of well-being. Fuel your body and mind with goodness.

Dear Light Being,

Today is your birthday. Come out of the shadows and reveal yourself and your gifts. The world is ready and waiting for you. We have waited far too long. Life is too short and we don't have much time. Let us see your great mind. The world is ready for you to appear with all of you. You are not alone. There are plenty of others like you that will understand. By you sharing yourself, others will share themselves, and that is really our purpose and why we are here. To see, really see all. We are so excited to meet you.

Our life is not a single birth, but rather a continuum of births and being reborn. Each time we are born, we awaken and shed the unwanted, shed the ego, and are alive in our true being. So, shed what needs to be shed, the pains, the sorrows, the fears, and meet me in the open field of possibility. It is your birthday today! Celebrate and bask in the rays of the sun. Unbound, wild, and free. There is no better time than now to open up to all your wonder and possibility.

And isn't it amazing that we join one another on the earth at this exact time with all the galaxies, supernovas, light years, sound waves, orbiting planets? Now is all of our time. That in all of history, cosmos, planets, that we share this time, this moment, this experience together. So, Happy, happy, happy birthday, Dear One.

So much gratitude that you join us today!

Yours beyond the Cosmos,
Ray of Light

Chapter 9:

Positive Life Practices and Living in Our Essence

> *"In the end*
> *these things matter most:*
> *How well did you love?*
> *How fully did you live?*
> *How deeply did you let go?"*
>
> —Jack Kornfield,
> *Buddha's Little Instruction Book*[1]

Living in our Magic

There is no one, not anyone, that is exactly like you. You have been placed on the Earth at this time to live in your magic. We are neuroindividuals forevermore—our uniqueness is embedded in our biology and in our minds through our autobiographical memories, perceptions, and behaviors. One of the greatest gifts I received from my teacher, Sam Christensen, is to live fully and completely in my essence. Learning to live in my essence was to face myself honestly and embrace all of me, the beauty, the shadow, the dreaming, the awake, and the hopeful. And my hope is that you live in your essence and embrace all of you. We are here to teach one another through our personal stories and share the core of our beating hearts.

Being a parent of a twice-exceptional child has been an experience filled with humility. It is in my biology to nurture, to fix, and to reduce pain and discomfort. Sometimes the pain and discomfort are exactly what are necessary to create change. Being the observer of our child's pain is excruciating. Our mirror neurons make empathy possible for us. But we do not have to get lost in the pain. We can develop an awareness of the pain and gain the knowledge that the pain we experience is useful information for better understanding ourselves. I offer you this: instead of taking the approach of trying to fix the pain and discomfort, embrace it as a starting point to nurture and grow.

For our children, it is essential to foster a child's strengths and see their innate goodness. For their development, we need to remove from their minds any notion that they are broken or not enough. They are exactly whole in all of their essence. We, as beings, are whole in our essence. When our child faces challenges, it is important to offer them support without stigma. Support may be given through tutors, coaches, psychologists, and professionals in the field. It might be listening to how they want to try out for a sport, or the school play, or how they want to give up violin lessons. Or, they might just want to talk to you for hours about Animal Crossing or Overwatch. When an individual is asking for attention through their speech and their actions it is not a simple ask. It is a big deal because they are being vulnerable with you, sharing what makes their heartbeat. As parents, guides, and educators it is our job to show up and be present, to listen and pay attention. Become a human scientist like Harri O'Kelley. Her approach is to follow her child's lead, offer encouragement and support, and allow the child to be the guide.

We as parents and educators see our children's light and must recognize that we are meant to help them shine in their one-of-a-kind way. Children have minds and bodies, just like adults—the difference is that their minds and bodies are developing rapidly. Children experience emotions, sensations, and have metacognition. They can teach us. Let them teach us.

For me, being a parent has been a humbling journey; to learn and admit how much I don't know, and to trust in the things I believe I know best. My son is my teacher and my equal. There is no one in the world that makes me laugh more than Spencer. He has taught me to be patient, trust, and have the faith to step back and out of the way so he can explore his essence. Together we discover his path and his magic. Many of my personal discoveries and neurohacks have come through trial and error. And there has been a good amount of error. The failures are as equal and valuable as the successes. Knowing what doesn't work is half the story, half the journey to discovering what will work. In my experience, I prefer to say, *I tried that and it was not for me* rather than *I could have tried that*—and never know. Exploration is messy and uncertain, but it is the foundation of expansion. Give yourself a break. If something isn't working, let it go and try something else. Give yourself the go-ahead to move on. Continue to explore and nurture the heart of your existence, the beats, rhythms, crescendos of your essence.

Cultivating Positive Neural Plasticity

> *Your beliefs become your thoughts,*
> *Your thoughts become your words,*
> *Your words become your actions,*
> *Your actions become your habits,*
> *Your habits become your values,*
> *Your values become your destiny.*
> —Ghandhi

We have the power to cultivate positive thinking patterns and shift our internal dialogue to reflect ourselves in a balanced light so we can modify our behaviors and habits to be more nurturing. We have the ability to live as empowered beings and we can shift our awareness and mindset to more supportive neural and behavior pathways. By actively guiding our mind, we can raise our awareness to shift our mindset and thinking patterns. This is a dynamic process. Changing our mindset, thoughts, and patterns does not happen overnight. It takes time to develop new thinking pathways. The shift in our conscious awareness happens through practice, patience, and perseverance until we gradually grow our mind into greater flexibility and neural plasticity.

Through actively cultivating awareness by shifting our focus, we build positive mental patterns and gain a greater metacognition that includes the thinking, emotional, and perceiving mind. When we practice these mental patterns, we literally shift our neural networks, shift our neural chemicals, and shift our brain and mind to be in alignment. New strengthened brain networks and patterns are the foundation for creating positive neural plasticity. When we practice and cultivate these positive thought processes and aspects of ourselves, we build new mind patterns and the nurturing behaviors become automatic.

Scientists like Phillippa Lally and her research team at University College London have discovered approximately how long it takes for humans to form an automatic habit.[2] Their study included 96 participants, each of whom chose a new habit. The participants reported daily whether they practiced the new habit and recorded whether or not the habit felt automatic. Participants varied in their choice of habits. For example, one participant chose to drink water at lunch every day and another chose to run fifteen minutes a day. Each of the habits and behaviors were specific to the participants. They recorded their particular behavior over a 12-week period. Scientists discovered that it takes approximately 66 days to create an automatic behavior, a little more than three times the number of days touted in popular science and self-help books—typically 21 days. According to Lally and team, that 66-day estimate is an approximation. In some cases, a habit was formed in just 18 days, and in others, it took as long as 254 days. Lally points out that this huge range is dependent on the type of behavior the person chooses and how much they practice the behavior.

The motivation to form a habit is highly individual. Some automatic behaviors require more time to develop to build the brain pattern and pathways for it to become an automatic behavior. This is an important lesson for us. When it takes more than 21 days to develop a habit, patience, practice, and perseverance are critical for cultivating neural plasticity and rewiring our mind. Neural plasticity is the brain's ability to form networks and pathways based on training the brain. This occurs through the brain's ability to develop neural patterns in response to repeated behaviors and actions. The brain has the ability to grow and adapt over time. Most importantly, scientists have uncovered this plasticity is in relation to the repeated brain activity and behavior. We can train neural patterns in how we think and in the stories we tell ourselves. We can approach the world with a greater ability, untangle old thinking patterns that can undermine the goodness, and activate new patterns that open us to living in the full expression of our essence and increase the goodness in life.

Rick Hanson, a psychologist and senior fellow of UC Berkeley's Greater Good Science Center, focuses his work on guiding people to train their brain to take in the good. In his approach, he writes about we can take positive aspects in our daily life and turn them into positive experiences.[3] For example, when someone greets us with compassion, we can actively take in the compassion and discover within us that *we* are compassionate. Another example is how we can, by bringing into our awareness things like flowers in bloom, or a stranger's smile, discover the goodness all around and develop our appreciation of those things in a lasting positive experience. Hanson also points out that we can enhance the length of a positive experience by savoring the experience. Specifically, through our awareness we can lengthen the positive experience by remaining present. Most experiences last from five to 20 seconds, so it is important to keep our attention on the experience and let it sink in. Fred Bryant, a psychologist at Loyola University, has found that when we center our attention on savoring experiences that are positive, these experiences are enhanced, which is directly related to our brain's neural activity.[4] As we take in the experience with greater awareness we begin to use more brain power, which is directly related to increasing the firing of neurons and our mind's memory. For example, when you receive a compliment, a good practice is to place your hand on your heart and take in a deep breath, and say thank you. Pay attention to how the compliment resonates throughout your body. This practice is savoring the experience. When we savor the experience and tune into how it feels in our body, we enhance the power of the positive experience. We integrate the positive feelings by connecting to our body and our present observations. This in turn elevates the reward in our mind and we have an influx of positive neurochemicals associated with positive experience which become more deeply encoded in our memory. When we enhance our active memory of the good we are more able to call upon these good experiences at any time—during easy times, challenging times, and neutral times. Having the ability to call on positive experiences through our imagination can open our minds and hearts and shift us into greater resilience, offering our mindset new possibilities. As Eckhart Tolle says, "The primary cause of unhappiness is never the situation but your thoughts about it." We have the power to shift our thought patterns, emotions, and behaviors so that we can build positive mind practices by enhancing our awareness and cultivating positive neural plasticity that directly nurtures our being.

Matters of Resilience

I was at the peak of the mountain Kalinchowk in Nepal when I made a commitment to complete this book, to rewrite, reinvent, and rebirth the story I planned to tell. I was on a five-day trek with my meditation group and we had silently hiked up the mountain. On this particular day, my meditation teacher, Raven Lee, asked me to surrender. Her words were, *"Be still, be silent, and allow for the space."* I am very good at doing and distracting myself, I was born to move and born to hike. I ascended the mountain alone, my footprints imprinting in the mountain dust, and the clouds slowly moving toward the peak of mountain.

One month prior to my trek, my publisher, James T. Webb, was on a sandy beach in Mexico when he suffered a heart attack and died. A gaping hole the size of the galaxy filled the center of my chest. In my grief, climbing a mountain seemed like a natural course to finding a new path.

For me, on that mountain, to be still was like trying to tie down a cheetah. Although Raven was not talking about physical stillness—she was talking about stillness in the mind. But my mind raced in forty thousand directions, trying to make sense of it all and intellectualize the loss of my friend and the realization that I would have to find a new home for my book.

The silence Raven described was not the act of speaking; she was talking about the inner dialogue and chatter that needed to be silenced. Meditation practice centers on clearing the mind through silence and stillness. Once that is achieved, the mind experiences spaciousness. The spaciousness is similar to the incubation period in creativity, where one releases the "thinking" mind by taking a break, and the unconscious mind swoops in and naturally makes the spontaneous connections.

During the five-day journey we walked through a damp forest. Our clothing was drenched from the humidity. We slipped and slid in the mud, and each step was a search for solid footing. Our local guides took us through the forest, circling the tracks of the wild cows. We were lost, far from home, and our muscles ached. At some point, leeches attacked all but two of us. I was not one of the lucky two. Two leeches attached at the core of my belly button and my friend Patil pulled them from my belly. The leeches attached so fiercely to my flesh that their fang marks are still visible on my skin. Leeches' parasitic nature is facilitated by the anesthetic properties of their saliva. Their prey does not initially feel the bite, giving the leech time to feast on its prey's blood before being discovered. We were outnumbered by the leeches. This was their forest, after all. We were visitors, lost, and off-course, and the leeches were living as they do in the forest. Disgusting as it was, the leech attack was a minor annoyance because our greater concern was making it through the forest alive. Our bodies were wrecked, and we longed for our basecamp. This trek felt far from a meditation retreat until our sage guide, Raven, asked, "When we have a weak body, is our mind weak?" We all replied, "Yes." And we all failed—most likely we were exhausted, not paying attention and trying to get out of the forest and make it to safety. Nevertheless, Raven said, "No, no, no, weak body, strong mind," meaning that through our suffering and pain we needed to cultivate a strong mind, adapt, and never give up.

Resilience is the process of recovering quickly from difficulties. The practice of resilience applies the principles to mentally and emotionally recover in response to a crisis and return to a balanced state. For me, walking through the damp forest so far away from home was a way to rebalance. I learned that through pain I had the ability to recover and move on. Pain is a transient state, just as experiencing joy is fleeting.

Nothing, not anything, is permanent and the more we can awaken to the flow of impermanence the sooner we can be liberated to take another step forward and climb another mountain. I could tell you about the resilience research and the science behind not giving up, but instead I wish to share that if I can get up and rebalance from trauma, so can you. We are not prisoners of our pain, and when we realize that, we can transform our mind and the stories we tell ourselves so that we are free. You can get up and try again. And again.

And as reluctant as I initially was to accept the healing processes of silence and stillness, that is exactly what I needed. I needed to embrace self-soothing, like a Ferberized baby that eventually surrenders. When I walked to my edge and softened, that is when the spaciousness arrived. I realized it was never about the book, it was about the loss of my dear friend and mentor. At the top of the mountain in the silence, as the clouds released drops of rain, I understood it didn't matter to anyone but me whether I wrote this book. Simply, if I wanted to write the book, I needed to write the book for me, because the topic is meaningful and valuable to *me*. I knew I would find a new publisher, I knew that it was a matter of time. It has taken me time, silence, hiking through faraway forests, meditating, kicking and screaming like a recalcitrant newborn baby. No one, not anyone, will hand you anything—you have to want it, *you* have to make it happen. And as I said, if I can do it, so can you.

> *"To give anything less than your best is to sacrifice the gift."*
> —Steve Prefontaine

Meditation, Mindfulness, and the Metta Mind

The seminal work of Jon Kabat-Zinn, in 1979, revolutionized the American culture by showing how the practice of mindfulness reduced the suffering of individuals who were struggling with physical and mental difficulties. Mindfulness is the practice of becoming presently aware of the current moment and is often an entry point into meditation. Mindfulness meditations are one of the many forms of guided meditation practices. Meditation is a practice that centers the mind and body to shift into greater awareness of oneself and one's environment. Meditation is not about doing, or getting somewhere; meditation is shifting one's awareness into the present moment. We live in a world where we have 24/7 access to information, and we are continuously navigating many attentional shifts. Guided meditation provides balance to focus the mind and one's attention. Through practicing meditation, the mind builds brain pathways centered on concentration and awareness. This is known as neural plasticity. Guided meditation improves attention, emotional balance, compassion, self-awareness, fear regulation, intuition, body regulation, communication skills, and mental flexibility. Guided meditation creates an overall sense of calm.

A foundational practice of meditation is focusing one's attention on their breath. The breath is a gateway into the present moment. Connecting to the flow of one's breath awakens the mind-body connection. I recommend starting small. Begin with a three-minute breath. Significantly, taking three diaphragm-deep breaths centers the nervous system and helps to calm the body and mind by releasing positive neurochemicals. Tuning into one's breath builds greater awareness and focus into the present moment.

Our in-tune awareness of our mind-body connection increases our understanding of our mental, physical, sensorial, and emotional states. Each of these states influence the others and dictates our behaviors and actions. The mind-body network informs us of our core motivations. Understanding our motivations provides us with insight to ascertain our experiences and our surroundings with greater wisdom. Meditation and breath awareness build a path to greater personal insight, truth, and liberation. As a world pioneer in guided meditation, Tara Brach explains, "Mindfulness is a pause—the space between stimulus and response: that's where choice lies." We have the power to shift our awareness, the power to step into our breath, the power to free our mind, so we can live a life with more openness and assemble networks in our brain and bridge pathways in the world for the greater good.

The Power of Breath

Before I began mindful meditation, I had no awareness of my breath or my body regulation. The first thing I noticed was that I breathed shallowly. I had no idea that my physiology was sending me messages to slow down. I often took half breaths. Oxygen barely reached to my chest and it did not pass my sternum. My breath was pushed out of my body with a lack of awareness. My body was starving. I neglected to oxygenate my muscles, bones, heart, organs, and especially my brain—and they were suffering. I often had the patience of a dog chasing a squirrel and I was overrun by emotional decision making. My lack of breath had many health consequences specific to anxiety, stress, muscle tension, and exhaustion. I was breathing myself sick. I needed to change my breath and change my mindset to restore my brain and body balance.

As I began my path of mindful awareness through an eight-week training in Mindfulness Based Stress Reduction (MBSR) at Insight LA, it became clearer to me that life is not a smooth sprint but rather an ultra-marathon across varied terrain. I needed to readjust my pacing to that of a long-distance runner, even walk slowly at times, crawl up a mountain, and pause under the shade of a tree. I needed to learn to breathe, mindfully. As I centered on my breath, I began to realize it was the simplest way to adjust my mood.

As I practiced and trained my mind, I first had to identify my breath in my body (*first step of awareness—where are you in your body?*) and tune in to my body. Then I needed to expand the breath in my body (*second step—visualize your breath being expanded in your body, deep belly breaths*) through my chest, abdomen, and all the way to the base of my spine. Finally, I learned to release the breath (*third step—exhale the breath and feel the breath move from the base of your spine all the way to the release through the nostrils*) with the same intentionality and identification of the breath moving through my body.[5] Who knew there is so much to breathing? Breathing is an automatic act carried out by the brain stem that I took for granted. As I investigated the breath, and my body, I learned my body was sending me signals to slow down, and allow for more oxygen to be released all throughout my body.

Neuroscience evidence shows that taking in a deep breath allows our nervous system to calm down, using the vagus nerve to activate the parasympathetic (relaxation) nervous system.[6] The activation of the vagus nerve through deep breathing releases positive neuro-hormones such as oxytocin and vasopressin to be released from the brain, telling our nervous system to relax, calm down, and feel better. These hormones—known as the soothing hormones—are essential for infant and pair bonding, when we experience feelings of deep love. These positive neurohormones allow our mind to reset away from negative emotions and thoughts. They reduce our emotional reactivity by calming the amygdala, our fear center in the brain, and by powering up the prefrontal cortex, the brain region essential for executive functioning and complex decision making.[7] A new study published in *Science*, reports that in the mouse brain, the higher order breathing center, known as the pre-Bötzinger complex, has rhythmic neural pulses for calming and arousal breathing.[8] These breath pace-maker neurons project to the locus coeruleus, a region of the brain responsible for calming, attention, and alarming throughout the brain.

Making a conscious decision to slow our breath has major health benefits: reducing anxiety, calming the emotional centers in the brain, and increasing clarity of thought by allowing the prefrontal cortex to engage in executive functioning. When we decide to stop and take a deep breath, we are using neuroscience and the power of our breath to change our mood, our mindset, and begin to rewire the mind for self-awareness and compassion.

Meditation Rewires Your Mind

Through evidence-based science, meditation has been proven to improve mental health conditions and emotional regulation by direct and indirect mechanism of the practice. Guided meditation develops our capacity to self-regulate, builds positive neural plasticity, enhances our awareness, increases compassion, and reinforces positive behavioral responses through building a greater metacognition and becoming a more self-actualized individual. Metacognition is the ability to understand one's own thought processes which encompass autobiographical memories, present perception from the five senses, emotional states, and behavioral responses. With greater metacognition, an individual can learn to be more present, flexible, and have a deep understanding of themselves and others. Meditation centers the mind so that an individual gains insight into greater awareness and has the ability to better regulate their emotional state based on clear understanding which minimizes the capacity of the emotional mind running the show. For conditions like anxiety, meditation rebalances the nervous system through release of neurotransmitters to shift the nervous system out of the "fight and flight" sympathetic activation and into the "rest and digest" parasympathetic response, restoring the sense of calm.

There is a wealth of studies supporting how meditation produces positive neurobiological and neurophysiological effects, including brain expansions, balancing neurotransmitters, and increasing alpha brain waves—all of which correspond with a calmer brain.[9] Studies have shown that meditation practices enhance neurotransmitter balance in the brain in many regions. For example, patients who practice mediation show a decrease in norepinephrine, a hormone that activates sympathetic activation, for the stress response.[10] Meditation has been shown to induce relaxing brain waves—the alpha brain waves—when measured via electroencephalogram. Individuals who meditated had an increase in the alpha brain waves in contrast to participants who did not meditate.[11] The brain is in a more relaxed and calm state when meditating and brain activity drives reactions and behaviors that are more balanced. Neurophysiological changes at the level of neurotransmitters and brain activity ultimately rewire the brain circuitry for neural pathways, constructing a more harmonious brain and way of being.

A research team at Harvard showed mindfulness stimulates neural plasticity where the brain rewires circuitry by reducing the volume of the stress circuitry and enhancing brain pathways related to having greater metacognition.[12] Specifically, researchers found that participants in an 8-week mindfulness-based stress reduction program had an increase in volume expansions of the prefrontal cortex (PFC), the region of the brain that allows for decision making, clear reasoning, motivation, attention, and planning. They further reported volume reductions in the amygdala part of the limbic cortex, the brain area responsible for fear and automatic emotional responses. Practicing guided mindful meditation alters brain anatomy where meditation increases in cortical thickness in brain regions associated with greater self-actualization. Scientists point out that brain areas responsible for attention, interoception, and processing emotional and sensory information were thicker in meditation participants and the expansions were shown in both the prefrontal cortex and right anterior insula. Intriguingly, prefrontal cortical thickness was most pronounced in older participants, proposing that meditation might offset age-related cortical thinning and even allow for the brain to age less over time. The team found that the thickness of the PFC and insula positively correlated with meditation experience. Not only does meditation reduce anxiety by releasing positive neurohormones, it rewires the brain to develop circuitry in a way that allows an individual to routinely use higher order thinking. The insular cortex is an essential area of the brain responsible for interpreting an individual's experiences of their feelings and emotions and is critical for interoception and for understanding the internal and external states of the mind and body specific to basic needs and desires (the sense that helps you understand and feel what's going on inside your body).[13]

Daniel J. Siegel points out the nine major functions of medial prefrontal cortex that improve with meditation practices.[14] Meditative practices enhance brain functioning through the expansion of the dorsal lateral prefrontal cortex, an area that has nine major functions: body regulation, in-tune communication, increasing emotional balance, greater adaptability in thinking, enhanced awareness, insight, fear regulation, morality, and intuition.

○ Body regulation is specific to the heart rate, temperature, breathing, and sweating.

○ In-tune communication is the ability to be more aware and aligned with verbal self-expression and tune into language and the motivations of others.

○ Increasing emotional equanimity allows one to be more emotionally centered in the presence of waves of emotion, and not get wrapped up in an emotion.

○ More flexible and creative thinking means one has adaptability and creative problem-solving abilities that allow for moving more freely in the world.

○ Greater awareness of empathy: empathy is the experience of understanding another person's thoughts, feelings, and condition. Empathy facilitates prosocial (helping) behaviors that come from within so that one behaves in a more compassionate manner.

○ Greater insight is the general bridge of knowledge of oneself, of others, and of how the world works so that one has enhanced self-awareness leading to a greater metacognition of motivations, actions, and behaviors.

○ Ability to regulate fear: where one is more able to regulate fear response better and use higher order thinking.

○ Morality: where one develops a better sense of knowing the difference between right and wrong and working toward the greater good.

○ Intuition is the ability to acquire knowledge without proof, evidence, or conscious reasoning, or without understanding how the knowledge was acquired, as well as an inner insight to unconscious pattern-recognition and the ability to understand something instinctively, without the need for conscious reasoning.

Meditation practices have been proven to reduce symptoms of anxiety, depression, PTSD, and trauma.[15] In a recent study, scientists offered a 12-week mindfulness-based cognitive therapy to children who had full-blown anxiety disorders and one parent with bipolar disorder.[16] Scientists obtained brain scans of the children as they watched emotional images prior to therapy and then after the mindfulness-based cognitive therapy. The results showed that children who had participated in mindfulness-based cognitive therapy had increased brain activity in their bilateral insula, the area of the brain involved in interoception, the sense that helps you understand and feel what is going on inside your body. Additionally, they reported an increase in activity in the right anterior cingulate cortex while the children were viewing the emotional stimuli. Right anterior cingulate cortex is the part of the brain that does the higher-order emotional processing. This finding shows that children with anxiety disorder build greater awareness of their internal states through the practice of meditation and can better understand their reactions to stimuli, which helps them to better process their emotions. Scientists also found there was decreased activity in the amygdala, the brain area that processes fear. Thus, children who practice meditation have a less automatic reaction in the brain when processing fear, they use higher order thinking to navigate through emotions, and build greater resilience patterns in their brain when processing negative information. They are, therefore, better self-regulated when dealing with challenging emotions.

Meditation practice has been shown to reduce stress levels, heart rate, chronic pain and, most encouraging, reduce the brain activity of the mind in response to stressful stimuli. We live in a stressful world where things are constantly pulling our attention. We need to learn to manage the stress through our brain, bodily sensations, and responses. Meditation provides a life of being aware and living in the present moment. Deep diaphragmic breathing activates the vagus nerve and allows for the release of good neurochemicals for calming, soothing, and positive feelings and bodily sensations. Meditation activates the parasympathetic nervous system, which calms the central nervous system, mind, and entire body. Meditation is also a proven method of rewiring the brain for more emotional balance, releasing positive neurochemicals, and reducing the symptoms related to anxiety and depression. Meditation allows for thinking with greater awareness and brings one into the present moment. Tara Brach describes in her meditation teaching that the mind's awareness is about going to the edge of the difficult feeling and, when at that edge, softening. This softening permits compassion for yourself and for others. Specifically, practicing a loving-kindness meditation develops prosocial behavior by cultivating greater compassion for self and others.[17] Meditation brings greater awareness of our thoughts, feelings, and emotions and helps us find ways to let emotions pass through rather than becoming stuck in the emotion. We have the ability to guide our mind to higher-order thinking so that we are not lost in the emotional reactivity but are aware of what it actually is and can respond from our heart wisdom. We can, through meditation, rewire the brain to awaken to our reality, build positive neuroplasticity centered on emotional equanimity, and step into a new age of our true nature and existence of being. Meditation is the connection to our greater wisdom, our freedom, our compassion, and joining the forces of the heart and the mind.

Kick Start Your Compassionate Brain

Metta meditation, also known as the benevolence meditation, or loving-kindness meditation, originated in Asia, and is now practiced throughout the world. The intention of a loving-kindness practice is to greet each life experience with kindness. Loving-kindness is not about "good' feelings or repeating positive affirmations but is the intention to come from a place of true kindness for yourself, others, and the planet. Loving-kindness practice builds great self-awareness and self-compassion. Raising our awareness of our self-compassion allows us to have more compassion for the entire world. Loving-kindness frees the mind into a more neutral and healing space, where there is less judgment, self-doubt, anxiety, and emotional reaction and action. Loving-kindness is a practice that focuses on the cultivation of kindness in every form of life through our experiences, emotions, bodily sensations, and thought patterns. Cultivating a loving-kindness mind state centers you experiencing life presently with kindness and loving awareness. As Mother Teresa said, "Every time you smile at someone, it is an action of love, a gift to that person, a beautiful thing." A loving-kindness practice is factually better for our health and increases well-being. Studies show that a loving-kindness practice develops prosocial behavior by focusing on compassion and cultivating more compassionate behavior. People who engage in a daily loving-kindness practice have consistently reported in numerous studies an increase in positive emotions and interpersonal connections, and they better understood complex thoughts in themselves and others. We are often hard on ourselves and others, full of expectations that can cause us to miss out on the good life. The cultivation of self-compassion is critical for health outcomes, and personal growth. The intention to begin loving-kindness focuses on being compassionate to ourselves, first and foremost. Remember to put on your own oxygen mask first and nourish your self-compassion.

Make peace with imperfection. Perfection impedes advancement. I suffer from major perfectionism and if I let it rule me and did not get over myself, this book would still be buried in my hard drive. Bottom line, there is no perfect and nothing is ever complete. Growth is leaping into the unknown and being ready to fall flat on your face. Then get back up again. Self-compassion for your successes and failures and letting go of expectations opens you to the present moment. Embrace your beautiful imperfections.

Saying no is saying yes to yourself. When I was a little girl my favorite book was Shel Silverstein's *The Giving Tree* for two reasons: the tree and giving. Trees are our lifeline: the process of photosynthesis gives us oxygen to breathe. Our symbiosis amazes me. A tree is my church, Aspen, magnolia, redwood, maple, pine, and oak. In the book, the tree gave and gave and gave until it was only a stump, and the little boy took and took and took. What I realized was that I was giving to the point that I was a stump, depleted and with nothing left to give, lacking simple photosynthesis. My physical, mental, and emotional health was suffering when I gave out of expectation rather than of my own intention. A lightbulb moment occurred when a dear friend told me, *You have to practice discernment, listen to your intuition, and release the guilt.* I was full of guilt and did things out of others' expectations rather than what was at my heart center. Now I give myself space to decide when it feels right to give, symbiosis, and when it does not serve me, parasitic. It is necessary for me to discern whether a relationship is nurturing to both parties and when it is not and I can let it go. When I say no to things that do not match my vibrational frequency and say yes to things that interest me, I have more time to sit, watch, and listen to trees in the wind and breathe the oxygen they release.

Meditation leader Tara Brach points out that when we say yes to everything it is an act of violence to ourselves, meaning that we as humans are limited in our abilities and saying yes to everything means we sacrifice our mental, physical, and emotional health. You have a choice. When you say no to things that deplete, you are saying yes to yourself. That is the art of practicing true self-compassion.

Impermanence is in everything. Nothing is permanent, not the good, the difficult or the neutral. Recognize that the "good" moment will pass just as the "difficult" moment or situation that weighs on your heart will. Neutral is the homeostatic balance of the good and difficult. Too often as humans we cling to the "good" moments or feelings and "fight off" the difficult emotions and situations. The cycle of elevation and lack creates a homeostatic imbalance. When we open ourselves to the ebb and flow of the of the human experience and emotions, and the impermanence of a moment or a feeling, we are in tune and can recognize the moment is already fleeing. Good, difficult, and neutral are beautifully intertwined and actually one and the same. When you develop self-compassion, you recognize your situation, tune into running thoughts in your mind, and identify your emotions, you are better equipped to regain a homeostatic balance of your life and be present for what really is.

Name it until you tame it. I recently learned this practice in a mediation class with world-leading meditation and dharma teacher Jack Kornfield, and it has been a powerful tool. When we name all the challenges we are experiencing, we allow the dragons in our mind to come to light and we learn they are not as scary as we'd imagined. Give voice to the pain points within yourself, your children, elders, and loved ones. Naming the "dragon" inherently reduces pain and suffering and calms the nervous system response. Sometimes naming can be as simple as one word or phrase: "logistics overload," "disaster thinking," or "illness." You can also be an active compassionate sounding board when someone shares their fears. Listening with compassion helps them and you to tame your responses to both real and imagined fear. Much of the time, people want others to listen to their needs and confirm that they are safe. Remember, when you help someone work through a challenging moment, have compassion for yourself as well. Notice your reactions and tendencies as you care for others and remain open to your process. Importantly, Jack Kornfield reminds us, "If your compassion does not include yourself, it is incomplete."

Learn to ride the waves of your emotions. Emotions evolved to cause us to take action. They are a form of information. We have the power to direct our mind to the emotional state and story we desire. Recognizing the presence of emotion is our very first step in understanding our physiological and safety needs. In addition, at any moment, we can experience many emotions simultaneously. When we identify our underlying emotions, we begin to understand our motivations, reactions, and behaviors. We also have awareness of how emotions drive our experience. That awareness is what we need to discern which emotion we would like to drive our experience and which emotion we would rather have pass through us like a wave. An emotion is a chemical reaction of an experience. Thus, an emotion is a process. It has a beginning, a middle, and an end—like a wave. "Riding the waves of the emotion," means allowing emotions to exist without judging or desiring the emotions to be different. Allow your waves of emotion to exist like an ocean. Sometimes emotions are more choppy and other times emotions are smoother. Just realize that emotional waves are part of the human experience. Remind yourself, I am caught in a current of emotion and this is a human experience. Or, I am a human experiencing waves of emotion. You do not have to drown in an emotion, you have the power to release the emotion, and you can choose to ride the wave and let it pass. As Jon Kabat-Zinn says, "You can't stop the waves, but you can learn to surf."

Be an agent of compassion. When tension is high and nervous systems are heightened, we forget our friend, Compassion. We get short-tempered and lose compassion for ourselves and others. Be kind to yourself, especially if you are having an emotional reaction to the stream of news, or if you feel your productivity is slipping as you review your to-do list. Find your friend Compassion and give yourself a hug.

We are often too hard on ourselves. Remember when a stream of negative self-talk arises, pause and ask yourself, would I say this to my best friend? The answer is most likely no. So, treat yourself as you would your very best friend. As for compassion for others, realize that other people, including family members, all tend to respond differently. Have compassion for the way they respond to life's challenges. When someone responds differently than you do, realize it is *their* response. It has nothing to do with you. Greet them with compassion. We can all use a giant hug—and when we embrace one another with compassion we diffuse feelings of anger, resentment and otherizing. When we practice compassion, we can elevate our mind and global consciousness to live in a more harmonious, balanced, and peaceful society.

> *"Love and compassion are necessities, not luxuries. Without them, humanity cannot survive."*
>
> —Dalai Lama XIV

Community & Social Connection is Key for Meaning and Longevity

Meaningful social connection is the one of the greatest factors for humans to experience optimal health and longevity. Humans are meant to be social beings, connect with other humans, and share in a collective experience. Social connection is necessary for our well-being and our livelihood. It is a core physiological need for living a meaningful life. When we experience social connections our pleasure centers are activated and we begin to develop a deep sense of meaning and connectedness. It is embedded in our biology that we are born to connect, this begins with our primary caretaker, where trust and bonding neurochemicals like oxytocin and vasopressin shape our social circuitry. Our social connectedness is reliant on our abilities and growth as a species. Our development of social relationships is directly related to our early exposure to social relationships. Studies find that when an individual experiences negative social encounters, their social development is hindered and as a result they fail to form adequate social relationships.[18] More often than not, people who experience negative social interactions are at greater risk for mental illness.

Being neurodiverse has its set of challenges. An individual can feel they are different from their family members, peers, and community and may seek to find like-minded individuals. All humans search for deep and meaningful connections. James T. Webb, a champion and world leader for gifted and 2e kids, often talked about how social and emotional needs get overlooked in these children and adults. In our culture, we focus heavily on building their scholastic opportunities when in fact these children and adults need social engagement and a community. Jim pointed out that many of his clients in therapy needed a friend, someone to talk to and hear what they had to say. He described a therapist as a confidante, and a friend, and said that everyone is looking for someone to connect with and with whom to share their stories. Science shows that having three deep and meaningful social connections provides one with a greater sense of well-being in life and vastly improves longevity.[19] When we have these deep social connections, our brain social networks are satisfied. We are wired to connect with other beings. The connections need to be part of a feeling of a deeper sense of a community. A reflection of our existence is in the balance of mirroring one another, in sharing in a collective experience, in sharing ourselves, in being seen, and in seeing others.

For example, we know that when individuals are engaged in social connection, they mirror one another and their brain waves match one another and fire in synchrony. Additionally, when individuals are connected, their heart rate, blood pressure, and level of muscle tension matches and they reflect one another. We build social connections based on interests and causes. Often, when we participate in social activities, the connections spontaneously arise as we connect over shared interests and passions. Being connected is one of the greatest ways to live a meaningful and purposeful life. When we find human connection, we experience a greater sense of meaning and belonging, and we experience the reward of feeling and being socially connected. Being connected can be transformational, as author and special education advocate Leo Buscaglia (also known as "Dr. Love") said, "Too often we underestimate the power of a touch, a smile, a kind word, a listening ear, an honest compliment, or the smallest act of caring, all of which have the potential to turn a life around."

Socialness is in our DNA. It begins with our ability to step outside ourselves, see others, and offer a hand. What seems like a simple act—that we care to see the other person, or when someone shares themselves with you—it is not really a simple act at all; it is a big deal and it requires your full attention. When we encounter the collective connectedness, oneness, we experience considerable life satisfaction and increase our ability to thrive. In a recent study, Laura Edinger-Schons found that people who believe in the concept of oneness, where everything in the universe is connected, have increased life satisfaction in comparison to people who do not believe in oneness.[20] She conducted two survey studies in Germany that included 75,000 participants. The survey posed a series of questions that focused on ascertaining whether participants believed in oneness. The findings reported that those participants with a higher "oneness" score reported they had more life satisfaction. Social connection, community, and an openness to a greater sense of oneness enrich and enhance one's quality of life and well-being. When we feel social connection and experience greater connectedness, our mind, body, and spirit have an increase in positive reward and pleasure. Being in synchrony with others enhances prosocial bonds and promotes a feeling of greater meaning in life and a wish to contribute to society in positive ways— all of which produces an entire global elevation.

> "A human being is a part of the whole called by us universe, a part limited in time and space. He experiences himself, his thoughts and feeling as something separated from the rest, a kind of optical delusion of his consciousness. This delusion is a kind of prison for us, restricting us to our personal desires and to affection for a few persons nearest to us. Our task must be to free ourselves from this prison by widening our circle of compassion to embrace all living creatures and the whole of nature in its beauty."
>
> —Albert Einstein

Nurturing Ourselves with Nature

Nature is a rich powerful source that can invigorate and heal us. Hippocrates said, "Nature itself is the best physician." We do not need to travel far to connect with nature. Nature is all around us. Even in the city we can find nature. There are birds, trees, flowers, breezes, mountains, and natural bodies of water like the ocean and streams. Once we bring nature into our awareness, we experience a greater sense of connectedness. We are part of nature, and when we connect to our natural world, we can be better attuned to the symbiosis throughout our environment. Simply connecting to nature calms the nervous system, relaxes one's heart rate and blood pressure and can even relax the mind. The ancient art of forest bathing has been around since the beginning of time, and has been proven to help with mental conditions such as anxiety and depression, as well as supporting increased immune function.[21] Yoshifumi Miyazaki and his team of researchers in Japan conducted a meta-analysis of 52 studies on nature's effects on the nervous system and found that nature has restorative benefits for the nervous system by allowing for physiological relaxation and enhanced immune function. Time in nature can be used as preventative medicine. The symbiotic benefits of nature play a role in adjusting our physiology through our autonomic nervous system, brain activity, hormones, and immune activity, which has the capacity for healing. Nature is a reflection of us, matching our inner forest of thoughts, emotions, and physiological responses. Take the example of a flower sprouting from a crack in the concrete. To the naked eye, there is no soil for that flower to grow and sprout, but nature finds a way to thrive, and life can flourish in the most challenging circumstances. So can we. At times we are resilient in making do with the lot we have been handed in life. At other times we are like a full-grown willow tree grounded and rooted in our being, glorious with all the sun's rays and the minerals in the soil nurturing us. Even in the city, we know there is always new growth: think about our flower emerging from a crack in the concrete. Nature has the ability to ground and center us. An ancient practice I learned from Tenzin Wangyal Rinpoche is observing the spaciousness of nature. In his book, *Spontaneous*

Creativity, he points to how the spaciousness of nature can ignite our mind and influence our creative process.[22]

A recent study measured the brain activity of elderly individuals while they were walking in an urban setting to assess the effects of green space on mood and well-being. Participants reported their levels of engagement, excitement, and frustration as they walked. Those that experienced more green spaces filled with nature while walking in an urban setting reported increased excitement and engagement and decreased frustration.[23] This finding points out that green space can elevate one's mood, and nature can restore and rebalance one's mindset and enhance one's emotional stability. In another study, scientists found that parks support an increase of well-being in visitors.[24] According to new research from investigators from University of Alabama at Birmingham Department of Occupational Therapy, spending 20 minutes in an urban park can increase happiness. This result was independent of whether a person exercised during their visit to the park. Most important, park visitors reported greater emotional well-being.[25] This further supports the theory that green spaces provide increased mental, emotional, and physical well-being.

E.O. Wilson writes, "Just being surrounded by bountiful nature rejuvenates and inspires us." In Denmark, scientists from Aarhus University used satellite date and mapped green space around homes over a 28-year period and found that children who lived in greener neighborhoods had 55% less risk of having mental health conditions later in life.[26] Scientists controlled for socioeconomic status, urbanization, and past history of family members with mental health conditions. Green space directly impacts mental health; individuals with greater access to nature have a greater likelihood of having better health outcomes. Nature can provide hope and healing in times of challenge. The impact of greenery has health benefits related to calming the nervous system through hormones, biofeedback, and immune responses. Also, nature inspires. Nature is connectedness. Nature reminds us of our oneness and is the equalizer. Humanity and nature are woven together through all of time. Nature and green spaces are healing.

Even the sounds of nature have been reported to relax and soothe the nervous system. Neuroscientists found that listening to "green" sounds—sounds of nature—increases relaxation of mind and body by activating the parasympathetic nervous system, reducing the heart rate, stress hormones, and anxiety. Tranquil sounds, like a bird chirping or a running stream are restorative and good for calming your nervous system.[27] By contrast, they reported unnatural sounds, like freeways, garden blowers, and sirens activate the stress response because these sounds are more dissonant. Natural sounds are more harmonious and soothe the nervous system.

On multiple levels, nature, green spaces and nature's sounds are restorative for the mind-body balance. Many scientific studies provide evidence-based research that shows being immersed in nature calms the nervous system through the senses, both through visual absorption of nature, and through hearing the sounds of nature. Experiencing nature can aid in the development of emotional balance and can reduce mental health conditions such as anxiety, depression, and chronic stress. Connecting and immersing ourselves in nature has been proven effective for opening our creativity and enhancing our mood and optimism.

> *"Nature holds the key to our aesthetic, intellectual, cognitive and even spiritual satisfaction."*
>
> —E.O. Wilson

Spread Your Wings and Fly

> *We delight in the beauty of the butterfly, but rarely admit the changes it has gone through to achieve that beauty.*
>
> —Maya Angelou

Our growth stems from our failures, our successes, and our ability to rise to the occasion and dream for a new day—despite our current circumstance. Our belief and hope that things will get better, be better, even in the face of our challenges, is what gives us the ability to transform ourselves and our lives. Anyone who has ever tried for something and failed time and time again has found that rising and getting back up again is worth it. That their efforts, their contribution, their wisdom led the world in the direction of a greater good.

As Jane Goodall says, "Every individual matters. Every individual has a role to play. Every individual makes a difference." I believe in this statement. We are all here on Earth at this exact time to teach one another and to create for the betterment of the world and humanity. For us to reach our highest selves and our maximum potential we need to move beyond surviving and learn the ways we can thrive. Thriving begins with our ability to play from our strengths and understand our neuroindividuality.

World leader in cognitive diversity, Susan Baum, has dedicated her life to nurturing talent development. Her method is simple: build from an individual's strengths and bring in supports when needed. When an individual feels safe in their environment and safe with their teachers, they are open to learning, are willing to take more risks, and have more flexible and adaptive thinking. In contrast, if an individual is stressed, they are not. They are in their fear mind and not able to think flexibly, or perhaps not even able to think at all, which has massive implications for their cognitive development. Stress interferes with learning and inhibits creativity. Thus, safety is the first element in reaching an individual. When a person feels safe, they experience trust and their natural abilities flow. Building an emotional connection centered on trust is necessary for them to have a sense of belonging in their community and with others.

Science shows, from the work of David Bennett's team at Rush University, that social connection is a key piece for healthy brain development and longevity.[28] As mentioned earlier, when people feel deep social connections with at least three people, they feel a greater sense of meaning and well-being. Having a sense of meaning and purpose is essential for life and health outcomes. Specifically, having a purpose in life was positively correlated with longevity and decreased incidences of dementia. Having a purpose and deep social connections in life are neuroprotective. When we feel we belong, we thrive and can explore deeper meaning and connection with higher levels of living in life. This sense of belonging comes from our mindset—that we are part of something, larger, and experiencing the sense of oneness.

The mind creates our narratives, thus it is crucial that we minimize negative self-talk in order to step into our full essence. More recently, negative self-talk has been associated with greater risks of dementia.[29] This makes sense: when we participate in negative self-talk, the monkey mind goes wild, activating stress circuitry, which can cause a cascade of hormones for immune activation and change baseline physiology. This causes greater inflammation and contributes to neuronal cell loss hindering our ability to see our gifts and true nature. It is essential to shift the mind-set to more optimistic thinking and feel, believe, and *know* there is hope. Science shows that when we can imagine positive outcomes we can conquer our fears.[30] Jon Kabat-Zinn says, "Maybe the fear is that we are less than we think we are, when the actuality of it is that we are much much more."

Optimistic thinking shifts the mindset and narrative. Our perception and emotional state are regulated by following our narrative. Our mind goes where the narrative flows. Invite the optimistic imagination, invite the positive. Our thoughts are powerful. We have the ability to drive our mind. We can drive our imagination and hope for the better. We are facing life with an array of choices. We can thrive, but to do so, each of us must continue to embrace our neuroindividuality and share our gifts, the gifts that no one else will ever have throughout all of time, the gifts that are ours alone. When we understand how deeply connected we are to everything, that we belong, we have a purpose which is our woven neuroindividuality, that is our transformation, that is when we begin to fly, that is when we live in our essence and live the life that we imagine and dream.

As E.O. Wilson says, "You are capable of more than you know. Choose a goal that seems right for you and strive to be the best, however hard the path. Aim high. Behave honorably. Prepare to be alone at times, and to endure failure. Persist! The world needs all you can give."

Acknowledgments

Gratitude and the completion of a book go hand in hand. *Insight into a Bright Mind* would not exist in its form without all of the love and encouragement I received on the way.

It begins with a thank you to James T. Webb for being the teacher and friend who saw this book in me and nurtured my voice in the beginning days. Thank you, Jan Webb, for our discussions as we grappled with our loss of Jim to a heart attack.

Thank you, Molly Isaacs-McLeod for your patience and conversations as we assembled the pieces to find the book's new path. I am delighted it found a home at Gifted Unlimited. Molly, I am grateful to have you as a partner and friend, your humor and compassion along the way opened the story in a way I never imagined.

Thank you to the many partners in the gifted and 2e community over the years for the sage discussions, like Barry Gelston, President of GHF Dialogue, Debbie Steinberg Kuntz, Founder of Bright and Quirky, Jean Harville, founder of Unleash Your Kid's Genius, Julie Skolnick, founder of Let's Talk 2e, the entire SENG team and community, Femke Hovinga, Ruth Karpinski, Lucy Hunt and Susanna Furfari of LAUSD, Susan Baum, Chris Wiebe and to my friends at Bridges and 2e News for encouraging my research along the way, I am grateful to be a part of Bridges Graduate School of Cognitive Diversity in Education. To all the people that came to my talks asking for the book, it is for you I never stopped. Thank you.

Thank you to all my meditation groups, sangha, teachers, and yogis, you nurtured peace, truth, and compassion within me.

To my dear friend Amy Deavoll, thank you for reading many drafts and for your shining light of support.

Thank you to John Allman for opening the door of his research laboratory at Caltech and guiding my dream to become a neuroscientist.

Thank you to my writing teachers, Pam Houston and Lidia Yuknavitch, I love your words.

Thank you to all of the people that I interviewed that shared their stories, who helped shape the backbone of the book, and who inspired the concept of neuroindividuality.

Susan Daniels, thank you for agreeing to write the foreword of my book, and for your book, *Living with Intensity*, which remains an inspiration to me.

Thank you to my editor, Lesley Dahl, for your gentle guidance, humor, and for the 1000 commas of clarity.

Thank you, Spotify, for the endless hours of music and inspiration. Thank you, my friends at the C.M. for creating a writing portal for my retreats and the late-night hours writing in the garden.

Thank you to my family, my mom, Loretta Anne Tetreault, for being loving awareness, and my dad, for always telling me to do what I love. Thanks to my sister Donna, as we wrote our books side by side and encouraged one another, and my brothers, David, for always seeing me, and Phil and Scott, for being part of my origin story. Thank you to all my adorable nieces and nephews. Many thanks to the bonus family I gained as an adult: Andrew, Shannon, John and Kathy, Shana and Deborah, Marissa and Jake.

My Spencer, my light, my teacher and the coolest person I have ever known, thank you for pushing me to be better. The day you were born goes down in my personal history as the best day of my life and every day after that one is better because you are in it. Thank you for all your work on my references, you supported me, because I am dyslexic, the assembly would have been daunting. Thank you, bright one.

Thank you, Billy, my one, my friend that patiently waited to ask me on a date as I showed you my histology book, who would have known that you would be the first my reader of my book and writings. I would not be who I am without all of your devotion and encouragement over the years. Thank you for all your proofreading, editing, and fact checking. Billy thank for the endless walks and talks about the brain and writing. Thank you for always listening. Thank you for seeing. Thank you, Billy, for being you.

Appendix and Supplementary Materials

My Favorite 2e/Gifted Resources, Communities, and Webinars:

Social Emotional Needs for the Gifted (SENG):
http://www.sengifted.org

National Association for the Gifted:
http://www.nagc.org

Davidson Institute:
https://www.davidsongifted.org/

2E News:
https://www.2enews.com

Gifted Homeschooler's Dialogue (GHF):
https://ghfdialogue.org/

Hoagies Gifted:
http://www.hoagiesgifted.org/gifted_adults.htm

Johns Hopkins Center for Talented Youth:
https://cty.jhu.edu

Belin-Blank Center:
https://belinblank.education.uiowa.edu/students/default.aspx

Bridges Graduate School for Cognitive Diversity:
https://graduateschool.bridges.edu

Gifted Unlimited:
https://www.giftedunlimitedllc.com/

Tilt Parenting:
https://tiltparenting.com

Bright & Quirky:
https://brightandquirky.com

Unleash Your Kid's Genius:
https://cf.jeanharville.com/masterclass?affiliate_id=2147288

With Understanding Comes the Calm:
https://www.withunderstandingcomescalm.com

The G Word Film:
https://www.thegwordfilm.com

California Gifted Network:
http://www.cagiftednetwork.com

Tutoring and Therapies:

The O'Kelley Lab and Mime as Therapy:
https://theokelleylab.com

Mr. Gelston's One Room School House:
https://www.mrgelston.com

Institute for Educational Advancement:
https://educationaladvancement.org/

H-Bar Tutoring:
http://www.hbartutoring.com/Welcome.html

Testing & Educational Services:

Summit Center:
https://summitcenter.us/home-page/

Gifted Ed Matters:
http://www.giftedandthriving.com

LAUSD GATE:
https://achieve.lausd.net/gate

Greater Los Angeles Gifted Children's Association:
http://www.giftedchildrenla.org/

Specialized High Schools & Early College Admissions:

Bridges Academy:
https://www.bridges.edu

Stanford Online High School:
https://onlinehighschool.stanford.edu/

Cal State Early Entrance Program (EPP):
http://www.calstatela.edu/academic/eep

Psychological and Health Services:

Summit Center:
https://summitcenter.us

Amend Group:
http://amendpsych.com/about-gifted-children/

S. Abigail McCarrel, LCSW, DCSW:
http://www.welcomehomefamilytherapy/

Matthew Zakreski:
http://www.evergreenassociates.com/

Nutritional Services:
https://nutritionally-fit.com/wendy-crump/

Vision Services:
https://www.optometrists.org/Stephey/

Meditation Organizations and Teachings:

UCLA MARC:
https://www.uclahealth.org/marc/default.cfm

Greater Good UC Berkeley:
https://greatergood.berkeley.edu

Spirit Rock:
https://www.spiritrock.org/

Insight LA:
https://insightla.org

Sounds True:
https://www.soundstrue.com

Buddhist Geeks:
>   https://www.buddhistgeeks.org/

Beyond the Cell:
>   https://www.beyondthecell.org

Radiant Heart Yoga and Wellness
>   https://radiantheartyogaandwellness.com

InsightTimer
>   https://insighttimer.com

MindUP
>   https://mindup.org

References

Aboitiz, F. "Brain Connections: Interhemispheric Fiber Systems and Anatomical Brain Asymmetries in Humans." [In Eng]. *Biological Research* 25, no. 2 (1992): 51-61. https://www.ncbi.nlm.nih.gov/pubmed/1365702.

Acharya, S., and S. Shukla. "Mirror Neurons: Enigma of the Metaphysical Modular Brain." [In Eng]. *Journal of Natural Science, Biology, and Medicine* 3, no. 2 (Jul 2012): 118-24. https://www.doi.org/10.4103/0976-9668.101878. https://www.ncbi.nlm.nih.gov/pubmed/23225972.

Adeyeye, T. E., E. H. Yeung, A. C. McLain, S. Lin, D. A. Lawrence, and E. M. Bell. "Wheeze and Food Allergies in Children Born Via Cesarean Delivery: The Upstate Kids Study." [In Eng]. *American Journal of Epidemiology* 188, no. 2 (Feb 1 2019): 355-62. https://www.doi.org/10.1093/aje/kwy257.

Adhikari, B. M., M. Norgaard, K. M. Quinn, J. Ampudia, J. Squirek, and M. Dhamala. "The Brain Network Underpinning Novel Melody Creation." [In Eng]. *Brain Connectivity* 6, no. 10 (Dec 2016): 772-85. https://www.doi.org/10.1089/brain.2016.0453.

Adriaanse, M., and D. A. Leffler. "Serum Markers in the Clinical Management of Celiac Disease." [In Eng]. *Digestive Diseases* 33, no. 2 (2015): 236-43. https://www.doi.org/10.1159/000371405.

Aguinis, Herman, Steven A. Culpepper, and Charles A. Pierce. "Differential Prediction Generalization in College Admissions Testing." *Journal of Educational Psychology* 108, no. 7 (2016): 1045-59. https://www.doi.org/10.1037/edu0000104.

Ahn, R. R., L. J. Miller, S. Milberger, and D. N. McIntosh. "Prevalence of Parents' Perceptions of Sensory Processing Disorders among Kindergarten Children." [In Eng]. *The American Journal of Occupational Therapy* 58, no. 3 (2004 May-Jun 2004): 287-93. https://www.doi.org/10.5014/ajot.58.3.287. https://www.ncbi.nlm.nih.gov/pubmed/15202626.

Allman, J. M., A. Hakeem, J. M. Erwin, and E. Nimchinsky. "The Anterior Cingulate Cortex. The Evolution of an Interface between Emotion and Cognition." [In Eng]. *Annals of the New York Academy of Sciences* 935 (May 2001): 107-17.

Allman, J. M., N. A. Tetreault, A. Y. Hakeem, K. F. Manaye, K. Semendeferi, J. M. Erwin, *et al.* "The Von Economo Neurons in Frontoinsular and Anterior Cingulate Cortex in Great Apes and Humans." [In Eng]. *Brain Structure & Function* 214, no. 5-6 (Jun 2010): 495-517. https://www.doi.org/10.1007/s00429-010-0254-0.

―――. "The Von Economo Neurons in the Frontoinsular and Anterior Cingulate Cortex." [In Eng]. *Annals of the New York Academy of Sciences* 1225 (Apr 2011): 59-71. https://www.doi.org/10.1111/j.1749-6632.2011.06011.x.

Allman, J. M., N. A. Tetreault, A. Y. Hakeem, and S. Park. "The Von Economo Neurons in Apes and Humans." [In Eng]. *The American Journal of Human Biology* 23, no. 1 (Jan-Feb 2011): 5-21. https://www.doi.org/10.1002/ajhb.21136.

Allman, J. M., K. K. Watson, N. A. Tetreault, and A. Y. Hakeem. "Intuition and Autism: A Possible Role for Von Economo Neurons." [In Eng]. *Trends in Cognitive Sciences* 9, no. 8 (Aug 2005): 367-73. https://www.doi.org/10.1016/j.tics.2005.06.008.

Alnæs, D., T. Kaufmann, N. T. Doan, A. Córdova-Palomera, Y. Wang, F. Bettella, T. Moberget, O. A. Andreassen, and L. T. Westlye. "Association of Heritable Cognitive Ability and Psychopathology with White Matter Properties in Children and Adolescents." [In Eng]. *JAMA Psychiatry* 75, no. 3 (03 2018): 287-95. https://www.doi.org/10.1001/jamapsychiatry.2017.4277. https://www.ncbi.nlm.nih.gov/pubmed/29365026.

Alvarez, J. A., and E. Emory. "Executive Function and the Frontal Lobes: A Meta-Analytic Review." [In Eng]. *Neuropsychology Review* 16, no. 1 (Mar 2006): 17-42. https://www.doi.org/10.1007/s11065-006-9002-x.

American Psychiatric Association., and American Psychiatric Association. DSM-5 Task Force. *Diagnostic and Statistical Manual of Mental Disorders : Dsm-5.* 5th ed. Washington, D.C.: American Psychiatric Association, 2013.

ANCA Consulting Inc. "Naturally Autistic." 2017, accessed 6/23/2020, from https://www.naturallyautistic.com/founders/297-2/.

Andreasen, N. C., M. Flaum, V. Swayze, 2nd, D. S. O'Leary, R. Alliger, G. Cohen, J. Ehrhardt, and W. T. Yuh. "Intelligence and Brain Structure in Normal Individuals." [In Eng]. *The American Journal of Psychiatry* 150, no. 1 (Jan 1993): 130-4. https://www.doi.org/10.1176/ajp.150.1.130.

Andrews, S., D. A. Ellis, H. Shaw, and L. Piwek. "Beyond Self-Report: Tools to Compare Estimated and Real-World Smartphone Use." [In Eng]. *PLoS One* 10, no. 10 (2015): e0139004. https://www.doi.org/10.1371/journal.pone.0139004.

Arain, M., M. Haque, L. Johal, P. Mathur, W. Nel, A. Rais, R. Sandhu, and S. Sharma. "Maturation of the Adolescent Brain." [In Eng]. *Neuropsychiatric Disease and Treatment* 9 (2013): 449-61. https://www.doi.org/10.2147/NDT.S39776. https://www.ncbi.nlm.nih.gov/pubmed/23579318.

Arcaro, M. J., and M. S. Livingstone. "A Hierarchical, Retinotopic Proto-Organization of the Primate Visual System at Birth." [In Eng]. *eLife* 6 (Jul 3 2017). https://www.doi.org/10.7554/eLife.26196.

Arora, M., A. Reichenberg, C. Willfors, C. Austin, C. Gennings, S. Berggren, P. Lichtenstein, *et al.* "Fetal and Postnatal Metal Dysregulation in Autism." [In Eng]. *Nature Communications* 8 (Jun 1 2017): 15493. https://www.doi.org/10.1038/ncomms15493.

Ashar, Y. K., J. R. Andrews-Hanna, S. Dimidjian, and T. D. Wager. "Empathic Care and Distress: Predictive Brain Markers and Dissociable Brain Systems." [In Eng]. *Neuron* 94, no. 6 (Jun 21 2017): 1263-73.e4. https://www.doi.org/10.1016/j.neuron.2017.05.014.

Aziz-Zadeh, L., S. L. Liew, and F. Dandekar. "Exploring the Neural Correlates of Visual Creativity." [In Eng]. *Social Cognitive and Affective Neuroscience* 8, no. 4 (Apr 2013): 475-80. https://www.doi.org/10.1093/scan/nss021.

Açbay, O., A. F. Celik, P. Kadioğlu, S. Göksel, and S. Gündoğdu. "Helicobacter Pylori-Induced Gastritis May Contribute to Occurrence of Postprandial Symptomatic Hypoglycemia." [In Eng]. *Digestive Diseases and Sciences* 44, no. 9 (Sep 1999): 1837-42. https://www.doi.org/10.1023/a:1018842606388.

Badawy, Rebecca L., Brooke A. Gazdag, Jeffrey R. Bentley, and Robyn L. Brouer. "Are All Impostors Created Equal? Exploring Gender Differences in the Impostor Phenomenon-Performance Link." *Personality and Individual Differences* 131 (2018/09/01/ 2018): 156-63. https://www.doi.org/10.1016/j.paid.2018.04.044. http://www.sciencedirect.com/science/article/pii/S0191886918302435.

Bankard, Joseph. "Training Emotion Cultivates Morality: How Loving-Kindness Meditation Hones Compassion and Increases Prosocial Behavior." *Journal of Religion and Health* 54, no. 6 (2015): 2324-43.

Baron-Cohen S, Hammer J. "Parents of Children with Asperger Syndrome: What is the Cognitive Phenotype?" *Journal of Cognitive Neuroscience* 9, no 4 (July 1997)548-54. https://www.doi.org/10.1162/jocn.1997.9.4.548.

Baron-Cohen, S. "The Autistic Child's Theory of Mind: A Case of Specific Developmental Delay." [In Eng]. *Journal of Child Psychology and Psychiatry* 30, no. 2 (Mar 1989): 285-97. https://www.doi.org/10.1111/j.1469-7610.1989.tb00241.x.

Baron-Cohen, Simon. "Does Autism Occur More Often in Families of Physicists, Engineers, and Mathematicians?" Autism 2, no. 3 (1998): 296-301. https://www.doi.org/10.1177/1362361398023008. https://journals.sagepub.com/doi/abs/10.1177/1362361398023008.

Bartzokis, G. "Age-Related Myelin Breakdown: A Developmental Model of Cognitive Decline and Alzheimer's Disease." [In Eng]. *Neurobiology of Aging* 25, no. 1 (Jan 2004): 5-18; author reply 49-62. https://www.doi.org/10.1016/j.neurobiolaging.2003.03.001. https://www.ncbi.nlm.nih.gov/pubmed/14675724.

Bastiaansen, J. A. C. J., M. Thioux, and C. Keysers. "Evidence for Mirror Systems in Emotions." [In Eng]. *Philosophical transactions of the Royal Society of London. Series B, Biological sciences* 364, no. 1528 (2009): 2391-404. https://www.doi.org/10.1098/rstb.2009.0058. https://pubmed.ncbi.nlm.nih.gov/19620110. https://www.ncbi.nlm.nih.gov/pmc/ articles/PMC2865077/.

Bauman, M. L., and T. L. Kemper. "Neuroanatomic Observations of the Brain in Autism: A Review and Future Directions." [In Eng]. *International Journal of Developmental Neuroscience* 23, no. 2-3 (Apr-May 2005): 183-7. https://www.doi.org/10.1016/j. ijdevneu.2004.09.006.

Beaty, R. E., M. Benedek, S. B. Kaufman, and P. J. Silvia. "Default and Executive Network Coupling Supports Creative Idea Production." [In Eng]. *Scientific Reports* 5 (Jun 17 2015): 10964. https://www.doi.org/10.1038/srep10964.

Beaty, R. E., Y. N. Kenett, A. P. Christensen, M. D. Rosenberg, M. Benedek,Q. Chen, A. Fink, *et al.* "Robust Prediction of Individual Creative Ability from Brain Functional Connectivity." [In Eng]. *Proceedings of the National Academy of Sciences of the United States of America* 115, no. 5 (Jan 30 2018): 1087-92. https://www.doi.org/10.1073/ pnas.1713532115.

Beaty, Roger E. "The Neuroscience of Musical Improvisation." *Neuroscience & Biobehavioral Reviews* 51 (2015/04/01/ 2015): 108-17. https://www. doi.org/10.1016/j.neubiorev.2015.01.004. http://www.sciencedirect. com/science/article/pii/S0149763415000068.

Bemporad, J. R. "Adult Recollections of a Formerly Autistic Child." [In Eng]. *The Journal of Autism and Developmental Disorders* 9, no. 2 (Jun 1979): 179-97. https://www.doi.org/10.1007/bf01531533.

Benbow, Camilla Persson. "Intellectually Gifted Students Also Suffer from Immune Disorders." *Behavioral and Brain Sciences* 8, no. 3 (1985): 442-42. https:// www.doi.org/10.1017/S0140525X00001059. https://www.cambridge. org/core/article/intellectually-gifted-students-also-suffer-from-immune-disorders/06EC219AD0004EB467AB0D372B-07F7BC.

———. "Physiological Correlates of Extreme Intellectual Precocity." *Neuro-psychologia* 24, no. 5 (1986/01/01/ 1986): 719-25. https://www.doi. org/10.1016/0028-3932(86)90011-4. http://www.sciencedirect.com/ science/article/pii/0028393286900114.

Benhayon, D., A. Youk, F. N. McCarthy, S. Davis, D. J. Keljo, A. Bousvaros, D. Fairclough, et al. "Characterization of Relations among Sleep, Inflammation, and Psychiatric Dysfunction in Depressed Youth with Crohn Disease." [In Eng]. *The Journal of Pediatric Gastroenterology and Nutrition* 57, no. 3 (Sep 2013): 335-42. https://www.doi.org/10.1097/ MPG.0b013e31829641df.

Benjamin, L. T. J. "The Birth of American Intelligence Testing." *Monitor on Psychology*, 2008. http://www.apa.org/monitor/2009/01/assessment.

Benno, P., A. L. Dahlgren, R. Befrits, E. Norin, P. M. Hellström, and T. Midtvedt. "From IBS to DBS: The Dysbiotic Bowel Syndrome." [In Eng]. *The Journal of Investigative Medicine - High Impact Case Reports* 4, no. 2 (Apr-Jun 2016): 2324709616648458. https://www. doi.org/10.1177/2324709616648458.

Benton, D., C. Williams, and A. Brown. "Impact of Consuming a Milk Drink Containing a Probiotic on Mood and Cognition." [In Eng]. *European Journal of Clinical Nutrition* 61, no. 3 (Mar 2007): 355-61. https:// www.doi.org/10.1038/ sj.ejcn.1602546.

Berger M, Gray JA, Roth BL. The expanded biology of serotonin. *The Annual Review of Medicine* 60 (2009):355-66. https://www.doi.org/10.1146/ annurev.med.60.042307.110802

Berkman, E. T., L. E. Kahn, and J. S. Merchant. "Training-Induced Changes in Inhibitory Control Network Activity." [In Eng]. *Journal of Neuroscience* 34, no. 1 (Jan 1 2014): 149-57. https://www.doi.org/10.1523/jneurosci.3564-13.2014.

Berkowitz, Aaron L. "The Cognitive Neuroscience of Improvisation." In *The Oxford Handbook of Critical Improvisation Studies, Volume 1*, edited by G.E. Lewis and B. Piekut: Oxford University Press, 2016.

Bernhardt, B. C., and T. Singer. "The Neural Basis of Empathy." [In Eng]. *The Annual Review of Neuroscience* 35 (2012): 1-23. https://www.doi.org/10.1146/annurev-neuro-062111-150536.

Berninger, Virginia Wise, and Beverly J. Wolf. *Teaching Students with Dyslexia and Dysgraphia : Lessons from Teaching and Science*. Baltimore: Paul H. Brookes Pub. Co., 2009.

Best, Catherine, Shruti Arora, Fiona Porter, and Martin Doherty. "The Relationship between Subthreshold Autistic Traits, Ambiguous Figure Perception and Divergent Thinking." *Journal of Autism and Developmental Disorders* 45, no. 12 (2015): 4064-73. https://doi.org/10.1007/s10803-015-2518-2

Bisho, G. H., and J. M. Smith. "The Size of Nerve Fibers Supplying Cerebral Cortex." [In Eng]. *Experimental Neurology, a Journal of Neuroscience Research* 9 (Jun 1964): 483-501. https://www.doi.org/10.1016/0014-4886(64)90056-1. https://www.ncbi.nlm.nih.gov/pubmed/14188535.

Blakemore, Sarah-Jayne, and Uta Frith. *The Learning Brain : Lessons for Education*. Malden, MA, USA: Blackwell, 2005.

Blanche, E. I., G. Reinoso, M. C. Chang, and S. Bodison. "Proprioceptive Processing Difficulties among Children with Autism Spectrum Disorders and Developmental Disabilities." [In Eng]. *The American Journal of Occupational Therapy* 66, no. 5 (Sep-Oct 2012): 621-4. https://www.doi.org/10.5014/ajot.2012.004234.

Blaser, M. J., and S. Falkow. "What Are the Consequences of the Disappearing Human Microbiota?" [In Eng]. *Nature Reviews Microbiology* 7, no. 12 (Dec 2009): 887-94. https://www.doi.org/10.1038/nrmicro2245.

Blum, Kenneth, Amanda Lih-Chuan Chen, Eric R Braverman, David E Comings, Thomas JH Chen, Vanessa Arcuri, Seth H Blum, *et al.* "Attention-Deficit-Hyperactivity Disorder and Reward Deficiency Syndrome." *Neuropsychiatric Disease and Treatment* (2008).

Bonder, M. J., E. F. Tigchelaar, X. Cai, G. Trynka, M. C. Cenit, B. Hrdlickova, H. Zhong, *et al.* "The Influence of a Short-Term Gluten-Free Diet on the Human Gut Microbiome." [In Eng]. *Genome Medicine* 8, no. 1 (Apr 21 2016): 45. https://www.doi.org/10.1186/s13073-016-0295-y.

Boring Co., The. (n.d.) "FAQ." [Website.] Accessed 6/24/20 from https://www.boringcompany.com/faq

Boswell, M., Y. Lu, W. Boswell, M. Savage, K. Hildreth, R. Salinas, C. A. Walter, and R. B. Walter. "Fluorescent Light Incites a Conserved Immune and Inflammatory Genetic Response within Vertebrate Organs (Danio Rerio, Oryzias Latipes and Mus Musculus)." [In Eng]. *Genes (Basel)* 10, no. 4 (Apr 3 2019). https://www.doi.org/10.3390/genes10040271.

Boyle, Patricia A., Aron S. Buchman, Robert S. Wilson, Lei Yu, Julie A. Schneider, and David A. Bennett. "Effect of Purpose in Life on the Relation between Alzheimer Disease Pathologic Changes on Cognitive Function in Advanced Age." *Archives of General Psychiatry* 69, no. 5 (2012): 499-504. https://www.doi.org/10.1001/archgenpsychiatry.2011.1487.

Bralten, J., C. U. Greven, B. Franke, M. Mennes, M. P. Zwiers, N. N. Rommelse, C. Hartman, *et al.* "Voxel-Based Morphometry Analysis Reveals Frontal Brain Differences in Participants with ADHD and Their Unaffected Siblings." [In Eng]. *The Journal of Psychiatry & Neuroscience* 41, no. 4 (Jun 2016): 272-9. https://www.doi.org/10.1503/jpn.140377.

Bravata, Dena M., Sharon A. Watts, Autumn L. Keefer, Divya K. Madhusudhan, Katie T. Taylor, Dani M. Clark, Ross S. Nelson, Kevin O. Cokley, and Heather K. Hagg. "Prevalence, Predictors, and Treatment of Impostor Syndrome: A Systematic Review." *Journal of General Internal Medicine* 35, no. 4 (Apr 1 2020): 1252-75. https://www.doi.org/10.1007/s11606-019-05364-1.

Brodmann, Korbinian. *Vergleichende Lokalisationslehre Der Grosshirnrinde in Ihren Prinzipien Dargestellt Auf Grund Des Zellenbaues.* [Comparative localization theory of the cerebral cortex presented in its principles on the basis of the cell structure] Barth, 1909.

Bruya, B., and Y. Y. Tang. "Is Attention Really Effort? Revisiting Daniel Kahneman's Influential 1973 Book." [In Eng]. *Frontiers in Psychology* 9 (2018): 1133. https://www.doi.org/10.3389/fpsyg.2018.01133. https://www.ncbi.nlm.nih.gov/pubmed/30237773.

Bryant, Fred B, Erica D Chadwick, and Katharina Kluwe. "Understanding the Processes That Regulate Positive Emotional Experience: Unsolved Problems and Future Directions for Theory and Research on Savoring." *International Journal of Wellbeing* 1, no. 1 (2011).

Bryant, Fred Boyd, and Joseph Veroff. *Savoring : A New Model of Positive Experience.* Mahwah, N.J.: Lawrence Erlbaum Associates, Publishers, 2007.

Buie, T., D. B. Campbell, G. J. Fuchs, 3rd, G. T. Furuta, J. Levy, J. Vandewater, A. H. Whitaker, *et al.* "Evaluation, Diagnosis, and Treatment of Gastrointestinal Disorders in Individuals with ASDS: A Consensus Report." [In Eng]. *Pediatrics* 125 Suppl 1 (Jan 2010): S1-18. https://www.doi.org/10.1542/peds.2009-1878C.

Bush, G., P. Luu, and M. I. Posner. "Cognitive and Emotional Influences in Anterior Cingulate Cortex." [In Eng]. *Trends in Cognitive Sciences* 4, no. 6 (Jun 2000): 215-22. https://www.doi.org/10.1016/s1364-6613(00)01483-2.

Cahill, L., and J. L. McGaugh. "A Novel Demonstration of Enhanced Memory Associated with Emotional Arousal." [In Eng]. *Consciousness and Cognition* 4, no. 4 (Dec 1995): 410-21. https://www.doi.org/10.1006/ccog.1995.1048.

Cahn, B. R., and J. Polich. "Meditation States and Traits: EEG, ERP, and Neuroimaging Studies." [In Eng]. *Psychological Bulletin* 132, no. 2 (Mar 2006): 180-211. https://www.doi.org/10.1037/0033-2909.132.2.180.

Cammarota, G., S. Pecere, G. Ianiro, L. Masucci, and D. Currò. "Principles of DNA-Based Gut Microbiota Assessment and Therapeutic Efficacy of Fecal Microbiota Transplantation in Gastrointestinal Diseases." [In Eng]. *Digestive Diseases* 34, no. 3 (2016): 279-85. https://www.doi.org/10.1159/000443362.

Campbell, A. W. "Autoimmunity and the Gut." [In Eng]. *Autoimmune Diseases* 2014 (2014): 152428. https://www.doi.org/10.1155/2014/152428.

Cantor, Pamela, David Osher, Juliette Berg, Lily Steyer, and Todd Rose. "Malleability, Plasticity, and Individuality: How Children Learn and Develop in Context." *Applied Developmental Science* 23, no. 4 (2019/10/02 2019): 307-37. https://www.doi.org/10.1080/10888691.2017.1398649.

Carr, L., M. Iacoboni, M. C. Dubeau, J. C. Mazziotta, and G. L. Lenzi. "Neural Mechanisms of Empathy in Humans: A Relay from Neural Systems for Imitation to Limbic Areas." [In Eng]. *Proceedings of the National Academy of Sciences of the United States of America*

100, no. 9 (Apr 2003): 5497-502. https://www.doi.org/10.1073/pnas.0935845100. https://www.ncbi.nlm.nih.gov/pubmed/12682281.

Carter, C. S., A. J. Grippo, H. Pournajafi-Nazarloo, M. G. Ruscio, and S. W. Porges. "Oxytocin, Vasopressin and Sociality." [In Eng]. *Progress in Brain Research* 170 (2008): 331-6. https://www.doi.org/10.1016/s0079-6123(08)00427-5.

Casanova, M. F., D. P. Buxhoeveden, A. E. Switala, and E. Roy. "Neuronal Density and Architecture (Gray Level Index) in the Brains of Autistic Patients." [In Eng]. *The Journal of Child Neurology* 17, no. 7 (Jul 2002): 515-21. https://doi.org/10.1177/088307380201700708. https://www.ncbi.nlm.nih.gov/pubmed/12269731.

Catani, M., and M. Thiebaut de Schotten. "A Diffusion Tensor Imaging Tractography Atlas for Virtual in Vivo Dissections." [In Eng]. *Cortex* 44, no. 8 (Sep 2008): 1105-32. https://www.doi.org/10.1016/j.cortex.2008.05.004. https://www.ncbi.nlm.nih.gov/pubmed/18619589.

Cattell, Raymond B. *Abilities : Their Structure, Growth, and Action.* Boston,: Houghton Mifflin, 1971.

Celiac.org. "Home Page." 2020, accessed 6/23/2020, 2020, https://celiac.org/.

Center for Talented Youth, Johns Hopkins University. "CTY Eligibility Policy." Updated October 9, 2018, 2018, accessed 6/27/2020, https://cty.jhu.edu/talent/eligibility/policy.html.

Cerruti, C. "Building a Functional Multiple Intelligences Theory to Advance Educational Neuroscience." [In Eng]. *Frontiers in Psychology* 4 (2013): 950. https://www.doi.org/10.3389/fpsyg.2013.00950. https://www.ncbi.nlm.nih.gov/pubmed/24391613.

Cesaroni, Laura, and Malcolm Garber. "Exploring the Experience of Autism through Firsthand Accounts." *Journal of Autism and Developmental Disorders* 21, no. 3 (1991/09/01 1991): 303-13. https://www.doi.org/10.1007/BF02207327.

Chandler, S., I. Carcani-Rathwell, T. Charman, A. Pickles, T. Loucas, D. Meldrum, E. Simonoff, P. Sullivan, and G. Baird. "Parent-Reported Gastro-Intestinal Symptoms in Children with Autism Spectrum Disorders." [In Eng]. *The Journal of Autism and Developmental Disorders* 43, no. 12 (Dec 2013): 2737-47. https://www.doi.org/10.1007/s10803-013-1768-0.

Chang, Hsin-Jen, and Ching-Chih Kuo. "Overexcitabilities: Empirical Studies and Application." *Learning and Individual Differences* 23 (2013/02/01/

2013): 53-63. https://www.doi.org/10.1016/j.lindif.2012.10.010. http://www.sciencedirect.com/science/article/pii/S1041608012001501.

Chen, Mu-Hong, Tung-Ping Su, Ying-Sheue Chen, Ju-Wei Hsu, Kai-Lin Huang, Wen-Han Chang, Tzeng-Ji Chen, and Ya-Mei Bai. "Comorbidity of Allergic and Autoimmune Diseases among Patients with Adhd:A Nationwide Population-Based Study." *Journal of Attention Disorders* 21, no. 3 (2017): 219-27. https://www.doi.org/10.1177/1087054712474686. https://journals.sagepub.com/doi/abs/10.1177/1087054712474686.

Cheung, S. G., A. R. Goldenthal, A. C. Uhlemann, J. J. Mann, J. M. Miller, and M. E. Sublette. "Systematic Review of Gut Microbiota and Major Depression." [In Eng]. *Frontiers in Psychiatry* 10 (2019): 34. https://www.doi.org/10.3389/fpsyt.2019.00034. https://www.ncbi.nlm.nih.gov/pubmed/30804820.

Cho, J. H., and S. R. Brant. "Recent Insights into the Genetics of Inflammatory Bowel Disease." [In Eng]. *Gastroenterology* 140, no. 6 (May 2011): 1704-12. https://www.doi.org/10.1053/j.gastro.2011.02.046.

Choi, Y. Y., N. A. Shamosh, S. H. Cho, C. G. DeYoung, M. J. Lee, J. M. Lee, S. I. Kim, *et al.* "Multiple Bases of Human Intelligence Revealed by Cortical Thickness and Neural Activation." [In Eng]. *Journal of Neuroscience* 28, no. 41 (Oct 2008): 10323-9. https://www.doi.org/10.1523/JNEUROSCI.3259-08.2008. https://www.ncbi.nlm.nih.gov/pubmed/18842891.

Chopra, Deepak, "Why Meditate?" [Blog] March 5, 2017, accessed 6/23/20 from https://www.deepakchopra.com/blog/article/4701.

Christensen, Sam. Interview by Nicole A. Tetreault. In-Person. Burbank, CA. April 23, 2018.

Church, T. S., D. M. Thomas, C. Tudor-Locke, P. T. Katzmarzyk, C. P. Earnest, R. Q. Rodarte, C. K. Martin, S. N. Blair, and C. Bouchard. "Trends over 5 Decades in U.S. Occupation-Related Physical Activity and Their Associations with Obesity." [In Eng]. *PLoS One* 6, no. 5 (2011): e19657. https://www.doi.org/10.1371/journal.pone.0019657.

Clance, Pauline Rose, and Suzanne Ament Imes. "The Imposter Phenomenon in High Achieving Women: Dynamics and Therapeutic Intervention." *Psychotherapy: Theory, Research & Practice* 15, no. 3 (1978): 241-47. https://www.doi.org/10.1037/h0086006.

Clark, David M., and Adrian Wells. "A Cognitive Model of Social Phobia." In *Social Phobia: Diagnosis, Assessment, and Treatment*, 69-93. New York, NY, US: The Guilford Press, 1995.

Clarke, T. K., M. K. Lupton, A. M. Fernandez-Pujals, J. Starr, G. Davies, S. Cox, A. Pattie, *et al.* "Common Polygenic Risk for Autism Spectrum Disorder (Asd) Is Associated with Cognitive Ability in the General Population." *Molecular Psychiatry* 21, no. 3 (2016/03/01 2016):419-25. https://www.doi.org/10.1038/mp.2015.12.

Colom, R., M. Burgaleta, F. J. Román, S. Karama, J. Alvarez-Linera, F. J. Abad, K. Martínez, MÁ Quiroga, and R. J. Haier. "Neuroanatomic Overlap between Intelligence and Cognitive Factors: Morphometry Methods Provide Support for the Key Role of the Frontal Lobes." [In Eng]. *Neuroimage* 72 (May 15 2013): 143-52. https://www.doi.org/10.1016/j.neuroimage.2013.01.032.

Colom, R., R. E. Jung, and R. J. Haier. "Distributed Brain Sites for the G-Factor of Intelligence." [In Eng]. *Neuroimage* 31, no. 3 (Jul 1 2006):1359-65. https://www.doi.org/10.1016/j.neuroimage.2006.01.006.

Colom, R., S. Karama, R. E. Jung, and R. J. Haier. "Human Intelligence and Brain Networks." [In Eng]. *Dialogues in Clinical Neuroscience* 12, no. 4 (2010): 489-501.

Coplan, J. D., S. Hodulik, S. J. Mathew, X. Mao, P. R. Hof, J. M. Gorman, and D. C. Shungu. "The Relationship between Intelligence and Anxiety: An Association with Subcortical White Matter Metabolism." [In Eng]. *Frontiers in Evolutionary Neuroscience* 3 (2011): 8. https://www.doi.org/10.3389/fnevo.2011.00008.

Clinical Trials.gov "Full Text View - Clinical Trials.G ov." Clinicaltrials.gov, 2018. https://clinicaltrials.gov/ct2/show/ NCT03567707?term=vaginal+seeding.

Coplan, Jeremy D., *et al.*. "Decreased Choline and Creatine Concentrations in Centrum Semiovale in Patients with Generalized Anxiety Disorder: Relationship to Iq and Early Trauma." *Journal of Psychiatric Research: Neuroimaging* 147, no. 1 (2006/06/30/ 2006): 27-39. https://www.doi.org/10.1016/j.pscychresns.2005.12.011. http://www.sciencedirect.com/science/article/pii/S0925492706000035.

Coplan, Jeremy, Sarah Hodulik, Sanjay Mathew, Xiangling Mao, Patrick Hof, Jack Gorman, and Dikoma Shungu. "The Relationship between Intelligence and Anxiety: An Association with Subcortical White Matter Metabolism." [In English]. Original Research. *Frontiers in Evolutionary*

Neuroscience 3, no. 8 (2012-February-01 2012). https://doi.org/10.3389/ fnevo.2011.00008. https://www.frontiersin.org/article/10.3389/ fnevo.2011.00008.

Corkindale, G. (2008, May 7). "Overcoming Imposter Syndrome." *Harvard Business Review.* Retrieved from https://hbr.org/2008/05/ overcoming-imposter-syndrome

Cortiella, Candace, and Sheldon H Horowitz. "The State of Learning Disabilities: Facts, Trends and Emerging Issues." *New York: National center for learning disabilities* 25 (2014): 2-45.

Cortland, Ken. Email Correspondence Interview with Nicole A. Tetreault. January 13, 2020.

Cossu, G., S. Boria, C. Copioli, R. Bracceschi, V. Giuberti, E. Santelli, and V. Gallese. "Motor Representation of Actions in Children with Autism." [In Eng]. *PLoS One* 7, no. 9 (2012): e44779. https://www.doi. org/10.1371/journal.pone.0044779.

Costa, M., S. J. Brookes, and G. W. Hennig. "Anatomy and Physiology of the Enteric Nervous System." [In Eng]. *Gut* 47 Suppl 4, no. Suppl 4 (Dec 2000): iv15-9; discussion iv26. https://www.doi.org/10.1136/gut.47. suppl_4.iv15.

Cotton, S., K. M. Kraemer, R. W. Sears, J. R. Strawn, R. S. Wasson, N. McCune, J. Welge, *et al.* "Mindfulness-Based Cognitive Therapy for Children and Adolescents with Anxiety Disorders at-Risk for Bipolar Disorder: A Psychoeducation Waitlist Controlled Pilot Trial." [In Eng]. *Early Intervention in Psychiatry* 14, no. 2 (Apr 2020): 211-19. https:// www.doi.org/10.1111/eip.12848.

Coury, D. L., P. Ashwood, A. Fasano, G. Fuchs, M. Geraghty, A. Kaul, G. Mawe, P. Patterson, and N. E. Jones. "Gastrointestinal Conditions in Children with Autism Spectrum Disorder: Developing a Research Agenda." [In Eng]. *Pediatrics* 130 Suppl 2 (Nov 2012): S160-8. https://www.doi. org/10.1542/peds.2012-0900N.

Cowen, A. S., and D. Keltner. "Self-Report Captures 27 Distinct Categories of Emotion Bridged by Continuous Gradients." [In Eng]. *Proceedings of the National Academy of Sciences of the United States of America* 114, no. 38 (09 2017): E7900-E09. https://www.doi.org/10.1073/ pnas.1702247114. https://www.ncbi.nlm.nih.gov/pubmed/28874542.

Crespi, B. J. "Autism as a Disorder of High Intelligence." [In Eng]. *Frontiers in Neuroscience* 10 (2016): 300. https://www.doi.org/10.3389/ fnins.2016.00300.

Critchley, H. D. "Neural Mechanisms of Autonomic, Affective, and Cognitive Integration." [In Eng]. *The Journal of Comparative Neurology* 493, no. 1 (Dec 5 2005): 154-66. https://www.doi.org/10.1002/cne.20749.

Critchley, H. D., C. J. Mathias, O. Josephs, J. O'Doherty, S. Zanini, B. K. Dewar, L. Cipolotti, T. Shallice, and R. J. Dolan. "Human Cingulate Cortex and Autonomic Control: Converging Neuroimaging and Clinical Evidence." [In Eng]. *Brain* 126, no. Pt 10 (Oct 2003): 2139-52. https://www.doi.org/10.1093/brain/awg216.

Cuddy, Amy Joy Casselberry. *Presence : Bringing Your Boldest Self to Your Biggest Challenges.* First edition. ed. New York: Little, Brown and Company, 2015.

Crump, Wendy. Interview by Nicole A. Tetreault. Telephone. June 18, 2018.

Culpepper, S. A., H. Aguinis, J. L. Kern, and R. Millsap. "High-Stakes Testing Case Study: A Latent Variable Approach for Assessing Measurement and Prediction Invariance." [In Eng]. *Psychometrika* 84, no. 1 (Mar 2019): 285-309. https://www.doi.org/10.1007/s11336-018-9649-2.

Curiati, J. A., E. Bocchi, J. O. Freire, A. C. Arantes, M. Braga, Y. Garcia, G. Guimarães, and W. J. Fo. "Meditation Reduces Sympathetic Activation and Improves the Quality of Life in Elderly Patients with Optimally Treated Heart Failure: A Prospective Randomized Study." [In Eng]. *The Journal of Alternative and Complementary Medicine: Paradigm, Practice, and Policy Advancing Integrative Health* 11, no. 3 (Jun 2005): 465-72. https://www.doi.org/10.1089/acm.2005.11.465.

D'Eufemia, P., M. Celli, R. Finocchiaro, L. Pacifico, L. Viozzi, M. Zaccagnini,E. Cardi, and O. Giardini. "Abnormal Intestinal Permeability in Children with Autism." [In Eng]. *Acta Paediatrica* 85, no. 9 (Sep 1996): 1076-. https://www.doi.org/10.1111/j.1651-2227.1996.tb14220.x.

Damasio, Antonio, and Gil B. Carvalho. "The Nature of Feelings: Evolutionary and Neurobiological Origins." *Nature Reviews Neuroscience* 14, no. 2 (Feb 1 2013): 143-52. https://www.doi.org/10.1038/nrn3403.

Daniels, Susan, and Michael M. Piechowski. *Living with Intensity : Emotional Development of Gifted Children, Adolescents, and Adults.* Scottsdale, AZ: Great Potential Press, 2009.

Danielson, Melissa L, Rebecca H Bitsko, Reem M Ghandour, Joseph R Holbrook, Michael D Kogan, and Stephen J Blumberg. "Prevalence of Parent-Reported Adhd Diagnosis and Associated Treatment among Us Children and Adolescents, 2016." *Journal of Clinical Child & Adolescent*

Psychology 47, no. 2 (2018): 199-212. https://doi.org/10.1080/1537 4416.2017.1417860

Danielsson, S., I. C. Gillberg, E. Billstedt, C. Gillberg, and I. Olsson. "Epilepsy in Young Adults with Autism: A Prospective Population-Based Follow-up Study of 120 Individuals Diagnosed in Childhood." [In Eng]. *Epilepsia* 46, no. 6 (Jun 2005): 918-23. https://www.doi. org/10.1111/j.1528-1167.2005.57504.x.

Dantzer, R. "Cytokine, Sickness Behavior, and Depression." [In Eng]. *Neurologic Clinics* 24, no. 3 (Aug 2006): 441-60. https://www.doi. org/10.1016/j.ncl.2006.03.003.

Dąbrowski, Kazimierz.. "[Higher Emotions and Objectivity in Evaluation]." [In Fre]. *Annales Médico-Psychologiques* 2, no. 5 (Dec 1969): 589-613. Les emotions supérieures et l'objectivité d'évaluation.

———. "[on Positive Disintegration. An Outline of the Theory Concerning the Psychological Development of Man through Unbalanced States, Nervous States, Neuroses and Psychoses]." [In Fre]. *Annales Médico-Psychologiques* 117(2) (Nov 1959): 643-68.

———. "On the Philosophy of Development through Positive Disintegration and Secondary Integration." *Dialectics and Humanism* 3 (1976): 131-44.

———. "[Psychotherapy of Neuroses and Psychoneuroses Based on the Theory of Positive Disintegration.] Part 1." *Zdrowie Psychiczne* 5 (1964): 19-26.

———. "[Remarks on Typology Based on the Theory of Positive Disintegration]." [In Fre]. *Annales Médico-Psychologiques* 118(2) (Oct 1960): 401-6.

———. "[the Principal Dynamisms of Disintegration at Multiple Levels]." [In Fre]. *Annales Médico-Psychologiques* 119(1) (Feb 1961): 225-34.

———. "The Theory of Positive Disintegration." *International Journal of Psychiatry*, no. 2 (1966): 229-44.

———. *Psychoneurosis Is Not an Illness: Neuroses and Psychoneuroses from the Perspective of Positive Disintegration.* London,: Gryf Publications, 1972.

Dąbrowski, Kazimierz, Andrzej Kawczak, and Michael Marian Piechowski. *Mental Growth through Positive Disintegration.* London,: Gryf Publications, 1970.

Dąbrowski, Kazimierz, and Michael M. Piechowski. *Theory of Levels of Emotional Development.* 2 vols. Oceanside, N.Y.: Dabor Science Publications, 1977.

de Magistris, L., V. Familiari, A. Pascotto, A. Sapone, A. Frolli, P. Iardino, M. Carteni, *et al.* "Alterations of the Intestinal Barrier in Patients with Autism Spectrum Disorders and in Their First-Degree Relatives." [In Eng]. *The Journal of Pediatric Gastroenterology and Nutrition* 51, no. 4 (Oct 2010): 418-24. https://doi.org/10.1097/MPG.0b013e3181dcc4a5.

de Mattos, B. R., M. P. Garcia, J. B. Nogueira, L. N. Paiatto, C. G. Albuquerque, C. L. Souza, L. G. Fernandes, W. M. Tamashiro, and P. U. Simioni. "Inflammatory Bowel Disease: An Overview of Immune Mechanisms and Biological Treatments." [In Eng]. *Mediators of Inflammation* 2015 (2015): 493012. https://www.doi.org/10.1155/2015/493012.

Deci, Edward L., and Richard Flaste. *Why We Do What We Do : The Dynamics of Personal Autonomy.* New York: Putnam's Sons, 1995.

Delville, Y., J. T. David, K. Taravosh-Lahn, and J. C. Wommack. "Stress and the Development of Agonistic Behavior in Golden Hamsters." [In Eng]. *Hormones and Behavior* 44, no. 3 (Sep 2003): 263-70. https://www.doi.org/10.1016/s0018-506x(03)00130-2. https://www.ncbi.nlm.nih.gov/pubmed/14609548.

Denny-Brown, D., and B. Q. Banker. "Amorphosynthesis from Left Parietal Lesion." [In Eng]. *AMA Archives of Neurology & Psychiatry* 71, no. 3 (Mar 1954): 302-13. https://www.doi.org/10.1001/archneurpsyc.1954.02320390032003.

Desco, M., F. J. Navas-Sanchez, J. Sanchez-González, S. Reig, O. Robles, C. Franco, J. A. Guzmán-De-Villoria, *et al.* "Mathematically Gifted Adolescents Use More Extensive and More Bilateral Areas of the Fronto-Parietal Network Than Controls During Executive Functioning and Fluid Reasoning Tasks." [In Eng]. *Neuroimage* 57, no. 1 (Jul 1 2011): 281-92. https://www.doi.org/10.1016/j.neuroimage.2011.03.063.

Dessein, R., M. Chamaillard, and S. Danese. "Innate Immunity in Crohn's Disease: The Reverse Side of the Medal." [In Eng]. *J Clin Gastroenterol* 42 Suppl 3 Pt 1 (Sep 2008): S144-7. https://www.doi.org/10.1097/MCG.0b013e3181662c90.

DeYoung, C. G., J. B. Hirsh, M. S. Shane, X. Papademetris, N. Rajeevan, and J. R. Gray. "Testing Predictions from Personality Neuroscience. Brain Structure and the Big Five." [In Eng]. *Psychol Sci* 21, no. 6 (Jun 2010): 820-8. https://www.doi.org/10.1177/0956797610370159.

Diamond, A. "Executive Functions." [In Eng]. *Annu Rev Psychol* 64 (2013): 135-68. https://www.doi.org/10.1146/annurev-psych-113011-143750. https://www.ncbi.nlm.nih.gov/pubmed/23020641.

Diamond, Marian Cleeves. *Enriching Heredity : The Impact of the Environment on the Anatomy of the Brain.* New York, London: Free Press; Collier Macmillan, 1988.

Digre, K. B., and K. C. Brennan. "Shedding Light on Photophobia." [In Eng]. *Journal of Neuro-Ophthalmology* 32, no. 1 (Mar 2012): 68-81. https://www.doi.org/10.1097/WNO.0b013e3182474548. https://www.ncbi.nlm.nih.gov/pubmed/22330853.

Dixon-Roman, Ezekiel, Howard Everson, and John McArdle. "Race, Poverty and Sat Scores: Modeling the Influences of Family Income on Black and White High School Students' SAT Performance." *Teachers College Record* 115 (May 1 2013). https://www.researchgate.net/publication/280232788_Race_Poverty_and_SAT_Scores_Modeling_the_Influences_of_Family_Income_on_Black_and_White_High_School_Students%27_SAT_Performance

Dominguez-Bello, M. G., E. K. Costello, M. Contreras, M. Magris, G. Hidalgo, N. Fierer, and R. Knight. "Delivery Mode Shapes the Acquisition and Structure of the Initial Microbiota across Multiple Body Habitats in Newborns." [In Eng]. *Proceedings of the National Academy of Sciences of the United States of America* 107, no. 26 (Jun 29 2010): 11971-5. https://www.doi.org/10.1073/pnas.1002601107.

Drinko, Clayton D. "The Improv Paradigm: Three Principles That Spur Creativity in the classroom." In *Creativity in Theatre: Theory and Action in Theatre/Drama Education*, edited by Suzanne Burgoyne, 35-48. Cham: Springer International Publishing, 2018.

Dunst, Beate, Mathias Benedek, Emanuel Jauk, Sabine Bergner, Karl Koschutnig, Markus Sommer, Anja Ischebeck, *et al.* "Neural Efficiency as a Function of Task Demands." [In Eng]. *Intelligence* 42, no. 100 (Apr 1 2014): 22-30. https://www.doi.org/10.1016/j.intell.2013.09.005. http://europepmc.org/abstract/MED/24489416. hhttps://europepmc.org/articles/ PMC3907682.

Durlak JA, Weissberg RP, Dymnicki AB, Taylor RD, Schellinger KB. The impact of enhancing students' social and emotional learning: a meta-analysis of school-based universal interventions. *Child Development* 2011 Jan-Feb;82(1):405-32. https://www.doi.org/10.1111/j.1467-8624.2010.01564.x.

Edinger-Schons, Laura Marie. "Oneness Beliefs and Their Effect on Life Satisfaction." *Psychology of Religion and Spirituality* (2019) https://www. doi.org/10.1037/ rel0000259.

Edwards, K. S., and M. Shin. "Media Multitasking and Implicit Learning." [In Eng]. Attention *Perception & Psychophysics* 79, no. 5 (Jul 2017): 1535- 49. https://doi.org/10.3758/s13414-017-1319-4.

Ekman, P., and W. V. Friesen. "Constants across Cultures in the Face and Emotion." [In Eng]. *Journal of Personality and Social Psychology* 17, no. 2 (Feb 1971): 124-9. https://www.doi.org/10.1037/h0030377. https://www.ncbi.nlm.nih.gov/ pubmed/5542557.

Emmons, R. A., and M. E. McCullough. "Counting Blessings Versus Burdens: An Experimental Investigation of Gratitude and Subjective Well-Being in Daily Life." [In Eng]. *Journal of Personality and Social Psychology* 84, no. 2 (Feb 2003): 377-89. https://www.doi.org/10.1037//0022- 3514.84.2.377. https://www.ncbi.nlm.nih.gov/pubmed/12585811.

Engemann, Kristine, Carsten Bøcker Pedersen, Lars Arge, Constantinos Tsirogiannis, Preben Bo Mortensen, and Jens-Christian Svenning. "Residential Green Space in Childhood Is Associated with Lower Risk of Psychiatric Disorders from Adolescence into Adulthood." *Proceedings of the National Academy of Sciences* 116, no. 11 (2019): 5188-93. https://www. doi.org/10.1073/pnas.1807504116. https://www.pnas.org/content/ pnas/116/11/5188.full.pdf.

Engström, I., and B. L. Lindquist. "Inflammatory Bowel Disease in Children and Adolescents: A Somatic and Psychiatric Investigation." [In Eng]. *Acta Paediatrica Scandinavica* 80, no. 6-7 (Jun-Jul 1991): 640-7. https:// www.doi.org/10.1111/j.1651-2227.1991.tb11923.x.

European Commission for Health and Consumers. Light Sensitivity, Scientific Committee on Emerging and Newly Identified Health Risks" (PDF). Director-General for Health and Consumers, European Commission. 2008. pp. 26–27. Accessed 6/24/20 from http://ec.europa.eu/health/ ph_risk/committees/04_scenihr/docs/scenihr_o_019.pdf

Evans, T., Bira, L., Gastelum, J. *et al.* Evidence for a mental health crisis in graduate education. *Nature Biotechnology* 36, 282–284 (2018) https:// www.doi.org/10.1038/ nbt.4089

Exton, M. S. "Infection-Induced Anorexia: Active Host Defence Strategy." [In Eng]. *Appetite* 29, no. 3 (Dec 1997): 369-83. https://www.doi. org/10.1006/appe.1997.0116.

Faber, Sarah E. M., and Anthony R. McIntosh. "Towards a Standard Model of Musical Improvisation." *European Journal of Neuroscience* 51, no. 3 (2020): 840-49. https://www.doi.org/10.1111/ejn.14567. https://onlinelibrary.wiley.com/doi/abs/10.1111/ejn.14567.

Faber Taylor A, Kuo FE. Is contact with nature important for healthy child development? State of the evidence. In: Spencer C, Blades M, editors. *Children and their environments: Learning, Using and Designing Spaces.* Cambridge, UK: Cambridge University Press; 2006. pp. 124–140.

Fairtest.Org. "2019 Sat Scores: Gaps between Demographic Groups Grows Larger." Updated September 24, 2019, accessed 6/27/2020, https://www.fairtest.org/2019-sat-scores-gaps-between-demographic-groups-gr.

Felsman, Peter, Sanuri Gunawardena, and Colleen M Seifert. "Improv Experience Promotes Divergent Thinking, Uncertainty Tolerance, and Affective Well-Being." *Thinking Skills and Creativity* 35 (2020): 100632. https://doi.org/10.1016/j.tsc.2020.100632

Fernández-Jaén, A., S. López-Martín, J. Albert, D. M. Fernández-Mayoralas,L. Fernández-Perrone, M. J. de La Peña, B. Calleja-Pérez, *et al.* "Cortical Thickness Differences in the Prefrontal Cortex in Children and Adolescents with Adhd in Relation to Dopamine Transporter (Dat1) Genotype." [In Eng]. *Journal of Psychiatric Research* 233, no. 3 (Sep 30 2015): 409-17. https://www.doi.org/10.1016/j.pscychresns.2015.07.005.

Ferreira, Ana, Catarina Nunes, Ana Rita Tedim, Mariana Cunha, Ana Ferreira, and Pedro Amorim. "Inter-Patient Variability and Predictive Factors of Propofol Requirements and Estimated Concentrations for Loss of Consciousness and Recovery." Conference: 43rd Annual Meeting of the Society for Neuroscience in Anesthesiology and Critical Care, San Diego, CA, October 2015.

Fine, E. J., C. C. Ionita, and L. Lohr. "The History of the Development of the Cerebellar Examination." [In Eng]. *Seminars in Neurology* 22, no. 4 (Dec 2002): 375-84. https://www.doi.org/10.1055/s-2002-36759.

Fjortoft I. The natural environment as a playground for children: The impact of outdoor play activities in pre-primary school children. *Early Childhood Education Journal.* 2001;29:111–117. https://doi.org/10.1023/A:1012576913074

Flett, G. L., Hewitt, P. L., & Dyck, D. G. (1989). Self-oriented perfectionism, neuroticism and anxiety. *Personality and Individual Differences, 10*(7), 731–735. https://www.doi.org/10.1016/0191-8869(89)90119-0

Fogassi, L., and P. F. Ferrari. "Mirror Systems." [In Eng]. *Wiley Interdisciplinary Reviews: Cognitive Science* 2, no. 1 (Jan 2011): 22-38. https://www.doi.org/10.1002/wcs.89.

Frost, R. O., Lahart, C. M., & Rosenblate, R. (1991). The development of perfectionism: A study of daughters and their parents. *Cognitive Therapy and Research,* 15(6), 469–489. https://www.doi.org/10.1007/BF01175730

Froh, J. J., W. J. Sefick, and R. A. Emmons. "Counting Blessings in Early Adolescents: An Experimental Study of Gratitude and Subjective Well-Being." [In Eng]. *The Journal of School Psychology* 46, no. 2 (Apr 2008): 213-33. https://doi.org/10.1016/j.jsp.2007.03.005. https://www.ncbi.nlm.nih.gov/pubmed/19083358.

Fukudo, S. "[Irritable Bowel Syndrome, Emotion Regulation, and Gut Microbiota]." [In jpn]. *Brain Nerve* 68, no. 6 (Jun 2016): 607-15. https://www.doi.org/10.11477/mf.1416200448.

Fung, B. J., S. Qi, D. Hassabis, N. Daw, and D. Mobbs. "Slow Escape Decisions Are Swayed by Trait Anxiety." [In Eng]. *Nature Human Behaviour* 3, no. 7 (07 2019): 702-08. https://www.doi.org/10.1038/s41562-019-0595-5. https://www.ncbi.nlm.nih.gov/pubmed/31110337.

Furness, J. B. "The Enteric Nervous System: Normal Functions and Enteric Neuropathies." [In Eng]. *Neurogastroenterology & Motility* 20 Suppl 1 (May 2008): 32-8. https://www.doi.org/10.1111/j.1365-2982.2008.01094.x.

Galaburda, Albert M. "Dyslexia—a Molecular Disorder of Neuronal Migration." *Annals of Dyslexia* 55, no. 2 (2005/12/01 2005): 151-65. https://www.doi.org/10.1007/s11881-005-0009-4.

Galipeau, H. J., J. L. McCarville, S. Huebener, O. Litwin, M. Meisel, Jabri, Y. Sanz, *et al.* "Intestinal Microbiota Modulates Gluten-Induced Immunopathology in Humanized Mice." [In Eng]. The American Journal of Pathology *Am J Pathol* 185, no. 11 (Nov 2015): 2969-82. https://www.doi.org/10.1016/j. ajpath.2015.07.018.

Gallese, V., L. Fadiga, L. Fogassi, and G. Rizzolatti. "Action Recognition in the Premotor Cortex." [In Eng]. *Brain* 119 (Pt 2) (Apr 1996): 593-609. https://www.doi.org/10.1093/brain/119.2.593. https://www.ncbi.nlm.nih.gov/pubmed/8800951.

Gardner, Howard. *Frames of Mind : The Theory of Multiple Intelligences.* New York: Basic Books, 1983.

————. *Intelligence Reframed : Multiple Intelligences for the 21st Century.* New York, NY: Basic Books, 1999.

Geake, J. G., and P. C. Hansen. "Neural Correlates of Intelligence as Revealed by fMRI of Fluid Analogies." [In Eng]. *Neuroimage* 26, no. 2 (Jun 2005): 555-64. https://www.doi.org/10.1016/j.neuroimage.2005.01.035.

Gelbard-Sagiv, H., E. Magidov, H. Sharon, T. Hendler, and Y. Nir. "Noradrenaline Modulates Visual Perception and Late Visually Evoked Activity." [In Eng]. *Current Biology* 28, no. 14 (07 2018): 2239-49. e6. https://doi.org/10.1016/j.cub.2018.05.051. https://www.ncbi.nlm.nih.gov/pubmed/29983318.

Genç, E., C. Fraenz, C. Schlüter, P. Friedrich, R. Hossiep, M. C. Voelkle, J. M. Ling, O. Güntürkün, and R. E. Jung. "Diffusion Markers of Dendritic Density and Arborization in Gray Matter Predict Differences in Intelligence." [In Eng]. *Nature Communications* 9, no. 1 (05 2018): 1905. https://doi.org/10.1038/s41467-018-04268-8. https://www.ncbi.nlm.nih.gov/ pubmed/29765024.

Gere, D. R., S. C. Capps, D. W. Mitchell, and E. Grubbs. "Sensory Sensitivities of Gifted Children." [In Eng]. *The American Journal of Occupational Therapy* 63, no. 3 (May-Jun 2009): 288-95; discussion 96-300. https://www.doi.org/10.5014/ ajot.63.3.288.

Gardner, H. (n.d.) "The components of MI." *MI Oasis* [Website.] Accessed 6/24/20 from https://www.multipleintelligencesoasis.org/the-components-of-mi

Gernsbacher, M. A., and M. Yergeau. "Empirical Failures of the Claim That Autistic People Lack a Theory of Mind." [In Eng]. *Archives of Scientific Psychology* 7, no. 1 (2019): 102-18. https://www.doi.org/10.1037/arc0000067.

Gignac GE, Vernon PA, Wickett JC. Factors influencing the relationship between brain size and intelligence. In: Nyborg H, editor. *The Scientific Study of General Intelligence: Tribute to Arthur R. Jensen.* Oxford; Pergamon: 2003

Gilbert, D. L., K. M. Isaacs, M. Augusta, L. K. Macneil, and S. H. Mostofsky. "Motor Cortex Inhibition: A Marker of Adhd Behavior and Motor Development in Children." [In Eng]. *Neurology* 76, no. 7 (Feb 15 2011):615-21. https://www.doi.org/10.1212/WNL.0b013e31820c2ebd.

Glasser, M. F., S. M. Smith, D. S. Marcus, J. L. Andersson, E. J. Auerbach, T. E. Behrens, T. S. Coalson, *et al.* "The Human Connectome Project's

Neuroimaging Approach." *Nature Neuroscience* 19, no. 9 (Aug 26 2016): 1175-87. https://www.doi.org/10.1038/nn.4361. https://www.ncbi.nlm.nih.gov/pubmed/27571196.

Gogtay, Nitin, Jay N. Giedd, Leslie Lusk, Kiralee M. Hayashi, Deanna Greenstein, A. Catherine Vaituzis, Tom F. Nugent, *et al.* "Dynamic Mapping of Human Cortical Development During Childhood through Early Adulthood." *Proceedings of the National Academy of Sciences of the United States of America* 101, no. 21 (2004): 8174. https://www.doi.org/10.1073/pnas.0402680101. http://www.pnas.org/content/101/21/8174.abstract.

Gomez, Rapson, Vasileios Stavropoulos, Alasdair Vance, and Mark D. Griffiths. "Gifted Children with ADHD: How Are They Different from Non-Gifted Children with ADHD?". *International Journal of Mental Health and Addiction* (2019/08/26 2019). https://www.doi.org/10.1007/s11469-019-00125-x. https://www.doi.org/10.1007/s11469-019-00125-x.

Gong, Q. Y., V. Sluming, A. Mayes, S. Keller, T. Barrick, E. Cezayirli, and N. Roberts. "Voxel-Based Morphometry and Stereology Provide Convergent Evidence of the Importance of Medial Prefrontal Cortex for Fluid Intelligence in Healthy Adults." [In Eng]. *Neuroimage* 25, no. 4 (May 1 2005): 1175-86. https://www.doi.org/10.1016/j.neuroimage.2004.12.044.

Gorrindo, P., K. C. Williams, E. B. Lee, L. S. Walker, S. G. McGrew, and P. Levitt. "Gastrointestinal Dysfunction in Autism: Parental Report, Clinical Evaluation, and Associated Factors." [In Eng]. *Autism Research* 5, no. 2 (Apr 2012): 101-8. https://www.doi.org/10.1002/aur.237.

Gottfried, Carmem, Victorio Bambini-Junior, Fiona Francis, Rudimar Riesgo, and Wilson Savino. "The Impact of Neuroimmune Alterations in Autism Spectrum Disorder." [In English]. Hypothesis and Theory. *Frontiers in Psychiatry* 6, no. 121 (2015-September-09 2015). https://doi.org/10.3389/fpsyt.2015.00121. https://www.frontiersin.org/article/10.3389/fpsyt.2015.00121.

Gould van Praag, C. D., S. N. Garfinkel, O. Sparasci, A. Mees, A. O. Philippides, M. Ware, C. Ottaviani, and H. D. Critchley. "Mind-Wandering and Alterations to Default Mode Network Connectivity When Listening to Naturalistic Versus Artificial Sounds." [In Eng]. *Scientific Reports* 7 (Mar 27 2017): 45273. https://www.doi.org/10.1038/srep45273.

Grandin, Temple. *Thinking in Pictures : And Other Reports from My Life with Autism.* 2nd Vintage Books ed. New York: Vintage Books, 2006.

Grandin, Temple, and Margaret Scariano. *Emergence, Labeled Autistic.* 1st ed. Novato, CA: Arena Press, 1986.

Grant, A. M., and F. Gino. "A Little Thanks Goes a Long Way: Explaining Why Gratitude Expressions Motivate Prosocial Behavior." [In Eng]. *Journal of Personality and Social Psychology* 98, no. 6 (Jun 2010): 946-55. https://www.doi.org/10.1037/a0017935. https://www.ncbi.nlm.nih.gov/pubmed/20515249.

Gray, John. *Men Are from Mars, Women Are from Venus : A Practical Guide for Improving Communication and Getting What You Want in Your Relationships.* 1st ed. New York, NY: HarperCollins, 1992.

Greenley, R. N., K. A. Hommel, J. Nebel, T. Raboin, S. H. Li, P. Simpson, and L. Mackner. "A Meta-Analytic Review of the Psychosocial Adjustment of Youth with Inflammatory Bowel Disease." [In Eng]. *Journal of Pediatric Psychology* 35, no. 8 (Sep 2010): 857-69. https://www.doi.org/10.1093/jpepsy/jsp120.

Greenough, W. T., F. R. Volkmar, and J. M. Juraska. "Effects of Rearing Complexity on Dendritic Branching in Frontolateral and Temporal Cortex of the Rat." [In Eng]. *Experimental Neurology* 41, no. 2 (Nov 1973): 371-8. https://www.doi.org/10.1016/0014-4886(73)90278-1. https://www.ncbi.nlm.nih.gov/pubmed/4126876.

Grissom, Jason A., and Christopher Redding. "Discretion and Disproportionality:Explaining the Underrepresentation of High-Achieving Students of Color in Gifted Programs." *AERA Open* 2, no. 1 (2016): 2332858415622175. https://www.doi.org/10.1177/2332858415622175. https://journals.sagepub.com/doi/ abs/10.1177/2332858415622175.

Grossi, D., M. Longarzo, M. Quarantelli, E. Salvatore, C. Cavaliere, P. De Luca, L. Trojano, and M. Aiello. "Altered Functional Connectivity of Interoception in Illness Anxiety Disorder." [In Eng]. *Cortex* 86 (01 2017): 22-32. https://www.doi.org/10.1016/j.cortex.2016.10.018. https://www.ncbi.nlm.nih.gov/pubmed/27871020.

Guidi, Luiz G., Antonio Velayos-Baeza, Isabel Martinez-Garay, Anthony P. Monaco, Silvia Paracchini, Dorothy V. M. Bishop, and Zoltán Molnár. "The Neuronal Migration Hypothesis of Dyslexia: A Critical Evaluation 30 years On." *European Journal of Neuroscience* 48, no. 10 (2018): 3212-33. https://www.doi.org/10.1111/ejn.14149. https://onlinelibrary.wiley.com/ doi/abs/10.1111/ejn.14149.

Guyonnet, D., A. Schlumberger, L. Mhamdi, S. Jakob, and O. Chassany. "Fermented Milk Containing Bifidobacterium Lactis Dn-173 010 Improves Gastrointestinal Well-Being and Digestive Symptoms in Women Reporting Minor Digestive Symptoms: A Randomised, Double-Blind, Parallel, Controlled Study." [In Eng]. *British Journal of Nutrition* 102, no. 11 (Dec 2009): 1654-62. https://www.doi.org/10.1017/s0007114509990882.

Hadar, A., I. Hadas, A. Lazarovits, U. Alyagon, D. Eliraz, and A. Zangen. "Answering the Missed Call: Initial Exploration of Cognitive and Electrophysiological Changes Associated with Smartphone Use and Abuse." [In Eng]. *PLoS One* 12, no. 7 (2017): e0180094. https://www.doi.org/10.1371/journal.pone.0180094.

Haier, R. J., R. E. Jung, R. A. Yeo, K. Head, and M. T. Alkire. "Structural Brain Variation and General Intelligence." [In Eng]. *Neuroimage* 23, no. 1 (Sep 2004): 425-33. https://www.doi.org/10.1016/j.neuroimage.2004.04.025.

Haier, R. J., D. H. Schroeder, C. Tang, K. Head, and R. Colom. "Gray Matter Correlates of Cognitive Ability Tests Used for Vocational Guidance." [In Eng]. *BMC Research Notes* 3 (Jul 22 2010): 206. https://www.doi.org/10.1186/1756-0500-3-206.

Haier, R. J., B. V. Siegel, Jr., A. MacLachlan, E. Soderling, S. Lottenberg, and M. S. Buchsbaum. "Regional Glucose Metabolic Changes after Learning a Complex Visuospatial/Motor Task: A Positron Emission Tomographic Study." [In Eng]. *Brain Research* 570, no. 1-2 (Jan 20 1992):134-43. https://www.doi.org/10.1016/0006-8993(92)90573-r.

Harvard Medical School, 2007. National Comorbidity Survey (NCS). (2017, August 21). Accessed 6/24/20 from https://www.hcp.med.harvard.edu/ncs/ index.php. Data Table 1: Lifetime prevalence DSM-IV/WMH-CIDI disorders by sex and cohort.

Haier, Richard J., Benjamin V. Siegel, Keith H. Nuechterlein, Erin Hazlett, Joseph C. Wu, Joanne Paek, Heather L. Browning, and Monte S. Buchsbaum. "Cortical Glucose Metabolic Rate Correlates of Abstract Reasoning and Attention Studied with Positron Emission Tomography." *Intelligence* 12, no. 2 (1988/04/01/ 1988): 199-217. https://www.doi.org/10.1016/0160-2896(88)90016-5. http://www.science-direct.com/science/article/pii/0160289688900165.

Hale, S., M. D. Bronik, and A. F. Fry. "Verbal and Spatial Working Memory in School-Age Children: Developmental Differences in Susceptibility to

Interference." [In Eng]. *Developmental Psychology* 33, no. 2 (Mar 1997): 364-71. https://www.doi.org/10.1037//0012-1649.33.2.364.

Hale, S., J. Myerson, and D. Wagstaff. "General Slowing of Nonverbal Information Processing: Evidence for a Power Law." [In Eng]. *The Journals of Gerontology* 42, no. 2 (Mar 1987): 131-6. https://www.doi.org/10.1093/geronj/42.2.131. https://www.ncbi.nlm.nih.gov/pubmed/3819335.

Hamachek, D.E. "Psychodynamics of Normal and Neurotic Perfectionism." *Psychology*, 15 (1978) 27-33. https://psycnet.apa.org/record/1979-08598-001

Hamilton, J. W. "Editorial and Miscellaneous. The Man through Whose Head an Iron Rod Passed Is Still Living". Ohio Medical and Surgical Journal. 13: 174. Reprinted." In *Medical and Surgical Reporter*, edited by D G. Brinton, 183. Philadelphia: Crissly & Markley, 1860.

Haney, C., Banks, W. C., & Zimbardo, P. G. (1973). "A Study of Prisoners and Guards in a Simulated Prison." *Naval Research Review*, 30, 4-17.

Haney, John Louis. The Name of William Shakespeare; a Study in Orthography. New York,: AMS Press, 1973.

Hanson, Rick. *Just One Thing : Developing a Buddha Brain One Simple Practice at a Time.* Oakland, CA: New Harbinger Publications, 2011.

Hanson, Rick, and Richard Mendius. *Buddha's Brain : The Practical Neuroscience of Happiness, Love & Wisdom.* Oakland, CA: New Harbinger Publications, 2009.

Hardiman, Mariale M., Ranjini Mahinda JohnBull, Deborah T. Carran, and Amy Shelton. "The Effects of Arts-Integrated Instruction on Memory for Science Content." *Trends in Neuroscience and Education* 14 (2019/03/01/2019): 25-32. https://www.doi.org/10.1016/j.tine.2019.02.002. http://www.sciencedirect.com/science/article/pii/S2211949317300558.

Harris, Bethany, Timothy Regan, Jordan Schueler, and Sherecce A. Fields. "Problematic Mobile Phone and Smartphone Use Scales: A Systematic Review." [In Eng]. *Frontiers in psychology* 11 (2020): 672-72. https://doi.org/10.3389/fpsyg.2020.00672. https://pubmed.ncbi.nlm.nih.gov/32431636. https://www.ncbi.nlm.nih.gov/pmc/articles/ PMC7214716/.

Hart, W., P. H. Slee, H. G. Schipper, R. P. Koopmans, and P. A. Kager. "[Clinical Reasoning and Decision Making in Practice. A Depressive Foreign Woman with Symptoms of Malaise]." [In Dut]. *Ned Tijdschr Geneeskd* 148, no. 16 (Apr 17 2004): 771-6. Klinisch denken en beslissen in de praktijk. Een depressieve buitenlandse vrouw met klachten van malaise.

Hebb, D. O. *The Organization of Behavior : A Neuropsychological Theory.* Mahwah, N.J.: L. Erlbaum Associates, 2002.

Herculano-Houzel, S. "The Human Brain in Numbers: A Linearly Scaled-up Primate Brain." [In Eng]. *Front Hum Neurosci* 3 (2009): 31. https://www.doi.org/10.3389/neuro.09.031.2009.

Herculano-Houzel, S., C. E. Collins, P. Wong, and J. H. Kaas. "Cellular Scaling Rules for Primate Brains." [In Eng]. *Proceedings of the National Academy of Sciences of the United States of America* 104, no. 9 (Feb 27 2007): 3562-7. https://www.doi.org/10.1073/ pnas.0611396104.

Herculano-Houzel, S., and R. Lent. "Isotropic Fractionator: A Simple, Rapid Method for the Quantification of Total Cell and Neuron Numbers in the Brain." [In Eng]. *Journal of Neuroscience* 25, no. 10 (Mar 9 2005): 2518-21. https://www.doi.org/10.1523/jneurosci.4526-04.2005.

Hewitt, P. L., and G. L. Flett. "Perfectionism in the Self and Social Contexts: Conceptualization, Assessment, and Association with Psychopathology." [In Eng]. *Journal of Personality and Social Psychology* 60, no. 3 (Mar 1991): 456-70. https://www.doi.org/10.1037//0022-3514.60.3.456. https://www.ncbi.nlm.nih.gov/ pubmed/2027080.

Hildreth, Eugene A. "Some Common Allergic Emergencies." *Medical Clinics of North America* 50, no. 5 (1966/09/01/ 1966): 1313-24. https://www.doi.org/10.1016/S0025-7125(16)33127-3. http://www.sciencedirect.com/science/article/pii/S0025712516331273.

Hofeldt, F. D. "Reactive Hypoglycemia." [In Eng]. *Endocrinology and Metabolism Clinics of North America* 18, no. 1 (Mar 1989): 185-201.

Holtzman RE, Rebok GW, Saczynski JS, Kouzis AC, Wilcox Doyle K, Eaton WW. Social network characteristics and cognition in middle-aged and older adults. *The Journals of Gerontology. Series B, Psychological Sciences and Social Sciences.* 2004 Nov;59(6):P278-84. https://www.doi.org/10.1093/geronb/59.6.p278. PMID: 15576855.

Hoogman, M., J. Bralten, D. P. Hibar, M. Mennes, M. P. Zwiers, L. S.J. Schweren, K. J. E. van Hulzen, *et al.* "Subcortical Brain Volume Differences in Participants with Attention Deficit Hyperactivity Disorder in Children and Adults: A Cross-Sectional Mega-Analysis." [In Eng]. *Lancet Psychiatry* 4, no. 4 (Apr 2017): 310-19. https://www.doi.org/10.1016/s2215-0366(17)30049-4.

Horn, A., D. Ostwald, M. Reisert, and F. Blankenburg. "The Structural-Functional Connectome and the Default Mode Network of the Human

Brain." [In Eng]. *Neuroimage* 102 Pt 1 (Nov 2014): 142-51. https://doi.org/10.1016/j.neuroimage.2013.09.069. https://www.ncbi.nlm.nih.gov/pubmed/24099851.

Horvath, K., J. C. Papadimitriou, A. Rabsztyn, C. Drachenberg, and J. T. Tildon. "Gastrointestinal Abnormalities in Children with Autistic Disorder." [In Eng]. *The Journal of Pediatrics* 135, no. 5 (Nov 1999): 559-63. https://doi.org/10.1016/s0022-3476(99)70052-1.

Houghton, L. A., M. Heitkemper, M. Crowell, A. Emmanuel, A. Halpert, J. A. McRoberts, and B. Toner. "Age, Gender and Women's Health and the Patient." [In Eng]. *Gastroenterology* (Feb 15 2016). https://www.doi.org/10.1053/j.gastro.2016.02.017.

Howland, R. H. "Vagus Nerve Stimulation." [In Eng]. *Current Behavioral Neuroscience Reports* 1, no. 2 (Jun 2014): 64-73. https://www.doi.org/10.1007/ s40473-014-0010-5.

Hölzel, Britta K., James Carmody, Mark Vangel, Christina Congleton, Sita M. Yerramsetti, Tim Gard, and Sara W. Lazar. "Mindfulness Practice Leads to Increases in Regional Brain Gray Matter Density." *Journal of Psychiatric Research: Neuroimaging* 191, no. 1 (2011/01/30/ 2011): 36-43. https://www.doi.org/10.1016/j.pscychresns.2010.08.006. http://www.science-direct.com/science/article/pii/S092549271000288X.

Iacoboni, M., I. Molnar-Szakacs, V. Gallese, G. Buccino, J. C. Mazziotta, and G. Rizzolatti. "Grasping the Intentions of Others with One's Own Mirror Neuron System." [In Eng]. *PLoS Biol* 3, no. 3 (Mar 2005): e79. https://www.doi.org/10.1371/journal.pbio.0030079. https://www.ncbi.nlm.nih.gov/pubmed/15736981.

Ingram, J. L., S. M. Peckham, B. Tisdale, and P. M. Rodier. "Prenatal Exposure of Rats to Valproic Acid Reproduces the Cerebellar Anomalies Associated with Autism." [In Eng]. *Neurotoxicology and Teratology* 22, no. 3 (May-Jun 2000): 319-24. https://www.doi.org/10.1016/s0892-0362(99)00083-5.

Ioannou, S., A. P. Key, R. A. Muscatello, M. Klemencic, and B. A. Corbett. "Peer Actors and Theater Techniques Play Pivotal Roles in Improving Social Play and Anxiety for Children with Autism." [In Eng]. *Frontiers in Psychology* 11 (2020): 908. https://www.doi.org/10.3389/fpsyg.2020.00908.

Jacobson, L. A., D. Crocetti, D. Dirlikov, K. Slifer, M. B. Denckla, S. H. Mostofsky, and E. M. Mahone. "Anomalous Brain Development Is Evident in Preschoolers with Attention-Deficit/Hyperactivity Disorder." [In Eng]. *The Journal of the International Neuropsychological Society* 24, no. 6 (Jul 2018): 531-39. https://doi.org/10.1017/s1355617718000103.

Janka, Z. "[Neuroscience of Mental Flexibility]." [In Hun]. *Orvosi hetilap* 158, no. 45 (Nov 2017): 1771-86. https://www.doi.org/10.1556/650.2017.30906. https://www.ncbi.nlm.nih.gov/pubmed/29135273.

Jauk, E., M. Benedek, B. Dunst, and A. C. Neubauer. "The Relationship between Intelligence and Creativity: New Support for the Threshold Hypothesis by Means of Empirical Breakpoint Detection." [In Eng]. *Intelligence* 41, no. 4 (Jul 2013): 212-21. https://www.doi.org/10.1016/j. intell.2013.03.003.

Jeon, H., and S. H. Lee. "From Neurons to Social Beings: Short Review of the Mirror Neuron System Research and Its Socio-Psychological and Psychiatric Implications." [In Eng]. *Clinical Psychopharmacology and Neuroscience* 16, no. 1 (Feb 2018): 18-31. https://www.doi.org/10.9758/ cpn.2018.16.1.18. https://www.ncbi.nlm.nih.gov/pubmed/29397663.

Joel, D., Z. Berman, I. Tavor, N. Wexler, O. Gaber, Y. Stein, N. Shefi, *et al.* "Sex Beyond the Genitalia: The Human Brain Mosaic." *Proceedings of the National Academy of Sciences of the United States of America* 112, no. 50 (Dec 15 2015): 15468-73. https://www.doi.org/10.1073/ pnas.1509654112. https://www.ncbi.nlm.nih.gov/pubmed/26621705.

Joel, D., and A. Fausto-Sterling. "Beyond Sex Differences: New Approaches for Thinking About Variation in Brain Structure and Function." [In Eng]. *Philosophical Transactions of the Royal Society B: Biological Sciences* 371, no. 1688 (Feb 19 2016): 20150451. https://www.doi.org/10.1098/ rstb.2015.0451.

Johnson, Christine Cole, MD. "Babies born by C-section at risk of developing allergies," *Presentation at American American Academy of Allergy, Asthma and Immunology San Antonio, Texas,* (2013); https://www. eurekalert. org/pub_releases/2013-02/hfhs-sbb022113.php

Jones, A. M. "A Five Year Physiological Case Study of an Olympic Runner." [In Eng]. *British Journal of Sports Medicine* 32, no. 1 (Mar 1998): 39-43. https://www.doi.org/10.1136/bjsm.32.1.39.

Jung, R. E., and R. J. Haier. "The Parieto-Frontal Integration Theory (P-Fit) of Intelligence: Converging Neuroimaging Evidence." [In Eng]. *Behavioral and Brain Sciences* 30, no. 2 (Apr 2007): 135-54; discussion 54-87. https://www.doi.org/10.1017/s0140525x07001185.

Kabat-Zinn, J., L. Lipworth, and R. Burney. "The Clinical Use of Mindfulness Meditation for the Self-Regulation of Chronic Pain." [In Eng]. *The Journal of Behavioral Medicine* 8, no. 2 (Jun 1985): 163-90. https://

www.doi.org/10.1007/ BF00845519. https://www.ncbi.nlm.nih.gov/ pubmed/3897551.

Kabeerdoss, J., P. Jayakanthan, S. Pugazhendhi, and B. S. Ramakrishna. "Alterations of Mucosal Microbiota in the Colon of Patients with Inflammatory Bowel Disease Revealed by Real Time Polymerase Chain Reaction Amplification of 16s Ribosomal Ribonucleic Acid." [In Eng]. *Indian Journal of Medical Research* 142, no. 1 (Jul 2015): 23-32. https:// www.doi.org/10.4103/0971-5916.162091.

Kaldy, Zsuzsa, Ivy Giserman, Alice S. Carter, and Erik Blaser. "The Mechanisms Underlying the Asd Advantage in Visual Search." [In Eng]. *Journal of Autism and Developmental Disorders* 46, no. 5 (2016): 1513-27. https://www.doi.org/10.1007/s10803-013-1957-x. https:// pubmed.ncbi. nlm.nih.gov/24091470. https://www.ncbi.nlm.nih.gov/ pmc/articles/PMC3976471/.

Kanner, Leo. "Autistic Disturbances of Affective Contact." *Nervous Child* 2, no. 3 (1943): 217-50.

Karpinski, Ruth I., Audrey M. Kinase Kolb, Nicole A. Tetreault, and Thomas B. Borowski. "High Intelligence: A Risk Factor for Psychological and Physiological Overexcitabilities." *Intelligence* 66 (2018/01/01/ 2018):8-23. https://www.doi.org/10.1016/j.intell.2017.09.001. http://www. sciencedirect.com/science/article/pii/S0160289616303324.

Karwowski, Maciej, Jan Dul, Jacek Gralewski, Emanuel Jauk, Dorota M. Jankowska, Aleksandra Gajda, Michael H. Chruszczewski, and Mathias Benedek. "Is Creativity without Intelligence Possible? A Necessary Condition Analysis." *Intelligence* 57 (2016/07/01/ 2016): 105-17. https://www.doi.org/10.1016/j.intell.2016.04.006. http://www. sciencedirect.com/science/article/pii/S0160289616300289.

Keown, Damien. *Buddhism : A Very Short Introduction.* Very Short Introductions. Fully updated new edition. ed. Oxford: Oxford University Press, 2013.

Kersey, A. J., E. J. Braham, K. D. Csumitta, M. E. Libertus, and J. F. Cantlon. "No Intrinsic Gender Differences in Children's Earliest Numerical Abilities." [In Eng]. *NPJ Science of Learning* 3 (2018): 12. https://www. doi.org/10.1038/ s41539-018-0028-7.

Kersey, Alyssa J., Kelsey D. Csumitta, and Jessica F. Cantlon. "Gender Similarities in the Brain During Mathematics Development." *NPJ Science of Learning* 4, no. 1 (2019/11/08 2019): 19. https://www.doi.org/10.1038/ s41539-019-0057-x. https://www.doi.org/10.1038/s41539-019-0057-x.

Kimbrough, E., T. Magyari, P. Langenberg, M. Chesney, and B. Berman. "Mindfulness Intervention for Child Abuse Survivors." [In Eng]. *Journal of Clinical Psychology* 66, no. 1 (Jan 2010): 17-33. https://www.doi.org/10.1002/jclp.20624.

Kircanski, K., M. D. Lieberman, and M. G. Craske. "Feelings into Words: Contributions of Language to Exposure Therapy." [In Eng]. *Psychological Science* 23, no. 10 (Oct 2012): 1086-91. https://www.doi.org/10.1177/0956797612443830. https://www.ncbi.nlm.nih.gov/pubmed/22902568.

Klaassen, C. D., and J. Y. Cui. "Review: Mechanisms of How the Intestinal Microbiota Alters the Effects of Drugs and Bile Acids." [In Eng]. *Drug Metabolism & Disposition* 43, no. 10 (Oct 2015): 1505-21. https://www.doi.org/10.1124/ dmd.115.065698.

Kohli, Sonali. "California Test Scores 2019: Half of Students Meet English Standards, Fewer Meet Math Standards." *Los Angeles Times* (Los Angeles), October 9, 2019 2019. https://www.latimes.com/california/story/2019-10-09/california-school-test-scores-2019.

Kolar, Dusan, Amanda Keller, Maria Golfinopoulos, Lucy Cumyn, Cassidy Syer, and Lily Hechtman. "Treatment of Adults with Attention-Deficit/Hyperactivity Disorder." *Neuropsychiatric Disease and Treatment* 4, no. 2 (2008): 389.

Krasnova, Hanna, Thomas Widjaja, Peter Buxmann, Helena Wenninger, and Izak Benbasat. "Research Note—Why Following Friends Can Hurt You: An Exploratory Investigation of the Effects of Envy on Social Networking Sites among College-Age Users." *Information Systems Research* 26, no. 3 (2015): 585-605.

Kross, E., M. G. Berman, W. Mischel, E. E. Smith, and T. D. Wager. "Social Rejection Shares Somatosensory Representations with Physical Pain." [In Eng]. *Proceedings of the National Academy of Sciences of the United States of America* 108, no. 15 (Apr 12 2011): 6270-5. https://www.doi.org/10.1073/pnas.1102693108.

Kyeong, S., J. Kim, D. J. Kim, H. E. Kim, and J. J. Kim. "Effects of Gratitude Meditation on Neural Network Functional Connectivity and Brain-Heart Coupling." [In Eng]. *Scientific Reports* 7, no. 1 (07 2017): 5058. https://doi.org/10.1038/s41598-017-05520-9. https://www.ncbi.nlm.nih.gov/ pubmed/28698643.

Lally, Phillippa, Cornelia HM Van Jaarsveld, Henry WW Potts, and Jane Wardle. "How Are Habits Formed: Modelling Habit Formation in the

Real World." *European Journal of Social Psychology* 40, no. 6 (2010): 998-1009, https://www.doi.org/10.1002/ejsp.674.

Landrigan, P. J. "What Causes Autism? Exploring the Environmental Contribution." [In Eng]. *Current Opinion in Pediatrics* 22, no. 2 (Apr 2010): 219-25. https://www.doi.org/10.1097/MOP.0b013e328336eb9a.

Laneri, D., S. Krach, F. M. Paulus, P. Kanske, V. Schuster, J. Sommer, andL. Müller-Pinzler. "Mindfulness Meditation Regulates Anterior Insula Activity During Empathy for Social Pain." [In Eng]. *Human Brain Mapping* 38, no. 8 (08 2017): 4034-46. https://www.doi.org/10.1002/hbm.23646. https://www.ncbi.nlm.nih.gov/pubmed/28504364.

Laren, Linda van. "Math Class Is Tough." In *Girl Culture : An Encyclopedia*, edited by Claudia Mitchell and Jacqueline Reid-Walsh, 423–24. Westport, Conn.: Greenwood Press, 2008.

Larner, AJ, and John P Leach. "Phineas Gage and the Beginnings of Neuro-psychology." *Advances in Clinical Neuroscience & Rehabilitation* 2, no. 3 (2002): 26.

Larsen, H. B. "Kenyan Dominance in Distance Running." [In Eng]. *Comparative Biochemistry and Physiology - Part A: Molecular & Integrative Physiology* 136, no. 1 (Sep 2003): 161-70. https://www.doi.org/10.1016/s1095-6433(03)00227-7.

Larsen, H. B., and A. W. Sheel. "The Kenyan Runners." [In Eng]. *Scandinavian Journal of Medicine & Science in Sports* 25 Suppl 4 (Dec 2015): 110-8. https://www.doi.org/10.1111/ sms.12573.

Lazar, S. W., C. E. Kerr, R. H. Wasserman, J. R. Gray, D. N. Greve,

M. T. Treadway, M. McGarvey, *et al.* "Meditation Experience Is Associated with Increased Cortical Thickness." [In Eng]. *Neuroreport* 16, no. 17 (Nov 28 2005): 1893-7. https://www.doi.org/10.1097/01.wnr.0000186598.66243.19.

Lee, K. H., Y. Y. Choi, J. R. Gray, S. H. Cho, J. H. Chae, S. Lee, and K. Kim. "Neural Correlates of Superior Intelligence: Stronger Recruitment of Posterior Parietal Cortex." [In Eng]. *Neuroimage* 29, no. 2 (Jan 15 2006): 578-86. https://www.doi.org/10.1016/j.neuroimage.2005.07.036.

Leekam, S. R., C. Nieto, S. J. Libby, L. Wing, and J. Gould. "Describing the Sensory Abnormalities of Children and Adults with Autism." [In Eng]. *The Journal of Autism and Developmental Disorders* 37, no. 5 (May 2007): 894-910. https://www.doi.org/10.1007/s10803-006-0218-7.

Legaz Arrese, A., E. Serrano Ostáriz, J. A. Jcasajús Mallén, and D. Munguía Izquierdo. "The Changes in Running Performance and Maximal Oxygen Uptake after Long-Term Training in Elite Athletes." [In Eng]. *Journal of Sports Medicine and Physical Fitness* 45, no. 4 (Dec 2005): 435-40.

Lereya, S. T., W. E. Copeland, E. J. Costello, and D. Wolke. "Adult Mental Health Consequences of Peer Bullying and Maltreatment in Childhood: Two Cohorts in Two Countries." [In Eng]. *Lancet Psychiatry* 2, no. 6 (Jun 2015): 524-31. https://www.doi.org/10.1016/S2215-0366(15)00165-0. https://www.ncbi.nlm.nih.gov/pubmed/26360448.

Lewis, George, and Benjamin Piekut. *The Oxford Handbook of Critical Improvisation Studies, Volume 1*. Oxford Handbooks. New York, N.Y.; Oxford, U.K.: Oxford University Press, 2016. https://books.google. com/books?id=ZTtADQAAQBAJ.

Liang, J., S. M. Sha, and K. C. Wu. "Role of the Intestinal Microbiota and Fecal Transplantation in Inflammatory Bowel Diseases." [In Eng]. *Journal of Digestive Diseases* 15, no. 12 (Dec 2014): 641-6. https://www.doi. org/10.1111/1751-2980.12211.

Libera, Anne, Neil Stevenson, and Kelly Leonard. "Chapter 11 - a Comedy Professor, Design Thinker, and Theatre Producer Walk into a Bar." In *Creativity and Humor*, edited by Sarah R. Luria, John Baer and James C. Kaufman, 231-42: Academic Press, 2019.

Lindberg, Sara M., Janet Shibley Hyde, Jennifer L. Petersen, and Marcia C. Linn. "New Trends in Gender and Mathematics Performance: A Meta-Analysis." *Psychological Bulletin* 136, no. 6 (2010): 1123-35. https:// www.doi.org/10.1037/a0021276.

Lipowski, Z. J. "Sensory and Information Inputs Overload: Behavioral Effects." [In Eng]. *Comprehensive Psychiatry* 16, no. 3 (1975 May-Jun 1975):199-221. https://www.doi.org/10.1016/0010-440x(75)90047-4. https:// www.ncbi.nlm.nih.gov/pubmed/1139919.

Liu, Siyuan, Ho Ming Chow, Yisheng Xu, Michael G. Erkkinen, Katherine E. Swett, Michael W. Eagle, Daniel A. Rizik-Baer, and Allen R. Braun. "Neural Correlates of Lyrical Improvisation: An fMRI Study of Freestyle Rap." *Scientific Reports* 2, no. 1 (2012/11/15 2012): 834. https://www. doi.org/10.1038/srep00834.

Liu, T., J. Shi, Q. Zhang, D. Zhao, and J. Yang. "Neural Mechanisms of Auditory Sensory Processing in Children with High Intelligence." [In Eng]. *Neuroreport* 18, no. 15 (Oct 8 2007): 1571-5. https://www.doi. org/10.1097/WNR.0b013e3282ef7640.

López-González, Mónica. *Cognitive Psychology Meets Art: Exploring Creativity, Language, and Emotion through Live Musical Improvisation in Film and Theatre.* Spie/Is&T Electronic Imaging. Vol. 9394: SPIE, 2015. https://doi.org/10.1117/12.2083880.

Lorenz, Edward. "Predictability: Does the Flap of a Butterfly's Wing in Brazil Set Off a Tornado in Texas?" Paper presented at the 139th meeting of the American Association for the Advancement of Science, Washington, D.C., December 29, 1972.

Loui, P. "Rapid and Flexible Creativity in Musical Improvisation: Review and a Model." [In Eng]. *Annals of the New York Academy of Sciences* (Mar 25 2018). https://www.doi.org/10.1111/nyas.13628.

Lyall, Kristen, Judy Van de Water, Paul Ashwood, and Irva Hertz-Picciotto. "Asthma and Allergies in Children with Autism Spectrum Disorders: Results from the Charge Study." *Autism Research* 8, no. 5 (2015): 567-74. https://www.doi.org/10.1002/aur.1471. https://onlinelibrary.wiley.com/doi/abs/10.1002/aur.1471.

Macmillan, M., and M. L. Lena. "Rehabilitating Phineas Gage." [In Eng]. *Neuropsychological Rehabilitation* 20, no. 5 (Oct 2010): 641-58. https://www.doi.org/10.1080/09602011003760527.

Maenner, M. J., K. A. Shaw, J. Baio, A. Washington, M. Patrick, M. DiRienzo, D. L. Christensen, *et al.* "Prevalence of Autism Spectrum Disorder among Children Aged 8 Years - Autism and Developmental Disabilities Monitoring Network, 11 Sites, United States, 2016." [In Eng]. *Morbidity and Mortality Weekly Report (MMWR) Surveillance Summaries* 69, no. 4 (Mar 27 2020): 1-12. https://www.doi.org/10.15585/mmwr.ss6904a1.

Maguire, E. A., K. Woollett, and H. J. Spiers. "London Taxi Drivers and Bus Drivers: A Structural Mri and Neuropsychological Analysis." [In Eng]. *Hippocampus* 16, no. 12 (2006): 1091-101. https://www.doi.org/10.1002/hipo.20233.

Malagon-Vina, H., S. Ciocchi, J. Passecker, G. Dorffner, and T. Klausberger. "Fluid Network Dynamics in the Prefrontal Cortex During Multiple Strategy Switching." [In Eng]. *Nature Communications* 9, no. 1 (Jan 22 2018): 309. https://www.doi.org/10.1038/s41467-017-02764-x.

Manninen, Sandra, Lauri Tuominen, Robin I. Dunbar, Tomi Karjalainen, Jussi Hirvonen, Eveliina Arponen, Riitta Hari, *et al.* "Social Laughter Triggers Endogenous Opioid Release in Humans." *The Journal of Neuroscience* 37, no. 25 (2017): 6125-31. https://www.doi.org/10.1523/jneurosci.0688-16.2017. https://www.jneurosci.org/content/jneuro/37/25/6125.full.pdf.

Mansueto, P., A. D'Alcamo, A. Seidita, and A. Carroccio. "Food Allergy in Irritable Bowel Syndrome: The Case of Non-Celiac Wheat Sensitivity." [In Eng]. *World Journal of Gastroenterology* 21, no. 23 (Jun 21 2015): 7089-109. https://www.doi.org/10.3748/wjg.v21.i23.7089.

Marasco, G., A. R. Di Biase, R. Schiumerini, L. H. Eusebi, L. Iughetti, F. Ravaioli, E. Scaioli, A. Colecchia, and D. Festi. "Gut Microbiota and Celiac Disease." [In Eng]. *Digestive Diseases and Sciences* 61, no. 6 (Jun 2016): 1461-72. https://www.doi.org/10.1007/s10620-015-4020-2.

Marchant, Natalie L., Lise R. Lovland, Rebecca Jones, Alexa Pichet Binette, Julie Gonneaud, Eider M. Arenaza-Urquijo, Gael Chételat, Sylvia Villeneuve, and for the PREVENT-AD Research Group. "Repetitive Negative Thinking Is Associated with Amyloid, Tau, and Cognitive Decline." *Alzheimer's & Dementia* https://www.doi.org/10.1002/alz.12116. https://alz-journals.onlinelibrary.wiley.com/ doi/abs/10.1002/alz.12116.

Marchesi, J. R., D. H. Adams, F. Fava, G. D. Hermes, G. M. Hirschfield, G. Hold, M. N. Quraishi, *et al.* "The Gut Microbiota and Host Health: A New Clinical Frontier." [In Eng]. *Gut* 65, no. 2 (Feb 2016): 330-9. https://www.doi.org/10.1136/gutjnl-2015-309990.

Markram, H., T. Rinaldi, and K. Markram. "The Intense World Syndrome— an Alternative Hypothesis for Autism." [In Eng]. *Frontiers in Neuroscience* 1, no. 1 (Nov 2007): 77-96. https://www.doi.org/10.3389/neuro.01.1.1.006.2007.

Markram, K., and H. Markram. "The Intense World Theory - a Unifying Theory of the Neurobiology of Autism." [In Eng]. *Frontiers in Human Neuroscience* 4 (2010): 224. https://www.doi.org/10.3389/fnhum.2010.00224.

Martin, E. I., K. J. Ressler, E. Binder, and C. B. Nemeroff. "The Neuro-biology of Anxiety Disorders: Brain Imaging, Genetics, and Psycho-neuroendocrinology." [In Eng]. *Psychiatric Clinics of North America* 32, no. 3 (Sep 2009): 549-75. https://www.doi.org/10.1016/j.psc.2009.05.004. https://www.ncbi.nlm.nih.gov/pubmed/19716990.

Martins, Marielza Regina Ismael, José Alexandre Bastos, Angela Traldi Cecato, Maria de Lourdes Souza Araujo, Rafael Ribeiro Magro, and Vinicios Alaminos. "Screening for Motor Dysgraphia in Public Schools." *Jornal de Pediatria* 89, no. 1 (2013/01/01/ 2013): 70-74. https://www.doi.org/10.1016/j.jped.2013.02.011. http://www.sciencedirect.com/science/article/pii/S0021755713000120.

Marwha, D., M. Halari, and L. Eliot. "Meta-Analysis Reveals a Lack of Sexual Dimorphism in Human Amygdala Volume." [In Eng]. *Neuroimage* 147

(Feb 15 2017): 282-94. https://www.doi.org/10.1016/j.neuroimage. 2016.12.021.

Maslow, A. H. (1943). A theory of human motivation. *Psychological Review*, 50(4), 370–396. https://www.doi.org/10.1037/h0054346

———. (1970). *Motivation and personality.* New York: Harper & Row.

———. (1971). *The farther reaches of human nature.* Arkana/PenguinBooks.

Mayer, E. A., R. Knight, S. K. Mazmanian, J. F. Cryan, and K. Tillisch. "Gut Microbes and the Brain: Paradigm Shift in Neuroscience." [In Eng]. *Journal of Neuroscience* 34, no. 46 (Nov 12 2014): 15490-6. https://www.doi.org/10.1523/jneurosci.3299-14.2014.

Mayer, E. A., K. Tillisch, and A. Gupta. "Gut/Brain Axis and the Microbiota." [In Eng]. *J Clin Invest* 125, no. 3 (Mar 2 2015): 926-38. https://www.doi.org/10.1172/jci76304.

Mayo Foundation for Medical Education and Research "Crohn's Disease." accessed 6/23/2020, http://www.mayoclinic.org/diseases-conditions/crohns-disease/basics/definition/ con-20032061.

———. "Reactive Hypoglycemia: What Can I Do?", Updated May 24, 2019, 2019, accessed 06/23/2020, 2020.

McCarthy, M. M. "Is Sexual Differentiation of Brain and Behavior Epigenetic?" [In Eng]. *Current Opinion in Behavioral Sciences* 25 (Feb 2019): 83-88. https://www.doi.org/10.1016/j.cobeha.2018.10.005.

McDaniel, Michael A. "Big-Brained People Are Smarter: A Meta-Analysis of the Relationship between in Vivo Brain Volume and Intelligence." *Intelligence* 33, no. 4 (2005/07/01/ 2005): 337-46. https://www.doi.org/10.1016/j.intell.2004.11.005. http://www.sciencedirect. com/science/article/pii/S0160289604001357.

McKavanagh, R., E. Buckley, and S. A. Chance. "Wider Minicolumns in Autism: A Neural Basis for Altered Processing?" [In Eng]. *Brain* 138, no. Pt 7 (Jul 2015): 2034-45. https://www.doi.org/10.1093/brain/awv110. https://www.ncbi.nlm.nih.gov/pubmed/25935724.

McKenna, Malcolm C., Susan K. Bell, and George Gaylord Simpson. *Classification of Mammals above the Species Level.* New York: Columbia University Press, 1997.

Medscape. "Hypoglycemia." WebMD, LLC. Updated July 23, 2020, accessed 3/10/2021. https://emedicine.medscape.com/article/122122-overview

Meerwijk, Esther L., Judith M. Ford, and Sandra J. Weiss. "Brain Regions Associated with Psychological Pain: Implications for a Neural Network and Its Relationship to Physical Pain." *Brain Imaging and Behavior* 7, no. 1 (2013/03/01 2013): 1-14. https://www.doi.org/10.1007/s11682-012-9179-y. https://www.doi.org/10.1007/s11682-012-9179-y.

Meilleur, Andrée-Anne S., Patricia Jelenic, and Laurent Mottron. "Prevalence of Clinically and Empirically Defined Talents and Strengths in Autism." [In Eng]. *Journal of Autism and Developmental Disorders* 45, no. 5 (2015): 1354-67. https://www.doi.org/10.1007/s10803-014-2296-2. https://pubmed.ncbi.nlm.nih.gov/25374134. https://www.ncbi.nlm.nih.gov/pmc/articles/PMC4544492/.

Meleine, M., and J. Matricon. "Gender-Related Differences in Irritable Bowel Syndrome: Potential Mechanisms of Sex Hormones." [In Eng]. *World Journal of Gastroenterology* 20, no. 22 (Jun 14 2014): 6725-43. https://www.doi.org/10.3748/wjg.v20.i22.6725.

Mendaglio, Sal. "Dąbrowski's Theory of Positive Disintegration: A Personality Theory for the 21st Century." In *Dąbrowski's Theory of Positive Disintegration*, edited by Sal Mendaglio, 13-40. Scottsdale, AZ: Great Potential Press, 2008.

Messaoudi, M., R. Lalonde, N. Violle, H. Javelot, D. Desor, A. Nejdi, J. F. Bisson, *et al.* "Assessment of Psychotropic-Like Properties of a Probiotic Formulation (Lactobacillus Helveticus R0052 and Bifidobacterium Longum R0175) in Rats and Human Subjects." [In eng]. *British Journal of Nutrition* 105, no. 5 (Mar 2011): 755-64. https://www.doi.org/10.1017/s0007114510004319.

Mezzacappa, E. S., R. M. Kelsey, and E. S. Katkin. "The Effects of Epinephrine Administration on Impedance Cardiographic Measures of Cardiovascular Function." [In Eng]. *International Journal of Psychophysiology* 31, no. 3 (Mar 1999): 189-96. https://www.doi.org/10.1016/s0167-8760(98)00058-0.

Miles, J. H. "Autism Spectrum Disorders—a Genetics Review." *Genet Med* 13, no. 4 (Apr 2011): 278-94. https://www.doi.org/10.1097/GIM.0b013e3181ff67ba. https://www.ncbi.nlm.nih.gov/pubmed/21358411.

Miles, Tim. "Some Problems in Determining the Prevalence of Dyslexia." *Electronic Journal in Educational Psychology* 2 (Oct 1 2004). http://repositorio.ual.es/bitstream/handle/10835/697/Art_4_43_eng.pdf?sequence=1&isAllowed=y

Miller, E. K., D. J. Freedman, and J. D. Wallis. "The Prefrontal Cortex: Categories, Concepts and Cognition." [In Eng]. *Philosophical*

Transactions of the Royal Society B: Biological Sciences 357, no. 1424 (Aug 29 2002): 1123-36. https://www.doi.org/10.1098/rstb.2002.1099.

Miller, J. J., K. Fletcher, and J. Kabat-Zinn. "Three-Year Follow-up and Clinical Implications of a Mindfulness Meditation-Based Stress Reduction Intervention in the Treatment of Anxiety Disorders." [In Eng]. *General Hospital Psychiatry* 17, no. 3 (May 1995): 192-200. https://www.doi.org/10.1016/0163-8343(95)00025-m.

Miller, Nancy B., R. Frank Falk, and Yinmei Huang. "Gender Identity and the Overexcitability Profiles of Gifted College Students." *Roeper Review* 31, no. 3 (2009/06/30 2009): 161-69. https://www.doi.org/10.1080/02783190902993920.

Miner-Williams, W. M., and P. J. Moughan. "Intestinal Barrier Dysfunction: Implications for Chronic Inflammatory Conditions of the Bowel." [In Eng]. *Nutrition Research Reviews* 29, no. 1 (Jun 2016): 40-59. https://www.doi.org/10.1017/s0954422416000019.

Moldavsky, M., and K. Sayal. "Knowledge and Attitudes About Attention-Deficit/Hyperactivity Disorder (ADHD) and Its Treatment: The Views of Children, Adolescents, Parents, Teachers and Healthcare Professionals." [In Eng]. *Current Psychiatry Reports* 15, no. 8 (Aug 2013): 377. https://www.doi.org/10.1007/s11920-013-0377-0.

Molloy, C. A., K. N. Dietrich, and A. Bhattacharya. "Postural Stability in Children with Autism Spectrum Disorder." [In Eng]. *The Journal of Autism and Developmental Disorders* 33, no. 6 (Dec 2003): 643-52. https://www.doi.org/10.1023/b:jadd.0000006001.00667.4c.

Murzin, Dmitry Yu. *Chemical Reaction Technology.* Berlin, Germany: Walter de Gruyter GmbH & Co KG, 2015.

Nagao-Kitamoto, H., S. Kitamoto, P. Kuffa, and N. Kamada. "Pathogenic Role of the Gut Microbiota in Gastrointestinal Diseases." [In Eng]. *Intestinal Research* 14, no. 2 (Apr 2016): 127-38. https://www.doi.org/10.5217/ir.2016.14.2.127.

National Association for Gifted Children (NAGC). "What Is Giftedness?" NAGC.org, 2020, accessed 6/24/2020, 2020, https://www.nagc.org/resources-publications/resources/what-giftedness.

National Center Against Bullying, (n.d.) "Types of bullying." Accessed 6/24/20 from https://www.ncab.org.au/bullying-advice/bullying-for-parents/types-of-bullying/

National Institute of Mental Health. (2017, November) "Any anxiety disorder." [Website.] Accessed 6/24/20 from https://www.nimh.nih.gov/health/statistics/ any-anxiety-disorder.shtml

———. (2018, February) "Depression." [Website.] National Institute of Health, 2019, Accessed 6/24/20 from https://www.nimh.nih.gov/health/topics/depression/index.shtml

———. "Major Depression." National Institute of Health, 2019, accessed 6/24/2020, from https://www.nimh.nih.gov/health/statistics/major-depression.shtml.

Namkung, H., S. H. Kim, and A. Sawa. "The Insula: An Underestimated Brain Area in Clinical Neuroscience, Psychiatry, and Neurology." [In Eng]. *Trends in Neurosciences* 40, no. 4 (Apr 2017): 200-07. https://www.doi.org/10.1016/j.tins.2017.02.002.

Nanda, M. K., G. K. LeMasters, L. Levin, M. E. Rothenberg, A. H. Assa'ad, N. Newman, D. Bernstein*, et al.* "Allergic Diseases and Internalizing Behaviors in Early Childhood." [In Eng]. *Pediatrics* 137, no. 1 (Jan 2016). https://www.doi.org/10.1542/peds.2015-1922.

Navarrete-Muñoz, Eva-María, Paula Fernández-Pires, Silvia Navarro-Amat, Miriam Hurtado-Pomares, Paula Peral-Gómez, Iris Juárez-Leal, *et al.* "Association between Adherence to the Antioxidant-Rich Mediterranean Diet and Sensory Processing Profile in School-Aged Children: The Spanish Cross-Sectional Inpros Project." [In Eng]. *Nutrients* 11, no. 5 (2019): 1007. https://www.doi.org/10.3390/nu11051007. https://pubmed.ncbi.nlm.nih.gov/31052555. https://www.ncbi.nlm.nih.gov/pmc/ articles/PMC6566151/.

Navas-Sánchez, Francisco J, Yasser Alemán-Gómez, Javier Sánchez-Gonzalez, Juan A Guzmán-De-Villoria, Carolina Franco *et al.* "White Matter Microstructure Correlates of Mathematical Giftedness and Intelligence Quotient." *Human brain mapping* 35, no. 6 (2014): 2619-31. https://doi.org/10.1002/hbm.22355

Neihart, Maureen, Steven I. Pfeiffer, and Tracy L. Cross. *The Social and Emotional Development of Gifted Children : What Do We Know?* Second edition. ed. Waco, Texas: Prufrock Press Inc., 2016.

Neisser, Ulric, Gwyneth Boodoo, Thomas J. Bouchard Jr, A. Wade Boykin, Nathan Brody, Stephen J. Ceci, Diane F. Halpern, *et al.* "Intelligence: Knowns and Unknowns." *American Psychologist* 51, no. 2 (1996):77-101. https://www.doi.org/10.1037/0003-066X.51.2.77.

Nestor, P. G., M. Nakamura, M. Niznikiewicz, J. J. Levitt, D. T. Newell, M. E. Shenton, and R. W. McCarley. "Attentional Control and Intelligence: MRI Orbital Frontal Gray Matter and Neuropsychological Correlates." [In Eng]. *Behavioural Neurology* 2015 (2015): 354186. https://www.doi.org/10.1155/2015/354186.

Nestor, P. G., M. Nakamura, M. Niznikiewicz, E. Thompson, J. J. Levitt, V. Choate, M. E. Shenton, and R. W. McCarley. "In Search of the Functional Neuroanatomy of Sociality: MRI Subdivisions of Orbital Frontal Cortex and Social Cognition." [In Eng]. *Social Cognitive and Affective Neuroscience* 8, no. 4 (Apr 2013): 460-7. https://www.doi.org/10.1093/scan/nss018.

Neu, J., and J. Rushing. "Cesarean Versus Vaginal Delivery: Long-Term Infant Outcomes and the Hygiene Hypothesis." [In Eng]. *Clinics in Perinatology* 38, no. 2 (Jun 2011): 321-31. https://www.doi.org/10.1016/j.clp.2011.03.008.

Newberg, A. B., and J. Iversen. "The Neural Basis of the Complex Mental Task of Meditation: Neurotransmitter and Neurochemical Considerations." [In Eng]. *Medical Hypotheses* 61, no. 2 (Aug 2003): 282-91. https://www.doi.org/10.1016/s0306-9877(03)00175-0.

Newman, M. G., S. J. Llera, T. M. Erickson, A. Przeworski, and L. G. Castonguay. "Worry and Generalized Anxiety Disorder: A Review and Theoretical Synthesis of Evidence on Nature, Etiology, Mechanisms, and Treatment." [In Eng]. *Annual Review of Clinical Psychology* 9 (2013): 275-97. https://doi.org/10.1146/annurev-clinpsy-050212-185544. https://www.ncbi.nlm.nih.gov/pubmed/23537486.

Nibali, L., B. Henderson, S. T. Sadiq, and N. Donos. "Genetic Dysbiosis: The Role of Microbial Insults in Chronic Inflammatory Diseases." [In engJournal of Oral Microbiology 6 (2014). https://www.doi.org/10.3402/jom.v6.22962.

Nigg, J. T., and K. Holton. "Restriction and Elimination Diets in Adhd Treatment." [In Eng]. *Child and Adolescent Psychiatric Clinics of North America* 23, no. 4 (Oct 2014): 937-53. https://www.doi.org/10.1016/j.chc.2014.05.010.

Niles, Barbara L., Julie Klunk-Gillis, Donna J. Ryngala, Amy K. Silberbogen, Amy Paysnick, and Erika J. Wolf. "Comparing Mindfulness and Psychoeducation Treatments for Combat-Related Ptsd Using a Telehealth Approach." *Psychological Trauma: Theory, Research, Practice, and Policy* 4, no. 5 (2012): 538-47. https://www.doi.org/10.1037/a0026161.

Nolen-Hoeksema, S. "The Role of Rumination in Depressive Disorders and Mixed Anxiety/Depressive Symptoms." [In Eng]. *Journal of Abnormal Psychology* 109, no. 3 (Aug 2000): 504-11.

Nishizawa, Susan. Interview by Nicole A. Tetreault. In-person. Pasadena, CA May 25, 2018.

Norgaard, Martin, Laura A. Stambaugh, and Heston McCranie. "The Effect of Jazz Improvisation Instruction on Measures of Executive Function in Middle School Band Students." *Journal of Research in Music Education* 67, no. 3 (2019): 339-54. https://www.doi.org/10.1177/0022429419863038. https://journals.sagepub.com/doi/abs/10.1177/0022429419863038.

Nussbaum, N. L. "ADHD and Female Specific Concerns: A Review of the Literature and Clinical Implications." [In Eng]. *Journal of Attention Disorders* 16, no. 2 (Feb 2012): 87-100. https://www.doi.org/10.1177/1087054711416909.

O'Boyle, M. W., R. Cunnington, T. J. Silk, D. Vaughan, G. Jackson, A. Syngeniotis, and G. F. Egan. "Mathematically Gifted Male Adolescents Activate a Unique Brain Network During Mental Rotation." [In Eng]. *Cognitive Brain Research* 25, no. 2 (Oct 2005): 583-7. https://www.doi.org/10.1016/j.cogbrainres.2005.08.004.

Odgers, Candice. "Smartphones Are Bad for Some Teens, Not All." [In Eng]. *Nature* 554, no. 7693 (2018): 432-34. https://www.doi.org/10.1038/d41586-018-02109-8. https://pubmed.ncbi.nlm.nih.gov/29469108. https://www.ncbi.nlm.nih.gov/pmc/articles/PMC6121807/.

Ohtani, T., P. G. Nestor, S. Bouix, D. Newell, E. D. Melonakos, R. W. McCarley, M. E. Shenton, and M. Kubicki. "Exploring the Neural Substrates of Attentional Control and Human Intelligence: Diffusion Tensor Imaging of Prefrontal White Matter Tractography in Healthy Cognition." [In Eng]. *Neuroscience* 341 (01 2017): 52-60. https://www.doi.org/10.1016/j.neuroscience.2016.11.002. https://www.ncbi.nlm.nih. gov/pubmed/27840231.

Ohtani, T., P. G. Nestor, S. Bouix, Y. Saito, T. Hosokawa, and M. Kubicki. "Medial Frontal White and Gray Matter Contributions to General Intelligence." [In Eng]. *PLoS One* 9, no. 12 (2014): e112691. https://doi.org/10.1371/journal.pone.0112691.

Oishi, K., A. V. Faria, J. Hsu, D. Tippett, S. Mori, and A. E. Hillis. "Critical Role of the Right Uncinate Fasciculus in Emotional Empathy." [In Eng]. *Ann Neurol* 77, no. 1 (Jan 2015): 68-74. https://www.doi.org/10.1002/ana.24300.

Olson, I. R., R. J. Von Der Heide, K. H. Alm, and G. Vyas. "Development of the Uncinate Fasciculus: Implications for Theory and Developmental Disorders." [In Eng]. *Dev Cogn Neurosci* 14 (Aug 2015): 50-61. https://doi.org/10.1016/j.dcn.2015.06.003.

Otu-Nyarko, C. G., A. Gedalia, A. C. Karpinski, A. Kolomensky, and P. E. Hyman. "Disability in Children and Adolescents with Irritable Bowel Syndrome and/or Fibromyalgia." [In Eng]. *The Journal of Pediatric Gastroenterology and Nutrition* 61, no. 5 (Nov 2015): 558-60. https://www.doi.org/10.1097/mpg.0000000000000886.

O'Kelley, Harri. Interview by Nicole A. Tetreault. In-person. Los Angeles, CA. April 29, 2018.

O'Kelley, Jordan. Interview by Nicole A. Tetreault. In-person. Los Angeles, CA. April 29, 2018.

Owen, J. P., E. J. Marco, S. Desai, E. Fourie, J. Harris, S. S. Hill, A. B. Arnett, and P. Mukherjee. "Abnormal White Matter Microstructure in Children with Sensory Processing Disorders." [In Eng]. *NeuroImage: Clinical* 2 (2013):844-53. https://www.doi.org/10.1016/j.nicl.2013.06.009. https://www.ncbi.nlm.nih.gov/pubmed/24179836.

Pace, F., M. Pace, and G. Quartarone. "Probiotics in Digestive Diseases: Focus on *Lactobacillus* Gg." [In Eng]. *Minerva Gastroenterologica e Dietologica* 61, no. 4 (Dec 2015): 273-92. https://pubmed.ncbi.nlm.nih.gov/26657927/

Papathoma, E., M. Triga, S. Fouzas, and G. Dimitriou. "Cesarean Section Delivery and Development of Food Allergy and Atopic Dermatitis in Early Childhood." [In Eng]. *Pediatric Allergy, Immunology, and Pulmonology* 27, no. 4 (Jun 2016): 419-24. https://www.doi.org/10.1111/pai.12552.

Parker, W. D. (2000, Summer). Healthy perfectionism in the gifted. *Journal of Secondary Gifted Education, 11*(4), 173+. *Gale Academic Onefile*, Gale Document Number: GALE|A154401003

Paulsen, O., and T. J. Sejnowski. "Natural Patterns of Activity and Long-Term Synaptic Plasticity." [In Eng]. *Current Opinion in Neurobiology* 10, no. 2 (Apr 2000): 172-9. https://www.doi.org/10.1016/s0959-4388(00)00076-3.

Penke, L., S. M. Maniega, M. E. Bastin, M. C. Valdés Hernández, C. Murray, N. A. Royle, J. M. Starr, J. M. Wardlaw, and I. J. Deary. "Brain White Matter Tract Integrity as a Neural Foundation for General Intelligence." [In Eng]. *Molecular Psychiatry* 17, no. 10 (Oct 2012): 1026-30. https://

www.doi.org/10.1038/mp.2012.66. https://www.ncbi.nlm.nih.gov/pubmed/22614288.

Penney, Alexander M, Victoria C Miedema, and Dwight Mazmanian. "Intelligence and Emotional Disorders: Is the Worrying and Ruminating Mind a More Intelligent Mind?". *Personality and Individual Differences* 74 (2015): 90-93. https://doi.org/10.1016/j.paid.2014.10.005

Peppers, K. H., S. Eisbach, S. Atkins, J. M. Poole, and A. Derouin. "An Intervention to Promote Sleep and Reduce Adhd Symptoms." [In Eng]. *The Journal of Pediatrics Health Care* 30, no. 6 (Nov-Dec 2016): e43-e48. https://www.doi.org/10.1016/j.pedhc.2016.07.008.

Perry, V Hugh. "Contribution of Systemic Inflammation to Chronic Neurodegeneration." *Acta neuropathologica* 120, no. 3 (2010): 277-86, https://www.doi.org/10.1007/s00401-010-0722-x

Petanjek, Z., M. Judaš, G. Šimic, M. R. Rasin, H. B. Uylings, P. Rakic, and I. Kostovic. "Extraordinary Neoteny of Synaptic Spines in the Human Prefrontal Cortex." [In Eng]. *Proceedings of the National Academy of Sciences of the United States of America* 108, no. 32 (Aug 9 2011): 13281-6. https://www.doi.org/10.1073/pnas.1105108108.

Pfefferbaum, A., E. V. Sullivan, and D. Carmelli. "Genetic Regulation of Regional Microstructure of the Corpus Callosum in Late Life." [In Eng]. *Neuroreport* 12, no. 8 (Jun 2001): 1677-81. https://www.doi.org/10.1097/00001756-200106130-00032. https://www.ncbi.nlm.nih.gov/pubmed/11409738.

Phan, K. L., T. Wager, S. F. Taylor, and I. Liberzon. "Functional Neuroanatomy of Emotion: A Meta-Analysis of Emotion Activation Studies in PET and fMRI." [In Eng]. *Neuroimage* 16, no. 2 (Jun 2002): 331-48. https://www.doi.org/10.1006/nimg.2002.1087.

Philippine Explorer. "Furry Mascot of Rp Forest Lives on Borrowed Time." Philippine Explorer, Global Nation, Updated October 8, 2006, 2006, accessed 6/24/2020, from http://www.inq7.net/globalnation/sec_phe/2005/jan/19-01.htm.

Philipsen, Alexandra, Bernd Feige, Bernd Hesslinger, Dieter Ebert, Christine Carl, Magdolna Hornyak, Klaus Lieb, Ulrich Voderholzer, and Dieter Riemann. "Sleep in Adults with Attention-Deficit/Hyperactivity Disorder: A Controlled Polysomnographic Study Including Spectral Analysis of the Sleep EEG." *Sleep* 28, no. 7 (2005): 877-84. https://doi.org/10.1093/sleep/28.7.877

Piechowski, M. M. "Emotional Development and Emotional Giftedness.". In *Handbook of Gifted Education*, edited by Nicholas Colangelo and Gary A. Davis, 285-306. Boston: Allyn and Bacon, 1991.

―――. "Developmental Potential." In *New Voices in Counseling the Gifted*, edited by N. Colangelo & R. T. Zaffrann, 25-57. Dubuque, IA: Kendall Hunt, 1979.

―――. *"Mellow out," They Say, If I Only Could: Intensities and Sensitivities of the Young and Bright*. Madison, Wis.: Yunasa Books, 2006.

Piercy, Katrina L, Richard P Troiano, Rachel M Ballard, Susan A Carlson, Janet E Fulton, Deborah A Galuska, Stephanie M George, and Richard D Olson. "The Physical Activity Guidelines for Americans." *JAMA* 320, no. 19 (2018): 2020-28. https://doi.org/10.1001/jama.2018.14854

Plutchik, Robert. *Emotion: Theory, research, and experience: Vol. 1. Theories of emotion*, 1, New York: Academic, 1980.

Posthuma, D., E. J. De Geus, W. F. Baaré, H. E. Hulshoff Pol, R. S. Kahn, and D. I. Boomsma. "The Association between Brain Volume and Intelligence Is of Genetic Origin." [In Eng]. *Nature Neuroscience* 5, no. 2 (Feb 2002): 83-4. https://www.doi.org/10.1038/nn0202-83. https://www.ncbi.nlm.nih.gov/pubmed/11818967.

Postma, Dr. Michael. *The Inconvenient Student: Critical Issues in the Identification and Education of Twice-Exceptional Students*. New York: Royal Fireworks Publishing, 2017.

Postma, Dr. Michael. Interview by Nicole A. Tetreault. Telephone. December 15, 2017.

Primack, Brian A, Ariel Shensa, César G Escobar-Viera, Erica L Barrett, Jaime E Sidani, Jason B Colditz, and A Everette James. "Use of Multiple Social Media Platforms and Symptoms of Depression and Anxiety: A Nationally-Representative Study among Us Young Adults." *Computers in Human Behavior* 69 (2017): 1-9. https://doi.org/10.1016/j.chb.2016.11.013

Proctor, S. L., N. G. Hoffmann, and S. Allison. "The Effectiveness of Interactive Journaling in Reducing Recidivism among Substance-Dependent Jail Inmates." [In Eng]. *International Journal of Offender Therapy and Comparative Criminology* 56, no. 2 (Apr 2012): 317-32. https://www.doi.org/10.1177/0306624x11399274.

Public Policy Institute of California. "Poverty in California." Updated November 12, 2019, accessed 6/24/2020, https://www. ppic.org/publication/poverty-in-california/.

Pässler, Katja, Andrea Beinicke, and Benedikt Hell. "Interests and Intelligence: A Meta-Analysis." *Intelligence* 50 (May 1 2015): 30-51. https://www.doi.org/10.1016/j.intell.2015.02.001. http://www.sciencedirect.com/science/article/pii/S0160289615000197.

Qi, S., D. Hassabis, J. Sun, F. Guo, N. Daw, and D. Mobbs. "How Cognitive and Reactive Fear Circuits Optimize Escape Decisions in Humans." [In Eng]. *Proceedings of the National Academy of Sciences of the United States of America* 115, no. 12 (03 2018): 3186-91. https://www.doi.org/10.1073/pnas.1712314115. https://www.ncbi.nlm.nih.gov/pubmed/29507207.

Quinlan, E. B., E. D. Barker, Q. Luo, T. Banaschewski, A. L. W. Bokde, U. Bromberg, C. Büchel, et al. "Peer Victimization and Its Impact on Adolescent Brain Development and Psychopathology." [In Eng]. *Molecular Psychiatry* (Dec 2018). https://www.doi.org/10.1038/s41380-018-0297-9. https://www.ncbi.nlm.nih.gov/pubmed/30542059.

Radel, Rémi, Karen Davranche, Marion Fournier, and Arne Dietrich. "The Role of (Dis)Inhibition in Creativity: Decreased Inhibition Improves Idea Generation." *Cognition* 134 (2015/01/01/ 2015): 110-20. https://www.doi.org/10.1016/j.cognition.2014.09.001. http://www.sciencedirect.com/science/article/pii/S0010027714001826.

Razuk, M., F. Perrin-Fievez, C. L. Gerard, H. Peyre, J. A. Barela, and M. P. Bucci. "Effect of Colored Filters on Reading Capabilities in Dyslexic Children." [In Eng]. *Research In Developmental Disabilities* 83 (Dec 2018): 1-7. https://www.doi.org/10.1016/j.ridd.2018.07.006. https://www.ncbi.nlm.nih.gov/ pubmed/30048864.

Reddan, M. C., T. D. Wager, and D. Schiller. "Attenuating Neural Threat Expression with Imagination." [In Eng]. *Neuron* 100, no. 4 (Nov 2018): 994-1005.e4. https://www.doi.org/10.1016/j.neuron.2018.10.047. https://www.ncbi.nlm.nih.gov/pubmed/30465766.

Reddy, Ajitha. "The Eugenic Origins of IQ Testing: Implications for Post-Atkins Litigation." *DePaul Law Review* 57 (2007): 667.

Ritchie, S. J., M. E. Bastin, E. M. Tucker-Drob, S. M. Maniega, L. E. Engelhardt, S. R. Cox, N. A. Royle, et al. "Coupled Changes in Brain White Matter Microstructure and Fluid Intelligence in Later Life." [In Eng]. *Journal of Neuroscience* 35, no. 22 (Jun 2015): 8672-82. https://www.doi.org/10.1523/JNEUROSCI.0862-15.2015. https://www.ncbi.nlm.nih. gov/pubmed/26041932.

Rizzolatti, G., and M. Fabbri-Destro. "The Mirror System and Its Role in Social Cognition." [In Eng]. *Current Opinion in Neurobiology* 18, no. 2 (Apr 2008): 179-84. https://www.doi.org/10.1016/j.conb.2008.08.001. https://www.ncbi.nlm.nih.gov/pubmed/18706501.

Roberts, Miles, and Frank Kohn. "Habitat Use, Foraging Behavior, and Activity Patterns in Reproducing Western Tarsiers, *Tarsius Bancanus*, in Captivity: A Managment Synthesis." *Zoo Biology* 12, no. 2 (Jan 1 1993): 217-32. https://www.doi.org/10.1002/zoo.1430120207.

Rogers, K, and L Silverman. "A Study of 241 Profoundly Gifted Children." Paper presented at the 44th annual convention of the National Association for Gifted Children, Little Rock, AR., 1997.

Rutter, M. "Incidence of Autism Spectrum Disorders: Changes over Time and Their Meaning." [In Eng]. *Acta Paediatrica* 94, no. 1 (Jan 2005): 2-15. https://www.doi.org/10.1111/j.1651-2227.2005.tb01779.x.

Saarela, M. V., Y. Hlushchuk, A. C. Williams, M. Schürmann, E. Kalso, and R. Hari. "The Compassionate Brain: Humans Detect Intensity of Pain from Another's Face." [In Eng]. *Cerebral Cortex* 17, no. 1 (Jan 2007): 230-7. https://www.doi.org/10.1093/cercor/bhj141. https://www.ncbi.nlm.nih.gov/pubmed/16495434.

Saggar, Manish, Eve-Marie Quintin, Eliza Kienitz, Nicholas T. Bott, Zhaochun Sun, Wei-Chen Hong, Yin-hsuan Chien, *et al.* "Pictionary-Based fMRI Paradigm to Study the Neural Correlates of Spontaneous Improvisation and Figural Creativity." *Scientific Reports* 5, no. 1 (May 28 2015): 10894. https://www.doi.org/10.1038/srep10894.

Said, C. P., J. V. Haxby, and A. Todorov. "Brain Systems for Assessing the Affective Value of Faces." [In Eng]. *Philosophical Transactions of the Royal Society B: Biological Sciences* 366, no. 1571 (Jun 2011): 1660-70. https://www.doi.org/10.1098/rstb.2010.0351. https://www.ncbi.nlm.nih.gov/pubmed/21536552.

Sakai, T., H. Makino, E. Ishikawa, K. Oishi, and A. Kushiro. "Fermented Milk Containing Lactobacillus Casei Strain Shirota Reduces Incidence of Hard or Lumpy Stools in Healthy Population." [In Eng]. *International Journal of Food Science and Nutrition* 62, no. 4 (Jun 2011): 423-30. https://www.doi.org/10.3109/09637486.2010.542408.

Sakulku, J. & Alexander F. (2011). The Impostor Phenomenon. *International Journal of Behavioral Science.* 6 (1): 73–92.

Sakellaridi, S., V. N. Christopoulos, T. Aflalo, K. W. Pejsa, E. R. Rosario, D. Ouellette, N. Pouratian, and R. A. Andersen. "Intrinsic Variable Learning for Brain-Machine Interface Control by Human Anterior Intraparietal Cortex." [In Eng]. *Neuron* 102, no. 3 (May 8 2019): 694-705.e3. https://www.doi.org/10.1016/j.neuron.2019.02.012.

Salminen, S., G. R. Gibson, A. L. McCartney, and E. Isolauri. "Influence of Mode of Delivery on Gut Microbiota Composition in Seven Year Old Children." [In Eng]. *Gut* 53, no. 9 (Sep 2004): 1388-9. https://www.doi.org/10.1136/gut.2004.041640.

Sampson, T. R., J. W. Debelius, T. Thron, S. Janssen, G. G. Shastri, Z. E. Ilhan, C. Challis, *et al.* "Gut Microbiota Regulate Motor Deficits and Neuroinflammation in a Model of Parkinson's Disease." [In Eng]. *Cell* 167, no. 6 (Dec 1 2016): 1469-80.e12. https://www.doi.org/10.1016/j.cell.2016.11.018.

Sampson, T. R., and S. K. Mazmanian. "Control of Brain Development, Function, and Behavior by the Microbiome." [In Eng]. *Cell Host & Microbe* 17, no. 5 (May 13 2015): 565-76. https://www.doi.org/10.1016/j.chom.2015.04.011.

Samson, F., L. Mottron, I. Soulières, and T. A. Zeffiro. "Enhanced Visual Functioning in Autism: An Ale Meta-Analysis." [In Eng]. *Human Brain Mapping* 33, no. 7 (Jul 2012): 1553-81. https://innovationscns.com/allergic-rhinitis-relationships-with-anxiety-and-mood-syndromes/ https://www.doi.org/10.1002/hbm.21307.

Sansone, R. A., and L. A. Sansone. "Allergic Rhinitis: Relationships with Anxiety and Mood Syndromes." [In Eng]. *Innovations in Clinical Neuroscience* 8, no. 7 (Jul 2011): 12-7. https://www.ncbi.nlm.nih.gov/pubmed/21860841

Sanz, Y. "Microbiome and Gluten." [In Eng]. *Annals of Nutrition and Metabolism* 67 Suppl 2 (2015): 28-41. https://www.doi.org/10.1159/000440991.

Sarrabayrouse, G., J. Alameddine, F. Altare, and F. Jotereau. "Microbiota-Specific Cd4cd8αα Tregs: Role in Intestinal Immune Homeostasis and Implications for Ibd." [In Eng]. *Frontiers in Immunology* 6 (2015): 522. https://doi.org/10.3389/fimmu.2015.00522.

Scahill, L., and M. Schwab-Stone. "Epidemiology of ADHD in School-Age Children." [In Eng]. *Child and Adolescent Psychiatric Clinics of North America* 9, no. 3 (Jul 2000): 541-55, vii. https://doi.org/10.1016/S1056-4993(18)30106-8

Schmithorst, V. J. "Developmental Sex Differences in the Relation of Neuroanatomical Connectivity to Intelligence." [In Eng]. *Intelligence* 37, no. 2 (Mar 2009): 164-73. https://www.doi.org/10.1016/j. intell.2008.07.001. https://www.ncbi.nlm.nih.gov/pubmed/21297966.

Schmithorst, V. J., M. Wilke, B. J. Dardzinski, and S. K. Holland. "Cognitive Functions Correlate with White Matter Architecture in a Normal Pediatric Population: A Diffusion Tensor MRI Study." [In Eng]. *Human Brain Mapping* 26, no. 2 (Oct 2005): 139-47. https://www. doi.org/10.1002/ hbm.20149.

Schmälzle, R., M. Brook O'Donnell, J. O. Garcia, C. N. Cascio, J. Bayer, D. S. Bassett, J. M. Vettel, and E. B. Falk. "Brain Connectivity Dynamics During Social Interaction Reflect Social Network Structure." [In Eng].*Proceedings of the National Academy of Sciences of the United States of America* 114, no. 20 (May 16 2017): 5153-58. https://doi.org/10.1073/pnas.1616130114.

Scullin, Michael K. "The Eight Hour Sleep Challenge During Final Exams Week." *Teaching of Psychology* 46, no. 1 (2019): 55-63. https://www. doi.org/10.1177/0098628318816142. https://journals.sagepub.com/ doi/ abs/10.1177/0098628318816142.

Shaw, P., D. Greenstein, J. Lerch, L. Clasen, R. Lenroot, N. Gogtay, A. Evans, J. Rapoport, and J. Giedd. "Intellectual Ability and Cortical Development in Children and Adolescents." [In Eng]. *Nature* 440, no. 7084 (Mar 30 2006): 676-9. https://www.doi.org/10.1038/nature04513.

Shaw, P., N. J. Kabani, J. P. Lerch, K. Eckstrand, R. Lenroot, N. Gogtay, D. Greenstein*, et al.* "Neurodevelopmental Trajectories of the Human Cerebral Cortex." [In Eng]. *Journal of Neuroscience* 28, no. 14 (Apr 2008): 3586-94. https://www.doi.org/10.1523/JNEUROSCI.5309-07.2008. https://www.ncbi.nlm.nih.gov/pubmed/18385317.

Shaw, P., W. S. Sharp, M. Morrison, K. Eckstrand, D. K. Greenstein, L. S. Clasen, A. C. Evans, and J. L. Rapoport. "Psychostimulant Treatment and the Developing Cortex in Attention Deficit Hyperactivity Disorder." [In Eng]. *The American Journal of Psychiatry* 166, no. 1 (Jan 2009): 58-63. https://www.doi.org/10.1176/appi.ajp.2008.08050781.

Shaw, Philip, K Eckstrand, W Sharp, J Blumenthal, JP Lerch, DEEA Greenstein, L Clasen*, et al.* "Attention-Deficit/Hyperactivity Disorder Is Characterized by a Delay in Cortical Maturation." *Proceedings of the National Academy of Sciences* 104, no. 49 (2007): 19649-54.

Shaw, Philip, Francois Lalonde, Claude Lepage, Cara Rabin, Kristen Eckstrand, Wendy Sharp, Deanna Greenstein*, et al.* "Development of Cortical Asymmetry in Typically Developing Children and Its Disruption in Attention-Deficit/Hyperactivity Disorder." *Archives of general psychiatry* 66, no. 8 (2009): 888-96.

Shaw, Philip, Jason Lerch, Deanna Greenstein, Wendy Sharp, Liv Clasen, Alan Evans, Jay Giedd, F Xavier Castellanos, and Judith Rapoport."Longitudinal Mapping of Cortical Thickness and Clinical Outcome in Children and Adolescents with Attention-Deficit/Hyperactivity Disorder." *Archives of General Psychiatry* 63, no. 5 (2006): 540-49.

Siegel, Daniel J. "Mindful Awareness, Mindsight, and Neural Integration." *The Humanistic Psychologist* 37, no. 2 (2009): 137-58. https://www.doi.org/10.1080/08873260902892220.

Siegel, Linda S. "Perspectives on Dyslexia." [In Eng]. *Paediatrics & child health* 11, no. 9 (2006): 581-87. https://www.doi.org/10.1093/pch/11.9.581. https://pubmed.ncbi.nlm.nih.gov/19030329. https://www.ncbi.nlm.nih.gov/pmc/articles/PMC2528651/.

Silverman, Linda K. "Asynchronous Development." In *The Social and Emotional Development of Gifted Children : What Do We Know?*, edited by Maureen Neihart, Steven I. Pfeiffer and Tracy L. Cross, xvi, 311 pages. Waco, Texas: Prufrock Press Inc., 2016.

Song, C., H. Ikei, and Y. Miyazaki. "Physiological Effects of Nature Therapy: A Review of the Research in Japan." [In Eng]. *Int J Environ Res Public Health* 13, no. 8 (Aug 3 2016). https://www.doi.org/10.3390/ijerph13080781.

Soulières, I., M. Dawson, F. Samson, E. B. Barbeau, C. P. Sahyoun, G. E. Strangman, T. A. Zeffiro, and L. Mottron. "Enhanced Visual Processing Contributes to Matrix Reasoning in Autism." [In Eng]. *Human Brain Mapping* 30, no. 12 (Dec 2009): 4082-107. https://www.doi.org/10.1002/hbm.20831.

Soulières, I., T. A. Zeffiro, M. L. Girard, and L. Mottron. "Enhanced Mental Image Mapping in Autism." [In Eng]. *Neuropsychologia* 49, no. 5 (Apr 2011): 848-57. https://www.doi.org/10.1016/j.neuropsychologia.2011.01.027.

Spolin, Viola. *Improvisation for the Theater; a Handbook of Teaching and Directing Techniques.* Evanston, Ill.: Northwestern University Press, 1963.

Steenbergen, L., R. Sellaro, S. van Hemert, J. A. Bosch, and L. S. Colzato. "A Randomized Controlled Trial to Test the Effect of Multispecies

Probiotics on Cognitive Reactivity to Sad Mood." [In Eng]. *Brain, Behavior, and Immunity* 48 (Aug 2015): 258-64. https://www.doi.org/10.1016/j.bbi.2015.04.003.

Stefanelli, T., A. Malesci, S. A. De La Rue, and S. Danese. "Anti-Adhesion Molecule Therapies in Inflammatory Bowel Disease: Touch and Go." [In Eng]. *Autoimmun Rev* 7, no. 5 (May 2008): 364-9. https://www.doi.org/10.1016/j.autrev.2008.01.002.

Stilling, R. M., F. J. Ryan, A. E. Hoban, F. Shanahan, G. Clarke, M. J. Claesson, T. G. Dinan, and J. F. Cryan. "Microbes & Neurodevelopment— Absence of Microbiota During Early Life Increases Activity-Related Transcriptional Pathways in the Amygdala." [In Eng]. *Brain, Behavior, and Immunity* 50 (Nov 2015): 209-20. https://www.doi.org/10.1016/j.bbi.2015.07.009.

Stimpson, C. D., N. A. Tetreault, J. M. Allman, B. Jacobs, C. Butti, *et al.* "Biochemical Specificity of Von Economo Neurons in Hominoids." [In Eng]. *The American Journal of Human Biology* 23, no. 1 (Jan-Feb 2011): 22-8. https://www.doi.org/10.1002/ajhb.21135.

Stoeber, J., and K. Otto. "Positive Conceptions of Perfectionism: Approaches, Evidence, Challenges." [In Eng]. *Personality and Social Psychology Review* 10, no. 4 (2006): 295-319. https://www.doi.org/10.1207/s15327957pspr1004_2. https:// www.ncbi.nlm.nih.gov/pubmed/17201590.

Stuckey, H. L., and J. Nobel. "The Connection between Art, Healing, and Public Health: A Review of Current Literature." [In Eng]. *American Journal of Public Health* 100, no. 2 (Feb 2010): 254-63. https://www.doi.org/10.2105/AJPH.2008.156497. https://www.ncbi.nlm.nih.gov/pubmed/20019311.

Sturgeon, John A, and Alex J Zautra. "Social Pain and Physical Pain: Shared Paths to Resilience." *Pain Management* 6, no. 1 (2016): 63-74. https://doi.org/10.2217/pmt.15.56. https://www.futuremedicine.com/doi/abs/10.2217/pmt.15.56.

Styles, Elizabeth A. *The Psychology of Attention, 2nd Ed.* The Psychology of Attention, 2nd Ed. New York, NY, US: Psychology Press, 2006.

Suskind, Ron. *Life, Animated : A Story of Sidekicks, Heroes, and Autism.* First edition. ed. New York: Kingswell, 2014.

Swanson, H. I. "Drug Metabolism by the Host and Gut Microbiota: A Partnership or Rivalry?" [In Eng]. *Drug Metabolism & Disposition* 43, no. 10 (Oct 2015): 1499-504. https://www.doi.org/10.1124/dmd.115.065714.

Szigethy, E. M., A. O. Youk, D. Benhayon, D. L. Fairclough, M. C. Newara, M. A. Kirshner, S. I. Bujoreanu, *et al.* "Depression Subtypes in Pediatric Inflammatory Bowel Disease." [In Eng]. *The Journal of Pediatric Gastroenterology and Nutrition* 58, no. 5 (May 2014): 574-81. https://www.doi.org/10.1097/ mpg.0000000000000262.

Tachibana, Atsumichi, J. Adam Noah, Yumie Ono, Daisuke Taguchi, and Shuichi Ueda. "Prefrontal Activation Related to Spontaneous Creativity with Rock Music Improvisation: A Functional near-Infrared Spectroscopy Study." *Scientific Reports* 9, no. 1 (Nov 5 2019):16044. https://www.doi.org/10.1038/s41598-019-52348-6.

Takeda, Naoya, Yuki Kishimoto, and Osamu Yokota. "Pick's Disease." In *Neurodegenerative Diseases*, edited by Shamim I. Ahmad, 300-16. New York, NY: Springer US, 2012.

Taylor, J. B. (2009). *My Stroke of Insight: A Brain Scientists Personal Journey.* New York: Plume.

Tang, Yi-Yuan, Britta K. Hölzel, and Michael I. Posner. "The Neuroscience of Mindfulness Meditation." *Nature Reviews Neuroscience* 16, no. 4 (2015/04/01 2015): 213-25. https://www.doi.org/10.1038/nrn3916.

Tavassoli, T., A. Brandes-Aitken, R. Chu, L. Porter, S. Schoen, L. J. Miller, M. R. Gerdes, *et al.* "Sensory over-Responsivity: Parent Report, Direct Assessment Measures, and Neural Architecture." [In Eng]. *Mol Autism* 10 (2019): 4. https://www.doi.org/10.1186/s13229-019-0255-7. https://www.ncbi.nlm.nih.gov/pubmed/30740199.

Taylor, C. T., S. Lyubomirsky, and M. B. Stein. "Upregulating the Positive Affect System in Anxiety and Depression: Outcomes of a Positive Activity Intervention." [In Eng]. *Depress Anxiety* 34, no. 3 (03 2017): 267-80. https://www.doi.org/10.1002/da.22593. https://www.ncbi.nlm.nih.gov/pubmed/28060463.

Tetreault, N.A. "Brain Fingerprints." Awesome Neuroscience, Updated April 14, 2017, 2017, accessed 6/24/2020, https://www.nicoletetreault.com/single-post/2017/04/14/Brain-Fingerprints.

———. "Neuroscience of Asynchronous Development in Bright Minds." 2e News, Updated May 16, 2019, accessed 6/24/2020 from https://www.2enews.com/child-development/neuroscience-of-asynchronous-development-in-bright-minds/.

Tetreault, N. A., A. Y. Hakeem, S. Jiang, B. A. Williams, E. Allman, B. J. Wold, and J. M. Allman. "Microglia in the Cerebral Cortex in Autism." [In Eng].

The Journal of Autism and Developmental Disorders 42, no. 12 (Dec 2012): 2569-84. https://doi.org/10.1007/s10803-012-1513-0. https://www.ncbi.nlm.nih.gov/pubmed/22466688.

Thaler, K. J., G. Gartlehner, C. Kien, M. G. Van Noord, S. Thakurta, R. C. M. Wines, R. A. Hansen, and M. S. McDonagh. "Drug Class Reviews." In *Drug Class Review: Targeted Immune Modulators: Final Update 3 Report.* Portland (OR): Oregon Health & Science University Copyright © 2012, Oregon Health & Science University, Portland, Oregon., 2012.

Theoharides, T. C., and R. Doyle. "Autism, Gut-Blood-Brain Barrier, and Mast Cells." [In Eng]. *Journal of Clinical Psychopharmacology* 28, no. 5 (Oct 2008): 479-83. https://www.doi.org/10.1097/JCP.0b013e3181845f48.

Thompson, D. A., Berg, K. M., & Shatford, L. A. (1987). "The heterogeneity of bulimic symptomatology: Cognitive and behavioral dimensions." *International Journal of Eating Disorders, 6*(2), 215–234. https://www.doi.org/10.1002/1098-108X(198703)6:2<215::AID-EAT2260060206>3.0.CO;2-J

Thompson, P. M., T. D. Cannon, K. L. Narr, T. van Erp, V. P. Poutanen, M. Huttunen, J. Lönnqvist, *et al.* "Genetic Influences on Brain Structure." [In Eng]. *Nature Neuroscience* 4, no. 12 (Dec 2001): 1253-8. https://www.doi.org/10.1038/nn758. https://www.ncbi.nlm.nih.gov/pubmed/11694885.

Tilley, S., C. Neale, A. Patuano, and S. Cinderby. "Older People's Experiences of Mobility and Mood in an Urban Environment: A Mixed Methods Approach Using Electroencephalography (Eeg) and Interviews." [In Eng]. *International Journal of Environmental Research and Public Health* 14, no. 2 (Feb 4 2017). https://doi.org/10.3390/ijerph14020151.

Tillisch, K., J. Labus, L. Kilpatrick, Z. Jiang, J. Stains, B. Ebrat, D. Guyonnet, *et al.* "Consumption of Fermented Milk Product with Probiotic Modulates Brain Activity." [In Eng]. *Gastroenterology* 144, no. 7 (Jun 2013): 1394-401, 401.e1-4. https://www.doi.org/10.1053/j.gastro.2013.02.043.

Toga, A. W., and P. M. Thompson. "Genetics of Brain Structure and Intelligence." [In Eng]. *The Annual Review of Neuroscience* 28 (2005): 1-23. https://doi.org/10.1146/annurev.neuro.28.061604.135655. https://www.ncbi. nlm.nih.gov/pubmed/15651931.

Torrente, F., A. Anthony, R. B. Heuschkel, M. A. Thomson, P. Ashwood, and S. H. Murch. "Focal-Enhanced Gastritis in Regressive Autism with Features Distinct from Crohn's and Helicobacter Pylori Gastritis." [In Eng].

American Journal of Gastroenterology 99, no. 4 (Apr 2004): 598-605. https://www.doi.org/10.1111/j.1572-0241.2004.04142.x.

Turnbaugh, P. J., R. E. Ley, M. Hamady, C. M. Fraser-Liggett, R. Knight, and J. I. Gordon. "The Human Microbiome Project." [In Eng]. *Nature* 449, no. 7164 (Oct 18 2007): 804-10. https://www.doi.org/10.1038/nature06244.

Tyler CW. "Evidence That Leonardo da Vinci Had Strabismus." *JAMA Ophthalmology.* 2019;137(1):82–86. https://www.doi.org/10.1001/jamaophthalmol.2018.3833

U.S. Department of Health and Human Services, "Crohn's Disease." 2020, accessed 6/23/2020, 2020, http://www.niddk.nih. gov/health-information/health-topics/digestive-diseases/crohns-disease/Pages/facts.aspx.

Urgesi, Cosimo, Salvatore M. Aglioti, Miran Skrap, and Franco Fabbro. "The Spiritual Brain: Selective Cortical Lesions Modulate Human Self-Transcendence." *Neuron* 65, no. 3 (Feb 11 2010): 309-19. https://www.doi.org/10.1016/j.neuron.2010.01.026. http://www.sciencedirect.com/science/article/pii/S0896627310000528.

Vaccarino, F. M., and K. M. Smith. "Increased Brain Size in Autism—What It Will Take to Solve a Mystery." [In Eng]. *Biological Psychiatry* 66, no. 4 (Aug 2009): 313-5. https://www.doi.org/10.1016/j.biopsych.2009.06.013. https://www.ncbi.nlm.nih.gov/pubmed/19643218.

Vaillancourt, T., H. L. Brittain, P. McDougall, and E. Duku. "Longitudinal Links between Childhood Peer Victimization, Internalizing and Externalizing Problems, and Academic Functioning: Developmental Cascades." [In Eng]. *Journal of Abnormal Child Psychology* 41, no. 8 (Nov 2013): 1203-15. https://www.doi.org/10.1007/s10802-013-9781-5. https://www.ncbi.nlm.nih.gov/pubmed/23907699.

Valizadeh, Seyed Abolfazl, Franziskus Liem, Susan Mérillat, Jürgen Hänggi, and Lutz Jäncke. "Identification of Individual Subjects on the Basis of Their Brain Anatomical Features." *Scientific Reports* 8, no. 1 (2018/04/04 2018): 5611. https://www.doi.org/10.1038/s41598-018-23696-6.

Vandvik, P. O., I. Wilhelmsen, C. Ihlebaek, and P. G. Farup. "Comorbidity of Irritable Bowel Syndrome in General Practice: A Striking Feature with Clinical Implications." [In Eng]. *Alimentary Pharmacology & Therapeutics* 20, no. 10 (Nov 15 2004): 1195-203. https://www.doi.org/10.1111/j.1365-2036.2004.02250.x.

Vickers, Brian. *Shakespeare, Co-Author: A Historical Study of Five Collaborative Plays.* Oxford ; New York: Oxford University Press, 2002.

Vighi, G., F. Marcucci, L. Sensi, G. Di Cara, and F. Frati. "Allergy and the Gastrointestinal System." [In Eng]. *Clinical & Experimental Immunology* 153 Suppl 1, no. Suppl 1 (Sep 2008): 3-6. https://www.doi.org/10.1111/j.1365-2249.2008.03713.x.

Vilensky, J. A., A. R. Damasio, and R. G. Maurer. "Gait Disturbances in Patients with Autistic Behavior: A Preliminary Study." [In Eng]. *Archives of neurology* 38, no. 10 (Oct 1981): 646-9. https://www.doi.org/10.1001/archneur.1981.00510100074013.

Volkow, Nora D, Gene-Jack Wang, Scott H Kollins, Tim L Wigal, Jeffrey H Newcorn, Frank Telang, Joanna S Fowler, *et al.* "Evaluating Dopamine Reward Pathway in ADHD: Clinical Implications." *JAMA* 302, no. 10 (2009): 1084-91. https://doi.org/10.1001/jama.2009.1308

Wallace, Caroline J. K., and Roumen Milev. "The Effects of Probiotics on Depressive Symptoms in Humans: A Systematic Review." [In Eng]. *Annals of general psychiatry* 16 (2017): 14-14. https://www.doi.org/10.1186/s12991-017-0138-2. https://pubmed.ncbi.nlm.nih.gov/28239408. https://www.ncbi.nlm.nih.gov/pmc/articles/PMC5319175/.

Wang, C. X., I. A. Hilburn, D. A. Wu, Y. Mizuhara, C. P. Cousté, J. N. H. Abrahams, S. E. Bernstein, *et al.* "Transduction of the Geomagnetic Field as Evidenced from Alpha-Band Activity in the Human Brain." [In Eng]. *eNeuro* 6, no. 2 (2019 Mar/Apr 2019). https://www.doi.org/10.1523/ENEURO.0483-18.2019. https://www.ncbi.nlm.nih.gov/pubmed/31028046.

Wangyal, Tenzin, and Marcy Vaughn. *Spontaneous Creativity : Meditations for Manifesting Your Positive Qualities.* First edition. ed. Carlsbad, California: Hay House, Inc., 2018.

Ward, Adrian F, Kristen Duke, Ayelet Gneezy, and Maarten W Bos. "Brain Drain: The Mere Presence of One's Own Smartphone Reduces Available Cognitive Capacity." *Journal of the Association for Consumer Research* 2, no. 2 (2017): 140-54.

Webb, James T. Interview by Nicole A. Tetreault. Telephone. July 27, 2017.

———., *et al.*, *Misdiagnosis and Dual Diagnoses of Gifted Children and Adults : Adhd, Bipolar, Ocd, Asperger's, Depression, and Other Disorders.* Second edition. ed. Tucson, AZ: Great Potential Press, Inc., 2016.

———. "Misdiagnosis and Dual Diagnosis of Gifted Children" *Outlook*, September/October, 2006 issue, Minnesota Council for the Gifted and Talented (MCGT).

Wellemeyer, James. "Wealthy Parents Spend up to $10,000 on SAT Prep for Their Kids." *MarketWatch*, July 7, 2019, Accessed 6/24/20 from https://www. marketwatch.com/story/some-wealthy-parents-are-dropping-up-to-10000-on-sat-test-prep-for-their-kids-2019-06-21.

Westrick, Paul A., Jessica P. Marini, Linda Young, Helen Ng, Doron Shmueli, and Emily Shaw. *Validity of the SAT®* for Predicting First-Year Grades and *Retention to the Second Year.* 2019. Accessed 6/24/20 from https://collegereadiness.collegeboard.org/pdf/national-sat-validity-study-overview-admissions-enrollment-leaders.pdf

Wheelwright, Sally, and Simon Baron-Cohen. "The Link between Autism and Skills Such as Engineering, Maths, Physics and Computing:A Reply to Jarrold and Routh, Autism,1998,2 (3):281-9." *Autism* 5, no. 2 (2001): 223-27. https://www.doi.org/10.1177/1362361301005002010. https://journals. sagepub.com/doi/abs/10.1177/1362361301005002010.

White, Mathew P., Ian Alcock, James Grellier, Benedict W. Wheeler, Terry Hartig, Sara L. Warber, Angie Bone, Michael H. Depledge, and Lora E. Fleming. "Spending at Least 120 Minutes a Week in Nature Is Associated with Good Health and Wellbeing." *Scientific Reports* 9, no. 1 (2019/06/13 2019): 7730. https://www.doi.org/10.1038/s41598-019-44097-3. https:// www.doi.org/10.1038/s41598-019-44097-3.

Wicker, B., C. Keysers, J. Plailly, J. P. Royet, V. Gallese, and G. Rizzolatti. "Both of Us Disgusted in My Insula: The Common Neural Basis of Seeing and Feeling Disgust." [In Eng]. *Neuron* 40, no. 3 (Oct 2003): 655-64. https://www.doi.org/10.1016/s0896-6273(03)00679-2. https://www. ncbi.nlm.nih.gov/pubmed/14642287.

Wiland, H. O., W. H. Henricks, and T. M. Daly. "Limited utilization of serologic testing in patients undergoing duodenal biopsy for celiac disease." [In Eng]. *BMC Gastroenterology* 13 (Nov 9 2013): 156. https://doi. org/10.1186/1471-230x-13-156.

Wilke, M., J. H. Sohn, A. W. Byars, and S. K. Holland. "Bright Spots: Correlations of Gray Matter Volume with Iq in a Normal Pediatric Population." [In Eng]. *Neuroimage* 20, no. 1 (Sep 2003): 202-15. https:// doi.org/10.1016/s1053-8119(03)00199-x.

Willing, B. P., S. L. Russell, and B. B. Finlay. "Shifting the Balance: Antibiotic Effects on Host-Microbiota Mutualism." [In Eng]. *Nature Reviews Microbiology* 9, no. 4 (Apr 2011): 233-43. https://www.doi.org/10.1038/ nrmicro2536.

Wittels, Harris. *Humblebrag : The Art of False Modesty.* 1st ed. New York: Grand Central Pub., 2012.

Woollett, K., and E. A. Maguire. "Acquiring "The Knowledge" Of London's Layout Drives Structural Brain Changes." [In Eng]. *Current Biology* 21, no. 24 (Dec 20 2011): 2109-14. https://www.doi.org/10.1016/j.cub.2011.11.018.

Wright, Barry, Penny Spikins, and Hannah Pearson. "Should Autism Spectrum Conditions Be Characterised in a More Positive Way in Our Modern World?" [In Eng]. *Medicina (Kaunas, Lithuania)* 56, no. 5 (2020): 233. https://www.doi.org/10.3390/medicina56050233. https://pubmed. ncbi.nlm.nih.gov/32413984. https://www.ncbi.nlm.nih.gov/pmc/articles/ PMC7279498/.

Xu, G., L. G. Snetselaar, J. Jing, B. Liu, L. Strathearn, and W. Bao. "Association of Food Allergy and Other Allergic Conditions with Autism Spectrum Disorder in Children." [In Eng]. *JAMA Network Open* 1, no. 2 (Jun 1 2018): e180279. https://www.doi.org/10.1001/jamanetworkopen.2018.0279.

Yackle, K., L. A. Schwarz, K. Kam, J. M. Sorokin, J. R. Huguenard, J. L. Feldman, L. Luo, and M. A. Krasnow. "Breathing Control Center Neurons That Promote Arousal in Mice." [In Eng]. *Science* 355, no. 6332 (Mar 31 2017): 1411-15. https://www.doi.org/10.1126/science.aai7984.

Young, S. (2010, November 29) "A pain-processing algorithm." [Pamphlet.] Accessed 6/27/2020 from https://www.shinzen.org/wp-content/ uploads/2016/12/ art_painprocessingalg.pdf

Yu, C., J. Li, Y. Liu, W. Qin, Y. Li, N. Shu, T. Jiang, and K. Li. "White Matter Tract Integrity and Intelligence in Patients with Mental Retardation and Healthy Adults." [In Eng]. *Neuroimage* 40, no. 4 (May 1 2008): 1533-41. https://www.doi.org/10.1016/j.neuroimage.2008.01.063.

Yue, X. D., C. L. Leung, and N. A. Hiranandani. "Adult Playfulness, Humor Styles, and Subjective Happiness." [In Eng]. *Psychological Reports* 119, no. 3 (Dec 2016): 630-40. https://www.doi.org/10.1177/0033294116662842.

Yuen, Hon K., and Gavin R. Jenkins. "Factors Associated with Changes in Subjective Well-Being Immediately after Urban Park Visit." *International Journal of Environmental Health Research* 30, no. 2 (2020/03/03 2020): 134-45. https://www.doi.org/10.1080/09603123.2019.1577368.

Yuknavitch, Lidia (author), and Alex Brewer (illustrator). *The Misfit's Manifesto.* Ted Books. First TED books hardcover edition. ed. New York: TED Books, Simon & Schuster, 2017.

Zablotsky, B., L. I. Black, M. J. Maenner, L. A. Schieve, and S. J. Blumberg. "Estimated Prevalence of Autism and Other Developmental Disabilities Following Questionnaire Changes in the 2014 National Health Interview Survey." [In Eng]. *National Health Statistics Reports*, no. 87 (Nov 13 2015): 1-20.

Zaharko, D. S., and J. M. Covey. "Arabinosyl-5-Azacytosine: Plasma Kinetics and Therapeutic Response (L1210) in Vitro and in Vivo in Mice." [In Eng]. *Investigational New Drugs* 3, no. 4 (1985): 323-9. https://www. doi.org/10.1007/ BF00170753. https://www.ncbi.nlm.nih.gov/ pubmed/2417983.

Zahn, R., J. Moll, M. Paiva, G. Garrido, F. Krueger, E. D. Huey, and J. Grafman. "The Neural Basis of Human Social Values: Evidence from Functional MRI." [In Eng]. *Cerebral Cortex* 19, no. 2 (Feb 2009): 276-83. https://www.doi.org/10.1093/cercor/bhn080. https://www. ncbi.nlm.nih. gov/pubmed/18502730.

Zhang, L., J. Q. Gan, and H. Wang. "Optimized Gamma Synchronization Enhances Functional Binding of Fronto-Parietal Cortices in Mathematically Gifted Adolescents During Deductive Reasoning." [In Eng]. *Frontiers in Human Neuroscience* 8 (2014): 430. https://www. doi.org/10.3389/fnhum.2014.00430. https://www.ncbi.nlm.nih.gov/ pubmed/24966829.

Zhuang, X., L. Xiong, L. Li, M. Li, and M. Chen. "Alterations of Gut Microbiota in Patients with Irritable Bowel Syndrome: A Systematic Review and Meta-Analysis." [In Eng]. *Journal of Gastroenterology and Hepatology* 32, no. 1 (Jan 2017): 28-38. https://www.doi.org/10.1111/jgh.13471.

Zope, S. A., and R. A. Zope. "Sudarshan Kriya Yoga: Breathing for Health." [In Eng]. *International Journal of Yoga* 6, no. 1 (Jan 2013): 4-10. https:// www.doi.org/10.4103/0973-6131.105935.

Endnotes

Chapter 1

1   Judy Singer, *Odd People In: The Birth of Community Amongst People on the Autism Spectrum: A personal exploration of a New Social Movement based on Neurological Diversity*. An Honours Thesis presented to the Faculty of Humanities and Social Science, the University of Technology, Sydney, 1998; Judy Singer, *Why can't you be normal for once in your life?: from a "Problem with No Name" to a new category of disability*. In Corker, M and French, S (Eds.) Disability Discourse (Open University Press UK 1999).

2   Harvey Blume, "Neurodiversity" *The Atlantic*. (Sept 30, 1998).

3   Korbinian Brodmann, *Vergleichende Lokalisationslehre der Grosshirnrinde in ihren Prinzipien dargestellt auf Grund des Zellenbaues* [Comparative localization theory of the cerebral cortex presented in its principles on the basis of the cell structure] (Barth, 1909).

4   Matthew F. Glasser *et al.*, "The Human Connectome Project's neuroimaging approach," *Nature Neuroscience* 19, no. 9 (Aug 26 2016), https://doi.org/10.1038/nn.4361.

5   Seyed Abolfazl Valizadeh *et al.*, "Identification of individual subjects on the basis of their brain anatomical features," *Scientific Reports* 8, no. 1 (April 4 2018), https://doi.org/10.1038/s41598-018-23696-6.

6   Donald O. Hebb, *The Organization of Behavior : A Neuropsychological Theory.* (Mahwah, N.J.: L. Erlbaum Associates, 2002).

7   Eleanor A. Maguire, Katherine Woollett, and Hugo J. Spiers, "London taxi drivers and bus drivers: a structural MRI and neuropsychological analysis," *Hippocampus* 16, no. 12 (2006), https://doi.org/10.1002/hipo.20233.

8   Elliot T. Berkman, Lauren E. Kahn, and Junaid S. Merchant, "Training-induced changesin inhibitory control network activity," *Journal of Neuroscience* 34, no. 1 (Jan 1 2014), https://doi.org/10.1523/jneurosci.3564-13.2014.

9   *Oz the Great and Powerful* [Motion picture]. directed by Sam Raimi; screen story by Mitchell Kapner ; screenplay by Mitchell Kapner and David Lindsay-Abaire ; produced by Joe Roth . (Walt Disney Studios Motion Pictures, 2013).

10   Sofia Sakellaridi, *et al.*, "Intrinsic Variable Learning for Brain-Machine InterfaceControl by Human Anterior Intraparietal Cortex," *Neuron* 102, no. 3 (May 8 2019), https://doi.org/10.1016/j.neuron.2019.02.012.

11   Pamela Cantor *et al.*, "Malleability, plasticity, and individuality: How children learn and develop in context," *Applied Developmental Science* 23, no. 4 (Feb 10 2019), https://doi.org/10.1080/10888691.2017.1398649.

12   *The Wizard of Oz* [Motion picture]. (1939) Directed by Victor Fleming, written by Noel Langley, Florence Ryerson, and Edgar Allen Woolf. United States: Metro-Goldwyn-Mayer.

13   Mariale M. Hardiman *et al.*, "The effects of arts-integrated instruction on memory forscience content," *Trends in Neuroscience and Education* 14 (Mar 1 2019), https://doi.org/10.1016/j.tine.2019.02.002.

14   L. Frank Baum. *The Wonderful Wizard of Oz*. (London, England: Penguin Books,1994.) (first published May 17th 1900).

15   J.W. Hamilton, "Editorial and Miscellaneous. The Man Through Whose Head an Iron Rod Passed Is Still Living". *Ohio Medical and Surgical Journal.* (Nov 17 1860). 13: 174. Reprinted: Samuel Worcester Butler; D G. Brinton, eds. Medical and Surgical Reporter. 5.Philadelphia: Crissly & Markley. p. 183.

16   Andrew J Larner and John P. Leach, "Phineas Gage and the beginnings ofneuropsychology," *Advances in Clinical Neuroscience & Rehabilitation* 2, no. 3 (2002).

17   Sarah-Jayne Blakemore and Uta Frith, *The Learning Brain: Lessons for Education* (Malden, MA, USA: Blackwell, 2005); D. Denny-Brown and B. Q. Banker, "Amorphosynthesisfrom left parietal lesion," *AMA Archives of Neurology and Psychiatry* 71, no. 3 (Mar 1954), https://doi.org/10.1001/archneurpsyc.1954.02320390032003.

18   Blakemore & Frith, "The Learning Brain." *Developmental Science* 8:6 (2005), pp 459– 471.

19   Cosimo Urgesi *et al.*, "The Spiritual Brain: Selective Cortical Lesions ModulateHuman Self-Transcendence," *Neuron* 65, no. 3 (Feb 11 2010), https://doi.org/10.1016/j.neuron.2010.01.026.

20   Naoya Takeda, Yuki Kishimoto, and Osamu Yokota, "Pick's Disease," in *Neurodegenerative Diseases*, ed. Shamim I. Ahmad (New York, NY: Springer US, 2012).

21   Edward J Fine, Catalina C Ionita, Linda Lohr, "The history of the development of thecerebellar examination," *Seminars in Neurology* 22, no. 4 (Dec 2002), https://doi.org/10.1055/s-2002-36759.

22   Daphna Joel *et al.*, "Sex beyond the genitalia: The human brain mosaic," *Proceedings of the National Academy of Sciences of the United States of America* 112, no. 50 (Dec 15 2015), https://doi.org/10.1073/pnas.1509654112.

23   Daphna Joel and Anne Fausto-Sterling, "Beyond sex differences: new approaches forthinking about variation in brain structure and function," *Philosophical Transactions of the Royal Society , B: Biological Sciences Sci* 371, no. 1688 (Feb 19 2016), https://doi.org/10.1098/rstb.2015.0451.

24   Dhruv Marwha, Meha Halari, Lise Eliot, "Meta-analysis reveals a lack of sexualdimorphism in human amygdala volume," *Neuroimage* 147 (Feb 15 2017), https://doi.org/10.1016/j.neuroimage.2016.12.021.

25   Margaret M. McCarthy, "Is Sexual Differentiation of Brain and Behavior Epigenetic?," *Current Opinion in Behavioral Sciences* 25 (Feb 2019), https://doi.org/10.1016/j.cobeha.2018.10.005.

26   Alyssa J. Kersey, Kelsey D. Csumitta, and Jessica F. Cantlon, "Gender similarities in the brain during mathematics development," *npj Science of Learning* 4, no. 1 (Nov 8 2019), https://doi.org/10.1038/s41539-019-0057-x.

27   Linda van Laren, "Math Class Is Tough," in *Girl culture : An Encyclopedia*, ed.Claudia Mitchell and Jacqueline Reid-Walsh (Westport, Conn.: Greenwood Press, 2008).

28   Alyssa J. Kersey *et al.*, "No intrinsic gender differences in children's earliest numericalabilities," *npj Science of Learning* 3 (2018), https://doi.org/10.1038/s41539-018-0028-7.

29   Sara M. Lindberg *et al.*, "New trends in gender and mathematics perfor- mance: A meta-analysis," *Psychological Bulletin* 136, no. 6 (2010), https:// doi.org/10.1037/a0021276.

30   Philip Shaw *et al.*, "Intellectual ability and cortical development in chil- dren and adolescents," *Nature* 440, no. 7084 (Mar 30, 2006), https:// doi.org/10.1038/nature04513.

31   Michael J Arcaro, and Margaret S Livingstone, "A hierarchical, retino- topic proto-organization of the primate visual system at birth," *eLife* 6 (Jul 3, 2017), https://doi.org/10.7554/eLife.26196.

32   Hugo Malagon-Vina *et al.*, "Fluid network dynamics in the prefrontal cortex during multiple strategy switching," *Nature Communications* 9, no. 1 (Jan 22, 2018), https://doi.org/10.1038/s41467-017-02764-x.

Chapter 2

1   John A Sturgeon and Alex J Zautra, "Social pain and physical pain: shared paths to resilience," *Pain Management* 6, no. 1 (2016), https:// doi.org/10.2217/pmt.15.56.

2   Research shows that long-term training can improve VO_2max, but even elite athletes reach a plateau where little physiological improvement occurs. A. Legaz Arrese *et al.*, "The changes in running performance and maximal oxygen uptake after long-term training in elite athletes," *The Journal of Sports Medicine and Physical Fitness* 45, no. 4 (Dec 2005).

3   Success of Kenyan elite runners has been attributed to a combination of genetic factors including maximal oxygen consumption (VO_2max), frac- tional VO_2max utilization, running economy (energetic cost of running) and body dimensions coupled with training that results in high utilization of natural potential. Henrik B. Larsen, "Kenyan dominance in distance running," *Comparative Biochemistry and Physiology – Part A: Molecular & Integrative Physiology* 136, no. 1 (Sep 2003), https://doi.org/10.1016/ s1095-6433(03)00227-7; Henrik B. Larsen and A. William Sheel, "The Kenyan runners," *Scandinavian Journal of Medicine & Science in Sports* 25 Suppl 4 (Dec 2015), https://doi.org/10.1111/sms.12573.

4   Paul A. Westrick *et al.*, *Validity of the SAT® for Predicting First-Year Grades and Retention to the Second Year*, (New York, NY: The College Board 2019).

5   Herman Aguinis, Steven A. Culpepper, and Charles A. Pierce, "Differ- ential prediction generalization in college admissions testing," *Journal of Educational Psychology* 108, no. 7 (2016), https://doi.org/10.1037/

edu0000104; Steven A. Culpepper *et al.*, "High-Stakes Testing Case Study: A Latent Variable Approach for Assessing Measurement and Prediction Invariance," *Psychometrika* 84, no. 1 (Mar 2019), https://doi.org/10.1007/s11336-018-9649-2.

6   Ezekiel Dixon-Román, Howard Everson, and John McArdle. "Race, Poverty and SAT Scores: Modeling the Influences of Family Income on Black and White High School Students' Sat Performance." *Teachers College Record* 115 (May 1, 2013).

7   Fairtest.org, "2019 SAT Scores: Gaps Between Demographic Groups Grows Larger," updated September 24, 2019, accessed 6/27/2020, https://www.fairtest.org/2019-sat-scores-gaps-between-demographic-groups-gr.

8   James Wellemeyer, "Wealthy Parents Spend up to $10,000 on SAT Prep for Their Kids.," *MarketWatch*, July 7, 2019, accessed 6/27/2020, http's://www.marketwatch.com/story/some-wealthy-parents-are-dropping-up-to-10000-on-sat-test-prep-for-their-kids-2019-06-21.

9   Center for Talented Youth. "CTY Eligibility Policy," updated October 9, 2018, accessed 6/27/2020, https://cty.jhu.edu/talent/eligibility/policy.html.

10   Albert M. Galaburda, "Dyslexia—A molecular disorder of neuronal migration," *Annals of Dyslexia* 55, no. 2 (December 1 2005), https://doi.org/10.1007/s11881-005-0009-4. Luiz G. Guidi *et al.*, "The neuronal migration hypothesis of dyslexia: A critical evaluation 30 years on," *European Journal of Neuroscience* 48, no. 10 (2018), https://doi.org/10.1111/ejn.14149.

11   Richard J. Haier *et al.*, "Cortical glucose metabolic rate correlates of abstract reasoning and attention studied with positron emission tomography," *Intelligence* 12, no. 2 (1988/04/01/ 1988), https://doi.org/10.1016/0160-2896(88)90016-5; Beate Dunst *et al.*, "Neural efficiency as a function of task demands," *Intelligence* 42, no. 100 (2014/01// 2014), https://doi.org/10.1016/j.intell.2013.09.005.

12   In 2019, fewer than half of California's public school students that participated in the state's standardized test met grade level standards for language and only 40% of students met the math standards for their grade level. Sonali Kohli, "California Test Scores 2019: Half of Students Meet English Standards, Fewer Meet Math Standards.," *Los Angeles Times* (Los Angeles), October 9, 2019, accessed June 27, 2020, https://www.latimes.com/california/story/2019-10-09/california-school-test-scores-2019.

13   In 2017, according to the California Poverty Measure (CPM), a joint research effort byPPIC and the Stanford Center on Poverty and Inequality, a comprehensive approach to gauging poverty in California that accounts for the cost of living and a range of family needs and resources, finds that children in Californians experience the highest rates of poverty (19.3%) and79.6% of poor Californians lived in families with at least one working adult (excluding families of only adults age 65 and older). Public Policy Institute of California, "Poverty in California," updated November 12, 2019, accessed 6/24/2020, https://www.ppic.org/publication/poverty-in-california/..

14   Candace Cortiella and Sheldon H Horowitz, "The state of learning disabilities: Facts,trends and emerging issues," *New York: National Center for Learning Disabilities* 25 (2014).

15   Edward Lorenz, "Predictability: does the flap of a butterfly's wing in Brazil set off atornado in Texas?" (paper presented at the 139th meeting of the American Association for theAdvancement of Science, Washington, D.C., December 29, 1972).

16   John Louis Haney, *The name of William Shakespeare; A Study in Orthography* (NewYork: AMS Press, 1973).

17   Brian Vickers, *Shakespeare, Co-Author: A Historical Study of Five CollaborativePlays* (Oxford ; New York: Oxford University Press, 2002). .

18   Quantifying the prevalence of "giftedness" naturally depends on how the term is defined. According to the National Association for Gifted Children, "many consider children who are in the top 10 percent in relation to a national and/or local norm to be a good guide for identification and services." National Association for Gifted Children "What Is Giftedness?," NAGC.org, 2020, accessed 6/24/2020, https://www.nagc.org/resources-publications/resources/what-giftedness. Importantly, some traditional measures of intelligence are inherently biased. Modern understanding of giftedness considers many different factors and a variety of measures not considered by the creators of some older IQ tests who, in some instances, were promoting the IQtest as a tool of eugenics. Ludy T. Benjamin, Jr., "The birth of American intelligence testing," *Monitor on Psychology*, 2008, http://www.apa.org/monitor/2009/01/assessment. Moreover, identifying gifted students implicates issues of racial equality, justice, and access to educational opportunity. A 2016 study has shown that a Black student is three times more likely to be identified as "gifted" when the student's teacher is also Black. Jason A. Grissom and ChristopherRedding, "Discretion

and Disproportionality:Explaining the Underrepresentation of High-Achieving Students of Color in Gifted Programs," *AERA Open* 2, no. 1 (2016), https://doi.org/10.1177/2332858415622175. For a recent guide to addressing racial equity issues in the gifted community, please see *Bright, Talented, and Black: A Guide for Families of Black Gifted Learners* (2nd Edition), by Joy Lawson Davis, Ed.D, available from Gifted Unlimited, LLC.

19   Melissa L Danielson *et al.*, "Prevalence of parent-reported ADHD diagnosis and associated treatment among US children and adolescents, 2016," *Journal of Clinical Child &Adolescent Psychology* 47, no. 2 (2018).

20   Matthew J. Maenner *et al.*, "Prevalence of Autism Spectrum Disorder Among ChildrenAged 8 Years -Autism and Developmental Disabilities Monitoring Network, 11 Sites, United States, 2016," *Morbidity and Mortality Weekly Report (MMWR) Surveillance Summaries* 69, no. 4 (Mar 27 2020), https://doi.org/10.15585/mmwr.ss6904a1.

21   Definitional questions make it challenging to determine the precise number of those considered "dyslexic." *See* Tim Miles, "Some problems in determining the prevalence of dyslexia," *Electronic Journal in Educational Psychology* 2 (10/01 2004).

22   Virginia Wise Berninger and Beverly J. Wolf, *Teaching Students with Dyslexia and Dysgraphia: Lessons from Teaching and Science* (Baltimore: Paul H. Brookes Pub. Co., 2009). Onesurvey found dysgraphia in 22% of sixth-graders screened. Marielza Regina Ismael Martins *et al.*, "Screening for Motor Dysgraphia in Public Schools," *Jornal de Pediatria* 89, no. 1 (January 1, 2013), https://doi.org/10.1016/j.jped.2013.02.011.

23   National Institute of Mental Health, "NIMH » Major Depression," *National Institute of Health*, 2019, accessed 6/24/2020, https://www.nimh.nih.gov/health/statistics/major-depression.shtml.

24   Ruth I. Karpinski *et al.*, "High intelligence: A risk factor for psychological andphysiological overexcitabilities," *Intelligence* 66 (Jan 1, 2018), https://doi.org/10.1016/j.intell.2017.09.001.

25   Cantor *et al.*, "Malleability, plasticity, and individuality: How children learn anddevelop in context."

Chapter 3

1   Ulric Neisser *et al.*, "Intelligence: Knowns and unknowns," *American Psychologist* 51, no. 2 (1996), https://doi.org/10.1037/0003-066X.51.2.77.

2   Raymond B. Cattell, *Abilities : Their Structure, Growth, and Action* (Boston,: HoughtonMifflin, 1971).

3   Arthur W. Toga and Paul M. Thompson, "Genetics of brain structure and intelligence,"*Annual Review of Neuroscience* 28 (2005), https://doi.org/10.1146/annurev.neuro.28.061604.135655.

4   Howard E. Gardner, *Frames of Mind : The Theory of Multiple Intelligences.* 1st ed.(New York: Basic Books. 1983).

5   Howard E. Gardner, *Intelligence Reframed: Multiple Intelligences for the 21st Century.*(New York: Basic Books 1999).

6   Carlo Cerruti, "Building a functional multiple intelligences theory to advance educational neuroscience," *Frontiers in Psychology* 4 (2013), https://doi.org/10.3389/fpsyg.2013.00950.

7   Howard E. Gardner, "The components of MI." *MI Oasis* [Website.] https://www.multipleintelligencesoasis.org/the-components-of-mi. Accessed Sept 3 2020.

8   Marian Cleeves Diamond, *Enriching Heredity : The Impact of the Environment on theAnatomy of the Brain* (New York, London: Free Press; Collier Macmillan, 1988).

9   William T. Greenough, Fred R. Volkmar, and Janice M. Juraska, "Effects of rearing complexity on dendritic branching in frontolateral and temporal cortex of the rat," *Experimental Neurology* 41, no. 2 (Nov 1973), https://doi.org/10.1016/0014-4886(73)90278-1. Diamond, *Enriching heredity.*

10   Gilles Gignac, Philip A. Vernon, John C. Wickett, "Factors influencing the relationship between brain size and intelligence," In *The Scientific Study of General Intelligence:Tribute to Arthur R. Jensen,* edited by Nyborg H, editor. (Oxford; Pergamon, 2003) https://doi.org/10.1016/B978-008043793-4/50042-8; Daniëlle Posthuma, "The association between brain volume and intelligence is of genetic origin." *Nature Neuroscience.* 2002;5:83–84. https://doi.org/10.1038/nn0202-83; Yu Yong Choi, *et al.*, "Multiple bases of human intelligence revealed by cortical thickness and neural activation," *Journal of Neuroscience.* 2008 Oct 8;28(41):10323-9. https://doi.org/10.1523/JNEUROSCI.3259-08.2008"

11 Paul M. Thompson, *et al.*, "Genetic influences on brain structure," *Nature Neuroscience.* 2001Dec;4(12):1253-8.

12 osthuma, "The association between brain volume and intelligence is of genetic origin."; Adolf Pfefferbaum, Edith V. Sullivan, Dorit Carmelli, "Genetic regulation of regionalmicrostructure of the corpus callosum in late life," *Neuroreport.* (Jun 13 2001);12(8):1677-81. https://doi.org/10.1097/00001756-200106130-00032.

13 Michael McDaniel, "Big-brained people are smarter: A meta-analysis of the relationship between in vivo brain volume and intelligence," *Intelligence* (July-Aug 2005) 33.337-346. https://doi.org/10.1016/j.intell.2004.11.005.

14 Nancy C. Andreasen, *et al.*. "Intelligence and brain structure in normal individuals," *Am J Psychiatry.* (Jan 1993);150(1):130-4, https://doi.org/10.1176/appi.ajp.2015.15060709; Marko Wilke M, *et al.*, "Bright spots: correlations of gray matter volume with IQ in a normal pediatric population," *Neuroimage.* (Sept 2003);20(1):202-15, https://doi.org/10.1016/s1053-8119(03)00199-x; Richard J. Haier, *et al.*, "Structural brain variation and general intelligence," *Neuroimage* 23(1) (Sept 2004):425-33, https://doi.org/10.1016/j.neuroimage.2004.04.025; Choi,"Multiple bases of human intelligence revealed by cortical thickness and neural activation."

15 Philip Shaw *et al.*, "Neurodevelopmental trajectories of the human cerebral cortex," *Journal of Neuroscience* 28, no. 14 (Apr 2008), https://doi.org/10.1523/JNEUROSCI.5309-07.2008.

16 Mariam Arain, *et al.* "Maturation of the adolescent brain." *Neuropsychiatric Disease and Treatment* vol. 9 (2013): 449-61. https://doi.org/10.2147/NDT.S39776.

17 Shaw, *et al.*, "Intellectual ability and cortical development in children andadolescents."

18 Manuel Desco *et al.*, "Mathematically gifted adolescents use more extensive and more bilateral areas of the fronto-parietal network than controls during executive functioning and fluidreasoning tasks," *NeuroImage* 57, no. 1 (Jul 1 2011), https://doi.org/10.1016/j.neuroimage.2011.03.063.

19 John G. Geake, and Peter C. Hansen. "Neural correlates of intelligence as revealed byfMRI of fluid analogies." *NeuroImage* vol. 26,2 (2005): 555-64. https://doi.org/10.1016/j.neuroimage.2005.01.035.

20   Flora M. Vaccarino, and Karen Müller Smith. "Increased brain size in autism—what it will take to solve a mystery." *Biological psychiatry* vol. 66,4 (2009): 313-5. https://doi.org/10.1016/j.biopsych.2009.06.013.

21   Rebecca McKavanagh, *et al.* "Wider minicolumns in autism: a neural basis for altered processing?." *Brain : A Journal Of Neurology* vol. 138,Pt 7 (2015): 2034-45. https://doi.org/10.1093/brain/awv110; Manuel F Casanova, *et al.* "Neuronal density and architecture (Gray Level Index) in the brains of autistic patients," *Journal of Child Neurology* vol. 17,7 (2002): 515-21. https://doi.org/10.1177/088307380201700708.

22   Erhan Genç, *et al.* "Diffusion markers of dendritic density and arborization in gray matter predict differences in intelligence." *Nature Communications* vol. 9,1 1905. (May 15 2018), https://doi.org/10.1038/s41467-018-04268-8.

23   Edward M. Miller, "Intelligence and brain myelination – A hypothesis," *Personality and Individual Differences* 17(6) (1994):803–32, https://doi.org/10.1016/0191-8869(94)90049-3; Francisco Aboitiz, "Brain connections: interhemispheric fiber systems and anatomical brain asymmetries in humans," *Biological research* vol. 25,2 (1992): 51-61; Geo H. Bishop, Jeanne M. Smith, "The size of nerve fibers supplying cerebral cortex," *Experimental Neurology* 59 (1964):483–501 https://doi.org/10.1016/0014-4886(64)90056-1; Dag Alnæs, *et al.* "Association of Heritable Cognitive Ability and Psychopathology With White Matter Properties in Children and Adolescents." *JAMA Psychiatry* vol. 75,3 (2018): 287-295, https://doi.org/10.1001/jamapsychiatry.2017.4277; Yu Yong Choi, *et al.* "Multiple bases of human intelligence revealed by cortical thickness and neural activation." *The Journal of Neuroscience : the Official Journal of the Society for Neuroscience* vol. 28,41 (2008): 10323-9, https://doi.org/10.1523/JNEUROSCI.3259-08.2008; Rex E Jung, and Richard J Haier. "The Parieto-Frontal Integration Theory (P-FIT) of intelligence: converging neuroimaging evidence." *The Behavioral and Brain Sciences* vol. 30,2 (2007): 135-54; discussion 154-87, https://doi.org/10.1017/S0140525X07001185.

24   Sandra Hale, Michelle D. Bronik, and Astrid F. Fry, "Verbal and spatial working memory in school-age children: developmental differences in susceptibility to interference," *Developmental Psychology* 33(2) (1997):364-371. https://doi.org/10.1037//0012-1649.33.2.364; Sandra Hale, Joel Myerson, and David Wagstaff, "General slowing of nonverbal information processing: evidence for a power law." *Journal of Gerontology* vol. 42,2 (1987): 131-6. https://doi.org/10.1093/

geronj/42.2.131; George Bartzokis, "Age-related myelin breakdown: a developmental model of cognitive decline and Alzheimer's disease." *Neurobiology of Aging* vol. 25,1 (2004): 5-18; author reply 49-62. https:// doi.org/10.1016/j.neurobiolaging.2003.03.001; Stuart J. Ritchie, *et al.* "Coupled changes in brain white matter microstructure and fluid intelligence in later life." *The Journal of Neuroscience : The Official Journal of the Society for Neuroscience* vol. 35,22 (2015): 8672-82. https://doi. org/10.1523/JNEUROSCI.0862-15.2015.

25 Vincent J Schmithorst, *et al.* "Cognitive functions correlate with white matter architecture in a normal pediatric population: a diffusion tensor MRI study." *Human Brain Mapping* vol. 26,2 (2005): 139-47. https:// doi.org/10.1002/hbm.20149; Vincent J Schmithorst, "Developmental sex differences in the relation of neuroanatomical connectivity to intelligence,"*Intelligence.* 2009 Mar;37(2):164-173; https://doi.org/10.1016/j. intell.2008.07.001; Francisco J Navas-Sánchez, *et al.*, "White matter microstructure correlates of mathematical giftedness and intelligence quotient." *Human Brain Mapping* vol. 35,6 (2014): 2619-31. https:// doi.org/10.1002/hbm.22355.

26 Lars Penke, *et al.* "Brain white matter tract integrity as a neural foundation for generalintelligence." *Molecular Psychiatry* vol. 17,10 (2012): 1026-30. https://doi.org/10.1038/mp.2012.66.

27 Michael W. O'Boyle, *et al.* "Mathematically gifted male adolescents activate a unique brain network during mental rotation." *Brain Research. Cognitive Brain Research* vol. 25,2 (2005): 583-7. https://doi. org/10.1016/j.cogbrainres.2005.08.004; Kun Ho Lee, *et al.* "Neural correlates of superior intelligence: stronger recruitment of posterior parietal cortex." vol. 29,2 (2006): 578-86. https://doi.org/10.1016/j. neuroimage.2005.07.036; Li Zhang, *et al.*, "Optimized Gamma Synchronization Enhances Functional Binding of Fronto-Parietal Cortices in Mathematically Gifted Adolescents during Deductive Reasoning." *Frontiers in Human Neuroscience* vol. 8 430. 11 Jun. 2014, https://doi.org/10.3389/fnhum.2014.00430.

28 Desco *et al.*, "Mathematically gifted adolescents use more extensive and more bilateralareas of the fronto-parietal network than controls during executive functioning and fluid reasoning tasks."

29 Navas-Sánchez, *et al.*, "White matter microstructure correlates of mathematicalgiftedness and intelligence quotient."

30   Qi-Yong Gong, *et al.* "Voxel-based morphometry and stereology provide convergentevidence of the importance of medial prefrontal cortex for fluid intelligence in healthy adults."*NeuroImage* vol. 25,4 (2005): 1175-86. https://doi.org/10.1016/j.neuroimage.2004.12.044.

31   James T. Webb, Edward R. Amend, and Paul Beljan. *Misdiagnosis and Dual Diagnoses of Gifted Children and Adults : ADHD, bipolar, OCD, Asperger's, depression, and other disorders*, Second edition. ed. (Tucson,AZ: Great Potential Press, Inc., 2016).; Karpinski *et al.*, "High intelligence: A risk factor for psychological and physiological overexcitabilities."; Susan Daniels and Michael M. Piechowski, *Living with Intensity : Emotional Development of Gifted Children, Adolescents, and Adults* (Scottsdale, AZ: Great Potential Press, 2009).

32   Chunshui Yu, *et al.* "White matter tract integrity and intelligence in patients withmental retardation and healthy adults." *NeuroImage* vol. 40,4 (2008): 1533-41. https://doi.org/10.1016/j.neuroimage.2008.01.063.

33   Oishi, Kenichi *et al.* "Critical role of the right uncinate fasciculus in emotional empathy." Annals of neurology vol. 77,1 (2015): 68-74. https://doi.org/10.1002/ana.24300.

34   Kyongsik Yun, *et al.* "Mathematically gifted adolescents have deficiencies in socialvaluation and mentalization." *PloS One* vol. 6,4 e18224. 4 Apr. 2011, https://doi.org/10.1371/journal.pone.0018224.

35   Karpinski *et al.*, "High intelligence: A risk factor for psychological and physiologicaloverexcitabilities."

36   Roger E. Beaty, *et al.* "Robust prediction of individual creative ability from brain functional connectivity." *Proceedings of the National Academy of Sciences of the United Statesof America* vol. 115,5 (2018): 1087-1092. https://doi.org/10.1073/pnas.1713532115.

37   Andreas Horn, *et al.* "The structural-functional connectome and the default modenetwork of the human brain." *NeuroImage* vol. 102 Pt 1 (2014): 142-51. https://doi.org/10.1016/j.neuroimage.2013.09.069.

38   Zoltán Janka, "A mentális rugalmasság idegtudománya" [Neuroscience of mental flexibility], [Article in Hu] *Orvosi hetilap* [Hungarian Medical Journal] 158, no. 45 (Nov 2017), https://doi.org/10.1556/650.2017.30906.

39   Roger E. Beaty, *et al.* "Default and Executive Network Coupling Supports CreativeIdea Production," *Scientific Reports* vol. 5 10964 (17 Jun. 2015), https://doi.org/10.1038/srep10964.

40   Adele Diamond, "Executive functions," *Annual Review of Psychology* vol. 64 (2013): 135-68. https://doi.org/10.1146/annurev-psych-113011-143750.

41   Beaty *et al.*, "Robust prediction of individual creative ability from brain functionalconnectivity."

Chapter 4

1   Roianne R. Ahn, *et al.* "Prevalence of parents' perceptions of sensory processing disorders among kindergarten children." *The American Journal of Occupational Therapy : Official Publication of the American Occupational Therapy Association* vol. 58,3 (2004): 287-93. https://doi.org/10.5014/ajot.58.3.287.

2   Douglas R Gere, *et al.* "Sensory sensitivities of gifted children." *The American Journal of Occupational Therapy : Official Publication of the American Occupational Therapy Association* vol. 63,3 (2009): 288-95; discussion 296-300. https://doi.org/10.5014/ajot.63.3.288.

3   Tongran Liu, *et al.*, "Neural mechanisms of auditory sensory processing in children withhigh intelligence," *Neuroreport,* 18(15) (2007):1571-5, https://doi.org/10.1097/wnr.0b013e3282ef7640.

4   Cassandra D Gould van Praag, *et al.* "Mind-wandering and alterations to default mode network connectivity when listening to naturalistic versus artificial sounds." *Scientific Reports* vol. 7 45273. 27 Mar. 2017, https://doi.org/10.1038/srep45273.

5   Gould van Praag, *et al.*, "Mind-wandering and alterations to default mode networkconnectivity when listening to naturalistic versus artificial sounds."

6   Director-General for Health and Consumers, European Commission "Light Sensitivity," Scientific Committee on Emerging and Newly Identified Health Risks" (2008): 26–27. accessed 6/24/2020 from http://ec.europa.eu/health/ph_risk/committees/04_scenihr/docs/scenihr_o_019.pdf.

7   Kathleen B Digre, and K C Brennan. "Shedding light on photophobia." *Journal ofNeuro-Ophthalmology : The Official Journal of the North American Neuro-OphthalmologySociety* vol. 32,1 (2012): 68-81. https://doi.org/10.1097/WNO.0b013e3182474548.

8   Mikki Boswell *et al.*, "Fluorescent Light Incites a Conserved Immune and InflammatoryGenetic Response within Vertebrate Organs (Danio

Rerio, Oryzias Latipes and Mus Musculus),"*Genes (Basel)* 10, no. 4 (Apr 3, 2019), https://doi.org/10.3390/genes10040271.

9　Milena Razuk, *et al.* "Effect of colored filters on reading capabilities in dyslexicchildren." *Research in Developmental Disabilities* vol. 83 (2018): 1-7. https://doi.org/10.1016/j.ridd.2018.07.006.

10　Christopher W. Tyler, "Evidence That Leonardo da Vinci Had Strabismus," *JAMAOphthalmol.* 2019;137(1):82–86. https://doi.org/10.1001/jamaophthalmol.2018.3833.

11　Webb, *et al.*, *Misdiagnosis and Dual Diagnoses of Gifted Children and Adults.*

12　Webb, et *al.*, *Misdiagnosis and Dual Diagnoses of Gifted Children and Adults.*

13　Gere, *et al.* "Sensory sensitivities of gifted children."

14　Eva-María Navarrete-Muñoz *et al.*, "Association between Adherence to the Antioxidant-Rich Mediterranean Diet and Sensory Processing Profile in School-Aged Children:The Spanish Cross-Sectional InProS Project," *Nutrients* 11, no. 5 (2019), https://doi.org/10.3390/nu11051007.

15　Elizabeth I. Martin, *et al.* "The neurobiology of anxiety disorders: brain imaging, genetics, and psychoneuroendocrinology." *Clinics in Laboratory Medicine* vol. 30,4 (2010): 865-91. https://doi.org/10.1016/j.cll.2010.07.006.

16　Z. J. Lipowski, Sensory and Information Inputs Overload: Behavioral Effects. *Comprehensive Psychiatry*, 16(3) (1975): 199-221.

17　Hagar Gelbard-Sagiv, *et al.*, "Noradrenaline Modulates Visual Perception and LateVisually Evoked Activity." *Current Biology : CB* vol. 28,14 (2018): 2239-2249.e6. https://doi.org/10.1016/j.cub.2018.05.051.

18　Taylor A Faber, Frances E. Kuo. "Is contact with nature important for healthy child development? State of the evidence." In: Spencer C, Blades M, editors. *Children and Their Environments: Learning, Using and Designing Spaces.* Cambridge, UK: Cambridge University Press; 2006. pp. 124–140; Ingunn Fjørtoft, "The Natural Environment as a Playground for Children: The Impact of Outdoor Play Activities in Pre-Primary School Children." *Early Childhood Education Journal* 29 (2001): 111–117 https://doi.org/10.1023/A:1012576913074.

19　Connie X Wang, *et al.* "Transduction of the Geomagnetic Field as Evidenced fromalpha-Band Activity in the Human Brain." *eNeuro* vol.

6,2 ENEURO.0483-18.2019. 26 Apr.2019, https://doi.org/10.1523/ENEURO.0483-18.2019.

Chapter 5

1 Deepak Chopra, "Why meditate?" (March 5, 2017) accessed 6/24/2020 fromwww.deepakchopra.com/blog/article/4701 .

2 Brian Bruya, and Yi-Yuan Tang. "Is Attention Really Effort? Revisiting Daniel Kahneman's Influential 1973 Book *Attention and Effort.*" *Frontiers in Psychology* vol. 9 1133.(Sep. 6 2018), https://doi.org/10.3389/fpsyg.2018.01133.

3 Marianne Cumella Reddan, *et al.* "Attenuating Neural Threat Expression with Imagination." *Neuron* vol. 100,4 (2018): 994-1005.e4. https://doi.org/10.1016/j.neuron.2018.10.047.

4 Jill Bolte Taylor, *My Stroke of Insight: A Brain Scientist's Personal Journey.* (NewYork: Plume, 2009).

5 Paul Ekman, and W V Friesen. "Constants across cultures in the face and emotion." *Journal of Personality and Social Psychology* vol. 17,2 (1971): 124-9. https://doi.org/10.1037/h0030377.

6 Robert Plutchik, *Emotion: Theory, Research, and Experience: Vol. 1. Theories ofemotion,* 1, (New York: Academic, 1980).

7 Alan S Cowen, and Dacher Keltner. "Self-report captures 27 distinct categories of emotion bridged by continuous gradients." *Proceedings of the National Academy of Sciences ofthe United States of America* vol. 114,38 (2017): E7900-E7909. https://doi.org/10.1073/pnas.1702247114.

8 Philippe Verduyn, and Saskia Lavrijsen, "Which emotions last longest and why: The role of event importance and rumination." *Motivation and Emotion* 39, 119–127 (2015). https://doi.org/10.1007/s11031-014-9445-y.

9 Katharina Kircanski, *et al.* "Feelings into words: contributions of language to exposuretherapy." *Psychological Science* vol. 23,10 (2012): 1086-91. https://doi.org/10.1177/0956797612443830.

10 Ralf Schmälzle, *et al.* "Brain connectivity dynamics during social interaction reflect social network structure." *Proceedings of the National Academy of Sciences of the United Statesof America* vol. 114,20 (2017): 5153-5158. https://doi.org/10.1073/pnas.1616130114.

11   George Bush, Phan Luu and Pichael I. Posner, "Cognitive and emotional influences in anterior cingulate cortex." *Trends in Cognitive Sciences* vol. 4,6 (2000): 215-222. https://doi.org/10.1016/s1364-6613(00)01483-2.

12   Antonio Damasio and Gil B. Carvalho, "The nature of feelings: evolutionary and neurobiological origins," *Nature Reviews Neuroscience* 14, no. 2 (February 1, 2003) https://doi.org/10.1038/nrn3403.

13   Vittorio Gallese, *et al.*, "Action recognition in the premotor cortex," *Brain*, 119(2) (April 1996):593–609, https://doi.org/10.1093/brain/119.2.593.

14   Sourya Acharya, and Samarth Shukla. "Mirror neurons: Enigma of the metaphysical modular brain." *Journal of Natural Science, Biology, and Medicine vol.* 3,2 (2012): 118-24. https://doi.org/10.4103/0976-9668.101878; Hyeonjin Jeon, and Seung-Hwan Lee. "From Neurons to Social Beings: Short Review of the Mirror Neuron System Research and Its Socio-Psychological and Psychiatric Implications." *Clinical Psychopharmacology and Neuroscience : The Official Scientific Journal of the Korean College of Neuropsychopharmacology* vol. 16,1 (2018): 18-31. https://doi.org/10.9758/cpn.2018.16.1.18.

15   Christopher P. Said *et al.* "Brain systems for assessing the affective value of faces." *Philosophical Transactions of the Royal Society of London. Series B, Biological sciences* vol.366,1571 (2011): 1660-70. https://doi.org/10.1098/rstb.2010.0351.

16   Giacomo Rizzolatti and Maddalena Fabbri-Destro. "The mirror system and its role in social cognition." *Current Opinion in Neurobiology* vol. 18,2 (2008): 179-84. https://doi.org/10.1016/j.conb.2008.08.001.

17   Marco Iacoboni, *et al.* "Grasping the intentions of others with one's own mirror neuron system." *PLoS Biology* vol. 3,3 (2005): e79. https://doi.org/10.1371/journal.pbio.0030079.

18   Laurie Carr, *et al.* "Neural mechanisms of empathy in humans: a relay from neural systems for imitation to limbic areas." *Proceedings of the National Academy of Sciences of the United States of America* vol. 100,9 (2003): 5497-502. https://doi.org/10.1073/pnas.0935845100.

19   Bruno Wicker, *et al.* "Both of us disgusted in My insula: the common neural basis of seeing and feeling disgust." *Neuron* vol. 40,3 (2003): 655-64. https://doi.org/10.1016/s0896-6273(03)00679-2; Miiamaaria V Saarela, *et al.* "The compassionate brain: humans detect intensity of

pain from another's face." *Cerebral Cortex* (New York, N.Y.: 1991) vol. 17,1 (2007): 230-7. https://doi.org/10.1093/cercor/bhj141.

20 Webb, *et al.*, *Misdiagnosis and Dual Diagnoses of Gifted Children and Adults.*

21 Toshiyuki Ohtani, *et al.* "Exploring the neural substrates of attentional control and human intelligence: Diffusion tensor imaging of prefrontal white matter tractography in healthycognition." *Neuroscience* vol. 341 (2017): 52-60. https://doi.org/10.1016/j.neuroscience.2016.11.002.

22 Plutchik, *Emotion.*

23 Webb, *et al.*, *Misdiagnosis and Dual Diagnoses of Gifted Children and Adults.*

24 Glasser, "The Human Connectome Project's neuroimaging approach."

25 Alexander M Penney, Victoria C. Miedema, & Dwight Mazmanian, "Intelligence and emotional disorders: Is the worrying and ruminating mind a more intelligent mind?" *Personalityand Individual Differences,* (205) *74*, 90-93 https://doi.org/10.1016/j.paid.2014.10.005.

26 Webb, *et al.*, *Misdiagnosis and Dual Diagnoses of Gifted Children and Adults.*

27 Karpinski *et al.*, "High intelligence: A risk factor for psychological and physiologicaloverexcitabilities."

28 Schmälzle, *et al.* "Brain connectivity dynamics during social interaction reflect socialnetwork structure."

29 Yoni K. Ashar, *et al.* "Empathic Care and Distress: Predictive Brain Markers andDissociable Brain Systems." *Neuron* vol. 94,6 (2017): 1263-1273.e4. https://doi.org/10.1016/j.neuron.2017.05.014.

30 Davide Laneri, *et al.* "Mindfulness meditation regulates anterior insula activity duringempathy for social pain." *Human Brain Mapping* vol. 38,8 (2017): 4034-4046. https://doi.org/10.1002/hbm.23646.

31 Nicole A. Tetreault, "Kick start your compassionate brain." *Awesome Neuroscience* [Blog]. (June 29, 2017) Accessed 6/27/2020 from https://www.nicoletetreault.com/single-post/2017/06/29/Kick-start-your-compassionate-brain.

32 Verduyn and Lavrijsen, "Which emotions last longest and why: The role of eventimportance and rumination."

33   Michelle G. Newman, *et al.* "Worry and generalized anxiety disorder: a review and theoretical synthesis of evidence on nature, etiology, mechanisms, and treatment." *Annual Review of Clinical Psychology* vol. 9 (2013): 275-97. https://doi.org/10.1146/annurev-clinpsy-050212-185544.

34   National Institute of Mental Health. (2017, November) Any anxiety disorder. [Website.] Accessed 6/27/2020 from https://www.nimh.nih.gov/health/statistics/any-anxiety-disorder.shtml.

35   Harvard Medical School, "Data Table 1: Lifetime prevalence DSM-IV/WMH-CIDI disorders by sex and cohort." *National Comorbidity Survey (NCS)* (August 21 2017). Accessed 6/27/2020 from https://www.hcp.med.harvard.edu/ncs/index.php..

36   Ronald C. Kessler, *et al.* "Prevalence, severity, and comorbidity of 12-month DSM-IV disorders in the National Comorbidity Survey Replication." *Archives of General Psychiatry* vol. 62,6 (2005): 617-27. https://doi.org/10.1001/archpsyc.62.6.617.

37   National Institute of Mental Health. "Any anxiety disorder." [.

38   Song Qi, *et al.* "How cognitive and reactive fear circuits optimize escape decisions in humans." *Proceedings of the National Academy of Sciences of the United States of America* vol.115,12 (2018): 3186-3191. https://doi.org/10.1073/pnas.1712314115; Bowen J Fung, *et al.* "Slow escape decisions are swayed by trait anxiety." *Nature Human Behaviour* vol. 3,7 (2019): 702-708. https://doi.org/10.1038/s41562-019-0595-5.

39   Qi, "How cognitive and reactive fear circuits optimize escape decisions in humans."

40   Webb, *et al.*, *Misdiagnosis and Dual Diagnoses of Gifted Children and Adults.*

41   Karpinski *et al.*, "High intelligence: A risk factor for psychological and physiologicaloverexcitabilities."

42   Ohtani, "Exploring the neural substrates of attentional control and human intelligence."

43   Dario Grossi, *et al.* "Altered functional connectivity of interoception in illness anxiety disorder." *Cortex; A Journal Devoted to the Study of the Nervous System and Behavior* vol. 86 (2017): 22-32. https://doi.org/10.1016/j.cortex.2016.10.018.

44   Webb, *et al.*, *Misdiagnosis and Dual Diagnoses of Gifted Children and Adults;* Kazimerez Dąbrowski, and Michael M. Piechowski, M.M. (1977) *Theory of levels of emotionaldevelopment* (Vols. 1 & 2). Oceanside, NY: Dabor Science. (Out of print).

45   Nicole A. Tetreault, "Brain fingerprints." *Awesome Neuroscience* [Blog]. (April 14, 2017) Accessed 6/27/2020 from https://www.nicoletetreault. com/single-post/2017/04/14/Brain-Fingerprints.

46   Nicole A. Tetreault, "Kick start your compassionate brain."

47   Nicole A. Tetreault, N. "Three minute mindful breath." *Awesome Neuroscience* [Blog]. (April 14, 2017) Accessed 6/27/2020 from https://www.nicoletetreault.com/single-post/2017/04/14/Three-minute-mindful-breath.

48   Reddan, "Attenuating Neural Threat Expression with Imagination."

49   *Free Solo* [Motion Picture]. directed and produced by Elizabeth Chai Vasarhelyi and Jimmy Chin. (2018).United States: Little Monster Films, Itinerant Media, Parkes+MacDonald/Image Nation, National Geographic Documentary Films.

50   Bryce Donovan, "The Science of Risk: How a Neuroscientist and Professional Climber Learned from One Another." March 18, 2019. The Medical University of South Carolina. Accessed June 27, 2020. https://web.musc.edu/about/news-center/2019/03/18/how-a-neuro-scientist-and-professional-climber-learned-from-one-another.

51   Dena M. Bravata *et al.*, "Prevalence, Predictors, and Treatment of Impostor Syndrome: a Systematic Review," *Journal of General Internal Medicine* 35, no. 4 (April 1, 2020), https://doi.org/10.1007/s11606-019-05364-1.

52   Pauline Rose Clance and Suzanne Ament Imes, "The imposter phenom-enon in highachieving women: dynamics and therapeutic intervention." *Psychotherapy: Theory, Research and Practice.* 15(3) (1978): 241–247 https://doi.org/10.1037/h0086006; Pauline Rose Clance, *The Impostor Phenomenon: When Success Makes You Feel Like a Fake.* (Toronto: Bantam Books; 1985).

53   Rebecca L. Badawy *et al.*, "Are all impostors created equal? Exploring gender differences in the impostor phenomenon-performance link," *Personality and Individual Differences* 131 (September 1, 2018), https:// doi.org/10.1016/j.paid.2018.04.044,.

54   Amy J.C. Cuddy, *Presence: Bringing Your Boldest Self to Your Biggest Challenges* (New York: Little, Brown and Company; First Edition 2015).

55   Clance and Imes, " The imposter phenomenon in high achieving women: dynamics andtherapeutic intervention."

56   Jaruwan Sakulku, "The Impostor Phenomenon." *International Journal of Behavioral Science.* 6(1) (2011): 73–92, https://doi.org/10.14456/ijbs.2011.6.

57   Valeria Young, *The Secret Thoughts of Successful Women: Why Capable People Suffer from the Impostor Syndrome and How to Thrive in Spite of It.* (New York: Crown Business, 2011).

58   Chopra, "Why meditate?"

59   Gill Corkindale, G. "Overcoming Imposter Syndrome," *Harvard Business Review.* (May 7 2008). Accessed 6/27/2020 from https://hbr.org/2008/05/overcoming-imposter-syndrome; Webb,*et al.*, *Misdiagnosis and Dual Diagnoses of Gifted Children and Adults.*

60   Don E. Hamachek, "Psychodynamics of normal and neurotic perfectionism,"*Psychology: A Journal of Human Behavior*, 15(1) (1978):27–33, https://psycnet.apa.org/record/1979-08598-001.

61   Joachim Stoeber,and Kathleen Otto. "Positive conceptions of perfectionism: approaches, evidence, challenges." *Personality and Social Psychology Review : An Official Journal of the Society for Personality and Social Psychology, Inc* vol. 10,4 (2006): 295-319.https://doi.org/10.1207/s15327957pspr1004_2.

62   Randy O. Frost, Cathleen M. Lahart, and Robin Rosenblate, "The development of perfectionism: A study of daughters and their parents," *Cognitive Therapy and Research*, 15(6), (1991): 469–489, https://doi.org/10.1007/BF01175730.

63   P.L. Hewitt and G.L. Flett, " Perfectionism in the self and social contexts: Conceptualization, assessment, and association with psychopathology," *Journal of Personality and Social Psychology,* 60(3) (1991):456–470. https://doi.org/10.1037/0022-3514.60.3.456.

64   S toeber and Otto, "Positive Conceptions of Perfectionism: Approaches, Evidence,Challenges."

65   Wayne D. Parker, "Healthy perfectionism in the gifted," *Journal of Secondary Gifted Education, 11*(4), (Summer 2000):173+. https://doi.org/10.4219/jsge-2000-632.

66   Gordon L. Flett, Paul L. Hewitt and Dennis G. Dyck, "Self-oriented perfectionism, neuroticism and anxiety," *Personality and Individual Differences, 10*(7) (1989):731–735. https://doi.org/10.1016/0191-8869(89)90119-0; P.L. Hewitt, *et al.* "Validation of a measure of perfectionism." *Journal of Personality Assessment* vol. 53,1 (1989): 133-44. https://doi.org/10.1207/s15327752jpa5301_14; Deborah A. Thompson, Kathleen M. Berg, and Lisa A. Shatford, "The heterogeneity of bulimic symptomatology: Cognitive and behavioral dimensions," *International Journal of Eating Disorders, 6*(2) (1987): 215–234. https://doi.org/10.1002/1098-108X(198703)6:2<215::AID-EAT2260060206>3.0.CO;2-J.

67   National Institute of Mental Health, "Depression." [Website.] (2018, February)Accessed 6/24/2020 from https://www.nimh.nih.gov/health/topics/depression/index.shtml.

68   Stephanie G Cheung, *et al.* "Systematic Review of Gut Microbiota and Major Depression." *Frontiers in Psychiatry* vol. 10 34. (Feb. 11, 2019) https://doi.org/10.3389/fpsyt.2019.00034.

69   National Institute of Mental Health,"Depression."

70   John A. Sturgeon and Alex J. Zautra, "Social pain and physical pain: shared paths toresilience," *Pain Management.* 6(1) (2016):63-74. https://doi.org/10.2217/pmt.15.56.

71   Teresa M. Evans, *et al.* "Evidence for a mental health crisis in graduate education." *Nature Biotechnology* vol. 36,3 (2018): 282-284. https://doi.org/10.1038/nbt.4089.

72   Karpinski *et al.*, "High intelligence: A risk factor for psychological and physiologicaloverexcitabilities."

73   Heather L. Stuckey, and Jeremy Nobel. "The connection between art, healing, and public health: a review of current literature." *American Journal of Public Health* vol. 100,2 (2010): 254-63. https://doi.org/10.2105/AJPH.2008.156497.

74   National Centre Against Bullying, (n.d.) "Types of bullying." Alannah & Madeline Foundation. Accessed 6/24/2020 fromhttps://www.ncab.org.au/bullying-advice/bullying-for-parents/types-of-bullying/.

75   *Back to the Future.* [Motion Picture]. (1985). directed by Robert Zemeckis, written by Robert Zemeckis & Bob Gale; produced by Bob Gale and Neil Canton. United States: Amblin Entertainment & Universal Pictures.

76   Tracy Vaillancourt, Shelley Hymel, and Patricia McDougall, "The Biological Underpinnings of Peer Victimization: Understanding Why and How the Effects of Bullying Can Last a Lifetime," *Theory into Practice*. 52. (2013):241-248. https://doi.org/10.1080/00405841.2013.829726.

77   Vaillancourt, "The Biological Underpinnings of Peer Victimization."

78   Erin Burke Quinlan, *et al.*, "Peer victimization and its impact on adolescent brain development and psychopathology," *Molecular Psychiatry*, (Dec. 12 2018), https://doi.org/10.1038/s41380-018-0297-9.

79   Craig Haney, Curtis Banks, and Philip G. Zimbardo, "A study of prisoners and guardsin a simulated prison." *Naval Research Review*, 30 (1973): 4-17, https://www.researchgate.net/publication/235356446.

80   Yvon Delville, *et al.*, "Stress and the development of agonistic behavior in goldenhamsters," *Hormones and Behavior* vol. 44,3 (2003): 263-70. https://doi.org/10.1016/s0018-506x(03)00130-2.

81   Dieter Wolke, and Suzet Tanya Lereya. "Long-term effects of bullying." *Archives ofDisease in Childhood* vol. 100,9 (2015): 879-85. https://doi.org/10.1136/archdischild-2014-306667.

82   Schmälzle, *et al.* "Brain connectivity dynamics during social interaction reflect socialnetwork structure."

83   Damien Keown, *Buddhism: A Very Short Introduction*. (Oxford: Oxford University Press, 2013). pp. 50–52. .

84   Shinzen Young, "A pain-processing algorithm." [Pamphlet.] (November 29, 2010) accessed 6/24/2020 from https://www.shinzen.org/wp-content/uploads/2016/12/art_painprocessingalg.pdf.

85   Verduyn and Lavrijsen, "Which emotions last longest and why: The role of eventimportance and rumination. "

86   Robert A Emmons, and Michael E McCullough. "Counting blessings versus burdens: an experimental investigation of gratitude and subjective well-being in daily life." *Journal of Personality and Social Psychology* vol. 84,2 (2003): 377-89. https://doi.org/10.1037//0022-3514.84.2.377; Jeffrey J Froh, *et al.* "Counting blessings in early adolescents: an experimental study of gratitude and subjective well-being." *Journal of School Psychology* vol. 46,2 (2008): 213-33. https://doi.org/10.1016/j.jsp.2007.03.005.

87   Sunghyon Kyeong, *et al.*, "Effects of gratitude meditation on neural network functional connectivity and brain-heart coupling," *Scientific Reports* vol. 7,1 5058, (Jul. 11 2017), https://doi.org/10.1038/

s41598-017-05520-9; Roland Zahn, *et al.*, "The neural basis of human social values: evidence from functional MRI," *Cerebral Cortex* (New York, N.Y.: 1991) vol. 19,2 (2009): 276-83. https://doi.org/10.1093/cercor/bhn080.

88   Charles T. Taylor, Sonja Lyubomirsky, and Murray B Stein, "Upregulating the positiveaffect system in anxiety and depression: Outcomes of a positive activity intervention." *Depression and Anxiety* vol. 34,3 (2017): 267-280. https://doi.org/10.1002/da.22593.

89   Adam M. Grant, and Francesca Gino. "A little thanks goes a long way: Explaining why gratitude expressions motivate prosocial behavior." *Journal of Personality and Social Psychology* vol. 98,6 (2010): 946-55. https://doi.org/10.1037/a0017935.

Chapter 6

1   Chopra, "Why meditate?"

2   The study of attention, and the wide variety of theories around attention as understood in psychology are beyond the scope of this book. Elizabeth A. Styles, *The psychology of attention, 2nd ed*, The psychology of attention, 2nd ed., (New York, NY, US: Psychology Press,2006).

3   J. A. C. J. Bastiaansen, M. Thioux, and C. Keysers, "Evidence for mirror systems in emotions," Philosophical Transactions of the Royal Society of London. Series B, Biological Sciences 364, no. 1528 (2009), https://doi.org/10.1098/rstb.2009.0058.

4   Nitin Gogtay *et al.*, "Dynamic mapping of human cortical development during childhood through early adulthood," *Proceedings of the National Academy of Sciences of the United States of America* 101, no. 21 (2004), https://doi.org/10.1073/pnas.0402680101.

5   Danielson et al., "Prevalence of parent-reported ADHD diagnosis and associated treatment among US children and adolescents, 2016."

6   Philip Shaw et al., "Longitudinal mapping of cortical thickness and clinical outcome in children and adolescents with attention-deficit/hyperactivity disorder," Archives of General Psychiatry 63, no. 5 (2006); Janita Bralten *et al.*, "Voxel-based morphometry analysis reveals frontal brain differences in participants with ADHD and their unaffected siblings," *J Psychiatry Neurosci* 41, no. 4 (Jun 2016), https://doi.org/10.1503/jpn.140377.

7   Lisa A. Jacobson *et al.*, "Anomalous Brain Development Is Evident in Preschoolers With Attention-Deficit/Hyperactivity Disorder," *J*

Int Neuropsychol Soc 24, no. 6 (Jul 2018), https://doi.org/10.1017/s1355617718000103.

8   Martine Hoogman *et al.*, "Subcortical brain volume differences in participants with attention deficit hyperactivity disorder in children and adults: a cross-sectional mega-analysis," *Lancet Psychiatry* 4, no. 4 (Apr 2017), https://doi.org/10.1016/s2215-0366(17)30049-4.

9   Philip Shaw *et al.*, "Attention-deficit/hyperactivity disorder is characterized by a delay in cortical maturation," *Proceedings of the National Academy of Sciences* 104, no. 49 (2007).

10   D. L. Gilbert *et al.*, "Motor cortex inhibition: a marker of ADHD behavior and motor development in children," *Neurology* 76, no. 7 (Feb 15 2011), https://doi.org/10.1212/WNL.0b013e31820c2ebd.

11   Shaw *et al.*, "Neurodevelopmental trajectories of the human cerebral cortex."

12   Shaw *et al.*, "Neurodevelopmental trajectories of the human cerebral cortex."; Alberto Fernández-Jaén *et al.*, "Cortical thickness differences in the prefrontal cortex in children and adolescents with ADHD in relation to dopamine transporter (DAT1) genotype," *Journal of Psychiatric Research* 233, no. 3 (Sep 30 2015), https://doi.org/10.1016/j.pscychresns.2015.07.005.

13   Nancy L. Nussbaum, "ADHD and female specific concerns: a review of the literature and clinical implications," *Journal of Attention Disorders* 16, no. 2 (Feb 2012), https://doi.org/10.1177/1087054711416909.

14   Maria Moldavsky and Kapil Sayal, "Knowledge and attitudes about attention-deficit/hyperactivity disorder (ADHD) and its treatment: the views of children, adolescents, parents, teachers and healthcare professionals," *Current Psychiatry Reports* 15, no. 8 (Aug 2013), https://doi.org/10.1007/s11920-013-0377-0.

15   Lidia Yuknavitch (author) and Alex Brewer (illustrator), *The Misfit's Manifesto*, First TED books hardcover edition. ed., TED books, (New York: TED Books, Simon & Schuster, 2017).

16   Rapson Gomez *et al.*, "Gifted Children with ADHD: How Are They Different from Non-gifted Children with ADHD?," *International Journal of Mental Health and Addiction* (2019/08/26 2019), https://doi.org/10.1007/s11469-019-00125-x, https://doi.org/10.1007/s11469-019-00125-x.

17   Gilbert *et al.*, "Motor cortex inhibition: a marker of ADHD behavior and motordevelopment in children."

18   Katrina L Piercy *et al.*, "The physical activity guidelines for Americans," *Jama* 320,no. 19 (2018).

19   Timothy S. Church *et al.*, "Trends over 5 decades in U.S. occupation-related physicalactivity and their associations with obesity," *PLoS One* 6, no. 5 (2011), https://doi.org/10.1371/journal.pone.0019657.

20   Brian A. Primack *et al.*, "Use of multiple social media platforms and symptoms of depression and anxiety: A nationally-representative study among U.S. young adults," *Computersin Human Behavior* 69 (April 1 2017), https://doi.org/10.1016/j.chb.2016.11.013.

21   Mike Allen, "Sean Parker Unloads on Facebook: 'God Only Knows What It's Doing to Our Children's Brains,'" *Axios*, (December 15, 2017), accessed 6/27/2020 from https://www.axios.com/sean-parker-unloads-on-facebook-2508036343.html.

22   Bethany Harris *et al.*, "Problematic Mobile Phone and Smartphone Use Scales: A Systematic Review," *Frontiers in Psychology* 11 (2020), https://doi.org/10.3389/fpsyg.2020.00672.

23   Adrian F https://doi.org/10.3758/s13414-017-1319-4. Ward *et al.*, "Brain drain: The mere presence of one's own smartphone reduces available cognitive capacity," *Journal of the Association for Consumer Research* 2, no. 2 (2017).

24   Kathleen S. Edwards and Myoungju Shin, "Media multitasking and implicit learning," *Atten Percept Psychophys* 79, no. 5 (Jul 2017), https://doi.org/10.3758/s13414-017-1319-4.

25   Aviad Hadar *et al.*, "Answering the missed call: Initial exploration of cognitive andelectrophysiological changes associated with smartphone use and abuse," *PLoS One* 12, no. 7 (2017), https://doi.org/10.1371/journal.pone.0180094.

26   AVIVA, 2017. "UK: Sun, Sea and Selfies: Has Social Media Killed the Holiday Postcard?" Aviva.Com. June 20, 2017. https://www.aviva.com/newsroom/news-releases/2017/06/uk-sun-sea-and-selfies-has-social-media-killed-the-holiday-postcard-17781/.

27   Hanna Krasnova *et al.*, "Research note—why following friends can hurt you: an exploratory investigation of the effects of envy on social

networking sites among college-ageusers," *Information Systems Research* 26, no. 3 (2015).

28   Harris Wittels, *Humblebrag : The Art of False Modesty*, 1st ed. (New York: GrandCentral Pub., 2012).

29   Alexandra Philipsen *et al.*, "Sleep in adults with attention-deficit/ hyperactivity disorder: a controlled polysomnographic study including spectral analysis of the sleep EEG," *Sleep* 28, no. 7 (2005).

30   Samuele Cortese, *et al.*, "Sleep and alertness in children with attention-deficit/hyperactivity disorder: a systematic review of the literature, *Sleep* 29(4) (2006):504-511.https://pubmed.ncbi.nlm.nih.gov/16676784/.

31   Katherine H. Peppers, *et al.*, "An Intervention to Promote Sleep and Reduce ADHDSymptoms," *Journal of Pediatric Health Care* 30, no. 6 (Nov-Dec 2016), https://doi.org/10.1016/j.pedhc.2016.07.008.

32   Michael K. Scullin, "The Eight Hour Sleep Challenge During Final Exams Week," *Teaching of Psychology* 46, no. 1 (2019), https://doi.org/10.1177/0098628318816142.

33   Dusan Kolar *et al.*, "Treatment of adults with attention-deficit/hyperactivity disorder," *Neuropsychiatric Disease and Treatment* 4, no. 2 (2008). Nora D Volkow *et al.*, "Evaluating dopamine reward pathway in ADHD: clinical implications," *The Journal of the American Medical Association* 302, no. 10 (2009).

34   Kenneth Blum *et al.*, "Attention-deficit-hyperactivity disorder and reward deficiencysyndrome," *Neuropsychiatric disease and treatment* 4 no. 5 (2008): 893-918. https://doi.org/10.2147/ndt.s2627.

35   Ana Ferreira *et al.*, "Inter-Patient Variability and Predictive Factors of Propofol Requirements and Estimated Concentrations for Loss of Consciousness And Recovery" *Journal of Neurosurgical Anesthesiology* 27 (2015) :260–261.

36   Sameer A. Zope and Rakesh A. Zope, "Sudarshan kriya yoga: Breathing for health," *International Journal of Yoga* 6, no. 1 (Jan 2013), https://doi.org/10.4103/0973-6131.105935.

Chapter 7

1   Leo Kanner, "Autistic disturbances of affective contact," *Nervous child* 2, no. 3 (1943).

2   Judith H. Miles, "Autism spectrum disorders—a genetics review," *Genet Med* 13, no. 4 (Apr 2011), https://doi.org/10.1097/GIM. 0b013e3181ff67ba.

3   American Psychiatric Association. and American Psychiatric Association. DSM-5 TaskForce., *Diagnostic and Statistical Manual of Mental Disorders : DSM-5*, 5th ed. (Washington, D.C.: American Psychiatric Association, 2013).

4   M. Rutter, "Incidence of autism spectrum disorders: changes over time and their meaning," *Acta Paediatr* 94, no. 1 (Jan 2005), https://doi. org/10.1111/j.1651-2227.2005.tb01779.x; Maenner, et al, "Prevalence of Autism Spectrum Disorder Among Children Aged 8 Years — Autism and Developmental Disabilities Monitoring Network."

5   Miles, "Autism spectrum disorders—a genetics review."

6   Susanna Danielsson *et al.*, "Epilepsy in young adults with autism: a prospective population-based follow-up study of 120 individuals diagnosed in childhood," *Epilepsia* 46, no. 6 (Jun 2005), https://doi.org/10.1111/ j.1528-1167.2005.57504.x; Susan R. Leekam *et al.*, "Describing the sensory abnormalities of children and adults with autism," *Journal of Autism and Developmental Disorders* 37, no. 5 (May 2007), https://doi. org/10.1007/s10803-006-0218-7; Joel A. Vilensky, Antonio R. Damasio, Ralph G. Maurer, "Gait disturbances in patients with autistic behavior: a preliminary study," *Archives of neurology.* 38, no. 10 (Oct 1981), https:// doi.org/10.1001/archneur.1981.00510100074013; Karoly Horvath *et al.*, "Gastrointestinal abnormalities in children with autistic disorder," *The Journal of Pediatrics* 135, no. 5 (Nov 1999), https://doi.org/10.1016/ s0022-3476(99)70052-1; Laura de Magistris *et al.*, "Alterations of the intestinal barrier in patients with autism spectrum disorders and in their first-degree relatives," *Journal of Pediatric Gastroenterology and Nutrition* 51, no. 4 (Oct 2010), https://doi.org/10.1097/MPG.0b013e3181dcc4a5.

7   Danielsson *et al.*, "Epilepsy in young adults with autism: a prospective population-based follow-up study of 120 individuals diagnosed in childhood."

8   Jules R. Bemporad, "Adult recollections of a formerly autistic child," *Journal of Autism and Developmental Disorders* 9, no. 2 (Jun 1979), https://doi.org/10.1007/bf01531533; Temple Grandin and Margaret Scariano, *Emergence, Labeled Autistic*, 1st ed. (Novato, CA: Arena Press, 1986). Laura Cesaroni and Malcolm Garber, "Exploring the experience of autism through firsthand accounts," *Journal of Autism*

and Developmental Disorders 21, no. 3 (1991/09/011991), https://doi. org/10.1007/BF02207327.

9   Leekam *et al.*, "Describing the sensory abnormalities of children and adults withautism."

10   Vilensky, Damasio, and Maurer, "Gait disturbances in patients with autistic behavior: apreliminary study"; Margaret L. Bauman and Thomas L. Kemper, "Neuroanatomic observations of the brain in autism: a review and future directions," *International Journal of Developmental Neuroscience* 23, no. 2-3 (Apr-May 2005), https://doi.org/10.1016/j. ijdevneu.2004.09.006; Cynthia A. Molloy, Kim N. Dietrich and Amit Bhattacharya, "Postural stability in children with autism spectrum disorder," *Journal of Autism and Developmental Disorders* 33, no. 6 (Dec 2003), https://doi.org/10.1023/b:jadd.0000006001.00667.4c.

11   Henry Markram, Tania Rinaldi and Kamila Markram, "The intense world syndrome—an alternative hypothesis for autism," *Frontiers in Neuroscience* 1, no. 1 (Nov 2007), https://doi.org/10.3389/neuro. 01.1.1.006.2007.

12   Kamila Markram and Henry Markram, "The intense world theory – a unifying theory ofthe neurobiology of autism," *Frontiers in Human Neuroscience* 4 (2010), https://doi.org/10.3389/fnhum.2010.00224.

13   Kanner, "Autistic disturbances of affective contact."

14   Simon Baron-Cohen, "Does Autism Occur More Often in Families of Physicists,Engineers, and Mathematicians?," *Autism* 2, no. 3 (1998), https://doi.org/10.1177/1362361398023008.

15   Fabienne Samson *et al.*, "Enhanced visual functioning in autism: an ALE meta-analysis," *Human Brain Mapping* 33, no. 7 (Jul 2012), https://doi. org/10.1002/hbm.21307.

16   I. Soulières *et al.*, "Enhanced mental image mapping in autism," *Neuropsychologia* 49, no. 5 (Apr 2011), https://doi.org/10.1016/j. neuropsychologia.2011.01.027.

17   Zsuzsa Kaldy *et al.*, "The Mechanisms Underlying the ASD Advantage in Visual Search," *Journal of Autism and Developmental Disorders* 46, no. 5 (2016), https://doi.org/10.1007/s10803-013-1957-x; Andrée-Anne S. Meilleur, Patricia Jelenic, andLaurent Mottron, "Prevalence of clinically and empirically defined talents and strengths in autism," *Journal of Autism and Developmental Disorders* 45, no. 5 (2015), https://doi. org/10.1007/s10803-014-2296-2.

18   Simon Baron-Cohen, and J Hammer. "Parents of Children with Asperger Syndrome: What is the Cognitive Phenotype?." *Journal of Cognitive Neuroscience* vol. 9,4 (1997): 548-54.https://doi.org/10.1162/jocn.1997.9.4.548.

19   S. Baron-Cohen, "The autistic child's theory of mind: a case of specific developmentaldelay," *Journal of Child Psychology and Psychiatry* 30, no. 2 (Mar 1989), https://doi.org/10.1111/j.1469-7610.1989.tb00241.x.

20   M. A. Gernsbacher and M. Yergeau, "Empirical Failures of the Claim That Autistic People Lack a Theory of Mind," *Archives of Scientific Psychology* 7, no. 1 (2019), https://doi.org/10.1037/arc0000067.

21   Barry Wright, Penny Spikins, and Hannah Pearson, "Should Autism SpectrumConditions Be Characterised in a More Positive Way in Our Modern World?," *Medicina (Kaunas, Lithuania)* 56, no. 5 (2020), https://doi.org/10.3390/medicina56050233.

22   Dr. Michael Postma, *The Inconvenient Student: Critical Issues in the Identification andEducation of Twice-Exceptional Students* (Perfect Paperback, January 1, 2017).

23   Ron Suskind, *Life, Animated : A Story of Sidekicks, Heroes, and Autism*, First edition.ed. (New York: Kingswell, 2014).

24   Erna Imperatore Blanche, *et al.*, "Proprioceptive processing difficulties among children with autism spectrum disorders and developmental disabilities," *The American Journal of Occupational Therapy* 66, no. 5 (Sep-Oct 2012), https://doi.org/10.5014/ajot.2012.004234.

25   Giuseppe Cossu *et al.*, "Motor representation of actions in children with autism," *PLoS One* 7, no. 9 (2012), https://doi.org/10.1371/journal.pone.0044779.

26   Leonardo Fogassi and Pier Francesco Ferrari, "Mirror systems," *Wiley Interdisciplinary Reviews -Cognitive Science* 2, no. 1 (Jan 2011), https://doi.org/10.1002/wcs.89.

27   ANCA Consulting Inc. "Mission Statement – Naturally Autistic ANCA." 2010. *NaturallyAutistic.com.* January 21, 2010. https://www.naturally-autistic.com/founders/297-2/.

28   Viola Spolin, *Improvisation for the Theater; A Handbook of Teaching and Directing Techniques* (Evanston, Ill.: Northwestern University Press, 1963).

29 Clayton D. Drinko, "The Improv Paradigm: Three Principles that Spur Creativity in the Classroom," in *Creativity in Theatre: Theory and Action in Theatre/Drama Education*, ed. Suzanne Burgoyne (Cham: Springer International Publishing, 2018).

30 Rémi Radel *et al.*, "The role of (dis)inhibition in creativity: Decreased inhibition improves idea generation," *Cognition* 134 (2015/01/01/ 2015), https://doi.org/10.1016/j.cognition.2014.09.001.

31 Martin Norgaard, Laura A. Stambaugh, and Heston McCranie, "The Effect of Jazz Improvisation Instruction on Measures of Executive Function in Middle School Band Students," *Journal of Research in Music Education* 67, no. 3 (2019), https://doi.org/10.1177/0022429419863038.

32 Roger E. Beaty *et al.*, "Default and Executive Network Coupling Supports Creative Idea Production," *Sci Rep* 5 (Jun 17, 2015), https://doi.org/10.1038/srep10964.

33 Atsumichi Tachibana *et al.*, "Prefrontal activation related to spontaneous creativity with rock music improvisation: A functional near-infrared spectroscopy study," *Scientific Reports* 9, no. 1 (2019/11/05 2019), https://doi.org/10.1038/s41598-019-52348-6; Siyuan Liu *et al.*, "Neural Correlates of Lyrical Improvisation: An fMRI Study of Free-style Rap," *Scientific Reports* 2, no. 1 (2012/11/15 2012), https://doi.org/10.1038/srep00834; Manish Saggar *et al.*, "Pictionary-based fMRI paradigm to study the neural correlates of spontaneous improvisation and figural creativity," *Scientific Reports* 5, no. 1 (2015/05/28 2015), https://doi.org/10.1038/srep10894; Mónica López-González, "Cognitive psychology meets art: exploring creativity, language, and emotion through live musical improvisation in film and theatre," vol. 9394, *SPIE/IS&T Electronic Imaging*, (SPIE, 2015). https://doi.org/10.1117/12.2083880; Bhim M. Adhikari *et al.*, "The Brain Network Underpinning Novel Melody Creation," *Brain Connectivity* 6, no. 10 (Dec 2016), https://doi.org/10.1089/brain.2016.0453; Norgaard, Stambaugh, and McCranie, "The Effect of Jazz Improvisation Instruction on Measures of Executive Function in Middle School Band Students."; Sarah E. M. Faber and Anthony R. McIntosh, "Towards a standard model of musical improvisation," *European Journal of Neuroscience* 51, no. 3 (2020), https://doi.org/10.1111/ejn.14567.

34 Xiao D. Yue, Chun-Lok Leung, and Neelam A. Hiranandani, "Adult Playfulness, Humor Styles, and Subjective Happiness," *Psychological Reports* 119, no. 3 (Dec 2016), https://doi.org/10.1177/0033294116662842.

35 Sandra Manninen *et al.*, "Social Laughter Triggers Endogenous Opioid Release in Humans," *The Journal of Neuroscience* 37, no. 25 (2017), https://doi.org/10.1523/jneurosci.0688-16.2017.

36 Anne Libera, Neil Stevenson, and Kelly Leonard, "Chapter 11–A Comedy Professor, Design Thinker, and Theatre Producer Walk Into a Bar," in *Creativity and Humor*, ed. Sarah R. Luria, John Baer, and James C. Kaufman (Cambridge, Mass: Academic Press, 2019).

37 Sara Ioannou *et al.*, "Peer Actors and Theater Techniques Play Pivotal Roles in Improving Social Play and Anxiety for Children With Autism," *Frontiers in Psychology* 11 (2020), https://doi.org/10.3389/fpsyg.2020.00908.

38 Peter Felsman, Sanuri Gunawardena, and Colleen M Seifert, "Improv experience promotes divergent thinking, uncertainty tolerance, and affective well-being," *Thinking Skillsand Creativity* 35 (2020).

39 Lisa Aziz-Zadeh, Sook-Lei Liew, and Francesco Dandekar, "Exploring the neural correlates of visual creativity," *Social Cognitive and Affective Neuroscience* 8, no. 4 (Apr 2013), https://doi.org/10.1093/scan/nss021.

40 Catherine Best *et al.*, "The Relationship Between Subthreshold Autistic Traits, Ambiguous Figure Perception and Divergent Thinking," *Journal of Autism and Developmental Disorders* 45, no. 12 (Dec 2015), https://doi.org/10.1007/s10803-015-2518-2.

41 Isabelle Soulières *et al.*, "Enhanced visual processing contributes to matrix reasoning in autism," *Human Brain Mapping* 30, no. 12 (Dec 2009), https://doi.org/10.1002/hbm.20831.

42 Temple Grandin, *Thinking in Pictures : And Other Reports from My Life with Autism*, 2nd Vintage Books ed. (New York: Vintage Books, 2006).

Chapter 8

1 Dmitry Yu. Murzin, *Chemical Reaction Technology* (Berlin, Germany: Walter deGruyter GmbH & Co KG, 2015).

2 Martin J. Blaser and Stanley Falkow, "What are the consequences of the disappearing human microbiota?," *Nature Reviews Microbiology* 7, no. 12 (Dec 2009), https://doi.org/10.1038/nrmicro2245.

3 U.S. Centers for Disease Control and Prevention, "FastStats–Births–Method of Delivery." 2020. 2020. https://www.cdc.gov/nchs/fastats/delivery.htm; Josef Neu and Jona Rushing, "Cesarean versus vaginal

delivery: long-term infant outcomes and the hygiene hypothesis," *Clinics in Perinatology* 38, no. 2 (Jun 2011), https://doi.org/10.1016/j. clp.2011.03.008.

4   Benjamin P. Willing, Shannon L. Russell & B. Brett Finlay, "Shifting the balance: antibiotic effects on host-microbiota mutualism," *Nature Reviews Microbiology* 9, no. 4 (Apr 2011), https://doi.org/10.1038/nrmicro2536.

5   Neu and Rushing, "Cesarean versus vaginal delivery: long-term infant outcomes and the hygiene hypothesis."

6   Julia P. Owen *et al.*, "Abnormal white matter microstructure in children with sensory processing disorders," *NeuroImage: Clinical* 2 (2013), https://doi.org/10.1016/j.nicl.2013.06.009.

7   Neu and Rushing, "Cesarean versus vaginal delivery: long-term infant outcomes and the hygiene hypothesis."

8   Maria G. Dominguez-Bello *et al.*, "Delivery mode shapes the acquisition and structure of the initial microbiota across multiple body habitats in newborns," *Proceedings of the National Academy of Sciences of the United States of America* 107, no. 26 (Jun 29 2010), https://doi.org/10.1073/pnas.1002601107.

9   Christine Cole Johnson, MD, "Study: Babies born by C-section at risk of developing allergies" (Presentation at American American Academy of Allergy, Asthma and Immunology San Antonio, Texas, 2013). https://www.eurekalert.org/pub_releases/2013-02/hfhs-sbb022113.php.

10   S. Salminen *et al.*, "Influence of mode of delivery on gut microbiota composition in seven year old children," *Gut* 53, no. 9 (Sep 2004), https://doi.org/10.1136/gut.2004.041640.

11   U.S. National Library of Medicine, "Vaginal Microbiome Exposure and Immune Responses in C-Section Infants." ClinicalTrials. gov, 2018. Accessed 6/24/2020 https://clinicaltrials.gov/ct2/show/NCT03567707?term=vaginal+seeding.

12   John B. Furness, "The enteric nervous system: normal functions and enteric neuropathies," *Neurogastroenterology and Motility* 20 Suppl 1 (May 2008), https://doi.org/10.1111/j.1365-2982.2008.01094.x.

13   Suzana Herculano-Houzel and R. Lent, "Isotropic fractionator: a simple, rapid method for the quantification of total cell and neuron numbers in the brain," *Journal of Neuroscience* 25, no. 10 (Mar 9, 2005), https://

doi.org/10.1523/jneurosci.4526-04.2005. Suzana Herculano-Houzel *et al.*, "Cellular scaling rules for primate brains," *Proceedings of the National Academy of Sciences of the United States of America* 104, no. 9 (Feb 27, 2007), https://doi.org/10.1073/pnas.0611396104; Suzana Herculano-Houzel, "The human brain in numbers: a linearly scaled-up primate brain," *Frontiers in Human Neuroscience* 3 (2009), https://doi.org/10.3389/neuro.09.031.2009.

14   M. Costa, S. J. Brookes, and G. W. Hennig, "Anatomy and physiology of the entericnervous system," *Gut* 47 Suppl 4, no. Suppl 4 (Dec 2000), https://doi.org/10.1136/gut.47.suppl_4.iv15.

15   Berger, Miles *et al.* "The expanded biology of serotonin." *Annual Review of Medicine* vol. 60 (2009): 355-66. https://doi.org/10.1146/annurev.med.60.042307.110802.

16   David Benton, Claire Williams, and Amy Brown, "Impact of consuming a milk drink containinga probiotic on mood and cognition," *European Journal of Clinical Nutrition volume* 61, no. 3 (Mar 2007), https://doi.org/10.1038/sj.ejcn.1602546.

17   Caroline J. K. Wallace and Roumen Milev, "The effects of probiotics on depressivesymptoms in humans: a systematic review," *Annals of General Psychiatry* 16 (2017), https://doi.org/10.1186/s12991-017-0138-2.

18   Webb, *et al.*, *Misdiagnosis and Dual Diagnoses of Gifted Children and Adults*;Karpinski *et al.*, "High intelligence: A risk factor for psychological and physiological overexcitabilities"; Samson *et al.*, "Enhanced visual functioning in autism: an ALE meta-analysis."

19   Karpinski *et al.*, "High intelligence: A risk factor for psychological and physiologicaloverexcitabilities."

20   Patrizia D'Eufemia *et al.*, "Abnormal intestinal permeability in children with autism," *Acta Paediatr* 85, no. 9 (Sep 1996), https://doi.org/10.1111/j.1651-2227.1996.tb14220.x.

21   Phillip Gorrindo *et al.*, "Gastrointestinal dysfunction in autism: parental report, clinical evaluation, and associated factors," *Autism Res* 5, no. 2 (Apr 2012), https://doi.org/10.1002/aur.237. S. Chandler *et al.*, "Parent-reported gastro-intestinal symptoms in children with autism spectrum disorders," *Journal of Autism and Developmental Disorders* 43, no. 12 (Dec 2013), https://doi.org/10.1007/s10803-013-1768-0.

22 Daniel L. Coury *et al.*, "Gastrointestinal conditions in children with autism spectrumdisorder: developing a research agenda," *Pediatrics* 130 Suppl 2 (Nov 2012), https://doi.org/10.1542/peds.2012-0900N.

23 Gorrindo *et al.*, "Gastrointestinal dysfunction in autism: parental report, clinicalevaluation, and associated factors."

24 D'Eufemia *et al.*, "Abnormal intestinal permeability in children with autism"; de Magistris *et al.*, "Alterations of the intestinal barrier in patients with autism spectrum disorders and in their first-degree relatives."

25 Theoharis C. Theoharides and Robert Doyle, "Autism, gut-blood-brain barrier, andmast cells," *Journal of Clinical Psychopharmacology* 28, no. 5 (Oct 2008), https://doi.org/10.1097/JCP.0b013e3181845f48.

26 de Magistris *et al.*, "Alterations of the intestinal barrier in patients with autismspectrum disorders and in their first-degree relatives."

27 Franco Torrente *et al.*, "Focal-enhanced gastritis in regressive autism with featuresdistinct from Crohn's and Helicobacter pylori gastritis," *The American Journal of Gastroenterology* 99, no. 4 (Apr 2004), https://doi.org/10.1111/j.1572-0241.2004.04142.x.

28 Coury *et al.*, "Gastrointestinal conditions in children with autism spectrum disorder:developing a research agenda."

29 Timothy Buie *et al.*, "Evaluation, diagnosis, and treatment of gastrointestinal disordersin individuals with ASDs: a consensus report," *Pediatrics* 125 Suppl 1 (Jan 2010), https://doi.org/10.1542/peds.2009-1878C.

30 Webb, *et al.*, *Misdiagnosis and Dual Diagnoses of Gifted Children and Adults.*

31 Karpinski *et al.*, "High intelligence: A risk factor for psychological and physiologicaloverexcitabilities."

32 Linda K. Silverman, "Asynchronous development," in *The Social and Emotional Development of Gifted Children: What Do We Know?*, ed. M. Neihart *et al.* (Waco, TX: PrufrockPress, 2002).

33 Webb, *et al.*, *Misdiagnosis and Dual Diagnoses of Gifted Children and Adults.*

34 Eugene A.V Hildreth, "Some Common Allergic Emergencies," *Medical Clinics of NorthAmerica* 50, no. 5 (September 1966), https://doi.org/10.1016/S0025-7125(16)33127-3.

35 Camilla Persson Benbow, "Physiological correlates of extreme intellectual precocity," *Neuropsychologia* 24, no. 5 (1986), https://doi.org/10.1016/0028-3932(86)90011-4.

36   Silverman, "Asynchronous development"; Karen Rogers and Linda Silverman, "A study of 241 profoundly gifted children" (paper presented at the 44th annual convention of the National Association for Gifted Children, Little Rock, AR, 1997).

37   Webb, *Misdiagnosis and Dual Diagnoses of Gifted Children and Adults : ADHD, bipolar, OCD, Asperger's, depression, and other disorders.*

38   Silverman, "Asynchronous development."

39   Guifeng Xu *et al.*, "Association of Food Allergy and Other Allergic Conditions With Autism Spectrum Disorder in Children," *JAMA Netw Open* 1, no. 2 (Jun 1 2018), https://doi.org/10.1001/jamanetworkopen.2018.0279.

40   Joel T. Nigg and Kathleen Holton, "Restriction and elimination diets in ADHD treatment," *Child and Adolescent Psychiatric Clinics of North America* 23, no. 4 (Oct 2014), https://doi.org/10.1016/j.chc.2014.05.010.

41   Maya K. Nanda *et al.*, "Allergic Diseases and Internalizing Behaviors in Early Childhood," *Pediatrics* 137, no. 1 (Jan 2016), https://doi.org/10.1542/peds.2015-1922.

42   Nanda *et al.*, "Allergic Diseases and Internalizing Behaviors in Early Childhood."

43   Randy A Sansone and Lori A Sansone, "Allergic rhinitis: relationships with anxiety and mood syndromes," *Innovations in Clinical Neuroscience* 8, no. 7 (Jul 2011), https://www.ncbi.nlm.nih.gov/pmc/articles/PMC3159540 .

44   "The mutant who would come to be known simply as 'Logan' was born James Howlett…. As a boy, James was notably frail and prone to bouts of allergic attacks." Marvel Database, "James Howlett (Earth 616)/Expanded History." https://marvel.fandom.com/wiki/James_Howlett_(Earth_616)/Expanded_History; Andy Kubert (Illustrator), Adam Kubert (Illustrator), Bill Jemas (Contributor), Paul Jenkins (Contributor), Joe Quesada (Contributor), Kieron Gillen (Contributor) *Wolverine: Origin – The Complete Collection Hardcover* volume III of IV, (Marvel Comics January 24, 2017).

45   Andrew W. Campbell, "Autoimmunity and the gut," Autoimmune *Diseases*, vol. 2014, Article ID 152428, 12 pages, 2014. https://doi.org/10.1155/2014/152428.

46   G. Vighi *et al.*, "Allergy and the gastrointestinal system," *Clinical & Experimental Immunology* 153 Suppl1, no. Suppl 1 (Sep 2008), https:// doi.org/10.1111/j.1365-2249.2008.03713.x .

47   Karpinski *et al.*, "High intelligence: A risk factor for psychological and physiological overexcitabilities." Webb, *Misdiagnosis and Dual Diagnoses of Gifted Children and Adults;* Guifeng Xu *et al.*, "Association of Food Allergy and Other Allergic Conditions With Autism Spectrum Disorder in Children." Timothy R. Sampson and Sarkis K. Mazmanian, "Control of brain development, function, and behavior by the microbiome," *Cell Host Microbe* 17, no. 5 (May 13 2015), https://doi.org/10.1016/j. chom.2015.04.011. Nigg and Holton, "Restriction and elimination diets in ADHD treatment."

48   Campbell, "Autoimmunity and the gut."

49   Julian R. Marchesi *et al.*, "The gut microbiota and host health: a new clinical frontier," *Gut* 65, no. 2 (Feb 2016), https://doi.org/10.1136/ gutjnl-2015-309990.

50   Judy H. Cho and Steven R. Brant, "Recent insights into the genetics of inflammatory bowel disease," *Gastroenterology* 140, no. 6 (May 2011), https://doi.org/10.1053/j.gastro.2011.02.046. Rodrigue Dessein, Mathias Chamaillard, and Silvio Danese, "Innate immunity in Crohn's disease: the reverse side of the medal," *Journal of Clinical Gastroenterology* 42 Suppl 3 Pt 1 (Sep 2008), https://doi.org/10.1097/ MCG.0b013e3181662c90; Tommaso Stefanelli *et al.*, "Anti-adhesion molecule therapies in inflammatory bowel disease: touch and go," *Autoimmunity Reviews* 7, no. 5 (May 2008), https://doi.org/10.1016/j. autrev.2008.01.002.

51   Heather J. Galipeau *et al.*, "Intestinal microbiota modulates gluten-in-duced immunopathology in humanized mice," *The American Journal of Pathology* 185, no. 11 (Nov 2015), https://doi.org/10.1016/j. ajpath.2015.07.018.

52   Luigi Nibali *et al.*, "Genetic dysbiosis: the role of microbial insults in chronic inflammatory diseases," *Journal of Oral Microbiology* 6 (2014), https://doi.org/10.3402/jom.v6.22962.

53   Michael S. Exton, "Infection-induced anorexia: active host defence strategy," *Appetite* 29, no. 3 (Dec 1997), https://doi.org/10.1006/ appe.1997.0116; V. Hugh Perry, "Contribution of systemic inflamma-tion to chronic neurodegeneration," *Acta neuropathologica* 120, no. 3 (2010);https://doi.org/10.1007/s00401-010-0722-x.

54 Robert Dantzer, "Cytokine, sickness behavior, and depression." *Neurologic Clinics* vol. 24,3 (2006): 441-60, https://doi.org/10.1016/j.ncl.2006.03.003.

55 Sampson and Mazmanian, "Control of brain development, function, and behavior bythe microbiome."

56 Emeran A. Mayer *et al.*, "Gut microbes and the brain: paradigm shift in neuroscience,"*Journal of Neuroscience* 34, no. 46 (Nov 12 2014), https://doi.org/10.1523/jneurosci.3299-14.2014; Emeran A. Mayer, Kirsten Tillisch, and Arpana Gupta, "Gut/brain axis and the microbiota," *Journal of Clinical Investigation* 125, no. 3 (Mar 2 2015), https://doi.org/10.1172/jci76304. Roman M. Stilling *et al.*, "Microbes & neurodevelopment—Absence of microbiota during early life increases activity-related transcriptional pathways in the amygdala," *Brain, Behavior, & Immunity* 50 (Nov 2015), https://doi.org/10.1016/j.bbi.2015.07.009.

57 Per Olav Vandvik *et al.*, "Comorbidity of irritable bowel syndrome in general practice: astriking feature with clinical implications," *Alimentary Pharmacology & Therapeutics* 20, no. 10 (Nov 15 2004), https://doi.org/10.1111/j.1365-2036.2004.02250.x.

58 Sampson and Mazmanian, "Control of brain development, function, and behavior bythe microbiome."

59 Karpinski *et al.*, "High intelligence: A risk factor for psychological and physiologicaloverexcitabilities."

60 Jeremy D. Coplan *et al.*, "Decreased choline and creatine concentrations in centrum semiovale in patients with generalized anxiety disorder: Relationship to IQ and early trauma," *Journal of Psychiatric Researchearch: Neuroimaging* 147, no. 1 (June 30 2006), https://doi.org/10.1016/j.pscychresns.2005.12.011; Alexander M Penney, VictoriaC. Miedema, and Dwight Mazmanian, "Intelligence and emotional disorders: Is the worrying andruminating mind a more intelligent mind?," *Personality and Individual Differences* 74 (2015).

61 Penney, Miedema, and Mazmanian, "Intelligence and emotional disorders: Is theworrying and ruminating mind a more intelligent mind?"

62 Webb, *Misdiagnosis and Dual Diagnoses of Gifted Children and Adults : ADHD, bipolar, OCD, Asperger's, depression, and other disorders.*

63 Marc Jan Bonder *et al.*, "The influence of a short-term gluten-free diet on the humangut microbiome," *Genome Med* 8, no. 1 (Apr 21 2016), https://doi.org/10.1186/s13073-016-0295-y. Kristen Tillisch *et al.*,

"Consumption of fermented milk product with probiotic modulates brain activity," *Gastroenterology* 144, no. 7 (Jun 2013), https://doi.org/10.1053/j.gastro.2013.02.043.

64   Shin. Fukudo, "[Irritable Bowel Syndrome, Emotion Regulation, and Gut Microbiota]," *Brain Nerve*= Shinkei kenkyū no shinpo. 68, no. 6 (Jun 2016), https://doi.org/10.11477/mf.1416200448.

65   Michaël Messaoudi al., "Assessment of psychotropic-like properties of a probiotic formulation (*Lactobacillus helveticus* R0052 and *Bifidobacterium longum* R0175) in rats and human subjects," *British Journal of Nutrition* 105, no. 5 (Mar 2011), https://doi.org/10.1017/s0007114510004319.

66   Laura Steenbergen *et al.*, "A randomized controlled trial to test the effect of multispecies probiotics on cognitive reactivity to sad mood," *Brain, Behavior, & Immunity* 48 (Aug 2015),https://doi.org/10.1016/j.bbi.2015.04.003.

67   Tillisch *et al.*, "Consumption of fermented milk product with probiotic modulates brain activity."

68   Curtis D. Klaassen and Julia Yue Cui, "Review: Mechanisms of How the Intestinal Microbiota Alters the Effects of Drugs and Bile Acids," *Drug Metabolism and Disposition* 43, no. 10 (Oct 2015), https://doi.org/10.1124/dmd.115.065698.

69   Hollie I. Swanson, "Drug Metabolism by the Host and Gut Microbiota: A Partnershipor Rivalry?," *Drug Metabolism and Disposition* 43, no. 10 (Oct 2015), https://doi.org/10.1124/dmd.115.065714.

70   Webb, *Misdiagnosis and Dual Diagnoses of Gifted Children and Adults*.

71   Fred D. Hofeldt, "Reactive hypoglycemia," *Endocrinology and Metabolism Clinics of North America* 18, no. 1 (Mar 1989), https://doi.org/10.1016/0026-0495(75)90156-0.

72   Mayo Clinic, "Reactive Hypoglycemia: What Causes It?" 2019. Accessed 6/24/2020 https://www.mayoclinic.org/diseases-conditions/diabetes/expert-answers/reactive-hypoglycemia/faq-20057778.

73   Webb, *Misdiagnosis and Dual Diagnoses of Gifted Children and Adults*.

74   Webb, James T. "Misdiagnosis and Dual Diagnosis of Gifted Children" *Outlook*, September/October, 2006 issue, Minnesota Council for the Gifted and Talented (MCGT); Webb, *Misdiagnosis and Dual Diagnoses of*

Gifted Children and Adults : ADHD, bipolar, OCD, Asperger's, depression, and other disorders.

75   Elizabeth S. Mezzacappa, Robert M. Kelsey, Edward S. Katkin, "The effects of epinephrine administration on impedance cardiographic measures of cardiovascular function," *International Journal of Psychophysiology* 31, no. 3 (Mar 1999), https://doi.org/10.1016/s0167-8760(98)00058-0.

76   Francisco J Navas-Sánchez *et al.*, "White matter microstructure correlates of mathematical giftedness and intelligence quotient," *Human brain mapping* 35, no. 6 (2014); Desco *et al.*, "Mathematically gifted adolescents use more extensive and more bilateral areas of the fronto-parietal network than controls during executive functioning and fluid reasoning tasks."

77   Kaldy *et al.*, "The Mechanisms Underlying the ASD Advantage in Visual Search.";Navas-Sánchez *et al.*, "White matter microstructure correlates of mathematical giftedness andintelligence quotient."

78   Navas-Sánchez *et al.*, "White matter microstructure correlates of mathematical giftedness and intelligence quotient."

79   Oxford Biomedical Technologies, Inc. "The Patented Mediator Release Test (MRT®)"2020. Oxford Biomedical Technologies, Inc. June 25, 2020. https://www.nowleap.com/the-patented-mediator-release-test-mrt/.

Chapter 9

1   Jack Kornfield, *Buddha's Little Instruction Book* (New York: Bantam, 1994).

2   Phillippa Lally *et al.*, "How are habits formed: Modelling habit formation in the realworld," *European Journal of Social Psychology* 40, no. 6 (2010), https://doi.org/10.1002/ejsp.674.

3   Rick Hanson and Richard Mendius, *Buddha's Brain : The Practical Neuroscience ofHappiness, Love & Wisdom* (Oakland, CA: New Harbinger Publications, 2009).

4   Fred B Bryant, Erica D Chadwick, and Katharina Kluwe, "Understanding the processes that regulate positive emotional experience: Unsolved problems and future directions for theory and research on savoring," *International Journal of Wellbeing* 1, no. 1 (2011), http://dx.doi.org/ 10.5502/ijw.v1i1.18.

5   Zope and Zope, "Sudarshan kriya yoga: Breathing for health."

6   R. H. Howland, "Vagus Nerve Stimulation," *Current Behavioral Neuroscience Reports* 1, no. 2 (Jun2014), https://doi.org/10.1007/s40473-014-0010-5.

7   C. Sue Carter *et al.*, "Oxytocin, vasopressin and sociality," *Progress in Brain Research* 170 (2008), https://doi.org/10.1016/s0079-6123(08)00427-5.

8   Kevin Yackle *et al.*, "Breathing control center neurons that promote arousal in mice," *Science* 355, no. 6332 (Mar 31 2017), https://doi.org/10.1126/science.aai7984.

9   Yi-Yuan Tang, Britta K. Hölzel, and Michael I. Posner, "The neuroscience of mindfulness meditation," *Nature Reviews Neuroscience* 16, no. 4 (2015/04/01 2015), https://doi.org/10.1038/nrn3916, https://doi.org/10.1038/nrn3916; Britta K. Hölzel *et al.*, "Mindfulness practice leads to increases in regional brain gray matter density," *Journal of Psychiatric Research* 191, no. 1 (Jan 30 2011), https://doi.org/10.1016/j.pscychresns.2010.08.006; Andrew B. Newberg and John Iversen, "The neural basis of the complex mental task of meditation: neurotransmitter and neurochemical considerations," *Medical Hypotheses* 61, no. 2 (Aug 2003), https://doi.org/10.1016/s0306-9877(03)00175-0; B. Rael Cahn and J. Polich, "Meditation states and traits: EEG, ERP, and neuroimaging studies," *Psychological Bulletin* 132, no. 2 (Mar 2006), https://doi.org/10.1037/0033-2909.132.2.180.

10   José Antonio Curiati, *et al.*, "Meditation reduces sympathetic activation and improvesthe quality of life in elderly patients with optimally treated heart failure: a prospective randomized study," *Journal of Alternative and Complementary Medicine* 11, no. 3 (Jun 2005), https://doi.org/10.1089/acm.2005.11.465.

11   Cahn and Polich, "Meditation states and traits: EEG, ERP, and neuroimaging studies."

12   Hölzel *et al.*, "Mindfulness practice leads to increases in regional brain gray matterdensity."; Sara W. Lazar *et al.*, "Meditation experience is associated with increased cortical thickness," *Neuroreport* 16, no. 17 (Nov 28 2005), https://doi.org/10.1097/01.wnr.0000186598.66243.19.

13   Ho Namkung, Sun-Hong Kim, Akira Sawa, "The Insula: An Underestimated BrainArea in Clinical Neuroscience, Psychiatry, and Neurology," *Trends in Neurosciences* 40, no. 4 (Apr 2017), https://doi.org/10.1016/j.tins.2017.02.002.

14 Daniel J. Siegel, "Mindful awareness, mindsight, and neural integration," *The Humanistic Psychologist* 37, no. 2 (2009), https://doi.org/10.1080/08873260902892220.

15 John J.Miller, Ken Fletcher, Jon Kabat-Zinn, "Three-year follow-up and clinical implications of a mindfulness meditation-based stress reduction intervention in the treatment of anxiety disorders," *General Hospital Psychiatry* 17, no. 3 (May 1995), https://doi.org/10.1016/0163-8343(95)00025-m; Barbara L. Niles *et al.*, "Comparing mindfulness and psychoeducation treatments for combat-related PTSD using a telehealth approach," *Psychological Trauma: Theory, Research, Practice, and Policy* 4, no. 5 (2012), https://doi.org/10.1037/a0026161; Elizabeth Kimbrough *et al.*, "Mindfulness intervention for child abuse survivors," *Journal of Clinical Psychology* 66, no. 1 (Jan 2010), https://doi.org/10.1002/jclp.20624.

16 Sian Cotton *et al.*, "Mindfulness-based cognitive therapy for children and adolescents with anxiety disorders at-risk for bipolar disorder: A psychoeducation waitlist controlled pilot trial," *Early Intervention in Psychiatry* 14, no. 2 (Apr 2020), https://doi.org/10.1111/eip.12848.

17 Joseph Bankard, "Training emotion cultivates morality: How loving-kindness meditation hones compassion and increases prosocial behavior," *Journal of Religion and Health* 54, no. 6 (2015).

18 Joseph A Durlak, *et al.* "The impact of enhancing students' social and emotional learning: a meta-analysis of school-based universal interventions." *Child Development* vol. 82,1 (2011): 405-32. https://doi.org/10.1111/j.1467-8624.2010.01564.x.

19 Holtzman, Ronald E *et al.* "Social network characteristics and cognition in middle-aged and older adults." *The journals of gerontology. Series B, Psychological sciences and social sciences* vol. 59,6 (2004): P278-84. https://doi.org/10.1093/geronb/59.6.p278.

20 Laura Marie Edinger-Schons, "Oneness beliefs and their effect on life satisfaction," *Psychology of Religion and Spirituality* 12 no. 4(2020) 428-439 https://doi.org/10.1037/rel0000259.

21 Chorong Song, Harumi Ikei, and Yoshifumi Miyazaki, "Physiological Effects of Nature Therapy: A Review of the Research in Japan," *International Journal of Environmental Research and Public Health* 13, no. 8 (Aug 3 2016), https://doi.org/10.3390/ijerph13080781.

22   Tenzin Wangyal and Marcy Vaughn, *Spontaneous Creativity : Meditations for Manifesting Your Positive Qualities*, First edition. ed. (Carlsbad, California: Hay House, Inc.,2018).

23   Sara Tilley *et al.*, "Older People's Experiences of Mobility and Mood in an Urban Environment: A Mixed Methods Approach Using Electroencephalography (EEG) and Interviews," *International Journal of Environmental Research and Public Health* 14, no. 2 (Feb 4 2017), https://doi.org/10.3390/ijerph14020151.

24   Hon K. Yuen and Gavin R. Jenkins, "Factors associated with changes in subjective well-being immediately after urban park visit," *International Journal of Environmental Health Research* 30, no. 2 (March 3, 2020), https://doi.org/10.1080/09603123.2019.1577368.

25   Yuen and Jenkins, "Factors associated with changes in subjective well-beingimmediately after urban park visit."

26   Kristine Engemann *et al.*, "Residential green space in childhood is associated with lower risk of psychiatric disorders from adolescence into adulthood," *Proceedings of the National Academy of Sciences* 116, no. 11 (2019), https://doi.org/10.1073/pnas.1807504116.

27   Gould van Praag *et al.*, "Mind-wandering and alterations to default mode networkconnectivity when listening to naturalistic versus artificial sounds."

28   Patricia A. Boyle *et al.*, "Effect of Purpose in Life on the Relation Between Alzheimer Disease Pathologic Changes on Cognitive Function in Advanced Age," *Archives of General Psychiatry* 69, no. 5 (2012), https://doi.org/10.1001/archgenpsychiatry.2011.1487.

29   Natalie L. Marchant *et al.*, "Repetitive negative thinking is associated with amyloid,tau, and cognitive decline," *Alzheimer's & Dementia* 16, no. 7, https://doi.org/10.1002/alz.12116.

30   Reddan, "Attenuating Neural Threat Expression with Imagination."

Index

Y

Z

About the Author

Nicole Tetreault, Ph.D., is a neuroscientist, author, meditation teacher, and international speaker on topics of neurodiversity, neuro-development, creativity, mental health, and wellness.

Her first book, *Insight into a Bright Mind: A Neuroscientist's Personal Stories of Unique Thinking* (Gifted Unlimited, LLC, Goshen, KY, 2020 giftedunlimitedllc.com) explores groundbreaking research examining the experiences of unique, creative, and intense brains weaving interviews, storytelling, and literary science, while advocating for new directions to embrace human diversity and neurodiversity.

Nicole received her Ph.D. from California Institute of Technology (Caltech) in biology specializing in neurodevelopment and neurode-generative disorders. As the founder of Awesome Neuroscience, she is dedicated to translating the most promising neuroscience research and positive psychology for individuals to live their best life. Her approach centers on guiding individuals to mindfully develop greater self-awareness and compassion, while teaching them positive life practices. She is of a new generation of meditation teachers, fusing neuroscience with the ancient art of meditation to help ground people to embody their neuroindividual essence. Nicole has researched neurodiversity, including autism, giftedness, and 2e for over two decades and is passionate about sharing her knowledge and approach to neurodiversity. Being 2e herself, she understands the experience from the inside out.

Nicole has authored numerous academic papers on intelligence, autism, brain evolution, neuroanatomy, neuroinflammation, brain development, and behavior. Her popular science writings can be found in 2e Newsletter, Variations Magazine, GHF Dialogue, SENG Newsletter, Gifted Unlimited, and Great Potential Press.

As a Milton and Rosalind Chang Career Exploration Prize recipient from Caltech, Nicole founded a novel non-profit, Beyond the Cell, a transformative program to rehabilitate incarcerated women through teaching guided meditation, neuroscience, literature, and expressive writing to cultivate positive neural, mental, and behavioral patterns for healing. Nicole believes all beings have the ability to rewire their minds for positive neural plasticity to manifest a meaningful life. She designed Beyond the Cell's foundational teachings to lead incarcerated and post-incarcerated women to greater liberation. She is a committee member for PEN Los Angeles and supports PEN's mission of protecting free speech. She works and serves the community in the hope that we can each learn to transform our pain and create something beautiful.

She currently resides in sunny Los Angeles, California with her life partner, Billy, their son, Spencer and furry daughter, Star.

For more about Nicole, please visit nicoletetreault.com and beyondthecell.org.

CPSIA information can be obtained
at www.ICGtesting.com
Printed in the USA
BVHW040015060421
604237BV00015B/2237